Freedom Roots

Freedom Roots

Histories from the Caribbean

· ·

LAURENT DUBOIS & RICHARD LEE TURITS

The University of North Carolina Press Chapel Hill

Publication of this book was made possible by the generous support of the Dean's Office and the History Department of the College of William & Mary.

The University of North Carolina Press has been a member of the Green Press Initiative since 2003.

Library of Congress Cataloging-in-Publication Data
Names: Dubois, Laurent, 1971–author. | Turits, Richard Lee, author.
Title: Freedom roots : histories from the Caribbean / Laurent Dubois
    and Richard Lee Turits.
Description: Chapel Hill : University of North Carolina Press, [2019] |
    Includes bibliographical references and index.
Identifiers: LCCN 2019012190 | ISBN 9781469653600 (cloth : alk. paper) |
    ISBN 9781469672557 (pbk : alk. paper) | ISBN 9781469653617 (ebook)
Subjects: LCSH: Caribbean Area—History. | Caribbean Area—Foreign
    relations. | Caribbean Area—Social conditions. | Caribbean Area—Politics
    and government.
Classification: LCC F1621 .D83 2019 | DDC 972.9—dc23 LC record available
    at https://lccn.loc.gov/2019012190

Cover illustration: Edouard Duval-Carrié, *L'arbre allumée* (1991, oil on canvas). Used by permission of the artist.

For Anton, Gabriel, Hannah, and Katie

Contents

Freedom Roots

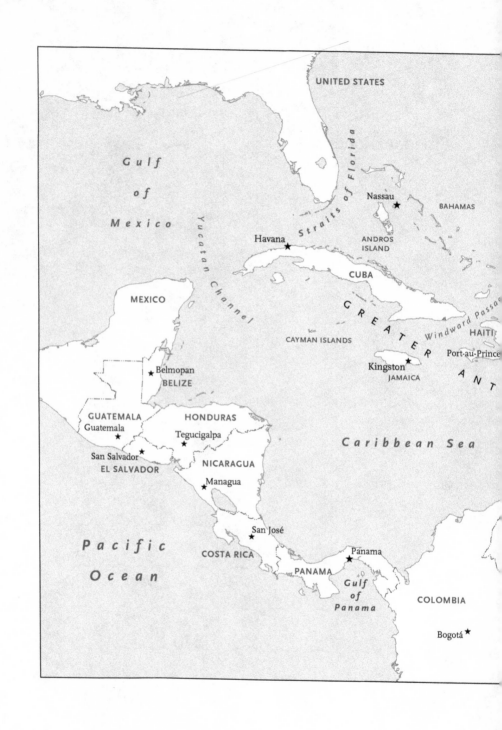

A t l a n t i c

O c e a n

TURKS & CAICOS ISLANDS

DOMINICAN
REPUBLIC

Canal de la Mona

San Juan

LEEWARD ISLANDS

VIRGIN ISLANDS

ANGUILLA

Santo
Domingo

BARBUDA

PUERTO
RICO

ANTIGUA

SAINT KITTS-NEVIS

St. John

MONTSERRAT

GUADELOUPE

Basse-Terre

ILLES

Roseau

DOMINICA

LESSER ANTILLES

Fort-de-France

MARTINIQUE

Castries

SAINT LUCIA

WINDWARD ISLANDS

SAINT VINCENT

BARBADOS

Kingstown

Bridgetown

ranjestad

ARUBA

CURAÇAO

BONAIRE

St. George's

GRENADA

Willemstad

Port of Spain

TRINIDAD & TOBAGO

Caracas

VENEZUELA

Georgetown

Paramaribo

GUYANA

SURINAME

Introduction

Caribbean Pasts

. . . . — as . . . .

To tell the history of the Caribbean is to tell the history of the world. For centuries the region has remained at the center of global transformations, at once a crossroads and a crucible for their unfolding. The Caribbean is a region deeply shaped and in enduring ways dominated by European and U.S. imperial projects, which across time and space have focused on implanting and sustaining extractive and exploitative systems of plantation agriculture. But the Caribbean is also a place where subjected peoples have never ceased, even under the most severe duress, contesting, imagining, and reinventing their worlds, creating rich cultural and political alternatives to those offered by imperial rule. In this book, we follow a particular itinerary though the history of these archipelagos by foregrounding the question of land. Through this optic, we tell the story of the construction of race and slavery, struggles over the meaning of freedom and sovereignty, and the invention of new practices and ways of life that sought to sustain autonomy within.

The Caribbean has experienced a particularly long period of colonialism, with virtually all of its populations having lived under three hundred years of colonial rule and many of them over four or even five centuries. This has created a region of remarkable complexity and diversity. As historian B. W. Higman notes, the islands of the contemporary Caribbean "are home to 24 distinct polities, one more than the total on the continental landmass." Thirteen of these are today sovereign nations, the others occupying a cascade of political forms of constrained autonomy linking them to European countries or the United States.[1] We focus on the "island Caribbean" rather than the "greater Caribbean," which includes a broader region stretching from North America to Central and South America.

Above all, we position the question of land—of how it is used, imagined, and contested in struggles for autonomy or wealth—as a centerpiece and continuing thread. From the beginnings of European colonization in the Caribbean in the late fifteenth century to the present day, those with economic means and political power have overseen the creation of plantation systems that relied on massive labor forces—for centuries, enslaved people—to produce goods for export from the region. Yet the populations of the Caribbean have also always generated and pursued alternative projects aimed at using the land as the foundation for economic autonomy and national independence. The meaning given to land by colonial administrators and planters was radically different from that given to land by enslaved people and those who, for generations after emancipation, sought to root their legal freedom in forms of economic and social autonomy at odds with planters' interest in labor exploitation. In histories from the Caribbean, we see the truth of historian Nigel Bolland's view that land is itself a complex category, not just a "geophysical determinant of social life" but something that is "itself socially produced and defined."[2]

· · · · · ·

The Haitian writer Jean Casimir calls this matrix of alternative cultural, political, and economic structures and practices the "counter-plantation system." Building on Casimir's ideas, Ángel Quintero Rivera urges us to think of the history of the Caribbean in terms of a "dialectical contradiction" between "plantation and counter-plantation," and between "slavery and escape." This constant struggle between "longings for freedom" and the realities imposed by empire and the plantation formed, he writes, the "shared skeleton of Caribbean culture," though the relative weights of and relationship between plantation and counter-plantation structures have varied over time and place.[3]

Some communities in the Caribbean were overwhelmingly defined by plantation logics and forces, others defined by a counterpoint between the plantation and counter-plantation. Still others became counter-plantation societies, as was the case for Spanish Santo Domingo after the sixteenth century and Haiti after 1804. Everywhere in the Caribbean, however, forms of the counter-plantation have existed in different ways, offering sanctuary and possibility to individuals and communities, and often supporting political movements seeking broader transformation. The history of the confrontation between and entanglement of these different projects, one that sees land primarily through the lens of extraction and the other as a means to autonomy for communities and individuals, is key to understanding the Caribbean past and its present.

Our book is rooted in the counter-plantation perspective. That perspective is that of the majority of the people who, from the period of slavery until the present day, have sought out spaces of freedom and autonomy for themselves in the midst of, and in many ways against, the dominant economic and political orders in which they lived. Though this has always been a resistant and insurgent perspective, struggling against powerful economic and political obstacles, we see it as the vital foundation for the crafting of better Caribbean futures. While our book accounts for the structures of colonialism and the plantation that have in many ways dominated Caribbean societies, we see our fundamental task as offering a history that does not accept the epistemologies of those systems and instead arises from the visions and practices of the region's majorities.

Conquest, the rise of the plantation, emancipation, overseas rule, revolution, and reform stretched out over many centuries. They were propelled by different imperial governments (Spanish, British, French, Dutch, Danish, and ultimately U.S.) in often far-apart historical periods and with diverse implications for indigenous-, African-, Asian-, and European-descended populations. While we touch on many parts of the Caribbean in this book, the chapters focus at times on particular regions and at other times specific nations, an approach that allows us to tell stories and analyze themes with a mixture of meaningful depth and illuminating breadth.

The first part of the book focuses on the colonial Caribbean, examining the Caribbean past from the late fifteenth century to the end of the nineteenth century by illuminating several key themes: indigeneity, plantation slavery, and emancipation and postemancipation struggles. We examine the indigenous Caribbean and early European colonization, then describe how a system of brutal plantation slavery emerged that propelled the expansion of the African slave trade and the European economy. We trace the roots of slavery in the Americas to late medieval southern Europe and the Atlantic Islands, where an active slave trade prevailed, shaping the worldviews and economic imagination of the first colonial rulers and entrepreneurs coming to the Caribbean. We also explore the concrete circumstances of slavery's construction in the region, focusing on the concatenation of forces that created the racial slavery that would dominate the Caribbean for centuries. We begin this treatment of "New World" slavery with Spanish Santo Domingo, the first plantation society in the Americas, which thrived in the mid-sixteenth century. We follow from there the plantation hurricane that would sweep powerfully, destructively, and for an elite few, lucratively across the Caribbean and much of the Americas.

Through these chapters, we remain attentive to the fissures, alternatives, and forms of opposition that were maintained and cultivated, starting with indigenous resistance and the earliest forms of *marronage* (escape from slavery) in the Caribbean. These were the first manifestations of a continuous pursuit of and escape to freedom on the part of Caribbean populations. We focus on the particular ways in which land was used both on and off plantations to craft alternative social and cultural realities that enabled the enslaved to envision and ultimately create different futures for themselves and generations to come. The history of freedom and emancipation in the region, in our view, is one that developed both within and outside the plantation, conceived of and articulated by enslaved peoples imagining different futures, and whose actions, through rebellion, escape, and more, spurred on the formal abolition of slavery.

The second part of the book, which begins in 1898, is focused on what we call the independent Caribbean—the independent nations of the region. We explore the independent Caribbean not because it is representative of the entire region. Finding representative histories would be difficult given the highly divergent political trajectories in the Caribbean during the twentieth century. Rather we have chosen this particular history because it was at the core of both regional and global developments, above all U.S. imperial expansion, revolutionary movements, and conservative and imperial reactions to them.

This part of the book focuses primarily on the three largest nations of the Caribbean—Cuba, Haiti, and the Dominican Republic—which were all independent at the turn of the twentieth century. We also analyze the history of nations in the English-speaking Caribbean, particularly Jamaica and Grenada, at the point when they gained independence in the 1960s and 1970s and their trajectories began to overlap with that of the older independent Caribbean. National sovereignty gave these countries a significant measure of autonomy in shaping their political projects during the twentieth century. Yet it also made them particularly vulnerable to the rise of a new overseas empire in the region: the United States. U.S. empire dramatically constrained and reshaped the independent Caribbean's political and economic possibilities.

The story of the twentieth-century independent Caribbean also reveals the continuing significance of land contests to the Caribbean past. Both U.S. domination and popular struggles against it in the region were deeply rooted in ongoing conflicts between plantation and counter-plantation forces. Hard-earned forms of popular land access and the defense of them in the early twentieth century impeded the development of state control over rural populations and economies, which both local elite groups and the U.S. government and corporations sought. Peasant autonomy and resistance, we argue, and what U.S. leaders perceived as failed central states—particularly in Haiti and the Dominican Republic—crucially shaped the long and repeated U.S. military occupations during these decades. They also help explain the postoccupation rise and the U.S. embrace of some of the most ruthless and iron-fisted dictators in Caribbean and Latin American history.

Land was also at the root, we stress, of the Cuban Revolution. The popular insurgencies led by Fidel Castro and others in the 1950s thrived in the countryside primarily in Cuba's Oriente Province, where they tapped into a decades-old battle for land between planters and independent peasants. Once it was victorious, the Cuban Revolution's sweeping agrarian reform at the expense of vast U.S. interests was a major impetus for U.S. economic and covert war against the Castro regime. That agrarian reform and other aspects of the Cuban Revolution's social priorities—but not its socialist or Soviet and Communist character—would, in turn, inspire attempts at egalitarian socioeconomic transformation in the Dominican Republic, Jamaica, Grenada, and Haiti.

This book emphasizes the prevailing forces that have come to shape and dominate the Caribbean but also the processes through which alternative possibilities were often articulated and sometimes enacted. We return to these alternatives throughout the book, in part because we see in them the seeds for different futures for the Caribbean. Our hope is that *Freedom Roots* will provide readers with a route for thinking productively about the Caribbean as a space shaped by empires and plantation economies but also one generating new and more just ways of envisioning the world and the place of Caribbean individuals, communities, and nations within it.

Part I **Land and Freedom**

Histories from the Colonial Caribbean

. . . .

1 The Indigenous Caribbean

In 1789, a Scottish naturalist named Alexander Anderson was determined to find a skull. The founder of the St. Vincent Botanical Gardens, the first of its kind in the Americas, he had studied the forests and plants of the island for years. He was also interested in the indigenous people who still lived on the island, a group who after several centuries of European colonization still remained autonomous. The "Yellow Caribs," he noted, "considered any attempt to disturb the ashes of their ancestors" as "the greatest of crimes." Undaunted, however, he rooted around in a burial site until he found a skull that he claimed was one of a chief of the Yellow Caribs. The skull ultimately was sent to Europe, where it was given as a gift to the German naturalist Johann Friedrich Blumenbach, who included an engraving of it in a 1795 work describing the human "races" as a representative of the "American" race.[1]

Since the arrival of Europeans in the Caribbean in 1492, the indigenous Caribbean has been the subject of many attempts to categorize, define, and contain. Any reconstruction of indigenous histories, either before or after Columbus, has to start with an understanding of the way power shapes the very language, categories, and geographies through which we tell this story. The broad outlines of this history are well known, and they are those of a cataclysm. Europeans arrived in the so-called New World and very quickly destroyed the populous and thriving native worlds through a combination of military conquest, enslavement, and disease. This story continues to haunt us and horrify us today. It was part of the large destruction of native populations throughout the Americas, in what Tzvetan Todorov and others have referred to as one of the greatest genocides in history.[2]

How we tell this story is not just about the past but also about the present. The stakes are high, notably for contemporary indigenous communities in the Greater Caribbean, including those in the Kalinago reserve in Dominica and the large population of Garifuna, descendants of a group deported from St. Vincent at the end of the eighteenth century, living in Central America. Today, the Garifuna are the largest group of people who tie themselves to the history of the indigenous Caribbean, and their contemporary life is a reminder that the long struggle to find spaces of sanctuary and autonomy within and against the colonial project is an ongoing one. When we depict the indigenous as having vanished in the face of European conquest, we end up erasing the indigenous entirely from our sense of the broader history of the region. But indigenous populations profoundly shaped the history of the Caribbean from the sixteenth through the eighteenth centuries. The "devastation" most often invoked when speaking about European-indigenous contacts in the Caribbean, while vital to our understanding of the history of the region, is only part of the story. Like other indigenous populations, those of the Caribbean have been subjected for centuries to a narrative in which they are doomed, vanishing, always on the verge of becoming nothing more than a memory. And yet the indigenous Caribbean is still here, in communities who identify as such as well as in many of the lifeways and cultural practices of the Caribbean. They have been told they are vanishing for over five hundred years, but they have refused to do so.

As historian Melanie Newton has argued, the "narrative of aboriginal disappearance" was one of the region's "foundational imperial myths," but it has also remained surprisingly present even in twentieth-century anticolonial texts from the Caribbean. "Thinking about the Caribbean as an aboriginal space," she argues, "and of indigeneity as a key site of struggle in Caribbean history, gives scholars new ways to expose colonial forms of knowledge and power." This chapter represents an attempt to respond to her call for a different approach to the history of the indigenous Caribbean. It focuses on the long chronology of conquest in the Caribbean, from Columbus's arrival in 1492 to the deportation of several thousand "Black Caribs" from St. Vincent in 1797. It is the story of how European empires moved into the Caribbean and how indigenous groups responded. The indigenous communities of the Caribbean suffered tremendously under European colonization, and yet many among them found ways not just to survive but to continue to cultivate independent worlds, to envision alternative futures for themselves that did not involve vanishing but rather continuing to live and thrive as individuals and communities. To narrate the history of the indigenous Caribbean in a different way, then, is also to be able to think differently about the future of the region. It is, as Newton writes, a necessary act aimed at rejecting "narratives crafted so that some certain people might get away with murder."[3]

Indigenous responses to European invaders were complex and varied, rooted in a longer history of social and political transformation and conflict.

Though it was defined most forcefully by violence and devastation, the European-indigenous encounters during these centuries also involved negotiation, exchange, and mixing. The indigenous response shaped the process of European expansion into the area, because resistance, particularly in the Lesser Antilles, helped to slow down and shape the course of colonization efforts. Military resistance took place in most areas of the Caribbean, and in a significant minority of cases it was successful. This was particularly the case in the Eastern Caribbean, where the communities of those who came to be known as "Caribs" managed to survive as independent nations, in practice, despite Spanish assertions of sovereignty and decades of attacks upon them and enslavement of those captured in raids and battle. The Caribs responded with raids of their own against European colonial settlements, including extensive ones in 1510s Puerto Rico with support from the local population. When France and England sought to gain footholds in the Eastern Caribbean, making some early inroads into the Americas, indigenous peoples combined continued military resistance with skillful negotiation and diplomacy, taking advantage of imperial rivalries and conflict in order to create what we might call, following Richard White, a Caribbean "Middle Ground." By 1660, the indigenous peoples had been pushed out of many islands but secured access to "reserve islands" through treaties with the French and English. These islands, St. Vincent and Dominica, were meant to be protected from European settlement and, therefore, serve as refuges of a kind for indigenous groups, including those driven out of other islands. But over the course of the eighteenth century, the booming plantation economy led to the creation of European settlements in St. Vincent and Dominica despite these earlier agreements. In 1797, the British deported several thousand indigenous people from St. Vincent in order to firmly secure the island for plantation agriculture. These deportees, however, created new communities in Central America while smaller indigenous communities have remained in both St. Vincent and Dominica to the present day.[4]

This history was, from the beginning, partly a struggle over categories and their meanings. European colonialism always combined colonialism in its rawest forms—of killing, enslavement, control—with the work of categorization and description such as that carried out by Anderson when he sought out a Carib skull. We see in this story how calling people certain things was also a way of attempting to write their history, or perhaps to write them out of history. But these categories in turn—most notably that of the Carib and therefore of the Caribbean itself—could shift and sway, the currents of meaning never stable and never fully under control. Those who took on the name Carib and used it to name themselves had their own ideas about what it meant and who they were and could be.

The Caribbean was the first site of European-indigenous encounter in the Americas, and the brutal treatment and rapid decimation of the communities invaded by the Spaniards were to be only the first in a long series of histories of such devastation. Although the devastation of the indigenous population of the Caribbean would prove to be far from unique, the first contacts that took place there remain of particular importance for understanding the broader history of European-indigenous encounter and conflict in the Americas. As Samuel Wilson noted, once the first Europeans had arrived in the Americas, "stories of their strange appearance and practices spread rapidly," and European trade items "entered into the existing trade networks" and often preceded the new arrivals. European diseases, too, spread rapidly and in advance of the invaders, and often made possible the invaders' progress, depopulating many areas and transforming them into what colonists opportunistically declared "empty lands."[5]

Still, there was no other moment after the first encounters in the Caribbean that were so powerfully defined by the profound lack of preparation, and utter surprise, that defined these first meetings. For this reason the Caribbean encounters of the late fifteenth century have been pored over by generations of scholars seeking to understand the beginnings of the broader history of the conquest of the Americas. It is tempting to see in these early contacts the patterns of misunderstanding, hostility, and destruction that would play out again and again and, in retrospect, can seem to have been inevitable and unstoppable. Yet it is also clear that there was much about these early encounters that was surprising and contingent and could well have gone a different way. That we are still living in the wake of the precise contours these encounters took is one reason to continue to return to them, and to attempt to account for and perhaps rewrite this history on different terms.

Traces of the Indigenous Caribbean

The year 1492 is a pivotal date in Caribbean and world history, perhaps one of the most powerful moments in which we can point to a "before" and an "after." That is also true in the sense that all histories of the pre-Columbian indigenous Caribbean are necessarily refracted through the lens of what happened when the Europeans arrived and of how they described the peoples they encountered. It has been and remains surprisingly difficult to tell the story of the indigenous Caribbean before European arrival without getting tangled up in the colonial categories generated about this so-called prehistory. In fact the categories and interpretations developed during the very first moments of encounter between Europeans and indigenous people profoundly shaped not just what happened at the time but the ways in which we have come to apprehend the world the Spanish encountered. While archaeological evidence has provided enormous insight about life in certain communities, the historical anthropology of the indigenous Caribbean is caught up in a common conundrum: the only existing written sources describing these communities were generated by various European writers invested, in various ways, in the processes of conquest, colonization, and missionary work. These writers included many European missionaries, such as Bartolomé de las Casas, Ramón Pané, and later Jean-Bapiste Labat. Their writings teach us a great deal about the ideological and discursive frameworks of European empire, but they provide us with only frustratingly distorted glimpses of a complex indigenous world. Their texts also represent a world in transition, shaped by reaction and response to European arrivals. So we need to be cautious in using them to understand what came before. It is, in other words, impossible to disentangle accounts of the indigenous Caribbean from the history of how such accounts came to be produced within the history of European empire in the region.

People tend to leave behind unruly traces of their existence. They are, of course, often not particularly sensitive or even aware of the needs of those who will come along later to try to figure out where and how they lived. Archaeologists depend on physical remains in tracking histories of movement and settlement. In reconstituting the history of indigenous communities in the Americas, they depend particularly strongly on ceramics. The construction and decoration of ceramics shift in recognizable ways over time, and so ceramics provide a particularly useful way of reconstituting and dating patterns of settlement and of migration. Among the earliest ceramics found in the Caribbean, for instance, are a large number of shards that show the repetition and consolidation of a style defined by "rules of complex symmetry" that govern "the conventional representation" of frogs, bats, and turtles. The prevalence of such aesthetic techniques, of course, really only proves that these techniques for ceramic production spread throughout the region. Archaeologists have sought to deduce patterns of movement, migration, and population from the patterns of ceramics, assuming that as people move they bring new styles of ceramics with them. Of course, ceramic styles themselves can potentially move between already established communities. Still, through analysis of ceramic as well as other physical remains, and historical and linguistic evidence, decades of archaeological research have provided a tentative map of the history of humans in the Caribbean in the millennia before the arrival of Europeans.[6]

While many of the mainland areas surrounding the Caribbean have been populated for tens of thousands of years, the earliest trace of human occupation in the islands of the Caribbean is on Trinidad from 5400 B.C. At that time, however, Trinidad may still have been attached to the nearby South American mainland, not yet actually the island it would eventually become. The islands of the Greater Caribbean seem to have been first settled by humans approximately six thousand years ago, between 4000 and 3500 B.C., most likely by migrants coming from Central America. Traces of settlements from this period have been found in Cuba, Haiti, Puerto Rico, the Dominican Republic, and Antigua. These early communities were "preceramic," but they did leave behind stone tools that have been found and examined by archaeologists. Very little is in fact known about their culture, although the groups called "Ciboney" or "Guanahatabey" who lived in Eastern Cuba at the time of the conquest may have been descended from these first migrants. They survived on hunting and fishing rather than farming. This was also true of another group of migrants archaeologists have argued moved into the area in the centuries before 2000 B.C. from South America, occupying many of the Lesser Antilles, where "traces of their small settlements are scattered today," and as far as Puerto Rico. Although this group too was preceramic, a later group of people archaeologists believe moved into the region after 500 B.C. did produce ceramics and so left traces that provide much more specific information about their history of migration. Archaeologists have dated early settlements to 530 B.C. in Martinique, 480 B.C. in Montserrat, and 430 B.C. in Puerto Rico, and they have found ceramic remains in most of the other Lesser Antilles.[7]

The migrants came from the tropical lowlands of South America, particularly the Orinoco River valley, which formed the "gateway" for migration to the Antilles. They brought with them both plants and agricultural techniques that would take root in the Caribbean. These horticultural techniques involved both the production of staple crops, particularly cassava, or manioc, in agricultural fields and the creation of small gardens bringing together a "seemingly chaotic" selection of trees and plants that produced fruit, peppers, beans, cotton, gourds, and perhaps tobacco as well. They also brought languages that became the dominant tongues spoken in the region by indigenous peoples at the time of the conquest, and since.[8]

Who were these migrants? And what should we call them? The answers have been the subject of much debate in recent decades. The scholarship that developed in the nineteenth and early twentieth centuries on the topic used the term "Arawak" to describe the indigenous peoples of the large islands of the western Caribbean. In recent decades, however, scholars have highlighted the fact that, as Peter Hulme writes, this term—and others often used today, including "Taíno"—were never "as far as we know, self-ascriptions." The first use of the term "Arawak" appeared in 1540 when the bishop of Cartagena used the term "Aruaca" to describe indigenous peoples in the northern regions of South America. By 1574 it appeared, according to Hulme, as an "established ethnic name" in a "geographical treatise." Like some other names that have come to describe indigenous groups in other parts of the Americas, it was originally a "contemptuous name" used by some of their indigenous neighbors in Guiana. It literally meant "meal-eaters," setting them apart for the importance of manioc in their diet. Eventually, some in the group began using the term to refer to themselves. Nineteenth-century scholars began using it to describe the language spoken by this group, and among linguists today the language family spoken across parts of the Guianas and among indigenous Caribbean groups, including the Garifuna, is called "Arawakan." Although these categories remain useful notably in linguistic discussions today, it is crucial to remember that neither Columbus nor the other Europeans who followed him into the Caribbean encountered any people who called themselves Arawak or identified themselves as such.[9]

The other term commonly used to describe the indigenous people who lived in the Western Caribbean at the time of colonization is "Taíno." This, too, is not a name the indigenous people used for themselves, and its contemporary use is also the result of the work of nineteenth-century scholars. At the time of the conquest, indigenous groups in the area, notably in Hispaniola, used the term "nitaíno" to describe the class of nobles within the society and also to describe something that was noble. But according to Peter Hulme, "Taíno" was first used as a general term to describe the "language of the Greater Antilles" only in 1836, and only in 1886 was it first broadened to describe the entire indigenous group Columbus had encountered in the Greater Antilles. By the end of the nineteenth century, it had become the standard term to describe the civilizations of the larger islands of the Western Caribbean. Many writers continued to use other words, notably in Puerto Rico, where the indigenous were often called Boriquén, a synonym still used today in Spanish for Puerto Rican. Like Arawak, then,

Taíno is a retroactive construction of a culture or people. This, of course, does not mean that some form of self-ascription did not exist, or that these groups did not "consider themselves a community of some sort." It simply startlingly highlights how little we really know about the worldview and self-vision of the indigenous people of the Greater Caribbean, and how powerfully the categories still used to write their history are the result of the projection of European colonists and later writers rather than something that emerged from the indigenous communities themselves.[10]

The dramatic destruction of many indigenous communities at the time of European conquest has tended to overshadow the tremendous diversity in these communities, as well as the fact that they themselves were sometimes in conflict with one another. During the two thousand years before European arrival, indigenous peoples in the Caribbean developed very different social, economic, and political systems in different parts of the Caribbean. Those in the Eastern Caribbean were mostly organized into relatively small, often quite mobile, and largely egalitarian communities focused on small-scale farming and fishing. In the larger islands, meanwhile, which were the first settled by Europeans, indigenous communities practiced larger-scale agriculture and had a more institutionalized social hierarchy.

The Eastern Caribbean, writes Louis Allaire, is made up of a "chain, or stepping stones, of mutually visible islands between the continent and the Greater Antilles, which afford almost uninterrupted landings all along the eastern edge of the Caribbean sea." It served as a "corridor for the movement of ideas, goods and individuals" over the course of the several thousand years that preceded European conquest. The communities that settled there were extremely mobile, and they carried on regular trade across the region and with South America, with which they likely had "sustained interaction." "The surrounding ocean," writes David Watters, "acted as an aquatic highway linking their islands and cultures rather than as a water barrier separating them." The presence of objects made from raw materials that were only available in South America clearly attests to these patterns of exchange. "Green stone" pendants that usually represented frogs, for instance, were important objects of exchange that circulated throughout northern regions of South America and in the Caribbean. So the practices of agriculture, religion, language, trade, and politics of those who lived on the islands were shaped by ongoing contact and communication with surrounding mainland regions.[11]

By the late fifteenth century, the Caribbean was "one of the most densely populated regions of the New World." There were particularly large populations on the island of Haiti or Quisqueya, which the Spanish would rename la isla Española or la Española, soon called Santo Domingo, and on the island of Boriquén, which the colonists would rechristen San Juan and then call Puerto Rico. The population of Haiti was perhaps in the hundreds of thousands by the late fifteenth century, comprising numerous small towns of one to two thousand, each governed by a cacique. "The villagers" in Haiti "were divided into two classes (nitaíno and naboría)," though the Spanish chroniclers "searched in vain for a still lower class, comparable to their own slaves" in Europe. By the decades before Columbus's arrival, villages were "organized into district chiefdoms, each ruled by one of the village chiefs in the district, and the district chiefdoms were in turn grouped into regional chiefdoms, each headed by the most prominent district chief." These chiefs, like the leaders of towns, were also called caciques, and their chiefdoms called *cacicazgos*. In the region of the island where Columbus first landed, in the north, a cacique named Guarionex was in command, while in other parts of the island were Guanagaric, Bohéchia, and Coanabo. Women could also be caciques, as was the case of Anacoana, who was killed in 1503 in a massacre by the Spanish. The caciques were "the heart of the system." It was around their particular abilities as leaders, rather than "the existence of permanent structures or institutions," that the political structure was organized. "They had forces able to carry out military activities but they did not have standing armies." They had a series of social privileges that included polygamy, military leadership, and oversight of labor in the community, which they at times used to organize large public projects. "The construction of public works such as roads, paths, ball fields, irrigation dikes, and agricultural terraces supported extensive communal life." One part of this communal life was organized around a ritual ball game played with a rubber ball on elaborate courts built in the center of many villages. The players, organized into teams, could not touch the ball with their hands, and used their shoulders, hips, legs, and heads to propel it forward toward the opposing goal.[12]

These communities practiced a sophisticated and highly productive method of farming that involved constructing *conucos*, or earth mounds several feet high and about ten feet around. This technique increased drainage and facilitated both weeding and harvesting. Some communities also seem to have constructed large irrigation systems in Quiskeya. Cassava and sweet potato were the most important of the crops grown in the *conucos*. The cassava was usually made into flour for bread, after the poisonous juice of the root was squeezed out in "basketry tubes" made for the purpose. Corn, beans, and squash were also grown, but on a smaller scale. Pineapple plants and fruit trees were cultivated. Spanish chroniclers described varied fishing techniques. Fish were caught with nets and hooks but also sometimes "stupefied with poison" and stored (as were turtles) in traps until it was time to eat them. Residents also "plucked iguanas off trees and decoyed wild parrots with tame birds," speared manatees, and ate dogs. Finally, they harvested wild vegetables and fruit, such as guava, from the forest. The guava was considered so delicious that it was also the food of the dead. Father Ramón Pané, who wrote an ethnographic account of the inhabitants of Haiti in 1498, was told that there was one part of the island called Coaybay. It was the "house and dwelling place of the dead." The dead hid there during the day, but at night went about and walked about, eating "a certain fruit that is called *guayaba* [guava]." The "lord of the said Coaybay," the first to inhabit it, was called Maquetairie Guayaba.[13]

Religious life in Haiti, or Quisqueya, was centered "on the worship of deities known as zemis," including two "supreme deities," one male and one female, and "lesser zemis," who included the "spirits of ancestors." The two "supreme gods" were Yúcahu Maórocaoti, who was "associated with the growth of cassava," and Attabeira, who was "a goddess of water, rivers and seas." The word "zemi" was used both for these deities and for the objects that represented them, "which were made from the remains of ancestors or from natural objects believed to be inhabited by powerful spirits." As Father Pané described it, most residents had zemis. "Some contain the bones of their fathers and mothers and relatives and ancestors; they are made of stone or of wood." Among the many zemis, there were some that spoke and others that caused "the things they eat to grow" or made rain and wind. Some zemis were represented through carved stone sculptures, many of which have been recovered by archaeologists. These stone sculptures may also have served to illustrate and embody stories about the past. The Haitian historian Emile Nau described the zemis evocatively as constantly "visible and present" figures who served as the "ministers of daily life."[14]

The power of caciques and other members of the elite was represented through their use of "duhos," carved wooden stools. They were used in rituals, particularly "such socially and politically charged events as the greeting and feasting of foreign dignitaries, allies and kin." Columbus and some who accompanied him, for instance, were invited to sit on duhos when they met with various caciques. The duhos also "facilitated communication with the supernatural," and in some cases caciques sat on one while a zemi was placed on another nearby as a way of signifying the important relationship between the two. The wood with which duhos were made seems also to have embodied the link with the spirit world. Pané noted that trees in fact participated in the making of wooden zemis. "When someone is walking along" and sees "a tree that is moving its roots, the man very fearfully stops and asks it who it is." Trees then demanded that a *behique*, a ritual specialist, be brought to speak to them, and provided instructions on how to build a zemi.[15]

Pané also noted that the people of Haiti had "their laws gathered in ancient songs, by which they govern themselves, as do the Moors by their scripture." The songs were called *areitos*, a term also used to describe the rituals in which they were sung. The word may have come from the verb *arit-ga*, "to remember, to recall," and in addition to carrying law also carried the history of the deeds of ancestors. The lyrics for the areitos were written by the caciques, who were "the interpreters of the collective and personal history, genealogists, those who crafted the culture's slogans and symbols." Their children were "the only ones allowed to play musical instruments." The content of these areitos has not survived. Nor did the caciques remain in place long enough to pass along areitos that could describe what happened when the Spanish arrived in 1492. We do get one passing glimpse of how the indigenous responded, however, in one story gathered by Pané. He describes one zemi known as Opiyelguabirán, who "has four feet, like a dog, they say, and is made of wood, and often at night he leaves the house and goes into the jungle." No matter how often people brought him back to their settlements, however—even if they tied him up with a rope—he would always escape back into the woods. When "the Christians arrived on the Island of Hispaniola," he escaped for good. The zemi, Pané writes, "escaped and went into a lagoon; and they followed his tracks as far as the lagoon, but they never saw him again, nor did they hear anything about him."[16]

Columbus Arrives

The indigenous world of the Caribbean was radically transformed by the arrival of Europeans in the late fifteenth century. Europe, too, would be remade by the encounter with a new continent. The voyage Columbus took in 1492 has long been understood as an epochal moment, a dramatic encounter, the beginning of what Edmund O'Gorman dubbed the "invention of America." Its immediate causes, though, were quite rooted in old conflicts and old dreams. After the Turkish conquest of Constantinople in the mid-fifteenth century, the overland spice trade from Asia to Europe became increasingly expensive, and Europeans began searching for other routes to Asia. In the second half of the fifteenth century, Portuguese ships increasingly journeyed down the African coast, building small "factories," or trading forts, where they traded for various kinds of merchandise, including slaves, many of whom were brought back to Iberia. Columbus, from Genoa in Italy, was part of this world of merchant voyages, working for Portuguese traders from 1476 to 1484. Throughout the 1480s, he sought sponsorship from different European monarchs for a voyage west across the ocean that he hoped would establish an oceanic trade route with Asia. In April 1492, the Spanish king and queen, respectively, of Aragon and Castile, fresh from having conquered the last Muslim region of Spain, Granada, agreed to sponsor Columbus's voyage, though he depended on support from Genoese merchants to finance his expedition. He left in August of 1492, heading west across the waters.[17]

The task of reconstructing what happened in October of 1492, when Columbus arrived in what would become known as the Caribbean, has preoccupied and indeed obsessed generations of scholars. Most of what we know about what happened comes from the "running journal" Columbus kept during the voyage, which he presented to the king and queen on his return to Spain. Before he left to return to the Caribbean on his second journey, he was given a copy of this journal to carry with him. However, both his original journal and the copy "eventually disappeared." Before they had disappeared, a young man named Bartolomé de las Casas—who would go on to become one of the great defenders of the indigenous peoples of the Americas—read one of the versions of the journal. At some point, probably in the 1530s, Las Casas produced a "partly quoted and partly summarized" version of Columbus's copy of the diary. This abstract itself was also lost, for 250 years, before being found in the late eighteenth century in a private library. It is Las Casas's refracted version that forms the basis of the modern-day published transcriptions of the journal to which scholars generally refer. When we read it, writes Peter Hulme, we are caught in "thickening layers of language" of "a transcription of an abstract of a copy of a lost original."[18]

How should we read this text? For the Colombian writer Gabriel García Márquez, the best way to read the journal is as a work of fiction. He terms it "the first masterwork of the literature of magical realism," a literary movement identified with a phrase coined by the Cuban writer Alejo Carpentier, and which García Márquez's own work has come to define. "From the first," García Márquez writes, "it was so contaminated by the magic of the Caribbean that even the history of the book itself makes an unlikely story." Through all its refractions, the text is a vivid, curious, and at times lyrical account of the voyage.[19]

After a numbing series of entries that repeat "He [Columbus] steered his route west" in late September and early October, the journal describes the first sight of land. (Las Casas was so excited about finally reaching that part of the manuscript himself that he made a drawing in the margin—a hand, or maybe a flame?—next to the note that announces "They find land.") It seems to have come just in time, for the entry for October 10 describes desperation among the crew. "Here the men could no longer stand it; they complained of the long voyage." Columbus responded by speaking of the "benefits they would secure," and then added "that it was useless to complain since he had come to find the Indies and thus had to continue the voyage until he found them, with the help of Our Lord." Luckily, the next day they saw hopeful signs—birds, and then, floating in the water, "a cane and a stick" and, more mysteriously, "another small stick that appeared to have been worked with iron." Then came "a small plank," some vegetation, and "a small stick loaded with barnacles." And then, that night, a light on the horizon. Columbus and several others on the ship saw something that looked like "a wax candle that rose and lifted up" on the horizon, promising an end to the journey.[20]

In the darkness the land appeared, and the ships cruised offshore until the dawn, when they approached an islet which, Columbus noted, "was called Guanahani in the language of the Indians," thought today to be in the Bahamas. "Soon they saw naked people," and Columbus and several crew members went ashore, where "they saw very green trees and many ponds and fruits of various kinds." They carried two green banners: the standard of the ship and "the royal banner." Columbus commanded his crew members to "be witnesses that, in the presence of all, he would take, as in fact he did take, possession of the said island for the king and for the queen his lords."[21]

At this point in Las Casas's version of the diary, he switches from the third to the first person, providing a direct quotation from Columbus, which allows him to continue to tell the story. In order "that they would be friendly to us," he explains, "to some I gave red caps, and glass beads which they put on their chests, and many other things of small value, in which they took so much pleasure and became so much our friends that it was a marvel." A lively trade developed, with the natives bringing out "parrots and cotton thread in balls and javelins and many other things," exchanging them for "small glass beads and bells." Columbus commented on the nakedness of those he saw, as well as on their youth—none were over thirty, he claimed. "Some of them paint themselves black," he wrote, "and they are the color of the Canarians"—the indigenous residents of the Canary Islands—"neither black nor white; and some of them paint themselves white, and some with red, and some of them with whatever they find." When Columbus showed them swords, they "took them by the edge and cut themselves." They had, he noted, "no iron." "They should be good and intelligent servants," he went on, having quickly determined what their future should be, "for I see that they say very quickly everything that is said to them." And they would "become Christians very easily," he noted, "for it seemed to me that they had no religion"—and, as he had indicated, no skill in arms and thus could not defend themselves. All of this was surely meant to entice the crown to continue supporting his ventures.[22]

Columbus also began his apprenticeship in the human geography of the Caribbean. Seeing some people with wounds on their bodies, he asked them where they came from. "They showed me how people from other islands nearby came there and tried to take them, and how they defended themselves." Columbus assumed that these raiders had come from *tierra firme*, the mainland, which he maintained was an extension of Asia. Others, though, would quickly recognize the land as a more truly unknown "New World," in the words of the Italian courtier Pedro Martyr in 1493. The globe was simply too big for Columbus to have reached "the Indies."[23]

All of this, of course, raises a question: How much did Columbus actually understand of what was being said? The encounter described in the document involved a remarkable level of incomprehension. Columbus and his crew were hearing a totally new language for the first time, as were those residents of Guanahani they encountered. Columbus didn't really have any help: the most linguistically able man on the voyage, Luis de Torres, a *converso* (a Jew who had converted to Catholicism amid the intensifying anti-Semitism of fifteenth-century Spain), spoke Hebrew, Chaldean, and "a little" Arabic. As Philippe Boucher puts it, when we talk about what Columbus "understood," what we are really saying is that this is what he concluded based on the "sign language and facial grimaces" of those he met.[24]

On his second day in the Caribbean, Columbus asked what he considered an urgent question: where was the gold? As he "labored" to find out "if there was any gold," Columbus noticed that some of the natives wore small pieces of the precious metal hanging from "a hole that they have in their noses." He was able to understand, he wrote, "by signs," that to the south there was "a king who had large vessels of it and had very much gold." Yet when he tried to convince his interlocutors to "go there," they made clear "they had no intention of going." He decided to set out with his crew, "to seek gold and precious stones."[25]

Columbus subsequently left and traveled to another part of the island, whose residents likely had already heard about his arrival. There was, Columbus's account suggests, already debate among the residents of the island about how to account for the arrival of these strange beings. According to his journal, as he approached a town, the natives swam out to the boats, "and we understood that they were asking us if we had come from the heavens." Some, including "one old man," got into the boat, while others called: "Come see the men who came from the heavens. Bring them something to eat and drink." Columbus's response, though, must have seemed strange, indeed alarming. He decided not to come ashore, worried about the reef he noticed circling the island. Still, he managed to capture and kidnap seven of those who had come to greet him, whom he "caused to be taken away." As he explained it to the Spanish king and queen to whom his journal was addressed, he did this "in order to carry them away to you and to learn our language and to return them." He was also apparently thinking ahead, it seems, when he explained that it would be easy to conquer the islands, for with "50 men" all of the residents "could be held in subjection and can be made to do whatever one might wish."[26]

Columbus would several times repeat the claim, one made again and again in the next centuries by European explorers, that the indigenous people saw him as having arrived from "the heavens." "They are firmly convinced," he wrote in a letter to a friend in 1493, "that I, with these ships and men came from the heavens, and in this belief they everywhere received me, after they had overcome their fear." This was not, he specified, because they were "ignorant," for they were "of very acute intelligence," and impressed Columbus with the fact that they were able to "navigate all these seas" and provided him with accounts of the region. They had "never seen people clothed or ships of such a kind" as the ones he was on. Of course Columbus and his crew had no idea what the inhabitants they encountered were saying when they swam out to meet them. And especially after several among them had been captured and taken away, opinions surely shifted in a hostile direction. "More likely," writes one scholar wryly, the indigenous peoples of the Bahamas "viewed Columbus and his crew as men from hell."[27]

Other scholars have presented a similar interpretation: the indigenous people just wanted the Spanish to leave, and as quickly as possible. Columbus suspected as much early on. Just three days after he arrived, he was told by some of those he had captured that he would find people elsewhere "wearing very large bracelets of gold on their legs and on their arms," but he concluded that these claims were simply "a ruse in order to flee." Peter Hulme suggests that indigenous people seem to have figured out early that if one told the Spanish there was much gold to be found in other lands, they would depart quickly. On the island he named la Isla Española, Columbus encountered one group who told him that there were enormous pieces of gold to be found on the neighboring island of Boriquén (Puerto Rico). As Hulme notes, there may be "a direct correlation between the natives' desire to see the back of the Spaniards and the size of the gold nuggets" they claimed he would find on the next island over. If that was the case, he adds, it is clear that the indigenous people on Hispaniola "were *very* keen to be left alone."[28]

As he moved through the archipelago, Columbus was also bewildered by the number of islands. "I saw so many islands that I did not know how to decide which one to go to first." He decided that he would go to the "largest." As he went, however, he thought of himself as "taking possession" of all that he saw: "My intention was not to pass by any island of which I did not take possession." He had an expansive sense of how such claims worked, seeming to see his ritualistic invocation of ownership standing in for a kind of imperial sovereignty by Spain itself. "If it is taken of one," he wrote, "it may be said that it is taken of all."[29]

While Columbus's first encounters with indigenous people took place on what he called the Lucayos, later renamed the Bahamas, it was on the larger island of Hispaniola (today shared by Haiti and the Dominican Republic) that he spent the most time. It was there that he developed what he considered to be lasting collaboration with at least one leader and created the first (though ill-fated and short-lived) settlement in the Americas. When one of his ships, the *Santa María*, crashed into a coral reef near what is today Cap-Haïtien, Columbus received the help of the local cacique, Guacanagarí, who "provided canoes and people to offload" the cargo of the ship, and then gave him and his men the two largest houses in the town to stay in. The trading between Columbus's men and the people in this town "netted more gold than any other part of the voyage," which was perhaps why he decided it would be a good place to leave behind a small settlement. He did not have much choice, anyway: he could not bring his entire crew back in the two remaining ships. Columbus left thirty-nine men behind "with instructions to obtain gold, find its source, trade peaceably with the Indians, and build a fortified tower from the timbers of the wrecked *Santa María*." He called the settlement la Navidad, in honor of what he took as a divine occurrence: his ship had run aground on Christmas Eve of 1492, and if it had not, he never would have stopped in the place and been welcomed by Guacanagarí. The place was, he later claimed in his letter to the King Ferdinand and Queen Isabella, "the best place in all the island for forming a settlement and nearest to the mines of gold."[30]

Columbus then left to travel back across the Atlantic, taking with him samples of gold, some parrots, and several indigenous people, probably captured under duress, to show off what he had found on his return. He arrived in Lisbon in March, and organized a procession that took him from Seville to Barcelona. People gathered along the route to see him and the indigenous people he had captured pass. Bartolomé de las Casas, who would become the most eloquent and famous defender of the indigenous peoples of the Americas, saw the parade in Seville. On display, he later wrote, were "seven brightly decorated Indians he brought back with him from the New World, along with some gorgeously colored parrots." Las Casas was also "especially impressed" by the sight of a "rubber ball that could bounce far higher than any ball he had known before," one of those used in the ball courts of Haiti. Las Casas's father, Pedro, a converso, joined Columbus's second expedition to the New World, and returned with an indigenous man whom he presented to his son. The man was freed soon afterward and returned to his home, but when Bartolomé traveled with his father to the Caribbean, he would once again have indigenous people in his service for many years. Only several years later, in 1514, did Las Casas truly begin his break with the system of servitude and coercion, turning instead to the relentless documentation and criticism of the system he knew firsthand. Las Casas's writings presented a wrenching and eloquent history of the "destruction of the Indies" that remains one of our central sources for understanding this moment of violent encounter.[31]

The greatest destruction that the Spanish wrought was that of the people. "It took only nine years," one historian notes, for the relationship between Europeans and indigenous peoples, which began in uncertainty and experimentation, to become essentially "relations of slavery and exploitation." "The worst thing about it was, of course, that Hispaniola became the model for relations throughout the New World."[32]

At first, the economy of the Spanish Caribbean had been based on forcing indigenous residents to extract gold from placer mines, in which the mineral was extracted from stream beds. Spanish officials divided up the native population and assigned them to work for specific colonists to whom they were "entrusted." Some "Christians" were allocated hundreds of Indians. And the gold economy thrived early on based on their coercion. Spanish massacres, overwork of forced laborers, the demolition of native social and political structures, and probably above all diseases to which the Indian population had no prior exposure and immunity led quickly to the death of the majority of these larger islands' native populations. Another factor leading to the Indians' extinction as an identifiable group was the scarcity of European women and the large numbers of native-Spanish unions and mixed-race children, who in the absence of entirely European-descended children would have been Europeans' only heirs. Under these conditions, people of partial indigenous ancestry appear to have been identified often as Europeans by officials. And some imported Indian slaves would be classified as "black," particularly as slavery became isolated mostly to people of African descent in the 1530s and 1540s.[33]

By 1518, the number of Indians "entrusted" to colonists had been reduced in la Isla Española to around fifteen thousand—a shocking figure for an island whose initial population upon contact with Europeans was in the hundreds of thousands. Many had fled into the island's untamed hills and woods and many had been forcibly assimilated, but most had perished. Twenty-five years later, the number of identified Indians would be in the hundreds.[34]

The Spanish crown, buttressed by the papacy, considered that it had laid claim to all of the islands of the Caribbean. But the focus of the Spanish on the Greater Antilles and the mainland, along with indigenous resistance, meant that at first many islands in the Eastern Caribbean remained unsettled. The incursions of English and French sailors and settlers into the area, of course, incited violent responses not only from the indigenous peoples but also from the Spanish. This was especially the case during times of war, notably during the years from 1585 to 1604, when the famous (or infamous) Francis Drake, along with other English privateers, repeatedly sacked and looted Spanish settlements in Santo Domingo, Cartagena, and elsewhere. Though the conflicts in the Americas were encouraged by parallel conflicts on the European continent, they also continued even when there was peace across the Atlantic. The Caribbean, like the rest of the Americas, was "beyond the line." French and Spanish diplomats agreed in 1559 that their negotiations for peace at home would still allow for war across the Atlantic. Spanish and English diplomats similarly drew up peace treaties in 1604 and 1630 that "deliberately sidestepped their rival pretensions in America."[35]

The various English and French sailors whom the indigenous peoples of the Eastern Caribbean encountered were part of a new wave of colonizers that would ultimately stake a claim to the islands of the Eastern Caribbean. Pirates, members of what Pierre Chaunu called an "international criminal organization" working loosely for European governments, struck the first blows against Spanish and Portuguese hegemony in the Americas and therefore opened the gate for a new phase of European colonization. Throughout the sixteenth century, ships heavy with silver and gold dug by indigenous slaves out of the mines of the Americas, predominantly in Mexico and Peru, constantly crossed the Atlantic. These floating treasure chests, often traveling relatively unarmed, were all-too-tempting prey for unscrupulous adventurers. The Spanish and Portuguese did their best to defend their ships against these marauders, at significant cost, while English and French governors saw that it was in their interest to support their activities against their enemies. By weakening the Spanish hold on the seas and setting up unofficial settlements in different parts of the Caribbean, the pirates opened the way for more permanent colonial settlement supported by European royal governments.[36]

Colonial projects were spurred on by the image of the Caribbean as a site of possibility spreading throughout Europe. Many European travelers romanticized the natural beauty of the Caribbean. "La Spañola is a marvel," wrote Columbus in his first letter describing his landfall in the Caribbean, which was translated and published in many languages soon afterward. He described harbors that "would not be believed without being seen" and mountains "of a thousand shapes" that were "filled with trees of a thousand kinds and tall, seeming to touch the sky." English privateer George Clifton, visiting Dominica in 1598, similarly described the mountainous country and wondered at the tall trees that "grow like good children of some happily civill body, without envie or oppression." Sir Henry Colt, visiting Barbados in 1631, marveled at the trees and the fruit they produced, reaching for the right metaphor when he described how the palmetto tree carried leaves "like a ladyes skreen fann, or peacocks tayle, the fruit like cabbidge but better."[37]

The Carmelite missionary Maurile de Saint-Michel, who traveled to the French colonies in the Eastern Caribbean in the 1650s, reflected on the many differences between the two worlds: "Here instead of bread we eat Cassava, which is very common and abundant; instead of beef we eat *lamentin* [manatee], which is a sort of sea dog caught along the shore; instead of chicken, large lizards that they make into a good soup." He also commented on the "excellent fruit," such as pineapples and guavas, to be had.[38]

Subsequent generations of European colonizers in the Caribbean would also focus on the beauty and variety of the natural world, often seemingly oblivious to the grim and brutal exploitation and oppression of the native and soon vast numbers of forcibly imported African peoples. Father Jean-Baptiste du Tertre, a Dominican missionary, devoted a volume to the natural history of the islands that included detailed engravings of many indigenous plants. A century later, the planter-historian Edward Long also devoted a volume of his history of Jamaica to the natural world. Such forms of wonder about the New World, however, did not rein in the impulses that began to shatter both the ecology and the existing indigenous worlds of the Caribbean.[39]

By the eighteenth century, the world of the plantation had quickly overtaken the indigenous forms of land use throughout much of the Caribbean, notably on the thriving colonies of Saint-Domingue and Jamaica. Writers at the time in these societies largely understood the indigenous as being consigned to history, though fascinating nonetheless. Long, for instance, found himself transfixed by the history of the indigenous civilizations of Jamaica. He described a "remarkable cave" outside a Spanish town that was "strewed with human bones," which he concluded were the "relicks of the last remnant of that unfortunate people, who perished here beneath the insupportable tyranny of their conquerors." After describing other nearby caves in which there were "large quantities of human bones, almost consumed by time," he wrote that they were the remains of indigenous people who had fled from their "savage invaders" into those caves. Though they "died miserably," he wrote, they left a "sad, though glorious, monument to future ages, of their having disdained to survive the loss of liberty and their country." Interestingly, Long also reported that there "runs a tradition among the Negroes, that a white person many years ago collected a vast pile" of bones and "consumed it to ashes." He did not explain the motivation attributed to this person, but the fact that this story was transmitted suggests interestingly that there was a concern within the slave community both about the presence of these bones and, perhaps, about attempts made to destroy them.[40]

A few decades later, the Martinican-born historian of Saint-Domingue, Médéric-Louis-Elie Moreau de Saint-Méry, similarly documented the many relics present throughout the colony, including some bones found in caves and what he called "fetishes," probably stone zemis, found in different parts of the colony. He described how slaves digging holes for cane on one sugar plantation kept turning up "new vestiges of the existence of this race now erased from the list of humans." Like Long, Moreau expressed sadness at the destruction of the indigenous communities. "The regret of the philosopher is awakened," wrote Moreau, "when he thinks about the fact that from a people so numerous, there is not one left to enlighten us on its history."[41]

For Long and Moreau, of course, regretting the lost civilizations of the Caribbean, and commenting on the barbarism that had destroyed them, was also a convenient distraction from the brutal system they actively participated in and defended: the plantation. What was ultimately built up on the Caribbean islands, in the wake of the wastelands of human devastation brought on by European settlement, was still another form of devastation, a highly profitable and productive one which reshaped not only the geography of the Caribbean itself but the economy, society, culture, and even intellectual history of much of the broader Atlantic world. The decimation of the indigenous population created an opening for the creation of a new order, one based on the mass importation of enslaved people from Africa in the Caribbean region. By the early eighteenth century, ships were leaving the Eastern Caribbean colonies with increasing regularity carrying a new kind of gold—sugar—across the Atlantic. Led by the Caribbean, much of the "New World" came "to resemble," as David Brion Davis has written, "the Death Furnace of the ancient god Moloch—consuming African slaves so increasing numbers of Europeans (and later, white Americans) could consume sugar, coffee, rice and tobacco."[42]

The indigenous world nonetheless remains in some ways in Caribbean culture, language, and economy. Although Europeans regularly suppressed indigenous names for places in the Caribbean and gave them new names—a dramatization of their power—a number of pre-Columbian names were maintained. Among these are Jamaica, the Caicos islands, Aruba (from Arubeira), Martinique (from Matinino), and Cuba (notwithstanding Spanish attempts to name this largest of the Caribbean islands "Juana" or "Fernandina"). Other terms from indigenous languages entered into European languages: the large seaworthy *canoas* that were central to pre-Columbian Caribbean cultures led to the use of the term "canoe" and its variants in several languages. The terms "hurricane" and "barbeque" also have origins in Caribbean languages, as does the term "cannibal." The term "tobacco," too, has its roots in the Caribbean, though like "cannibal" its use was founded on a misunderstanding. The term *tabaco* was used to describe the tube through which a hallucinogenic powder called cohoba was inhaled into the nose. Spanish confusion led to "the loss of the former term and the misapplication of the latter" to the plant itself.[43]

Indigenous agricultural techniques also profoundly shaped Caribbean culture. "The subsistence economy that developed in the sixteenth century, based on the sea's resources and heavily intercropped kitchen gardens," argues Samuel Wilson, "clearly comes in large part from pre-conquest, aboriginal economic practices." This contribution, however, was rarely documented and remains little acknowledged because the interaction from which it emerged was "largely between African people, both free and enslaved, and indigenous people." In addition to techniques of fishing and agriculture that would become central to the struggles for autonomy of slaves and ex-slaves, some aspects of religious practice may have been preserved. In this important sense, the history of the indigenous Caribbean lay the foundation for the long-term development of various forms of the counter-plantation in the region—a vital inheritance that needs to be recognized and understood.[44]

The presence of the indigenous past has long been recognized among Haitian political leaders and thinkers. When they declared independence from France, the founders of the country decided to return to the indigenous name of Haiti. This was a way of asserting a kind of legitimate sovereignty over the land, and part of a larger project of linking together the struggles of the enslaved against colonialism to earlier forms of resistance. "The African and the Indian," wrote Emile Nau in his 1854 study of the caciques of Haiti, "were linked together by their chains." Through this "community of suffering," their "destinies were intertwined." "Having inherited their servitude, we ultimately inherited their country." Nau made an early effort to write a history "by placing myself among them," one that historians continue to attempt to this day.[45]

The memory of indigenous resistance was kept alive in Haiti in other ways too. A song collected in 1893 from an elderly man by the Haitian writer Frédéric Marcelin at the ruins of the palace of Sans-Souci, in the north of Haiti, powerfully brings together the intertwined histories evoked by Nau. Marcelin and Nau argued the song dated back to the early nineteenth-century reign of Henry Christophe, though of course it could have been shaped and reshaped between then and the time they heard it sung. It explicitly connects the struggles of the slaves with those of earlier generations. Through the lyrics, the battles fought in different eras become one and the same, warriors speaking as one. The song begins by declaring that the "Butios"—indigenous priests—"have predicted victory" and asks for support from the zemis. "Our faces," it goes on, are covered in "Xagua," the plant traditionally used among indigenous communities to paint bodies. "We carry terror on our faces!" Then another symbol is invoked: that of the conch shell (the lambi), used as a call to revolt. And words from a song of Central African origin—"Aya bombé!"—become a chorus, repeated again and again.

> The lambi is sounding in the air
> No one can resist us
> Kill, exterminate, burn!
> Their skin will become the hammock
> For our children to sleep in
> Aya bombé, aya bombé![46]

The call to relentless violent resistance takes other evocative forms in the song: "Let us smash their hard heads / Just as in the season of ripeness / Guavas are crushed on the ground / Aya bombé, aya bombe!" "Our cause is just!" the song declares. "The land is ours. Let us defend it with our pointed arrows!" Alongside this fierceness there is also a kind of sadness, a recognition that resistance often can happen only through escape. In the song the military reality of the Haitian Revolution, in which insurgents' redoubts in the mountains became sanctuaries and hubs of resistance, is merged with earlier histories in which indigenous communities could find refuge only in the mountains of Bahoruco. A goddess figure named Mamona is evoked as a final refuge.

> To die free, we have to go higher
> Very high, even higher, always
> To where they can't climb!
> Their feet are not sure or agile
> The plain betrays us and hands us over to them
> But Bahoruco welcomes and keeps us
> O sacred mother, o saintly mountain
> O Mamona, ultimate refuge!
> Take our bonds, o faithful one
> Who will dare come and find us when we are in your arms?
> And in the hair of your vines?
> Aya bombé, aya bombé!

Caribs and Europeans

During the same period when Haitian revolutionaries were drawing on these histories of resistance, the Eastern Caribbean was the theater of a major military showdown between independent indigenous groups and colonial powers. In 1797, after a brutal war in St. Vincent, the British deported several thousand members of a group they called the "Black Caribs." It was an attempt to put an end to several centuries of conflict through which indigenous communities had sought to preserve autonomy in the face of expanding European colonialism.

The story of the Caribs of the Eastern Caribbean is, again, a story of the imbrication of categories and power. The interpretations of the indigenous Caribbean generated during Columbus's first voyage had an extremely tenuous relationship to the realities of the indigenous Caribbean. Nevertheless, these interpretations had profound and long-lasting consequences for European understandings of the region, and therefore for its inhabitants. Columbus's journal included several descriptions of indigenous people warning him about communities living on other islands who "eat human flesh." Supposedly, some described these fearsome people as "those of *caniba*, or *canima*"; others called them *Caníbales*, and some spoke of an island called Carib and of *Caribes*. Columbus also claimed that these dangerous peoples had been described as having "one eye and the face of a dog." As Philip Boucher notes, these creative visualizations "obviously reflected inherited classical and medieval notions about anthropophagi inhabiting the far ends of the earth" and may have had little to do with what the indigenous peoples were in fact saying. Hulme suggests that Columbus's interpretations of indigenous statements "had such obvious continuities with the classical Mediterranean paradigm that it is tempting to see the whole intricate web of colonial discourse as weaving itself in its own separate space entirely unaffected by any observation of or interchange with native Caribbean cultures." The deep irony, as Melanie Newton notes, is that in the course of the "first expression of Spain's annihilationist impulse in the Americas," it was "the Caribs who entered the imperial archive as 'man-eaters' and murderers."[47]

When Columbus's second voyage arrived in the Caribbean, hitting land in the Eastern Caribbean rather than on the larger islands where Columbus had stopped on the first voyage, he and his crew were quickly convinced that they had stumbled upon the *Caribes*. When some members of the expedition looted a village on the island that would later be named Guadeloupe, they came back with "four or five bones of the arms and legs of men." A chronicler and the principal physician of the journey, Diego Álvarez Chanca, concluded from this "that the islands were those of *Caribe*, which are inhabited by people who eat human flesh." An alternative explanation favored by some contemporary scholars, that such bones were likely those of deceased members of the community whose bodies were being prepared according to indigenous mortuary practices, was not entertained. The stories heard by Columbus on his first voyage about flesh-eating peoples were quickly confirmed in the minds of the Spanish, and the reputation of the indigenous groups of the Eastern Caribbean, the *Caníbales* or the Caribs, was, it seems, sealed for the long term. The term used for this group would give rise ultimately to the term "cannibal" and its variants in different languages to mean a human who had eaten human flesh.[48]

The designation of Caribs as cannibals quickly came to have both political and economic advantages. "With little cause to examine the plausibility of Columbus's reports, since the existence of 'cannibals' on the frontiers of 'civilization' had been accepted since classic times and the writings of Herodotus and Pliny," writes Neil Whitehead, "and with sound economic judgments to accept them, the Spanish crown soon enshrined the ethnographic judgment in law."[49]

As will be discussed in the following chapter, Spanish law permitted the enslavement of indigenous people across the empire who were taken as prisoners of war or of armed rebellion against Spanish conquest and rule. This was the case generally until the 1540s and remained the policy in some places until the end of the seventeenth century. Large numbers were seized illegally as well. In this legal context, the accusation against Caribs of cannibalism was used as an implicit part of the construction of a population as essentially warlike, that is, of a people who not only resisted Spanish conquest fiercely but could perhaps never be ruled, never acquiesce to Catholicism and the Spanish crown, never be loyal subjects. Designated Carib areas were thus fair game for slave raids at any time. One sixteenth-century Spanish chronicler, Juan de Castellanos, bemoaned the fact that in some areas indigenous communities were labeled Carib by officials "not because there they ate human flesh but because they defended their homes well." But it was not exactly that, either. Even in Eastern Caribbean areas where there was, in truth, no concerted effort at Spanish conquest and colonization, Spanish leaders sustained, and presented as inevitable, a state of constant war with indigenous communities. Much of the Eastern Caribbean and northern coast of South America became a slaving zone, a space largely outside the reach of formal colonization but that was raided consistently to sell enslaved laborers in Spanish settlements elsewhere, particularly Santo Domingo. All this helps explain the contradictory assessments of the same area as Carib or not Carib at different times and by different groups. Missionaries were often the most likely to assert that a particular area was not

Carib in attempts to protect residences from slave raids. The people inhabiting the island of Trinidad, for instance, were declared "Carib" in 1511, but after Bartolomé de las Casas intervened, this ascription—which functioned as a kind of condemnation—was reversed in 1518. These discrepant determinations reflected contradictory and changing political goals and interests. Those seeking to actively colonize certain areas with settlers or to evangelize tended not to describe those areas as Carib, while those who wanted to make them part of a slaving zone did.[50]

Over time, European writers added another justification for their wars and enslavement against surviving indigenous communities. They came to present those they described as "Caribs" as recent arrivals in the region, who had invaded and decimated the innocent and peaceful people who lived there before them. This characterization, one that survives in many accounts of the Caribbean, both mirrored and masked the actual historical processes underway by placing the invading Europeans in the role of liberators and defenders of the recently colonized, "true" indigenous residents in the region. Although many residents of la Isla Española and other islands of the Western Caribbean had in fact fought fiercely against the Spanish, the most common portrait that emerged by the mid- to late sixteenth century focused on these groups as relatively peaceful and docile. This portrait was in part the result of the writings of Bartolomé de las Casas, who eloquently protested Spanish excesses in the Caribbean by describing a simple and innocent people overrun by vicious colonists exercising unnecessary violence. By the time such historical narratives of the pre-Columbian Caribbean took root, it cost very little to present certain indigenous communities as innocent and peaceful in contrast to the Caribs. Indigenous communities were granted a level of humanity and innocence, for the most part posthumously, after they had been thoroughly dominated and decimated.[51]

Recent critiques of traditional understandings of the indigenous Caribbean have successfully challenged older orthodoxies about the region, but they have as yet not replaced them with a new consensus about what terms and categories most usefully describe the indigenous world that existed at the time of European arrival. Despite all of the difficulties in doing so, we still should ask what the indigenous people Columbus encountered, in fact, did say, and more broadly to what extent the expressions of fear and conflict that Europeans drew upon in inventing their map of the Caribbean were rooted in longer histories of settlement, war, and conquest in the region.

While the indigenous people of Cuba, Puerto Rico, and Hispaniola were overwhelmed, decimated, and assimilated by European colonization within a century, those in the Eastern Caribbean experienced this period in a very different way and secured, for a time, a different fate. They, too, were exposed to deadly European diseases. But because Eastern Caribbean communities preserved their hold over their islands and had only sporadic contact with sailors and merchant ships, Europeans had a less devastating impact there than in the Greater Caribbean. Though indigenous people suffered from the many slave raids carried out against them by the Spanish, they also boldly fought back, launching raids of their own against Puerto Rico and other Spanish settlements. Through the sixteenth and into the early seventeenth century, they maintained near complete control over the islands of the Eastern Caribbean. Some groups on Dominica and St. Vincent were a strong and important presence, shaping the course of imperial expansion through the eighteenth century. The successes of these groups depended on a combination of violent resistance, economic and ecological adaptation, and skillful diplomacy.

As the French and British moved into the region, they generated their own representations of the indigenous peoples that both drew on Spanish precedents and were shaped by local interactions and realities. The category of "Carib" ultimately took on a life of its own and became established as a true representation of the inhabitants of the Eastern Caribbean. Some of these inhabitants occasionally used the term to describe themselves but only, it seems, in certain circumstances. César de Rochefort, a French Protestant who traveled in the Caribbean in the late 1640s, wrote that the Caribs "never call themselves by this name among themselves, except when they are drunk and, with their head full of wine, jump and joyfully say, in their *baragouin* [jargon], 'I'm a good Carib.'" Beyond that, they only used the term as a way to identify themselves when involved in trade and communication with "foreigners," since they knew that this name "was known to them." Europeans' categories and stereotypes, then, were incorporated to some extent into the lives of indigenous communities, but as Neil Whitehead and Peter Hulme have written, "it is clear that by 1650 'Carib' had become as much a political category as a cultural one," and that as an identifying marker of indigenous identity, it had been forged in response to European encroachment. "Political alliances, cultural and social features, and a sense of ethnic identity were to an important degree the product of interaction with and resistance to European forces." But most residents of the Eastern Caribbean, according to seventeenth-century sources, still used terms other than "Carib" to describe themselves, particularly "Kalinago."[52]

The indigenous communities in the Eastern Caribbean lived lives that involved regular movement between islands, combining fishing and agriculture in a way that stretched across the archipelago. This was made possible by their "extraordinary seamanship, which turned the waters up and down the island chain into a highway." They maintained gardens on some of the "lower-lying, more arid islands," including Antigua and Barbados, which could "supply them with provisions on their travels." Their understanding of what the land was, and how it should be used, was radically different from the understanding of those who would be brought to the region with the European plantation model. What is striking, however, is how long the indigenous communities were able to maintain this alternative social and economic structure in the face of increasing pressure and encroachment. They did so in part by making use of the European presence, trading for goods with passing ships, even collaborating at times with settlers, while also fighting fiercely to maintain control and autonomy over both geographical space and their right to use it as they wished.[53]

During the sixteenth century, many ships traveled past the Eastern Caribbean on journeys to other parts of the Caribbean or to the mainland of South America. They often hit land there after the Atlantic crossing, in desperate need of fruit and fresh water. In 1530, the Spanish officially designated Dominica as a stopping point, and a few decades later it was known as the point where transatlantic convoys were to split up if some ships were heading to Mexico and others toward South America. Sailors therefore frequently came into contact with Caribs in the Eastern Caribbean as they sought sources of food and fresh water. Many of these encounters started out quite friendly. The French captain René Laudonnière, for instance, described a set of encounters with Caribs that took place when his boat stopped at Dominica, which he described as "full of hilles, and of very good smell," in 1564. When his ships anchored off the shore, "two Indians (inhabitants of that place) sayled towards us in two Canoas full of a fruit of great excellencie which they call *Ananas* [pineapples]." The two groups "traffiqued dayly," with the Caribs exchanging fruit "very liberally" for "things of small value." Such exchanges were sometimes shadowed, however, by the threat of violence. One of the individuals who approached them when they first arrived, in fact, upon seeing the French, went back to land and sought to escape. The French pursued him and brought him to the ship, where he explained that he was fearful of falling into Spanish hands, having been "taken once before." The Spanish, "as he shewed us, had cut of [off] his stones [testicles]." The French, too, had conflicts with the Caribs. Several sailors journeyed from Laudonnière's ships, ventured inland, and began to steal from the gardens of pineapples they found, "trampling through them without any discretion." A fight ensued, and one of the French sailors was shot and left behind. The French did not know if he was dead or taken prisoner, but they didn't stay to find out.[54]

In the 1580s Francis Drake stopped in Dominica and found "very personable and handsome strong men," with their skin colored red, who helped the British by carrying "on their bare shoulders fresh water to our ships boates, and fetching from their houses great store of Tabacco, as also a kind of bread which they fed on, called Cassavi, very white and souverie, and made of the roots of Cassavi." They also received a "cock & a henne," potatoes, and plantains. Another British pirate, Robert Davies, described stopping at Dominica in 1595 and trading for "plantans, pinos [pineapples], and potatos." Several sick sailors also found a "hot bath" along a river and "were soone recovered of their sicknesses." A few years later another British writer described trading in Dominica for "Tabacco, Pinos, Plantins, Potatoes and Peppers." He also noted that the Caribs spoke "some Spanish words," and he encountered a "King" wearing "a wide hanging garment of rich crimson Taffetie, a Spanish Rapier in his hand, and the modell of a Lyon in shining Brasse, hanging upon his breast." He did not reflect on the provenance of these clothes, but the near-constant war between Caribs and Spanish suggests it was probably not a gift.[55]

Charles Fleury, an early seventeenth-century French captain, described how boats "full of French, Dutch, English and Spanish" continued to stop along the islands to get fresh water and buy food, particularly fruits and cassava, from the Caribs. The Spanish, he claimed, never dared stay for long, for they were regarded with enormous suspicion, so that when the natives traded with them, they did so "holding a bow and arrow in one hand and the merchandise they wish to sell in the other." In contrast, Fleury claimed, the Caribs liked the French "above all other nations," and he described the overwhelming hospitality that the Caribs extended. Malnourished sailors were showered with food, and Carib hosts would wake them up "three or four times each night to touch the stomach of their guests, in order to see if it was still small and, if it was, they woke them up and made them eat." Sometimes the results were quite disastrous, as the sailors had intense pains in their stomachs from having eaten so much after weeks spent eating so little. Luckily, though, the Caribs had a cure for this, making them eat grease made from turtles that helped the sailors digest. According to Fleury, "without the use of the turtle grease, which softened our intestines, few French would have been saved and survived." The Caribs offered other kinds of medical care as well. A particularly menacing kind of insect, "finding the soles of our feet easier to penetrate" than those of the Caribs, dug into the feet of many of the sailors. The Caribs, though, tenderly pulled the insects out, and dressed the wounds they had caused through this surgery. They liked the company of the French, some Caribs told them, because the devil didn't attack when the French were with them.[56]

By the early 1600s, the Caribs had been trading and interacting with Europeans for over a century. They had clearly adapted to these occasional visits and had taken advantage of the opportunity to incorporate new animals and crops into their lives. When an ill-fated visit of English sailors returning from a failed expedition to Guiana began in 1605, the Carib residents of St. Lucia offered "Tobacco, Plantons, Potatoes, Pines, Sugar Canes and diverse other fruits, with Hens, Chickens, Turtles and Guanas." During later moments of trading, according to one chronicler of the journey, John Nicholl, the Caribs also offered pumpkins, calabashes, and guavas. The last fruit, Nicholl noted, grew as big as apples and were "verie pleasant to eat." They also had medicinal qualities, which the sailors likely learned from the Caribs: the "green ones" were, Nicholl wrote, "wholesome for the bloodie flux." The English were also learning other things: they hunted turtles by following the tracks the turtles left in the sand with their fins when they came onto the beaches to lay their eggs, then turning the turtles on their backs and waiting for them to die. Nicholl described impressive Carib gardens: a "most pleasant Garden of Potatoes" that was round and "encompassed by a greene Banke," and other "goodly Gardens" with an "abbundance of Cassada, Potatoes, Tobacco, Cotton-wool-trees, and Guiava trees." The Caribs also showed they had other important skills. When a dispute began with the English, the Caribs turned on them and massacred much of the crew. Familiarity had not bred sympathy: as the Caribs attacked the English, they named them "by our names as they hit us." Still, the reputation of the Caribs as purveyors of valuable goods continued during the next decades. In 1631, the English colonist Sir Henry Colt was disappointed when none of the Caribs of Dominica responded to the cannon shot fired by his captain as an invitation to trade. He was hoping to acquire one of the hammocks the Caribs made, which he had heard were of excellent quality.[57]

In time, roving bands of sailors and pirates began to set up small communities that lay the foundations for the colonization of various islands by the British, French, Dutch, and other European powers in the early decades of the seventeenth century. Two early ventures at colonizing the Eastern

Caribbean, the first at St. Lucia and the second in Grenada in 1609, ended in failure when the settlements were overrun and the settlers killed by Carib inhabitants. Several attempts to colonize Guiana by both the British and French ended in failure. The English tried in 1604, 1609, 1617, 1620, and again in 1629 and 1643, never with success. While some settlements were destroyed by disease, starvation, and indigenous resistance, others were destroyed by the Spanish. The English Providence Company, founded in 1630, set up colonies on three islands: Providence (today Santa Catalina), Henrietta (today San Andreas) along the Central American coast, and Tortuga, off the coast of la Isla Española. Although they set up some plantations and grew corn, tobacco, and cotton, they "soon diverted their energies to piratical expeditions against nearby Spanish settlements," according to Richard Dunn. Indeed, "Tortuga was an outright pirate lair" whose heyday generated a long-lasting and nearly mythical reputation as a hub of danger and dissipation. The Spanish took over Tortuga in 1635 and closed down the Providence Company in 1641.[58]

As Richard Dunn writes, the lesson was that "settlement was only feasible in sites removed as far as possible from contact with the Spanish and Indian population centers." In this sense, the home of the first successful settlements of both the English and the French was perfect. In 1622, the Englishman Thomas Warner was returning from Guiana when he stopped on the small island of St. Christopher, at the northern end of the chain of islands that make up the Lesser Antilles. The island, along with its neighbor Nevis, was known to many sailors, who frequently stopped to gather water, fell trees, and in one case catch a turtle so large it was a struggle to get it on board the ship. When Francis Drake stopped there in the mid-1580s, he noted that "there were not any people at all that we could heare of" on the island. But when Warner arrived in 1622, he found a group of Europeans there growing tobacco and was inspired to seek funding for the construction of a larger settlement focused on the production of this "rich commodity." There were a small number of indigenous inhabitants on St. Christopher, while Nevis was considered uninhabited. Warner succeeded in gaining investment from merchants and a license from the king to "traffick to and from the said islands" of St. Christopher, Nevis, Barbados, and Montserrat and to "transport men, and do all such things as settle a colony and advance trade there, to govern and rule all persons there." Several ships arrived in St. Christopher in 1624 and 1625 under Warner's command. In 1627, Warner was named governor-for-life of St. Christopher, and he remained there until his death in 1647.[59]

The British were not alone in St. Christopher, however. As Warner was raising money to support his settlement there, merchants at Rouen learned of a small community of Frenchmen on the island and decided to invest in a larger colonization effort. They placed Belin d'Esnambuc, who had experience in both the Caribbean and Brazil, in charge of the mission to St. Christopher. D'Esnambuc's effort led to the creation of the Compagnie de Saint-Christophe, which received a royal charter from Cardinal Richelieu, Louis XIII's minister, instructing it to bring settlers to St. Christopher, Barbados, and other islands "at the entrance of Peru." Several ships were sent from France in 1627 to expand the settlement in St. Christopher, carrying several hundred settlers recruited primarily from Normandy, though more than half died either on the journey or soon after their arrival in the Caribbean. In the same year, the French and British signed a treaty dividing up the island. The British occupied the center portion and the French both ends. They also united to destroy the small group of Caribs remaining on the island. The British and French efforts at the colonization of the Caribbean, which in time would evolve into a violent and ongoing war for supremacy in the region, began with cooperation on the same small stretch of land. Although a Spanish fleet attacked in 1629, the Spanish did not reoccupy the island, and the fledging French-English settlement grew and prospered during the next decades.[60]

In February 1627, meanwhile, the British set up a second colony in Barbados when "a small group of Englishmen arrived from England, bringing with them a handful of Africans captured during the sea voyage." Subjected to slave raiding during the sixteenth century, the indigenous population on the island had declined, and Barbados seems to have been uninhabited when the British arrived. Within a few decades, Barbados would be transformed from a small settlement into a thriving sugar colony, the first center of the "sugar revolution" of the seventeenth century and a prototype for the other colonies that would follow its transformation into a plantation society founded on the exploitation of a majority of enslaved Africans.[61]

Governor Thomas Warner had several children in the Caribbean, among them a boy whose mother was a Carib woman who was a servant in his household. He gave this boy the name Thomas and raised him as his son. The boy's life changed, however, when his father died in 1647 and the other members of the household began treating him as a servant, sending him to work in the fields. He ran away, back to Dominica, where his mother was from. There, thanks to his familiarity with the English, he became an important local leader, negotiating and navigating with the French and English, and he became known by the name of "Indian Warner." Both imperial powers sought to make use of him, but he was also adept at making use of them, playing them off against one another and keeping them each a bit unsure about exactly to whom he was loyal. He dealt closely with English and French colonists, at times participating in raids against different colonies. He was, write Peter Hulme and Neil Whitehead, "a figure who inhabited that treacherous zone 'between' cultures," moving "between two worlds, being seen at times on both sides as a valued intermediary, sometimes as a potential traitor." In 1660, he led a delegation of Caribs to Antigua to make peace with the English. In 1663, the governor of Barbados sent him on a visit to London, where he appeared at court, and then commissioned him as the deputy governor of the island of Dominica. He had instructions to keep the peace between English and French colonists, return any escaped slaves from nearby colonies, and prevent raids by the Caribs against the English. As an account by the French missionary Jean-Baptiste Du Tertre put it, the English, feeling "restricted" by the treaties that had made Dominica and St. Vincent Carib "reserves," "believed that Indian Warner was the most appropriate individual to get round this treaty, & to take possession by these means of the island of Dominica."[62]

Despite the confidence placed in him by English officials, there were some who always suspected his loyalty. Among them was his half-brother, Philip Warner, the son of Thomas Warner and his third wife, Anne. Following in his father's footsteps, Philip Warner had become the deputy governor of Antigua. When a group of Caribs from Dominica raided the colony in 1675, Philip Warner led a punitive expedition to take revenge for the "bloody and perfidious villainies" committed against the English. He was joined by Indian Warner, who led a party of Caribs from a different part of the island to join the English. Afterward, Indian Warner joined Philip Warner and his troops on their ship to celebrate the victory. But they had actually been drawn into a trap. Once Indian Warner and his Carib party were drunk, Philip Warner ordered them killed. They were overpowered by the larger number of Englishmen. Indian Warner's young son, seeing his father killed, asked to join him in death, and Philip Warner killed him as well, along with all the others of the group.[63]

What was the goal of the massacre? An English official explained that Indian Warner, "though he had an English commission," was "a great villain and took a French commission." The best policy, he insisted, was the complete annihilation of the Caribs. Others, however, were shocked at the slaughter, rightly understanding that this would only push the Caribs in the region more forcefully into an alliance with the French. The English crown demanded that "speedy and exemplary justice should be done upon the person guilty of this inhuman act," so that the "innocent blood that hath been so barbarously spilt be fully avenged." Officials worried rightly that the Caribs had been "alienated" by the action and suggested that there needed to be some "public demonstration" of "the detestation his Majesty and the whole nation" had of what Philip Warner had done, going so far as to suggest that one option would be "sending them some heads." Philip Warner was brought to England and imprisoned in the Tower of London to stand trial for the killing of Indian Warner. In his trial, he never sought to deny what he had done. His defense centered on justifying the killing by arguing that Indian Warner was, in fact, not English at all, but fully Carib. He denied that Indian Warner was Thomas Warner's son, producing testimony that claimed Indian Warner was just one of the "Indian slaves" who grew up in the household and "was never baptized or looked on as any other than a slave or negro's child." "Killing an Indian heathen," Philip Warner argued, was "not so great a crime as killing His Majesty's subjects." In the end, despite the strong initial reaction from the crown, Philip Warner had several powerful people on his side, and so he was acquitted of the crime. In this way, the English resolved the "problem" of Indian Warner, who, as Hulme and Whitehead note, was always a "source of ideological uncertainty."[64]

Predictably, the Warner affair ultimately solidified Carib hostility to the English. In 1681, two thousand Carib warriors in fifty pirogues (boats) attacked the small colony of Barbuda. The British responded with raids against St. Vincent and Dominica, burning hundreds of houses and pirogues and destroying provision grounds. But the Caribs largely escaped into the forest and returned to rebuild their communities soon after. The French understood the opportunity and cultivated increasingly strong links with Carib communities, notably by sending missionaries into their communities. The Dominican priest Father Labat, who lived in the Caribbean from 1693 to 1705, wrote extensively about Carib life. He acquired a Carib hammock, whose virtues as a traveling companion he extolled. "I carried one in my travels in Italy," he wrote, "where everyone knows the beds in hotels are generally very dirty." Attaching his hammock to doors or window frames with screws like bottle-openers, he slept happily, "without worrying about the lice, bedbugs and other trash that the beds of those lands are abundantly supplied with." He was, he wrote, surprised that such hammocks were not used by the military. This was only one aspect of Carib life that Labat found ingenious and that Europeans colonists readily appropriated. Labat described the techniques they used to capture parrots: they identified which trees the parrots were living in and then at night placed hot coals with a paste of hot peppers underneath them. The smoke confused and intoxicated the birds, who fell to the ground. The legs and wings of the parrots were then tied up, and they were trained not to bite, and to speak, rewarded for good behavior with food and for bad behavior with a puff of tobacco in their beaks.[65]

Among those Caribs Labat came to know was Indian Warner's mother, whom he visited in Dominica in 1700. People still called her Mrs. Warner, or "Madame Ouvernard," as he put it, even though it had been many decades since she had been sent back to the island after the death of Governor Thomas Warner. It was not her connection to the Englishman, however, that gave her the high status she had among the Caribs, but her "agedness": she was, he wrote, a hundred years old. Indian Warner, wrote Labat, was just one of many children she had had by Thomas Warner, so that "her Carbet [home], which is very large, was peopled with a marvelous number of sons, grandsons and great-grandsons." Labat was greeted warmly when he arrived, carrying "two bottles of rum," and Indian Warner's mother asked when another missionary named Raymond Breton, who had been there in the mid-seventeenth century "working futilely" to convert the Caribs, was coming back. That missionary had, in fact, been dead for thirty years, but Labat had learned that the Caribs refused to believe that someone was dead "until they had seen them in their grave." So he told them Breton "would come soon," which "gave pleasure to this good woman." With her "still lively eyes," she invited Labat and his party to stay a while and brought them hammocks so they could rest.[66]

The Garifuna

The indigenous worlds of the late seventeenth-century Caribbean are perhaps best conceived of as a space profoundly shaped by, and reconstituted through, the colonial experience. The arrival of Europeans starting in the late fifteenth century, writes Julie Chun Kim, had set off "a chain reaction of political and social reorganization." "Those who survived the initial rounds of decimation and assimilation responded by fleeing to the margins of Iberian control and regrouping as novel tribes and entities." Within the Caribbean, the eastern islands became a space of refuge, at least for a time. Because they lacked "the rich mineral deposits and concentrated population centers" of the larger islands, they were less of a focus of early Spanish colonization. In time, Kim argues, they became home to a "heterogeneous group of refugees" who were identified by the Spanish as "Carib." As the French and British began to colonize the Eastern Caribbean, these groups continued to resist and to seek out spaces of sanctuary. The islands of Dominica and St. Vincent, two islands with "mountainous, heavily wooded slopes," became such spaces of refuge, and over the course of the seventeenth and eighteenth centuries, places where new kinds of indigenous communities and societies developed as well. This was notably true in St. Vincent, where Carib communities not only were made up of "diverse Amerindian populations" but also included people of African descent from nearby islands. Father Labat described St. Vincent as "the center of the Carib Republic," and it became the center for a century of renewal and resistance to European colonialism. The population of the island had, by the late seventeenth century, "two hundred years' experience of Europeans—and of keeping them at arm's length."[67]

By that time, Barbados had become the center of the British Caribbean plantation complex, thriving thanks to its exploitation of a large population of enslaved people from Africa and their descendants. As some learned, the winds and prevailing currents meant that if you could get in a boat in Barbados, it didn't take long to sail the hundred miles to St. Vincent, which was a radically different world. Alexander Anderson noted in the late eighteenth century that from St. Vincent all the nearby islands could be seen "distinctly," and the reverse was true too. "From Barbados, St. Vincent was on some days visible to the naked eye," writes Paul Johnson. "It must have seemed close enough to reach out and touch its verdant peaks and to imagine a very different life there." It was an island to maroon to. (The English term "maroon" derived from the Spanish term for escaped slave as well as for escaped or wild animal, *cimarrón*, which in turn came from the term *cima*, meaning mountain top.) And starting early in the seventeenth century, some enslaved people seem to have done just that. This continued into the late eighteenth century: in 1778, when two enslaved people ran away from Barbados, the owners took out an advertisement in the *St. Vincent Gazette*, looking for them. Colonial officials in Barbados and elsewhere regularly requested that Caribs return any escaped slaves they caught, but this does not seem to have happened very often. Instead, people of African descent were gradually incorporated into the indigenous communities in a process whose contours are difficult to reconstruct. There are almost no archival traces of the process, but language provides a clue. The communities that came to be known as the Black Caribs of St. Vincent speak the Carib language, with very few if any traces of African language. This may have been because escaped African slaves arrived slowly and in small numbers, so that they had little choice but to adopt the Carib language. Even if there were, at times, larger groups of Africans arriving in St. Vincent, they may have spoken many different languages. In this case, Carib would have served as a kind of common language, a bit like different creole languages did in other contexts, except that it didn't have to be invented. "The Africans adopted, and were adopted by," argues Johnson, "the Island Carib tongue and religion." A linguistic study done centuries later among the descendants of the Black Caribs in Honduras found this still to be largely true: they continued to speak a language very similar to that of the seventeenth-century Caribs, with a significant number of loan-words from French probably incorporated during the eighteenth century. There was, however, one telling and powerful mark of the linguistic impact of Africans: the word for "person" or "persons," a key word, is the Bantu term *mutu*. The fact that the term for this word, a rather central one in any language, came from an African language is a striking trace of the broader ways in which various cultures and languages interacted and created a new culture over the centuries on St. Vincent.[68]

The question of from where the African-descended population of St. Vincent originally came itself became an increasingly political issue in the late eighteenth century. In the context of increasing conflict with the Black Caribs, an English colonist named William Young claimed that the community had been born when a slave ship headed to Barbados got off course and foundered at St. Vincent. He dated this event in 1675 and said the ship had come from Bight of Benin in West Africa. A hurricane did hit Barbados in that year, which could have caused a ship to blow off course. Other authors dated the shipwreck later, to 1712 or 1734. As Christopher Taylor notes, if this was the source of the population of African descent on St. Vincent, it would have had to be a "very big ship," because a report from 1676 claimed that there were as many as three thousand on the island. In fact, a report from 1667 already claimed that some Spanish slave ships had foundered in St. Vincent in 1635. All of this suggests that the growth of the population of African descent on St. Vincent was a gradual process, probably combining different moments of arrival—perhaps one or more shipwrecked slavers, and then a consistent stream of escaped slaves from Barbados and other parts of the Eastern Caribbean. Over time, the story of the 1675 shipwreck has solidified, however, and has become a key part of Black Caribs' accounts of their own history. It is, among other things, a way to root the community's history outside the plantation complex, a story of the encounter between free people from two sides of the Atlantic: Africans enslaved and transported, but never prisoners of the plantation, and Caribs, steadfastly refusing submission to the Europeans.[69]

What transpired in St. Vincent, largely unobserved and undocumented by European colonists, was a remarkable process of cultural encounter and mixing. Over the course of two centuries, African and indigenous Caribbean lifeways and visions shaped one another. The culture of the Caribs itself was by the early seventeenth century shaped by interactions with European colonization. As people of African descent—whether from slave ships or escaping from nearly plantation islands—joined these communities, they brought a variety of experiences and forms of knowledge. "Coastal Africans," notes Johnson, "were likely to have been excellent builders of large canoes," and would have found they had this in common with Caribs, who had long constructed canoes that could carry fifty people or more up and down the archipelago. Certain aspects of Carib culture, in addition to language, were widely shared, notably the practice of flattening the heads of infants to give them a distinctive, long forehead, which helped identify the group as distinct from others. European missionaries, both French and English, were active in these communities at different points in their history, and aspects of Christian practice were taken on. There were also very likely connections made between other types of religious practice. One account of the Black Caribs from the early eighteenth century described them putting the "hair and bones of their dead relatives in a calabash," believing that "the spirit of the dead speaks within it, warning them of the plans of their enemies." This could have been the "borrowing of a West African practice, making the exchange a two-way street," or else "an Island Carib ritual grammar whose structure would have been strikingly familiar to the Africans." The Black Caribs also used what Europeans described as "charms," notably to protect them in battle, along with a range of incantations to protect themselves from spirits. These observed practices were, however, clearly part of a much broader matrix of religious practice, one that remains deeply anchored in the contemporary communities descended from the Black Caribs.[70]

Despite the fact that both Dominica and St. Vincent had been declared "reserve islands" in 1660, there were persistent attempts by European colonists to settle on both. The Carib communities tolerated small settlements, as long as they remained contained in certain parts of the island and didn't move into the areas they considered theirs. Carib land use was rooted in a long tradition of indigenous agricultural activity that supplemented fishing and hunting with the use of forests for food and medicine, along with the planting of provision grounds in various locations. Caribs considered woodlands as commons to be used by particular families or groups of Caribs, maintaining an equilibrium with the forest as a result. It was a form of land use that was much more suited to the environment of the Caribbean than the aggressive, and destructive, plantation agriculture that multiplied on other islands during the period. The deforestation of islands like Antigua and Barbados happened startlingly early. It quickly led to a level of "ecological change" that was "dramatic and even unprecedented" in world history. English colonists often considered forests to be dangerous sources of "miasmas" and diseases, and some forests were destroyed simply for this reason. In 1677, Antigua was still covered with many trees, but the governor of the Leeward Islands had slaves clear the woods to create "more health for the English." Heavy logging for export and construction also contributed to the destruction of the forests. By the mid-sixteenth century, the consequences were clear: there were flash floods, rains that carried soil down hillsides, and problems finding the necessary water for the ever-thirsty cane fields. Dominica and St. Vincent, in contrast, remained heavily wooded, thanks to the Carib control of much of the land.[71]

English colonists, however, had developed a critique of indigenous land use that claimed that it was nothing short of a crime that left too much land unused. The writings of the Swiss jurist Emmerich de Vatel, translated into English in 1760, argued that those who left lands "uncultivated" had no right to occupy them, and went further, saying they deserved "to be exterminated as savage and pernicious beasts." While it might have been acceptable to use land in this way in earlier times, the human race had "so multiplied" that all land had to be used productively for agriculture, so that those who maintained a different form of land use were effectively usurpers, stealing it from those who would labor and use it to produce food for the growing population. Colonial administrators repeatedly described the Black Caribs in this way, complaining in 1765 that they lived on the land in an "irregular manner at a great distance from each other, without any subordination, claiming large tracts of woodland intervening of which they make no use," and also owned land elsewhere in St. Vincent which interfered with the creation of large plantations.[72]

There was also another problem: the Black Caribs living in the forests were, as one report in 1771 put it, "exempted from fear of punishment"— they were too free. They fought back against attempts to take their land, "constituting one of the most effective groups" of "resisters ever encountered during British colonial rule." The fear of an armed resistance rooted in a particular landscape in St. Vincent shaped the ways observers described the land itself. The Scottish botanist Alexander Anderson described the interior of St. Vincent as "the most wild, unbroken and inaccessible" of any in the Caribbean, along with parts of Dominica, "consisting of an aggregate of deep ravines or chasms, perpendicular precipices and conical topped mountains jumbled together in all forms and appearances that man can conceive from the wildest sportings of nature." A Methodist missionary, who almost died after tumbling off a precipice with his horse, wrote of the interior of St. Vincent as a place "full of serpentine involutions," where "opposition and defiance seemed to be presented both by rocks and bushes; and a complication of obstacles threatened to prohibit all access." The landscape was "both the residence and the empire of Danger."[73]

The 1748 Treaty of Aix-la-Chapelle signed between the French and the English had confirmed that St. Vincent was neutral territory that was not to be settled by either empire, but within a few decades efforts were underway to colonize the parts of the island still controlled by the Caribs. The Black Caribs understood quite clearly how European colonialism worked: the mapmakers and surveyors were the first wave of invaders. In 1768, a surveyor tasked with mapping out the route for an extension of a road through Black Carib territory was stopped by an armed group who told him they would "not have the Great Road go any further." To make themselves clear, they burned down his house and "three hundred well-armed warriors then proceeded to demolish" a new barrack that had been built along the road. The government cartographer of St. Vincent was also threatened, and he hid his "half-made survey maps in a field" to try to save them. The Caribs, however, "soon found and burned the hidden maps." Through such actions, over the course of several years, the Black Caribs stopped attempts to move into their territory. They were able to push back against colonial attitudes about the land, and "indigenous meanings of the environment survived" thanks to their resistance.[74]

As a result, the Black Caribs faced an increasingly strong attempt to write their history in a way that delegitimized their claim to the land they were defending. They were described as interlopers on the island, as invaders who had taken land away from the group that became known, in contrast, as the "Yellow Caribs," or sometimes the "Red Caribs." The story went that the latter group, the legitimate indigenous people of the island, had found themselves enslaved and ultimately displaced by the larger group of Black

Caribs. It was, notes Peter Hulme, "an absolute reversal" in the way in which the "Yellow Caribs" were portrayed: they were now meek, peaceful, and defenseless in the face of the invading "Black Caribs," just as the Arawak had once been portrayed in the face of the Caribs themselves.[75]

The "planter's version" of history, in which the Black Caribs were depicted as usurpers in conflict with the Yellow Caribs of Dominica, was so successfully codified that, like the dichotomy between peaceful Arawak and "warlike" Caribs, it has remained relatively ensconced to this day. But a French soldier who was sent by the French to St. Vincent in 1795, Alexandre Moreau de Jonnès, provided a starkly different perspective on the question of the population on the island from those of British observers. His memoirs about his time there were published many decades later, and he had a very nostalgic view of his stay on the island: "During the three months I spent in the mountain carbet with my Carib friends, my days were a tissue of silk and gold." "This was truly Eden," Moreau de Jonnès went on, "with its perpetual spring, its shady forests, its magnificent views, its flowering groves, its singing birds, adorned with the most varied and brilliant colors." He sketched a map containing all the main paths in the interior and described what Paul Johnson calls the "spirit geography" of the island, which included the "Black Forest" at the foot of the island's volcano and a place known as the "Cavern of Death," both inhabited by spirits. He met and allied with a broad range of Carib groups, and in sharp contrast to British accounts, claimed that the group he called the "Red Caribs" still far outnumbered the "Black Caribs." In fact, as Peter Hulme argues, this account suggests that St. Vincent seems to have been inhabited by about twelve main groups, mostly in the east of the island. These groups were organized not around racial identification but according to their own political and social organization. The British, writes Hulme, were applying a "one-drop rule" to the Caribs, seeing any group that had some African ancestry as "Black." "*Black* and *yellow*," however, were "colonizer's terms, ideological fictions built around the unmarked centrality of imperial whiteness." The reality was one of diversity, including some Caribs who had started to live on and cultivate small plantations on the island by the late eighteenth century.[76]

Yet the Caribs always made clear that they considered themselves indigenous and anchored in the territory. In the 1770s, English officials were making plans to remove them from the island entirely to make way for settlement by deporting them to "some unfrequented Part of the Coast of Africa or some desert Island adjacent thereto." It was a suggestion, notes Hulme, "full of ironies." "If anyone was native to St. Vincent, it was certainly not the English, so they were hardly in a position to remove anyone else." The Black Caribs "had been settled in the Caribbean for several centuries," and "in so far as they could be considered African they were hardly themselves responsible for being in the West Indies in the first place." In response to plans for deportation, the Black Caribs made clear they considered that their land in St. Vincent was "transmitted to them from their ancestors." It was land, furthermore, "in defense of which they would die."[77]

It was during the 1790s, during a period of revolution, emancipation, and imperial conflict, that the Black Caribs ultimately made their last stand. Led by their chief Joseph Chatoyer, who had led them in conflicts with colonists since the 1760s, they fought with the French in a bid to preserve their claim to the land. The alliance was an attempt to stop increasingly aggressive colonization of lands on St. Vincent they considered their own. The pace of ecological change on the island in the 1780s was startling. Alexander Anderson described how one stretch of the island, between the Morne Agarou River and the Souffrière volcano, was "one of the most impenetrable forests on St. Vincent" in 1784 and served as a "Carib track by which they communicated across the mountains from the windward to the leeward side of the island." Within a few years, this and other forests had "disappeared" and "many large, beautiful sugar estates had arisen in their places." With support from the French, who had abolished slavery on nearby Guadeloupe and used the island as a launching pad for attacks against nearby islands, the Black Caribs attacked plantations and colonial towns and for a time seemed poised for victory. The British sent a massive military mission to the Caribbean, which enabled them to defeat the Black Caribs. The Carib leader Joseph Chatoyer was killed in battle, helping to turn the tide in favor of the English. The war in St. Vincent and elsewhere in the Caribbean was brutal, "so horrific, even for the victors," that the "few survivors had not desire to talk about what they had been through." The planters of St. Vincent were able to do what they had long dreamed of, and deported the remaining Black Caribs. Over four thousand were brought to a tiny nearby island, where half died before the survivors were put into the holds of British navy ships, led by the warship *Experiment*, and then taken to the island of Roatan, off the coast of Spanish Honduras.[78]

This was, however, the beginning of a remarkable new history. The Black Caribs were soon transported to the coastal town of Trujillo, where they encountered a range of other groups resettled from the Caribbean, including Saint-Domingue. Trujillo was a small town, the Black Caribs became the majority, and over the next decades they found their way into different professions. They also took on important military roles, defending Trujillo against a British attack two years after their arrival and participating on various sides of the wars of independence that ended overseas Spanish rule and that reshaped the borders of Central America during the first decades of the nineteenth century. At one point, when two groups of Black Caribs were fighting on opposite sides in a battle to take Trujillo, they refused to fight one another. These conflicts, and the reprisals that sometimes followed, led to a series of migrations along the coast, and the Black Caribs settled in villages stretching from Guatemala and Honduras north to Belize. "They were extremely mobile, the pre-eminent sailors of the coastal waters," according to Virginia Kerns, and spoke many languages—including Spanish, English, and Mosquito, the language of an indigenous group in Central America with which they mixed at times. They also kept alive their indigenous Carib language to the present day.[79]

Today, the members of this group call themselves the Garifuna, a version of the term "Kalinago" used by the Caribs to describe themselves. St. Vincent remains a touchstone in their spiritual life because it is where their community was born. Central to their practice is the work of what are called *buyei*, a Carib term describing those who communicate with the spirits of ancestors. These spirits are understood as living in St. Vincent, and they have to travel across the waters to come to speak with the *buyei*. Sometimes, too, they are called to participate in large, multiple ceremonies known as *dügü*, which are held when a particular family ancestor has shown his or her displeasure by causing sickness or misfortune. "These rituals," writes Virginia Kerns, "center on mourning, the remembrance of the dead," and are "occasions when the living and the dead enjoy themselves." It is "a thrill" when the ancestors appear, writes Nancie González. "People laugh, cry, dance, hug and kiss, and generally behave as they would at a family reunion." These ceremonies are usually led by the women in a given family and are an occasion that brings the family—including those who have migrated away from the villages, including to the United States—back together. The returning ancestors expect a feast, and a few days before the *dügü* begins, men and women go out into the coastal waters. They return at dawn of the third day, writes Kerns, "with their catch: fish, conchs, crabs, and other fruits of the sea," and the ceremony begins. The ancestors themselves are seen as making the same journey, arriving from across the waters in St. Vincent. The altars at the *dügü* and other ritual events often, according to Paul Johnson, have "miniature hammocks, canoes, and sailing vessels" on them, and during rituals "participants recapitulate and remember repose on St. Vincent by resting in hammocks."[80]

"Our journey has been sad, my grandchild," the ancestors sing in one song. "We have been searching for our grandchildren. We have been crossing the deep ocean. For our descendants are far away." With these words, the ancestors insist on connection across the generations, on the continuity that stretches back to the forests of St. Vincent, and continues into a Garifuna future in Central America, New York, Los Angeles, and beyond. Recalling the name of one particular group of Caribs on St. Vincent, the Aurayuna, the song is a powerful reminder too of the distance traveled, the loss of one shore and the opening up of another. "We have been standing on the shore of the Aurayuna. On the resplendent shore of Aurayuna, shedding tears."[81]

2 The Worlds of the Plantation

Starting in the sixteenth century, the Caribbean was transformed into a world of plantations. This social order drew on preexisting legal, economic, social, and cultural practices, but what emerged in the Caribbean was unique within the larger sweep of world history. The Spanish developed the first American economies driven by sugar plantations in la Isla Española, soon also called Santo Domingo, and in Puerto Rico in the early 1500s, and the Portuguese soon followed suit in Brazil. Building on these historical foundations, the French and English similarly created Caribbean colonies that specialized almost exclusively in the production of plantation commodities for export: indigo and tobacco, coffee and cotton, but most of all sugar. In the process, they developed a social system that was anomalous in world history, one in which the vast majority of the population was enslaved. This system depended on a radical reconfiguration of the geography of the Caribbean, on carving up as much land as possible into plantations, and on creating ports that were the nodes of oceanic trade. The system's functioning also depended on the constant use of violence and terror in order to assure the subjection of the enslaved majority, and it entailed the conceptual, legal, and social deployment of new forms of racial hierarchy. In terms of the magnitude, duration, and legacy of horror, plantation slavery in the Americas finds few, if any, parallels in world history.[1]

The development of the Caribbean plantation complex had far-reaching global consequences. It propelled the expansion of the wealth and power of European societies, notably England and France. At the same time, it reshaped many societies in Africa, where the increasingly large slave trade had a devastating impact on many regions. Writing in 1770, the French priest Abbé Raynal, who oversaw the publication of a multivolume history of European colonialism, described the Caribbean colonies as "the principal cause of the rapid movement which stirs the universe." The establishment of slave plantation societies in the Caribbean also played a key role in forging the meaning and power of race and racism in Europe, the Americas, and beyond.[2]

Slavery had long been a part of societies across the globe. Yet in most of world history, the enslaved were a demographically small group, and virtually never did they reach the dimensions of those in the Caribbean, where they would make up in many societies as much as 85 to 90 percent of the population. Never before, furthermore, had slavery been so powerfully racialized. In late medieval southern Europe and the Middle East, both slave owners and the enslaved had diverse origins and represented many ethnic groups. In the Caribbean, slavery would be increasingly isolated to one particular group and one defined in racial terms, those of African descent. By the eighteenth century, even the white contract or "indentured" labor that had played an important role in the early plantations of the British and French Caribbean was abandoned, replaced by enslaved Africans and their progeny. This same pattern of racial slavery, first developed in the Caribbean, came to prevail throughout the Americas, and to some extent in Europe. Because what was constructed in the Caribbean ultimately became—along with the parallel system developed in Brazil during the same period—a model for other regions, notably North America, these developments had an enduring significance for and impact on societies throughout the world.

The formation, consolidation, and multiplication of racial discourses were at the center of this process. "The process of calling blackness into being and causing it to become inextricable from brute labor," writes Jennifer Morgan, "took place in legislative acts, laws, wills, bills of sale, and plantation inventories just as it did in journals and adventurers' tales of travels." The construction of racial ideas was always imbricated with gender, as Morgan argues. "Ideas about black sexuality and misconceptions about black female sexual behavior formed the cornerstone of Europeans and Euro-Americans' general attitudes towards slavery." Although men outnumbered women in the slave trade, data for eighteenth-century Jamaica, for instance, show this imbalance evening out over time. And in many slave societies, women made up a large portion of those working in the fields. As such, their labor power was fundamental to production on the plantation. "Women's lives under slavery," however, also "always included the possibilities of their wombs," and the "cost-benefit calculations of colonial slaveowners included the speculative value of a reproducing labor force." The brutality of Caribbean plantation societies was such that fertility rates were low and infant mortality high, with the result that deaths among the enslaved outpaced births and only constant imports from the slave trade maintained the laboring population. Yet the legislative, legal, and political debates about slavery often revolved around questions of sexuality and motherhood, and the actions and visions of enslaved women shaped the worlds of the plantation and of the colonial town. Recovering and documenting their stories, however, means confronting a particularly powerful set of elisions and silences in the archival record.[3]

In the late eighteenth century, Bryan Edwards, an English-born Jamaican planter and intellectual, wrote an extensive account of the history and functioning of this colonial world powered by the enslaved. "The plantation," he wrote, "ought to be a well-constructed machine, compounded of various wheels turning different ways, yet all contributing to the great end proposed; but if any one part runs too fast or too slow, in proportion to the rest, the main purpose is defeated." In a recent study focusing on late eighteenth-century Jamaica and Saint-Domingue, historians Trevor Burnard and John Garrigus similarly describe the structures of what they call "the plantation machine," which they argue ushered in "the first Western institutions to implement industrial-style production, deploying hundreds of workers factory-like in an array of complex interdependent tasks with complex attention to time." "The hallmarks of the large integrated plantation," they write, "were discipline, coordination, and coercion." Plantation discipline was achieved through the regular use of torture and execution by masters. Whipping was the most common punishment, and many slaves carried the scars on their backs. Father Labat, a priest who lived in the French Antilles in the late seventeenth century, described how quickly masters and overseers got used to this. While at first the sight of a slave being whipped "excited the compassion of those who were not used to it," he wrote, "you get used to it pretty quickly."[4]

Much like a hurricane transforming everything in its wake, the plantation system cycled through the Caribbean, expanding and contracting at disparate times in different colonies and thriving for shorter or longer durations. The plantation, Cuban writer Antonio Benítez-Rojo explains, "turns out to be one of the principal instruments for studying the area, if not indeed the most important." Generations of thinkers from the region, whose writings and theorizations we draw on throughout this chapter, have reflected on the powerful and ongoing legacies of the plantation structure on economy, society, culture, politics, and thought itself in the region. It did not dominate every corner of the region, and there were always people, communities, and ecologies outside of it, including indigenous peoples and maroon communities who carved out spaces of autonomy and sovereignty against tremendous odds. Still, the plantation has clearly been the main economic formation in the region, and resistance to it the core structuring of the Caribbean's major political struggles. It is the form that makes the Caribbean what Benítez-Rojo calls a "cultural meta-archipelago."[5]

At the same time, the plantation mutated and shifted in different times and places. While the expansion in plantation agriculture, and particularly in sugar plantations, had many parallel social and economic consequences wherever and whenever it took place, the particular timing of the plantation boom in each region also influenced its long-term impact and legacy. The first plantation society in the Americas developed in Spanish Santo Domingo, where the expansion of sugar during the first half of the sixteenth century led to a parallel expansion in the importation of enslaved indigenous and African laborers. This plantation society lasted about seventy-five years. Subsequently, in the late seventeenth and eighteenth centuries, British and French sugar colonies—first in Barbados, Guadeloupe, and Martinique, and then in Jamaica and Saint-Domingue—created a plantation system that ultimately imported an exponentially larger number of slaves and became central to European economies, lasting until the nineteenth century. Plantation systems would prevail on shifting islands in the Caribbean for varying periods of time over several centuries. Few were very long lived, but, altogether, plantation economies, and the massive trades that fed them, would have hugely transformative and pernicious effects. Those ranged from the death of at least two million enslaved people who perished in their forced transport and the millions more who died on plantations to the anchoring of the Americas in deep foundations of racial inequality, privilege, and disadvantage.[6]

Following the Haitian Revolution of 1791 to 1804, which transformed the French colony of Saint-Domingue into an independent nation, there was a second plantation boom in the Spanish Caribbean, this time in Puerto Rico and, above all, Cuba. Plantations in these colonies began to supply the mass quantities of sugar once produced in the former French colony and in many ways followed the trajectory of the French and British expansion of the previous century. Here, however, the rural plantation boom emerged with an existing population of small landholders, producing somewhat different demographic and social conditions in these societies than those in Jamaica and Saint-Domingue. The fact that the plantation boom took place in the nineteenth century also meant differences in the sources of the enslaved Africans brought to the Caribbean, in the ideologies and techniques of repression used to contain them, and in the strategies and ideals of the cycle of slave insurrections that helped pave the way for Cuba's first war of independence (1868–80).

The plantation models created in the Caribbean would become templates for certain of the colonies of the U.S. South. Settlers moved from overpopulated Barbados, where already by the late seventeenth century it was difficult to acquire land for plantations, to the Carolinas, founding colonies based on the Caribbean model. The laws, practices, and attitudes developed in the Caribbean thereby shaped slavery in North America. The colonies of the Caribbean and those of North America developed together, depending on one another for certain products, tied together in an Atlantic economy founded on the slave trade. And yet their destinies would diverge in startling ways by the end of the eighteenth century. When the North American colonies revolted against their British governors, the wealthiest colonies of the empire—those of the Caribbean—did not join in the revolt, in part because the fear of containing their slaves overshadowed a desire for independence. Although many slaves participated in the war—most often by joining the British, who held out the promise of emancipation—in its wake slavery was consolidated overall rather than destroyed, notwithstanding a movement, in general, toward gradually ending slavery in New England. In contrast, the victorious struggle for national independence that soon followed in Saint-Domingue, like the one that took place decades later in Cuba, was both a war for independence and a war against slavery.[7]

As the anthropologist Michel-Rolph Trouillot argues, the plantation is also at the root of much of contemporary Caribbean culture. The enslaved, subject to a brutal plantation regime, nevertheless were able to find and exploit spaces within that regime that enabled them to survive and resist, and in the process to generate new creole cultures. The process of creolization in the Caribbean, in which new cultures were born primarily out of the encounter between European and African-descended peoples, both living in new lands, "did not happen away from the plantation, but within it." This was possible because "slaves found a most fertile ground in the interstices of the system." "Afro-Caribbean cultural practices," Trouillot argues, "were born within the plantation but on the edges of particular plantations," in the spaces between "the logic of the system and the daily life of actual estates" that "provided a context full of minute opportunities for initiatives among the enslaved." These practices, in turn, were able to gnaw "at the logic of an imposed order and its daily manifestations of dominance." "Filtering in the interstices of the system, they conquered each and every inch of cultural territory they now occupy." This chapter offers a reading of the history of the plantation that emphasizes both its structure and its interstices, and focuses on the way in which the plantation was an attempt to order land and labor by controlling space and the ways it never fully succeeded.[8]

From Medieval to Modern Slavery

Slavery was a familiar practice for the first European colonists in the Americas. In much of medieval Spain and Italy, slavery had continued uninterrupted from ancient times. The number of enslaved people in parts of southern Europe was substantial even prior to the African-Atlantic slave trade. In the early 1400s, nearly one in ten persons in the Spanish city of Valencia was enslaved. In Genoa and Palermo at this time, the number of people owned by another person is believed to have varied between two and five percent. The enslaved represented significant populations in Seville, Barcelona, and Mallorca as well. The scale of slavery was small relative to the eventual extremes of Caribbean societies, the antebellum U.S. South, and regions of Brazil, but not compared with slavery at large in world history.[9]

The enslaved in southern Europe were of diverse origins. During the centuries before the African-Atlantic slave trade, in Europe as well as in North Africa and the Middle East, the commerce in bound humans was continually fed by wars and raids around Eastern Europe, Russia, and neighboring Black Sea lands populated by Orthodox Christian and Muslim peoples. Similarly, during the fourteenth century, Orthodox Greek Christians were enslaved and transported to be sold in Italy and Spain, in particular. Catholics did not consider Orthodox Christians co-religionists but rather enemies for not following the dictates of the pope. The latter, therefore, could be held in slavery if taken as prisoners of war or if legally purchased. Adding to this extraordinary diversity of "inhuman bondage," in David Brion Davis's phrase, Christian raids and invasions of Muslim regions of the Iberian Peninsula had generally produced the bulk of the bound population in Christian Spain and Portugal.[10]

Like slavery, the key plantation crop in the Caribbean, sugar, had an important Old World history. Sugar was long cultivated in parts of the Middle East and India, and it spread with Islam to North Africa and Southern Spain beginning in the eighth century. Here growers experimented with different strategies for planting, fertilizing, and irrigating cane fields and perfected the processes for grinding the cane to extract its juice (sometimes with water mills) and boiling down the cane juice to make sugar. Starting in the late eleventh century, the Christian crusaders who invaded Palestine and the Normans who invaded Sicily imitated Muslim sugar-cultivating practices, taking over existing sugar estates and building new ones. In this period, they also began to increase exports of sugar to Western Europe.[11]

Early sugar estates in the Muslim world were most often cultivated through sharecropping arrangements with tenants, but in some areas, notably Morocco, enslaved laborers were also used. The Christian European sugar estates ordinarily relied on a mix of enslaved and free laborers. After the Christians' loss of Acre—the last major city they held in Palestine—at the end of the thirteenth century, some of the sugar producers there retreated to other parts of the Mediterranean, including the Italian colony of Cyprus. The island boasted several large sugar estates that were worked by bond labor of various forms, including enslaved Arabs. One plantation in the mid-fifteenth century had four hundred laborers, making it as extensive as the largest of the sugar plantations that would be built in the New World. In the same era, Sicily, now in Christian European hands, also produced a substantial amount of sugar.[12]

The technologies of cultivation and processing and the technique of using some slave labor on the estates would ultimately be transferred first to a series of islands off the coast of Africa and then to the New World. The experience of sugar cultivation in the Mediterranean was, writes J. H. Galloway, "a school for the colonizers" who would follow in the Canary Islands, in Madeira, and later in "tropical America." For all its successes, however, the sugar industry in the Mediterranean faced environmental limits, particularly a cold winter that shortened the growing season for cane. In the tropics, this would not be a problem. Not long after New World sugar began arriving at European markets in a big way, the Mediterranean sugar economy, already weakened by various other forces, would decline and vanish. "In the Americas," notes Galloway, "with an abundance of land, an ideal climate, and a supply of slave labor, sugar production found scope to flourish."[13]

One of the factors that made New World plantations possible, the growing supply of enslaved laborers, depended on a major new trade route that Europeans opened for the buying and selling of people. In the 1440s, Europeans gained maritime access to sub-Saharan Africa for the first time. Enslaved people from this region had long been brought to the Mediterranean and elsewhere by North African traders crossing the Sahara.

But now Europeans could exploit, divert, and augment this trade with relative ease. They immediately began forcibly shipping enslaved Africans (more than one thousand per year over the coming decades) to Portugal and Spain, to their Atlantic island possessions, and subsequently to Santo Domingo and the New World. There the most unholy historical marriage of vast new supply and demand for slaves developed, ultimately on an unprecedented scale. The massive new supply of enslaved Africans quickly replaced the traditional sources of slavery, which were dwindling at the time due to new political and economic developments. For one, the Ottoman Empire's rapid expansion in the fifteenth century had created an escalating demand for slaves that diverted Black Sea slave trading away from southern Europe. In the same period, moreover, when Spain conquered the entire Iberian Peninsula, the eight-century-long struggle between Christian and Muslim rulers on the peninsula came to an end and with it the supply of enslaved prisoners of war or captives from those battles.[14]

The Italian merchants who had previously dominated the Black Sea slave trade now took their business west to Spain and Portugal, where, as historian David Brion Davis wrote, "they became pioneers in developing the African slave trade." The Italian influence was important in the Iberian region, notably in port towns like Seville, where there were many Genoans living in exile, including Christopher Columbus. And in the 1510s, Genoese entrepreneurs would be among the very first to invest their capital and bring large numbers of enslaved Africans to the Americas to work the earliest sugar plantations in Spanish Santo Domingo.[15]

Another prior history that helped shape the ideas and actions of early European colonists in the Americas was European expansion to numerous islands off the coast of Morocco. During the mid-fourteenth century, Spain invaded and annexed the Canary Islands. This small group of islands was inhabited by a population in the tens of thousands, the Guanches, who had migrated there from North Africa centuries before. In the early fifteenth century, a French knight and his followers who had sworn allegiance to the king of Castile (part of Spain) began conquering the islands' population according to the Spanish tradition of the *repartimiento* ("distribution"). In this system, an evolution from practices developed during the Christian seizure of Muslim regions of Spain, conquered peoples were divided up among the victors and forced to work for them. Spaniards and other Europeans captured and sold thousands of Guanches into slavery, exporting many to Spain and Portugal, while keeping others as family laborers. In some areas, the Guanches fought back ferociously and kept colonists at bay into the 1490s. But soon Spanish military conquest, brutal overwork, unfamiliar diseases, slave exports, and a measure of assimilation led not only to the native Guanches' defeat but to their near extinction as an identifiable group. During the 1500s, thousands of enslaved Africans were then imported into the Canary Islands to toil in a successful small sugar industry driven in part by Genoese capital.[16]

In a number of key ways, the experience of colonization in the Canaries anticipated on a small scale what would happen in the Caribbean and to some extent the Americas at large: the virtual extermination of indigenous groups and the importation of enslaved Africans who were put to work on sugar plantations. An additional continuity both from the past (Spanish "reconquest" of the Iberian Peninsula) and toward the future was that enslavement was permitted even of subjects claimed by the Spanish crown, but only if they were deemed prisoners taken during conquest or to stop their rebellion against its rule, that is, in a "good" or "just war." This practice reflected ongoing tensions between the crown's (and the pope's) interests in augmenting the Spanish (and Roman Catholic) empire by incorporating new populations as subjects and the mercenary and commercial interests in capturing, enslaving, and selling people along with other booty. Similar tensions would come to the fore again, and on a far larger scale, in Spanish colonization of the Caribbean and the Americas.[17]

Like Spain in the fifteenth century, Portugal also colonized areas off the coast of Africa where they developed slave plantations. On the tiny, unpopulated island of Madeira (three hundred square miles), north of the Canaries, a Portuguese settlement was created in 1420. The Portuguese set up sugar plantations, drawing on the technology and models developed in the Mediterranean during the previous centuries. By the mid-fifteenth century, sugar cultivation was well established on the island, and a water mill was constructed to process the cane. As the sugar estates expanded and became more profitable, their owners also came to depend more and more on enslaved labor, which by the end of the fifteenth century seems to have made up most of the labor force working the cane. Initially, the colonists had imported slaves from the Canary Islands and North Africa, but they ultimately turned to West Africa to supply the labor they needed. Eventually plantations in Madeira were exporting to Western Europe and even into the eastern Mediterranean an extraordinary amount of sugar, which rose from almost 900 tons per year in the late 1400s to as many as 2,500 at the beginning of the sixteenth century. One person familiar with the expanding and successful exploitation of slave labor on sugar plantations on Madeira and the Canaries was Christopher Columbus, who moved to Madeira in the late 1470s and worked in the sugar industry for a number of years.[18]

The Portuguese also developed a plantation site much farther south, on the island of São Tomé, off the coast of Central Africa. By 1495, this island was home to thriving plantations worked by enslaved Africans, which exported sugar to Antwerp, in present-day Belgium, which was "long the major refining and distributing center for Europe." Some of the investment in the São Tomé plantations came from wealthy Africans in Angola itself, and the island also became a depot for the slave trade out of West Africa. In 1507, there were by some accounts two thousand slaves working on plantations there, with another five to six thousand being held on the island on their way to being reexported.[19]

These developments on the Atlantic coast of Africa, in the Canary Islands, Madeira, and São Tomé, meant that, as Sidney Greenfield argues, large-scale plantations run on enslaved labor were not "invented as a response to the conditions of the New World tropics," but rather could be "brought to tropical America as an integrated system." And this meant that for many, if not most, of the Iberian migrants who traveled to the islands of the Caribbean in the early sixteenth century, slavery was a customary and doubtless timeless-seeming institution and sugar plantations worked largely by enslaved Africans were familiar enterprises.[20]

While slavery in southern Europe continued to be imagined as a diverse phenomenon excluding only co-religionists, enslaved Africans were increasingly becoming the main slave population. This racialization would soon cross the Atlantic to the Spanish Caribbean, where this process would continue until it was virtually complete. In the Americas, racialization would entail not only the lack of white slaves—for the Black Sea and Mediterranean slave trades no longer flowed into southern Europe—but also the collapse of a massive early sixteenth-century slave trade in indigenous people. During the decades of Iberian conquest and colonization, the population the Spanish named "Indians" had been continuously captured and enslaved in war and raids. But after the mid-1500s, slavery would be increasingly isolated to people of African descent in Spanish America.[21]

Spain's first American possession, Santo Domingo, a large island roughly the size of Portugal, had a population upon European contact perhaps in the hundreds of thousands. This native population would for the most part be divided up among the European settlers and forced to work for "Christians," as they typically identified themselves. From the crown's perspective, those who were compliant and obedient were not to be enslaved. But enslaved laborers were brought from Europe on the first ships that landed in Santo Domingo, and from the start colonists sought to import additional enslaved laborers both for domestic use and to mine gold, and by the late 1510s to cut sugar cane. The Spanish organized the trade by issuing licenses and fees to import a set number into Spain's American colonies. By the end of the 1510s, the number of these licenses had grown dramatically. In 1518, the Spanish king issued a license to the governor of La Bresse in Burgundy (part of present-day France) to export 4,000 slaves to the Americas, most going to Santo Domingo to mine gold and work in the fledgling sugar industry there. In addition to the authorized slave imports, a probably far greater number would be smuggled into Santo Domingo over the coming decades.[22]

The import of enslaved Africans into Santo Domingo in the first half of the sixteenth century went hand in hand with that of enslaved Indians from elsewhere in the Americas. They were generally captured in battle during Spanish conquest or in raids on islands and continental areas that Spanish authorities deemed to be economically "useless"—that is, without precious metals and overall without interest to European settlers. The populations of those areas were all opportunistically deemed to be at war with Spain, whether they were or not, and thus subject to legal capture and enslavement. Vast numbers of Indians were captured and exported from the Bahamas, the Lesser Antilles, the northern coast of South America, Nicaragua, and other places in the Greater Caribbean. Many perished in transport under dire conditions. Many others died in Santo Domingo from disease, violence, and exploitation, much as the natives of Santo Domingo continued to die until their final horrific demise as a people on the island.[23]

As Spain's empire spread across the Americas, the crown increasingly sought—with mixed results—to crack down on the illegal enslavement of indigenous Americans who had not, in fact, been captured in authorized warfare in areas considered still resistant to Spanish rule. Finally, in the 1540s, Spain simply banned altogether any new enslavement of free Indians, including prisoners of war, even though major exceptions would continue to be made. This increasingly left Africans and their descendants the only population laboring as slaves in Santo Domingo and Spanish America by the mid-sixteenth century.[24]

In these same early decades of the 1500s, many initially profitable gold mines in Santo Domingo were becoming unproductive. With the model of Madeira and the Canaries to draw on, Spanish colonists then turned increasingly toward sugar plantations and importing greater and greater numbers of slaves in hopes of resuscitating and expanding the economy. Santo

Domingo thus would develop the earliest sugar plantation economy and slave society in the Americas and become the motor and hub of a growing African-Atlantic slave trade linking Europe, Africa, and the Caribbean.

By midcentury, some 20,000 people were enslaved in Santo Domingo, and the island's sugar industry boomed through the brutal exploitation of their labor. Annual sugar exports to Spain totaled around 1,400 tons in 1543. A great deal of sugar was also sold as contraband to European rivals, and some was marketed within the region. Altogether, available figures suggest that the total production each year could be several times higher than sugar exports to Seville, historian Genaro Rodríguez Morel emphasizes. By 1568, more than thirty mills were reported to be in service, with many estates worked by between one hundred and three hundred enslaved laborers and several other estates of still greater size. An impressive cattle industry also added to Santo Domingo's wealth during this period, with some forty to sixty thousand hides sent to Spain per year from ranches worked by enslaved people. Slaves also worked on other types of agricultural estates and as servants and urban laborers, including some two thousand in the capital alone. Finally, slaves continued to mine ore from gold deposits that remained productive, an industry that, though in decline, remained important for decades after the sugar economy expanded. The large island of Santo Domingo, then, was not simply consumed by cane fields as had been the Atlantic islands off the coast of Africa, but rather was home to multiple lucrative industries while also being a key seat of imperial governance for the region (the Audiencia of Santo Domingo).[25]

In the mid-1500s, observers estimated the population of Spaniards on the island to be five to six thousand, far smaller than that of the enslaved. By midcentury, there was also a growing population of free persons of African descent as well as thousands of escaped slaves. At the same time, Santo Domingo's indigenous population was vanishing, though the number of people of partial Indian descent was surely significant and more enduring. The European colony named "Spanish Island" (la Isla Española), was already a majority African land.[26]

Although in the mid-sixteenth century Santo Domingo's plantation economy was ostensibly thriving, there was deep instability at its heart, which was not surprising for a society that sought to keep the vast majority in chains. This was also unsurprising given that the colonial state was weak, with limited repressive apparatus for an island as vast, mountainous, and wooded as Santo Domingo. In its dense, untamed terrain, enslaved people found it comparatively easy to escape, hide, and subsist on bountiful wildlife. Early on, large numbers of slaves were escaping into the countryside and joining in rebellion with Indians who resisted Spanish rule. In the 1540s, the number of escaped slaves was estimated to be well into the thousands. Many of these fugitives—some one thousand—were on the offensive. Maroon leaders with scores of rebels armed with stolen weapons burned sugar cane, mills, and houses and liberated the enslaved. In 1580, an inspector sent to Santo Domingo by the crown argued that it was only the fact that the enslaved on the island spoke different languages and came from different nations that kept them from uniting in one collective rebellion. Were they able to do that, he imagined, they would "easily" make themselves "lords of the land."[27]

The extent of slave escape, rebellion, and property damage surely contributed to what in the mid-1580s became Santo Domingo's downward spiral from which it never emerged. Production fell to a small fraction of what it had been by 1600, and it was virtually nonexistent by the 1640s. It is unclear what exactly led to the sugar industry's collapse. But slave resistance paired with high taxes levied to support state campaigns to recapture escaped slaves and fight rebels must have decreased productivity and profits. Furthermore, planters had to bear the costs of continually replacing the large numbers of escaped slaves while slave prices increased over time. These costs were compounded by the fact that by the 1580s the sugar industry faced substantial new competition because of expanding sugar cultivation in Spain and, most obviously, Brazil, where the sugar industry had taken off in this period and would soon expand to many times the size of Santo Domingo's at its peak. The increased supply of sugar and competition on the world market may have made it possible only for more efficient producers to thrive.[28]

In the late 1570s Dominican planters expanded ginger production. The industry thrived for four decades until it, too, failed amid increased global competition, low prices, and slave resistance. The cattle industry remained the only commercial option left, but even the export of hides was reduced to almost negligible levels in dramatic contrast to the large and lucrative sixteenth-century trade. By the mid-1600s, most Dominican planters were living as modest cattle ranchers who had limited wealth with which to import, purchase, or even continue to own enslaved laborers. Many Spaniards sold their slaves for needed cash. In some cases, the enslaved purchased their own freedom, for they found a variety of ways to accumulate the needed funds. Owners also had few resources available to pay slave catchers and to prevent slaves' permanent flight. The enslaved had been the majority of the population in the previous century. Now the largest part was families that had escaped or been freed from slavery, who were living independently, practicing itinerant agriculture, and hunting and raising wildlife on the open range.[29]

With little sugar production in the sixteenth century, Cuba would follow a path different from that of Santo Domingo and Puerto Rico (which had a history similar to that of Santo Domingo but on a smaller scale). In the late eighteenth century, the Haitian Revolution would lead to the collapse of slavery and sugar production in French Saint-Domingue. Although the revolution also had a destabilizing effect on neighboring Santo Domingo, it created an opening for a massive new plantation economy in Cuba that was aided by an earlier decrease in Spanish taxes on slave imports. "Liberation in Saint-Domingue," writes Ada Ferrer, "helped entrenched its denial in Cuba." Two centuries earlier, though, Havana, Cuba's capital, was already a bustling port city of the New World with half its population enslaved. As Alejandro de la Fuente shows, Havana's development at the end of the sixteenth century was vital to creating the broader economic network of the Spanish empire.

Havana's beginnings were difficult. In 1585, Francis Drake sailed with twenty-two ships from England on a mission to attack Spanish colonies in the Caribbean. He attacked both Santo Domingo and Cartegena de Indias on the mainland, which at the time was already the primary American port and market for the African-Atlantic slave trade. Governors in Havana were panicked, certain that their town would be the next to be attacked. They mobilized as many men as they could, rallying one thousand to defend the port, and stretched a chain across the Havana port's relatively narrow entrance. Prepared for the worst, they also readied two ships to flee as messengers in case the town fell "to the enemies of God and His Majesty."[30]

Drake, however, did not attack. Many of his men had died from tropical diseases, and he was likely discouraged by the state of Havana's defenses. Spared the attack, the city was nevertheless transformed by Drake's presence. The Spanish crown rushed to make sure they were prepared to fend off future such attacks. Drake's mission indicated that England was on the move, eager to conquer Spanish territories in the Caribbean. Spanish king Philip II hired an Italian military engineer to design and build fortifications throughout the Spanish Empire in the Greater Caribbean, from Mexico, Florida, and Cartagena to the ports in Santo Domingo, Puerto Rico, and Havana. A fort called La Fuerza already protected the interior of the harbor of Havana, but by the end of the 1580s, construction had begun on two more forts at the harbor's entrance, which was also equipped permanently with a chain, much like the one used to put a stop to Drake's attack. Contemporaries described the now-intensely fortified city as "impregnable." It would take more than a century and a half before Drake's dream of taking Havana would be realized by the English, who finally occupied the port city for almost a year in 1762.[31]

The well-protected port of Havana became one of the most important nodes of the Spanish empire in the Americas, and therefore of the larger Atlantic economy. In 1581, the Spanish government made Havana the gathering point for all ships heading back to Spain, which were taken under the protection of heavily armed warships whose duty was to protect the fleet from pirate attacks. Havana not only greeted ships, it also produced them, soon becoming America's largest shipbuilding city. For several decades in the late sixteenth century, small ships were built in the Havana harbor, but by the 1590s, often with support from the royal government, many large ships were built there, earning, de la Fuente recounts, "a reputation for quality, hardiness, and durability." The construction of these ships was a truly Atlantic endeavor. The crucial ingredients were provided in Havana: timber, harvested from the rich forests surrounding Havana, and labor, both free and enslaved. The forests around Havana provided mahogany, cedar, and oak, along with pine trees for ship masts. Local laborers also made ropes from fibers of hibiscus trees. Many of the other materials came by ship from far away: tar, some of it imported from the Canary Islands; "mainmasts from Norway"; and "cables from England and Flanders, French tools, and steel from Milan." Metals needed for anchors, chains, and nails were imported, an inconvenience the royal government sought to resolve by funding the construction of a local foundry in 1600. Master shipbuilders were recruited to the port, and they oversaw work carried out by free laborers as well as slaves, often African born, rented out for the purpose by their proprietors.[32]

Among Havana's population were a large number of free people of African descent. Some were quite prosperous, such as Cristóbal Mayorga, a merchant from Portugal who came to Cuba as a sailor on a slave ship and described his initial profession as "a pilot of the Angola trade." He established himself as a merchant, selling hides and other products in Cuba and beyond. Many free blacks, however, lived on the margins of Havana society, and their houses were usually in outlying sections of the town. They lived there with poorer whites but seem to have faced limited options even if they could afford better. One woman, Beatriz Nizardo, who sought to purchase a plot of land in a more central section of town in 1561 had her request refused by the town council, who told her to "request it in another place, close to the area where other free blacks are." On the one hand, in these earlier periods, some free people of color owned property and enjoyed certain privileges as heads of household, including participation in local elections. Many were able to gain access to land and some owned slaves. On the other hand, free people of African descent faced discriminatory laws that singled them out based on race—harsher punishments for the same crimes, sumptuary prohibitions, and restrictions on permissible jobs and commerce, for instance. For free people of color in the city, race was in some senses gaining "primacy . . . over freedom as a marker of status," writes de la Fuente.[33]

A tiny town in the mid-sixteenth century with only a few hundred residents, by the early seventeenth century Havana had grown exponentially, with four thousand or five thousand permanent free residents and as many enslaved. The armadas and fleets harbored in Havana on their way back to Spain provided a stream of residents: it was a favorite place for soldiers and seamen to jump ship to avoid returning home. Many had enlisted in Spain precisely for this reason, planning to gain free passage across the Atlantic and then desert once they were in the New World. Others emigrated from Spain with less subterfuge, paying their way, hoping to take advantage of the growing economic opportunities in Cuba. The majority of Spanish immigrants came from Andalusia in southern Spain, often from the regions around the major port of Seville, where it was easy to find a ship heading across the Atlantic. Many others came from different parts of Spain, as well as Portugal and other European countries. These arrivals drove the importation of another group that would become a central part of the population of Havana: enslaved Africans. Their importation dramatically increased in the 1590s, driven by demand from local residents and officials looking for workers to do hard labor. They came from throughout the continent, with a little over half arriving from West Africa. These included those described as Arara or, as they would be in Saint-Domingue a century later, Arada, often arriving from the slave factories at Whydah. About 40 percent of slaves arriving in the late sixteenth century came from the regions of Congo and Angola. There were also a small number of slaves from other regions, including one person from "Yndia of Portugal" (Portuguese Goa or another Portuguese-controlled part of what was then India), one from Turkey, and others from North Africa described as "Moors." Already, then, Havana was a densely multicultural and cosmopolitan space, in which roughly half the population was enslaved. "The Atlantic port city," writes de la Fuente, "had become a collection of African and European 'nations' living by the sea."[34]

The Plantation in the Eastern Caribbean

By the early seventeenth century, meanwhile, British and French settlers were beginning to colonize a series of islands in the Eastern Caribbean. These were the smaller islands, the Lesser Antilles that Spain had always claimed but never really colonized, cast off instead as small and "useless" other than as a slaving zone for its developed colonies through war against their populations, identified as "Carib."

The new European colonists started in St. Christopher, where in 1624–25 both British and French colonists arrived and began to build separate settlements. The two groups peaceably partitioned the island, with the French occupying both extremities and the British the center. The two groups rapidly developed a small, thriving plantation society. In 1646, when the Carmelite missionary Maurile de Saint Michel visited St. Christopher, he found the French governor there overseeing a large plantation complex. There were two mills on the plantation, which produced sugar, indigo, and ginger. White officers and artisans, as well as laborers, lived on the property, along with slaves, who were in a separate set of quarters the governor referred to as "his Angolan village" because of the origin of those who lived there. The mountains above harbored wild pigs that provided meat for the plantation, but also hid fugitive slaves who had "left their masters because of bad treatment" as well as escaped French and English "servants." Indeed, Maurile de Saint Michel noted, there were a number of Frenchmen "who became savages, hiding in the woods," including some of the passengers on the ship he had taken from France, who had "chosen this life, rather than suffer the pains of the poor servants." St. Christopher also startled him for its enormous diversity of cultures, which were reflected in the food consumed on the island. There were many different kinds of "peas," he noted, including "pois de Rome," green beans, English peas (brought from Virginia), and "pois d'Angole from Africa." There was a similar range of alcohol available. The Dutch on the island had brought beer, the French Normans cider, and Madeira and wine from Gascogne were also available, as were a series of locally produced drinks: the indigenous Ouicou, as well as a wine made from pineapples and "wine" made from sugar cane. The islands, Saint Michel also noted, were riven by a clear conflict: "We have to be wary of the negroes and savages," he wrote, "who would exterminate us if they could."[35]

Despite such worries, it was not long before the French settlers began thinking of expanding to other nearby islands. In 1625, the newly formed Compagnie des Indes d'Amerique funded colonization missions in Martinique and Guadeloupe. In 1664, control of the colonies was turned over to another company, the Compagnie des Indes Occidentales, which gained a monopoly on French Caribbean commerce. These companies granted concessions to settlers, who created a growing number of plantations during the seventeenth century, while a steady stream of white *engagés* (indentured laborers) and slaves were brought in to work on them. In 1655, there were thirteen thousand whites and ten thousand African slaves in the French Caribbean colonies. The Compagnie des Indies Occidentales's control of the colonies ended in 1674, when it was dissolved by the royal government, which took over the direct administration of the colonies. Martinique became the center of French empire in the Eastern Caribbean. The main town of the island, Fort Royal, was originally a small fort build to withstand raids by the indigenous Caribs, who continued to live on the eastern side of the island until the late 1650s. In 1669, the governor of the island decreed that the area surrounding the fort should be turned into a town. It remained heavily fortified, for there were frequent raids by pirates attracted by the ever-expanding cargoes of sugar and slaves. The rest of the island was fortified as well: above coves and around port towns, residents built small palisades, and by 1700 the island had eight larger forts. The defenses were concentrated wherever barrels of sugar were loaded onto ships.[36]

The center of early British colonization in the Caribbean was the island of Barbados, where colonists carried out a "sugar revolution" and created a new society that would become the prototype for many others in the Caribbean. A small island, only 166 square miles wide and "shaped like a leg of mutton," Barbados is relatively flat, without the tall mountains and rivers of most of the other islands in the Eastern Caribbean. The island was, however, "marvelously suited to agriculture," with a great deal of flat land. And because of its location "far east of the main Antillean chain," it "became the first Caribbean port of call for provision ships from Europe or slave ships from Africa."[37]

The colony's beginnings were difficult. When Sir Henry Colt visited the island in 1631, he found the plantations "raw and straggling." They "cultivated tobacco and cotton for export and wheat and corn for their own consumption," as well as raising some livestock. But they "had no horses or oxen, which made transportation difficult," and so had established their plantations near the sea, where the soil was of lower quality than inland. Much of the workforce, made up of indentured servants, was clearly suffering: the ship upon which Colt traveled was "continually overrun by servants who came on board hoping to escape from the island or at least avoid laboring in the fields," and the captain had to spend a day clearing off these visitors before departing. Nevertheless, the colonists were surviving. They ate wild hogs and stewed turtle, of which Colt wrote that "the taste is between fish and flesh of veale." One settler regaled Colt with "a feast of pigs, chickens, turkey, corn, cassava, and palm cabbage, boasting that he could entertain at the same rate every day of the year."[38]

Barbados expanded rapidly, its population growing from 1,227 taxpayers in 1635 to 8,707 in 1639. Most settlers planted tobacco. "Agriculture was labor intensive, and land distribution was skewed in favor of the big entrepreneurs." The plantations were worked by a mix of African slaves and European indentured laborers. Small farmers with little capital could also cultivate tobacco, and many, including indentured laborers who had served out their terms, grew the crop on small plots of land. Because of the stiff competition from Virginia tobacco, sales of the crop were never very successful, and planters who grew cotton as an alternative had limited success.[39]

Then, between 1640 and 1660, "the Barbados planters switched from tobacco and cotton to sugar and from white servants to black slaves." With the introduction of labor-intensive sugar plantations, the number of enslaved people in the colony increased exponentially. By the mid-1640s there were already "an estimated 5,680 to 6,400 slaves and 18,300 to 18,600 European males" on the island. By 1655 the slave population was 20,000, nearly as great as the white population of 23,000. "The island is inhabited by all sorts," wrote the English traveler Henry Whistler, who visited Barbados in 1655, "with English, French, Dutch, Scots, Irish, Spaniards," and "Indians and miserable Negroes born to perpetual slavery, they and their seed." He was not particularly impressed. "This island is the dunghill whereon England doth cast forth its rubbish," he lamented. "Rogues and whores and such like people are those which are generally brought here. A rogue in Europe would hardly make a cheater here." By 1673 there was a clear slave majority on the island of over 33,000, while the white population had actually declined to about 21,000. The trend continued during the next decades: in 1712, there were nearly 42,000 enslaved compared with only 12,500 whites. Barbados was already, as it would remain until the twentieth century, extremely densely populated.[40]

A rapid expansion of sugar production in Barbados would be the result of a historical conjuncture that brought together technical knowledge with an opening in the European market. Dutch merchants and planters played a pivotal role, introducing the techniques of sugar processing, which they were then using in their colony in Brazil, into Barbados and also supplying the African slaves that sustained the plantation boom. At the time "no other Caribbean island as yet produced sugar for the European market, and Brazil was a battleground between the Dutch and the Portuguese." The result was that the product produced in Barbados quickly found outlets in the European markets, beginning a long process through which sugar, once a relatively marginal part of European diets, was transformed from a luxury into a necessity and a staple.[41]

The social, economic, and ecological impact on Barbados was rapid and staggering. A visitor in 1655 declared it "one of the Richest spotes [sic] of ground" in the world, and it was, as Richard Dunn writes, the "richest colony in English America." "Land changed hands rapidly, population boomed, commerce accelerated, and prices climbed sky high." The price of land skyrocketed in the 1640s, with a "tenfold increase in seven years" of the worth of most land, and the better-situated plots increasing in value even more. There was, in fact, very little arable land on the "tight little island," less than one hundred thousand acres in all, and very rapidly the forests that remained on the island were cut down, so that "by the 1650s there was a timber shortage, and by the 1660s Barbados had less woodland than most districts in England." The forests that had once covered the island had almost completely disappeared. Plants introduced by the British would spread throughout the island, most importantly the "omnipresent grass," sugar cane.[42]

The sugar boom, with its "unholy union of sugar, slavery and the plantation system," led to the concentration of land in fewer and fewer hands. Because of the labor-intensive nature of the growing, harvesting, and processing of sugar, they had to be carried out on a larger scale than tobacco or cotton cultivation to be profitable. Those who were able to purchase enough land consolidated their holdings, but smaller landowners unable to bear the costs of setting up sugar plantations tended to sell their land. The number of agricultural properties on the island declined from 1,120 in 1645 to 745 in 1667, and a small elite increasingly controlled a larger and larger portion of arable land. By 1680, more than half of the arable land was owned by only 6.9 percent of the planters, and by 1750 about one-third of sugar planters in Barbados owned 56.9 percent of all agricultural properties. The colony was deeply shaped by "the rapid rise of a cohesive and potent master class" that, in the words of Richard Dunn, developed into "the most perfectly articulated colonial aristocracy in English America." The planters of Barbados were, by 1680, the "wealthiest men in British America."[43]

With the overpopulation and saturation of Barbados, the British increasingly coveted other islands, including French Martinique and Guadeloupe.

These islands had developed and sustained relatively diversified plantation economies during the seventeenth century. At first, there were relatively small plantations focused on the production of provisions for local consumption and tobacco for export. Tobacco was an attractive crop in the French Caribbean (as elsewhere) because it required little capital to begin producing it. Its importance was, however, short-lived. Changing colonial policies and competition from Virginia and other British colonies pushed settlers in other directions. Alongside these tobacco plantations there were already others focused exclusively on the production of sugar cane. It was these plantations that ultimately proved more successful and profitable, and as in Barbados, sugar cultivation became the major focus of the economy in both Martinique and Guadeloupe. While other crops, including cotton and indigo, were always cultivated along with sugar, these islands joined the "sugar revolution" and over the course of the eighteenth century steadily expanded their production and export of sugar to the French metropole.

The British ultimately helped the process along. During the Seven Years' War, they occupied Guadeloupe from 1759 to 1763, along with a shorter occupation of Martinique. Because Guadeloupe was in some ways less developed economically than Martinique, the British poured money and slaves into the island. Slave-trading ships usually headed to the more lucrative markets in Martinique and especially French Saint-Domingue, so Guadeloupe's planters had traditionally acquired their slaves through transshipment from Martinique or else contraband trade with other nearby islands. During their occupation, however, the British imported large numbers of slaves directly to the island. As a result, more slaves arrived in Guadeloupe directly from Africa on British ships during these four years than arrived on French ships during the entire eighteenth century. There was a massive increase in the number of sugar plantations, from 185 to 447, during this period. The British also expanded the port of Pointe-à-Pitre, turning it into the leading port of the island and condemning the administrative capital of Basse-Terre to second string from then on. During the same years (1762–63), a brief occupation of Havana by the British had a similar impact in helping to develop sugar production on the island.[44]

Jamaica

It was another island that became the center of the British Empire in the Caribbean: Jamaica. It was settled by the Spanish in the early 1500s, but it remained a marginal colony compared with the settlements in the rest of the Greater Antilles, Cuba, Santo Domingo, and Puerto Rico. In 1655, though there were a few sugar mills producing for local consumption, the total population was perhaps as small as 1,500 and "no more than 2,500." In that year, however, a British mission composed of 8,200 soldiers arrived on the island. Sent by the British leader Oliver Cromwell against Spanish possessions in the Caribbean as part of his "Western design," the mission was made up of 3,500 soldiers from Barbados, 1,200 from the other British Caribbean islands, and 3,500 sent from England. They arrived in Jamaica after a disorganized and disastrous attempt to conquer Spanish Santo Domingo during which several hundred soldiers had died. At first they had better luck in Jamaica, where the Spanish militia put up little resistance and the governor soon offered to surrender. Some Spanish commanders retreated inland, though, and they had valuable allies: groups of slaves and free people of African descent, many of whom had long lived in the mountains.[45]

Spanish Jamaica had been a loosely populated frontier society, and at the time of the British invasion there were a few hundred free people of African descent, many of them small farmers who also hunted the cattle and pigs that wandered in the mountains. There were also many slaves who were "allowed a great deal of practical freedom in their duties" as farmers and hunters. From among this group came the most serious resistance to the British invasion. Many among them were able to remain free, founding long-standing maroon communities in the mountains of Jamaica that exist to this day. As one member of such a community recalled in 1999, the Spanish "freed their slaves, and asked them to fight the British." Although the rallying of former slaves to the Spanish cause did not stop the British takeover, it did provide many individuals with an opportunity to create settlements in the hills, which were the foundation for the long-standing and powerful communities of maroons who would resist the British in the coming century. As another maroon recalled, the Spanish had carried his ancestors to Jamaica from the "Guinea Coast," but after the British takeover, "they did not want to work anymore" as slaves.[46]

While a few preserved their freedom, Jamaica grew into the most important British colony in the Americas, filled with flourishing plantations dependent on slave labor. Cromwell anticipated this possibility when he celebrated the conquest of Jamaica in a 1655 proclamation that declared the island "spacious in its extent, commodious in its harbors and rivers within itself, healthful by its situation, fertile in the nature of the soil," and therefore "generally fit and worthy to be planted and improved to the advantage, honor, and interest of this nation." In order to encourage its settlement, he declared that "every planter, or adventurer to that island" would be exempt from paying "customs or excise" on any goods brought to the island and that no taxes would be imposed on any commodities produced there and imported into "any dominions belonging to the commonwealth" of England. The commissioners sent to the island in 1656 were authorized to admit any people of the commonwealth, as long as they were Protestants, "to inhabit and plant upon any part of" Jamaica.[47]

Like other Caribbean societies, Jamaica fascinated and appalled many European visitors. In his popular 1697 account of a journey to Jamaica, Ned Ward offered a withering description of its society. As he recounted it, he had so "often heard such extravagant Encomiums of that Blessed Paradise" that he hoped a trip there might help him escape from the ill fortune he had suffered in England. His co-travelers on the ship included a woman who was going to find her "*Stray'd Husband, who, in Jamaica, had Feloniously taken to Wife (for the sake of Plantation) a Lacker-Fac'd Creoleon,*" that is, a locally born Creole woman, along with "a *Creoleon Captain, a Superanuated Mariner, an Independent Merchant, an Irish Kidnapper* . . . all going with one Design, to patch up their *Decay'd Fortunes.*" The journey, as he told it, included weathering a storm, which the passengers spent in "a doubteful Condition, between this World and the next." It also had its share of joys, such as watching "the Clouds, whose various Forms, and Beautious Colours, were Inimitable by the Pencil of the greatest Artist in the Universe," in which the enthralled shipborne saw "*Cities, Palaces, Groves, Fields* and *Gardens; Monuments, Castles, Armies, Bulls, Bears* and Dragons." It was "as if the Air above us had been Frozen into a *Looking-Glass,* and shew'd us by Reflection, all the Rarities of Nature." He found much less to admire about Jamaica itself, which he described as a "Sweating Chaos," and as much worse: "The Dunghill of the Universe, the Refuse of the whole Creation, the Clippings of the Elements, a shapeless pile of Rubbish confused'ly jumbl'd into an Emblem of the Chaos, neglected by Omnipotence when he formed the World into its admirable Order." The colony had become, he went on, "The Receptacle of Vagabonds, the Sanctuary of Bankrupts, and a Closestoll for the Purgers of our Prisons. As Sickly as a Hospital, as Dangerous as the Plague, as Hot as Hell, and as Wicked as the Devil." Ward satirized the inhabitants of Jamaica as pompous and greedy, highlighting the possibilities for transformation available on the island: "A *Broken Apothecary* will make there a *Topping Physician;* a *Barbers Prentice,* a good *Surgeon;* a *Bailiffs Follower,* a Passable *Lawyer;* and an *English Knave,* a very *Honest Fellow.*"[48]

Jamaica's largest town in the seventeenth century was Port Royal, famous as a haven for pirates and as a favorite site for them to spend their plunder. Its inhabitants and visitors had a wide range of taverns to choose from, such as the Black Dogg, the Chesire Cheese, and the Sign of Bacchuss. By 1672, according to the wealthy planter and great eighteenth-century historian of Jamaica Edward Long, there were eight hundred houses in the town, and the rents in "most of them" were "as high as any of that time in the heart of the city of London." Two decades later, in 1692, there were about two thousand houses and 3,500 inhabitants.[49]

Then, on June 7 of that year, a massive earthquake struck in the late morning and, wrote Long, in "two minutes time" destroyed most of the city. One survivor described seeing people in the streets with "lifted up hands begging God's assistance," while "the sand in the streets" rose up like "waves of the sea, lifting up all persons that stood upon it and immediately dropping down into pits," while water flooded in and rolled "those poor souls over and over." Many streets sank into the ocean, and, according to Long, "about two thousand Whites and Negroes perished" in Port Royal alone. A "great part of a rocky mountain" nearby fell down, and "buried a whole plantation lying at the foot of it." "Offensive stenches were emitted" from the fissures in the earth for weeks after the quake, the weather grew warmer, and "such prodigious swarms of muskeetos infested the coasts, as to astonish the inhabitants." In the wake of the catastrophe, sickness spread into nearby Kingston and other parts of the island, killing as many as three thousand people. "Thus fell the glory of Port Royal," concluded Long. Ever the historian, he added that "all the public records" were destroyed as well, "which proved a heavy loss." A fire destroyed much of the remaining city in 1703, and "as if Providence had decreed that it should never before revive to anything like its former splendor, what the earthquake and conflagration had spared was nearly demolished by a violent hurricane" in 1722.[50]

Although Port Royal was rebuilt and remained an important port in Jamaica, over the course of the eighteenth century it was overtaken in size and prominence by Kingston, which became the hub of an increasingly successful colony. Jamaica became the most profitable colony in the British Atlantic world, its planters the richest men in British America. They enjoyed opulent, transatlantic lifestyles. One such man was John Tharp, the son of a planter in Jamaica, who was educated at Eton and Trinity College of Cambridge. He acquired the three thousand-acre Good Hope plantation in Jamaica in 1767 and owned two other plantations, and by 1791 owned upwards of three thousand slaves. His plantation boasted a "sugar works, with a waterwheel turned by the Martha Brae River; a church; a slave hospital, a school for slaves' children; and houses for the slaves." Tharp also made profits purchasing slaves off ships arriving from the Middle Passage and selling them to other Jamaican planters.[51]

Tharp played important roles in the public life, serving in the House of Assembly of Jamaica, and in relations with the maroon communities of Trelawny Parish. His Great House at Good Hope "commanded a splendid view of the Cockpit country" and "exemplified the opulence" of the "slave-owning plantocracy" of the region. His house was a "central meeting place" for local planters, "both for social occasions and for discussions relating to the sugar industry." He and his guests ate their food off "fine silver plate, engraved with the head of an African man," or china decorated with "a similar head of an African slave enclosed by sheeves of sugarcane," which were "imported from England, as were wine and champagne." As a treat to his business contacts and family members in England, Tharp sometimes sent live turtles across the Atlantic for them. He used his fortune to acquire extensive landholdings in England: a six thousand-acre estate called Chippenham Park in Cambridgeshire, where his portrait and a map of his Jamaican plantation still hang to this day, as well as a "beautiful London house." William Beckford, whose father was the lord mayor of London in the mid-eighteenth century and who was the extremely wealthy absentee owner of the large Drax Hall Plantation in Jamaica, owned an object that more bluntly crystallized the relations of power that underpinned his wealth: a "blackamoor stool," in which a black man in a contorted position holds up a pillowed seat.[52]

Another Jamaican planter, Charles Price, owner of the Worthy Park Plantation in Jamaica, likely owned 1,800 slaves at the time of his death. Like Tharp, he participated in slave trading, at one point joining with two others in buying an entire cargo of slaves worth 16,000 pounds. He built a "magnificent mansion" on one of his many properties, called Decoy, complete with a triumphal arch overlooking cultivated plantation fields and an elaborate botanical garden. Many planters were avid botanists, including Hinton East, an Oxford-educated lawyer and planter who introduced a variety of plants on the island, including a baobab tree, native to the West African savannah. A search for East's baobab tree in the 1980s turned up nothing, though several other thriving baobabs were inventoried in Jamaica and they grow on islands throughout the Caribbean. Planters also brought in other imports: Charles Price introduced deer onto his estate, "the wild descendants of which were still roaming in some parts of Jamaica in

1850." Perhaps more fittingly, he was remembered until the mid-twentieth century by the "Charles Price rats," who carried his name because he was believed to have introduced them into the island to eradicate a native species of rodents.[53]

Many commentators in the eighteenth century saw the lifestyle of wealthy planters, particularly those who were Creoles—that is, born in the Americas—as excessively decadent. A visitor to the French colony of Saint-Domingue, established on the western half of Hispaniola starting in the late seventeenth century, similarly highlighted and satirized the possibilities for social mobility available in the colony in a series of poems. Whereas in France, he wrote, people gained advantages because of their "rank, courage / knowledge, possessions or blood," in Saint-Domingue all it took for people to think of themselves as a prominent "personality" was "being white." And among whites, he suggested, everyone exaggerated their importance, and even those who possessed a tiny parcel of land called themselves "*habitants*," or "planters."[54]

The extensive journals of the Jamaican planter Thomas Thistlewood are probably the most detailed window we have into the lives of planters. Thistlewood developed his skills as a horticulturalist and gathered an important collection of books that included the works of Voltaire and Montesquieu. At the same time, he was a brutal slave master who whipped his slaves weekly and devised appalling and degrading tortures for them. "How could an Enlightenment man also be a cruel tyrant?" asks Trevor Burnard in his study of Thistlewood. His answer is that Thistlewood, like the Enlightenment thinkers discussed above, in fact saw no contradiction between the two because he saw his slaves as "a species of humanity to whom normal rules of humanitarianism, liberty and justice need not apply."[55]

Over the course of the eighteenth century, planters throughout the Caribbean developed a rich political and juridical tradition that brought together demands for the same political rights as other subjects within their empires with an insistent defense of their own right to hold slaves. Throughout the early eighteenth century, in "contest after contest," planters in the British Caribbean had shown "that they were prepared to go to extraordinary lengths to defend their identities as English or British people by standing up to London authorities, royal governors, and any local supporters" who threatened to take away the privileges they considered were theirs as English subjects. They did so, however, not primarily by invocation of natural rights theory—whose potential for mobilization against slavery on the part of antislavery activists, both free and enslaved, would become glaringly clear by the end of the eighteenth century—but rather by using "English jurisprudential traditions, which provided clearer support for making categorical legal distinctions among various classes of people in the same society."[56]

The articulation of planter political ideology became increasingly conscious and sophisticated when it became a way to respond to the critiques of slavery that multiplied starting in the middle of the eighteenth century. Despite their rich engagement with a variety of political and juridical traditions, what ultimately dominated and shaped the political theories and horizons of the planters, were their foundations in a plantation society of great violence. There was no way to escape the fears and excesses of the slavery that surrounded the beautiful plantation homes. When Edward Long advocated the creation of a public school in Jamaica, he unwittingly exposed how much any such project was constrained and circumscribed by the realities of slavery. The school would need, he noted, a "defensible barrack" to "guard against any calamity likely to happen from insurrections among the Negroes." The garrison in this barrack, as well as the students, would have to be fed, of course, so Long advocated that "a Negroe market should be held there once a week, for poultry, hogs and such other provisions as these people usually deal in." At the same time, though, there should be "white servants" rather than slaves in the school itself, so that the students "might not, by a too early familiarity and intercourse with the Negroes, adopt their vices and broken English." The enslaved majority of Jamaica was at once a resource, because of the central place it played in providing provisions to the population, and a menace for both its potential insurrections and its potential cultural and social influence.[57]

At the core of planter practice and ideology was the consistent deployment of torture and rape as forms of control. As Heather Vermeulen argues, the control exercised over the enslaved by Thistlewood and other slave owners was always grounded in forms of sexual assault and humiliation. Thistlewood's "chief mode of surveying—and surveilling the landscapes under his control—was through the serial rapes of enslaved women, which he documented in his diaries." There was no contradiction, in his mind, between his sexual assaults of women and his "self-fashioning" as a man of the Enlightenment. In fact, the various forms of knowledge and power he exercised were deeply imbricated with one another: "his violence against enslaved women was central to his working-out of Enlightenment thought and plantation management." As Vermeulen notes, Thistlewood often raped women in the spaces that might otherwise offer some kind of refuge for them, in the slave quarters themselves, in provision grounds, or in areas near the plantation where they went to harvest food or simply to escape. Rape was used as a weapon of control over bodies and over space. These were "both acts of sexual terror and ways of marking the grounds—and people—under his surveillance." Rape, Vermeulen argues, should therefore be seen as central to planter practice and ideology, and integrated into any account of how we consider their intellectual and political history.[58]

The port towns of colonies like Barbados and Jamaica offered a different landscape, one in which enslaved people in some ways had more opportunities for autonomy than in the plantation sphere. In 1774, Kingston had a population of about 14,200, making it the third-largest town in British America, totaling about 7 percent of the total population of Jamaica. Forty percent of the colony's free people of African descent lived in Kingston. By 1788, there were over three thousand free people of African descent along with over sixteen thousand slaves in the town, so that Kingston had "more slaves and free people of color combined than in all the urban centers of British North America." These towns, then, were profoundly shaped economically, socially, and culturally by people of African descent, who found economic, social, and cultural opportunities there. In Port-au-Prince, the capital of colonial Saint-Domingue, many women of color were able to invest in real estate and participate in other important economic roles, such as merchant activities, for instance.[59]

Yet, as Marisa Fuentes has argued, urban areas were also landscapes of terror and violence for the enslaved, notably women who were under constant threat of sexual assault. Reconstructing how women would have seen, sensed, and moved through the town of Bridgetown, Barbados, in the eighteenth century, Fuentes notes that this was a space in which they encountered "spatial reminders of the looming violence of slavery." In the center of town was something called "the Cage," where enslaved runaways who had been captured were imprisoned and displayed. Built in 1657 along a public wharf, this was a key part of the lived experience of all residents in the town through the early nineteenth century. But punishments against slaves were also carried out in many other public locations, including near markets that were central spaces for enslaved economic and social activity. The public nature of torture was a critical part of maintaining the order of slavery. When, in 1768, a woman named Molly was hanged publicly after having been accused of poisoning a white man, her body was then gathered by community members who carried out a lengthy and elaborate funeral rite. This enraged the Barbados governor, who considered it an insult to the white population. He ordered that henceforth, the body of an enslaved person who was executed would be carried "immediately into the Sea," and saddled with weights "to sink it in the deep water, so that it may be impossible for the Negroes to take it up again." When this led to less public executions, however, the governor realized that "a secret punishment is a punishment half wasted," and issued new regulations to make sure the violence against enslaved bodies was maximally visible. Bodies were still rowed out to sea, or else thrown into wells, to make it impossible for communities to properly bury them and mourn. "Dumping the bodies at sea," notes Fuentes, also "served to remind the enslaved of their position by invoking the Middle Passage" and represented "a second death." Within the towns, the enslaved also constantly reencountered the trauma of the Middle Passage itself through the very visible arrival and auctioning of Africans, reminding those in Barbados "of their own moment of disembarkation and sale or the repeated terror of witnessing frightened captives led into a life of perpetual bondage and violence."[60]

While plantation societies across the Caribbean varied in many ways, they all depended on a nexus of legal, social, and economic practices in order to maintain and defend a particularly exploitative and brutal order. As Elsa Goveia argues in her classic study on eighteenth-century laws surrounding slavery, there was a striking consistency in the forms these laws took across different empires, despite very different European legal traditions. "The rule of force inherent in slavery produced comparable results in the Spanish, British, and French colonies of the West Indies." At the core of the legal order were always police regulations aimed at containing the potential threat posed by the majority population against the minority holding them in bondage. "Police regulations lay at the heart of the slave system," Goveia notes, and "without them, the system itself became impossible to maintain." The primary function of laws in this context was "either directly or indirectly repressive." And as Fuentes notes, in a system where the enslaved themselves could not testify in their own defense, notions of "guilt" and "innocence" were effectively "evacuated of meaning." The "slave laws collapsed on themselves," given that the human beings ensnared by them were considered commodities without any human agency of their own. In rare cases where white residents were tried for the murder of enslaved people, they were fined for "destroying property," having to pay the cost of those they killed to their legal owners.[61]

Enslaved people had to understand and analyze this illegitimate system in order to survive. Yet, under conditions of constant threat and constraint, they also found and cultivated spaces in which they created a different set of principles and ways of living, sustaining alternative visions and possibilities. These projects and practices lay the foundation for long-standing forms of community formation and activity within the Caribbean, whose history points to an alternative landscape. At the root of this alternative social order was a different religious and spiritual vision as well as a different vision of Caribbean land and of the communities it could and should sustain.

Within and beyond the Plantation

The majority of the population of Caribbean islands was by the early eighteenth century made up of enslaved, often African-born, survivors of the Middle Passage. The traumatic voyages of the Middle Passage would have shaped the slaves' perspectives on the plantation world. In 1714, the *Duke of Cambridge*, which had registered a cargo of 350 slaves when it left the Gambia, arrived in Barbados carrying only 100. Of the rest, eighty had been killed during an uprising, the rest presumably of diseases. The journey across the Atlantic was always accompanied by death, and it represented an entrance into exile in the midst of a brutal plantation world. That world, as Vincent Brown has shown, was shaped powerfully by the constant experience of death as a structuring and defining force. The death of the enslaved was so common that it was barely noted at the time, and in some ways the numbers of the dead are difficult to fathom. In the course of six weeks in the 1770s in colonial Saint-Domingue, as many as thirty thousand slaves died from disease and hunger during an anthrax epidemic.[62]

The journey from Africa is still recalled in a range of settings in the Caribbean. Among maroon communities in Jamaica, stories are told of how ancestors were able to preserve their secret powers and knowledge so that they could be used in Jamaica, sometimes by swallowing their "obeah," objects of spiritual power that connected them to spirits, and then fleeing into the woods on their arrival to "shit" them out. Contemporary maroons recount how Nanny, who emerged as a great leader in the eighteenth century, had ensured "the safe passage of her spiritual knowledge across the Atlantic by swallowing a special substance" that made her mute, making it impossible for the slavers to "extract any secrets from her."[63]

In Haiti, one Vodou song announces an act that more than one African-born slave must have carried out. The song begins by calling out to "Agwe Woyo," one of the family of *lwa* (gods) of Vodou called Agwe, who watches over the ocean and whose second name also probably refers to the kingdom of Oyo in West Africa. "Agwe Woyo, I'm going down / I'm going down to the Oceanside / I'm looking for my family!" Families were left behind, others perhaps lost in the ocean itself on the journey. Africa is also constantly evoked in Vodou songs that refer to Guinée as both a geographical homeland and a mythic place, often calling on gods and kings in Africa to provide assistance in a new and hostile world. Vodou itself emerged out of the encounter and dialogue between a wide range of religious practices and perspectives. The ports of Saint-Domingue received cargoes of enslaved people from seventy-six different African ports. The enslaved, of course, drew on all they carried with them—political ideals, intellectual histories, religious practices, fighting tactics, forms of healing, ideas about sexuality, and social organization—as they approached and confronted the plantation world.[64]

That was notably true in the area of healing. The medicinal knowledge of slaves, which was linked to their knowledge about, and often cultivation of, medicinal plants, was widely recognized by whites. Whites were also often dependent on the medicinal knowledge of slaves, which was based on knowledge both of plants they grew and of plants they harvested outside the plantations. Edward Long criticized whites who practiced medicine in Jamaica for their ignorance about the botany of the island, pointing out that in contrast, "many of the Negroes are well acquainted with the healing virtues of several herbs and plants, which a regular physician tramples underfoot, with no other idea of them, than they are not part of his *materia medica*, nor any better than useless weeds." Eighteenth-century observers in Barbados similarly noted the knowledge of herbal medicines among enslaved healers on the plantations.[65]

Knowledge of the medicinal properties of plants was of crucial importance for the enslaved. Even when plantation owners provided hospitals and medical care, as a certain number did in the French and British Caribbean in the second half of the eighteenth century, it was "oriented toward preserving the fitness of the labor force and its economic productivity" or "insuring its natural increase." European medicine was, in any case, of limited efficacy and often quite primitive in its treatments. As a result, the enslaved depended primarily on their own knowledge and their own specialists in confronting disease, caring for wounds, and managing the labor and delivery of children. Our understanding of the systems of healing they used is extremely fragmentary, for descriptions written by colonial observers were usually cursory and shaped by limited observation. Nevertheless, it seems clear that much of this healing took place through a holistic approach that saw a connection between physical and spiritual healing, notably through the identification of spiritual causes for physical ailments.[66]

As in many societies, some of those who could heal spiritual ailments could also inflict them. The existence of forms of spiritual attack among the enslaved, which were often associated in the minds of masters with the use of poison, gained the attention of slave owners and colonial administrators, who saw in them the potential for subversion and resistance on the part of slaves. A focus on the aggressive use of spiritual power among the enslaved tended to skew the perspective of whites who observed such practices. In the British Caribbean, the work of healers, as well as that of spiritual practitioners who used their powers to harm others, gradually came to be referred to as "Obeah"—a word that probably has an African etymology, though its precise origin remains unclear—and were increasingly criminalized in colonial law. The generalized term, however, in fact points to an extremely diverse range of practices, from the use of herbal remedies for common ailments to elaborate rituals of healing that called on realms of power beyond that of the living.[67]

There were those who escaped from slavery and formed or joined maroon communities. Other enslaved people, and free people of African descent, were able to find a space of freedom on the sea itself, as pirates. While most pirates were sailors who had escaped from the harsh life they experienced on merchant and military ships, where pay was low, the work dangerous, and the discipline harsh and brutal, there were also always those who had escaped from bondage in the Americas or had been freed from slave ships attacked by pirates. Slaves and sailors were the pillars of the Atlantic economy, creating and transporting the commodities that made fortunes for its planters and merchants, and yet they did not share in this wealth. As pirates, however, they could. When they were part of a band that captured a ship, they got a portion of the loot. National, social, and racial boundaries were less important in pirate bands than the value of each member in the pursuit of pillage, and there was a rough democracy on many ships. This world provided an escape and a refuge in the Atlantic for many men, and some women, who had few prospects elsewhere. By the early eighteenth century approximately a quarter of those in pirate bands were of African descent, both escaped slaves and free individuals from Africa and the Americas. Some of them were ship captains, leading crews of both whites and blacks, so that according to Kenneth Kinkor, pirate ships were "the first site of black power in the midst of the white world of the 18th century."

Pirates and maroons had different goals and different methods, but frequently their paths crossed and they served each other.[68]

The vast majority of Africans and people of African descent lived on plantations, where their lives were dominated by labor. Still, there were critical ways in which they found and cultivated spaces of autonomy. Much of the land on sugar plantations was devoted not to growing sugar cane but to supporting all the activities that made growing and harvesting the cane possible. On the large and successful Drax Hall Plantation in Jamaica, for instance, only about 10 percent of the land was devoted to growing sugar cane even though that was the main crop produced there. The rest was devoted to provision grounds and fields for raising cattle and other animals. The intensively "mono-crop" plantation at Drax Hall was embedded within "complex networks of local production."[69]

As B. W. Higman has shown in his richly detailed analysis of the history of the Montpelier Plantation in Jamaica, the spatial configuration and material worlds on any given plantation represented an extremely complex crossroads of practices and intentions layered onto a particular geographical space. While planters, of course, dominated much of the structure of plantation life, the enslaved "influenced the larger pattern of land and labor exploitation, both through resistance and accommodation." And, over generations, the enslaved made the space of the plantation their own in many ways. The owners of Montpelier over its history mostly lived elsewhere in Jamaica or in England, and overseers and other white residents rarely remained for long. "As a shared place, a locality, a place in which to live a life," Higman argues, "Montpelier existed only for the slave population and its post-emancipation children." In the spaces they could best control, the houses in the slave villages and the plots of land that surrounded them, they came to "establish their own spatial patterns of routes, land allocation, settlement pattern and household architecture." These models were "anathema" to the way the planters conceived of the landscape, going against the desire for "geometric order," which was also a form of control. "Within these small spaces, contained within the larger boundaries of the estate, the workers set out paths, walls, fences, yards, pens, buildings, graves and gardens following principles which demonstrated a distinct vision of the relationship between people and the land." In doing so, they drew both on African models and on new creole practices. They were particularly interested in creating "elements of refuge" in their lives, spaces that were invisible to the planters and overseers, where family and spiritual life, as well as independent economic activity, could be carried out.[70]

The planting and maintenance of trees were a crucial part of this. An 1818 visitor to another plantation in Jamaica, Hope Estate, described the village where the enslaved lived as seen from a distance as "a thick grove, formed of every kind of fruit tree known in the island. Coco-nuts, oranges, shaddocks, forbidden fruit, mangoes, avocado pears, ackees, naseberries," and other trees all came together "to form an impenetrable wood." Coming closer, he saw paths "leading into this apparent labyrinth," and inside individual houses surrounded by gardens. These houses and gardens could be home to a complex network of kin, such as those who in 1825 lived across three houses in the Montpelier Plantation village occupied by descendants of the sixty-three-year-old Bessy Warren, which included daughters, sons, and grandchildren, along with others not related by blood who were brought into the family group. A drawing of the village at Montpelier from 1820 shows an area thick with trees, hiding many of the houses. An 1840 visitor to a "hamlet" on a plantation in Westmoreland Parish noted admiringly the "variety and grandeur of the various trees" with which the community was "embowered."[71]

Trees provided cover and privacy, but they were also a vital economic resource for the fruit many of them produced. They were one part of a larger complex of food production carried out by the enslaved. Within and alongside the plantations, enslaved people developed another economy that both sustained and contested the world that surrounded them. Although the habit was not always officially sanctioned, a large number of plantation owners took care of the problem of providing sustenance to their slaves by placing the burden for it on them. The idea was simple: masters would grant the enslaved access to plots of land that were not useful for the cultivation of the main plantation crops, and allow them to grow provisions there for themselves. Masters would then save money, always a preoccupation, by cutting back on or entirely eliminating the provisions they provided to their slaves. The approach of allowing slaves to cultivate small plots, usually adjacent to their houses, was often combined with the maintenance of provision grounds on the plantations. These grounds were sometimes worked by gangs of slaves under direct supervision from overseers, but at other times were cultivated somewhat independently by the slaves. Provision grounds tended to be located on hilly land that could not be used for other crops, and therefore were often far away from the core of the plantations, so that slaves were burdened not only with cultivating them but also with walking relatively long distances back and forth from them.[72]

Most masters probably saw their granting of access to land as temporary and retractable, but the enslaved thought otherwise. What the plantation laborers grew and harvested in the provision grounds and on the garden plots around their houses were, Higman notes in his study of Montpelier, "regarded as theirs to consume or exchange." The enslaved on plantations throughout the Caribbean came to understand access to their plots as a basic right, and some considered this land an inheritance they could pass down to their children. They also saw these garden plots, conceived of originally as an economic opportunity for their masters, as an opportunity for themselves. Some were able to grow food and raise livestock not only for their own families but also for local markets that often served as crucial providers of food for white masters themselves. Ultimately the independent agricultural production of slaves lay the foundation for the strategies of land use and farming that would be drawn upon by ex-slaves in the postemancipation period.[73]

The origins of many agricultural techniques were "in the slaves' ancestral homelands of west and central Africa and, hence, the product of several thousand years of agricultural experimentation." They were also richly creole, a "syncretic adaptation worked out by African slaves who incorporated African and European elements into aboriginal systems that already existed in the islands." They used mounds of earth, a strategy probably derived from the *conucos* used by indigenous peoples, and strategies of intercropping that brought together a variety of crops in a way that helped sustain the soil in which they were grown. The crops they grew were often indigenous, as was the case for avocado, guava, and mango trees or root vegetables like manioc and yams. The enslaved also raised livestock, particularly pigs, goats, and chickens, sometimes tethering them on fallow land.[74]

The enslaved developed their agricultural skills and knowledge mostly on their own, with no guidance from masters in terms of what to plant and how to best make use of the soil in the small plots they had. Through trials and experimentation, they developed strategies for mixed cropping, taking advantage of the presence of plants from the New World, Europe, Africa, and later Asia. The result of this "vast amount of plant experimentation" was the creation of a "food forest," in which "plants of various shapes and sizes" were concentrated together in a way that root systems didn't compete with one another and trees, bushes, and smaller crops all found room in which to grow. Transmitted knowledge and experimentation enabled farmers to exercise an "ecological artistry" and develop gardens that limited the impact of pests and diseases and provided a consistent and sustainable source of food, medicine, and even ornamental plants. Among the creations that likely emerged from this period were "living fences" that used plants, often cacti, to create strong and self-sustaining barriers for containing livestock and keeping them out of their gardens.[75]

In late eighteenth-century Jamaica, Edward Long observed the expertise of the enslaved, noting for instance that they often cultivated the "Pigeon, or Angola Pea," because it was "perennial," did not "require much care," and bore "a great number of pods," all characteristics that would have made it attractive to those who had to struggle to carve out time to work their own gardens. The "Palm-Tree," which he wished was more common in Jamaica, was also "chiefly cultivated by the Negroes" for its roasted nuts, which tasted "very much like the outside fat of roasted mutton," and the nut-oil, used in cooking but also to lessen the pain of rheumatic aches. Other foods were consumed by both masters and slaves, such as plantains, which supplied "a principal part of the substance to the inhabitants, black and white," though the former usually ate it in broth with fish or meat, while the latter ate it boiled or roasted as a substitute for bread. Long also noted how important the crops grown by slaves were in the Jamaican economy. Whites in plantation societies were often dependent not only on the labor that slaves did under their command on the plantations but also on the labor slaves did independently on their own plots of land. John Luffman, writing of Antigua in 1788, described how some of the land granted to slaves was "industriously and advantageously cultivated," and admitted that during "such times of the year as vessels cannot come to these coasts with safety," it was thanks to the livestock raised by slaves that whites were "prevented from starving."[76]

Cultivation that slaves performed for their own consumption, exchange, or sale independently from the plantation was a crucial part of the economy of the plantation system. Yet it also created challenges to and breaches within that system. As Sidney Mintz wrote, many slaves, "even while still owned by others, gained access to the use of productive property, produced thereby quantities of goods that they could consume and also exchange and sell, used their earnings autonomously, and in these ways achieved at least some distance from the conventional meanings of their defined status."[77]

There was much about the cultivation of land by slaves that undermined the institutional and regulatory intent of the plantation regime. As Woodville Marshall has written:

Slaves cultivated land and disposed of its produce without supervision from their owners. Slaves worked their provision grounds in family groups. Slaves selected crops and determined the methods of cultivation. They did so, moreover, with an energy and enthusiasm that sharply contrasted with their work habits and low productivity in gang labour plantation export staples. . . . These achievements were particularly remarkable because they were secured mainly by the slaves themselves. Their owners contributed land and grudgingly donated small portions of the slaves' labour time, but they did not intend or expect more from the provision-ground system than a reduction in the cost of slave maintenance.

Building on the small, and self-serving, concessions of masters, slaves created for themselves an independent economic role in the slave society, and in the process ultimately transformed the regulations that governed their lives. Initially, most local regulations heavily restricted the movement of slaves and outlawed their participation in markets. But ultimately the centrality of the goods produced by slaves meant that colonial administrations had to grant "the formal concession of the slaves' right to attend market on a designated day," which gave them an opportunity to leave the plantation for the towns. By the latter half of the eighteenth century, notably in the British colonies, "customary arrangements had overturned legal restrictions, and what had grown outside the law had become recognized in law."[78]

In addition to creating a shift in the administrative regime that governed them, slaves also came to understand that they had certain customary rights, and acted to defend those rights when they were threatened. At some points the enslaved "openly protest[ed] the choice of market day and the organization of markets." They also "forced their owners to recognize rights of occupancy on portions of plantation ground," refusing to move "without notice or without replacement grounds being provided, and they could bequeath rights of occupancy as well as property."[79]

What was true in the British Caribbean was also true elsewhere. In the late eighteenth century in Guadeloupe, slaves diverted water from canals built to sustain fountains in the capital of Basse-Terre to irrigate their gardens, to the dismay of local officials. In Martinique by the 1840s, plots granted to slaves could sometimes be "quite extensive," as large as one or two acres. "In these gardens slaves grew sorrel, squash, cucumbers from France and Guinea, green peppers, hot peppers, calabash vines, okra and perhaps some tobacco. They also planted fruit trees and, if the master permitted, kept chickens there as well." The abolitionist Victor Schoelcher visited one plantation where he observed a large mango tree inconveniently growing in the middle of a cane field, but which the planter could not cut down because it was "owned" by a slave who understood it as his right both to own it and to pass it on to his descendants. The respect of the "property" of the slaves was so widespread, according to another observer, that a planter who disrespected it would risk being "dishonored" by other whites.[80]

As Jean Besson has written, this broader configuration developed by the enslaved represented a key component of "Caribbean cultural creativity" in the face of the structures of the colonial plantation system. The enslaved "developed the provision ground system well beyond the planter rationale," not only producing "surpluses for sale in internal markets beyond plantation boundaries" but using these practices "as the basis of kinship, community, and customary land tenure." These practices, notes Dale Tomich, created a space from which the plantation experience was "mediated and contested." The enslaved found ways to contest "the definition and meaning of time and space, labour and power." Though they originated within "the social and spatial boundaries of the plantation," they also "allowed for the construction of an alternative way of life that went beyond it." The beyond involved not just the opportunity to leave the plantation physically as the enslaved traveled to markets to sell what they produced on plots. It also involved the creation of alternative forms of relation and meaning. "The work of preparing the soil, planting, cultivating, harvesting" was all "organized through ritual, kinship and mutual obligation." "The provision grounds were important for aspects of slave life as diverse as kinship, religious belief, cuisine and healing practices." Some of this sense of possibility was captured in the name one official in Saint-Domingue gave to the provision grounds, une petite Guinée, suggesting that, in a sense, Africa itself was being re-created within and against the plantation world. According to the slave masters, the place of the slaves within this world was to be nothing but laborers with no past or future. But as Edouard Glissant has emphasized, the enslaved always worked to reconstitute a sense of their own history, upon which alternative futures could be founded. This work was done perhaps most powerfully through the constitution of new forms of kinship and community. Some childless slaves, notes Besson, "transmitted garden rights to their nearest kin or friends," in so doing rooting a "wider concept of community" in concrete practices linked to the use of land.[81]

Trouillot eloquently described how profoundly important these small forms of economic independence ultimately were for the ways that they created broader possibilities for autonomy, independence, and the creation of a different set of worlds:

> Time used on the provision grounds was also slave-controlled time to a large extent. It was time to develop new practices of labor cooperation, reminiscent of—yet different from—African models of work. Time to talk across the fences to a passing neighbor. Time to cross fences themselves and fish in adjacent rivers. It was time to create culture knowingly or unknowingly. Time to mark the work tempo with old songs. Time to learn rhythm while working and to enjoy both the rhythm and the work. Time to create new songs when the old ones faded away. Time to take care of the needs of the family. Time to meet a mate. Time to teach children how to climb a tree. Time indeed to develop modes of thought and codes of behavior that were to survive plantation slavery itself.

Provision grounds and garden plots, Trouillot explains, "provided a space quite distinct from the plantation fields congested with sugarcane, coffee, and cotton. Space where one learned to cherish root crops, plantains, bananas; space to raise and roast a pig, to run after a goat, or barbecue a chicken; space to bury the loved ones who passed away, or to worship the ancestors and to invent new gods when old ones were forgotten."[82]

The markets, where the enslaved gathered to trade and sell what they had produced, were also vital sites of autonomy and community. The practices surrounding marketing were shaped by experiences and memories of similar spaces in Africa. One German observer named Wilhelm Muller noted of markets on the Gold Coast in the 1660s that "only women" participated in these markets. These were, notes Jennifer Morgan, places where "women exchanged more than goods." As Muller wrote, while there they "strengthen their memories by zealously repeating the old stories," while "young people and children listen to such discourse with avid ears and absorb it into their hearts." In the Caribbean, women played a similarly central role in markets, which were also sites for much more than just economic exchange. "As their largest and most prominent meeting place," writes Natasha Lightfoot, "the market created the conditions for slaves to see themselves collectively, as a community with similar origins and a common cause." It was "a social world in which they realized alternative visions for their lives." "To a certain degree, the Sunday market *was* freedom."[83]

In 1831 in Antigua, as the movement for abolition gained increasing momentum in the British Empire, the colonial legislature abolished the Sunday market with the justification that it was preventing the enslaved from attending church. But when a magistrate rode into the market in the capital of St. John to enforce the decision, he encountered a crowd of several hundred ready to fight back. They were prepared "waiting, not with products to vend, but 'armed with strong bludgeons secured by twine to the wrists.'" A detachment of soldiers was sent into the market, but it took several hours of fighting to subdue the crowd. It was early evening when "the last company of 7 or 8 obstinate women" finally left the market. And in the next days, a number of fires were set on plantations, clearly in protest against the closing of the market. And, a few weeks later, a group of enslaved from one plantation collectively left on a Saturday, when they were supposed to be working in the fields, to go to protest the closing of the market on the steps of the Government House in St. John. As some of the enslaved explained to a Methodist missionary, they could accept that they could no longer go to market on Sunday—as long as they were given another day off from labor on the plantations to do so instead. When he told them to be patient and "see what would be done for them," they insisted that they deserved the protection of the law: "so them make Law for the Negro, so them make Law for Master." As with provision grounds, they had come to see marketing as an "inalienable right." To the missionary, they insisted: "Give us the Day."[84]

The plantation complex had, by the nineteenth century, shaped the environment, economy, and society of the Caribbean for several centuries. As a structure and a project, it would long outlast slavery itself. But it had also generated a series of practices and visions crafted to respond to, survive within, and seek to move beyond the plantation. The political engagement of the enslaved in the project of emancipation, which we explore in the next chapter, was rooted in the experiences and visions that they developed within and against the plantation.[85]

3 Emancipation and the Rooting of Freedom

The history of the abolition of slavery in the Caribbean begins with the maroons. Speaking to Kenneth Bilby in Jamaica in 1978, a man named Charles Bernard told a short story about the most famous of his maroon ancestors: "White man say, 'you fe work.' Grandy Nanny say, 'me not working!' And she tek the river, follow river! She follow river." These four sentences condense an epic struggle, a journey, that reshaped Jamaica and the British Empire. For contemporary maroon communities and many others in the Caribbean, this struggle is still as present as it is past. The ongoing work of securing and protecting sovereignty—over one's body, community, land, and nation—is a continuation of the project started by those ancestors who took the river, followed the river, and began to create islands of freedom in the midst of a world of plantation slavery centuries ago.[1]

The Jamaican maroons were, along with those of Suriname, the largest and most successful maroon communities in the Greater Caribbean. But marronage was a part of all slave societies in the Caribbean. It existed alongside what it sought to escape and negate: the plantation system. Maroon societies existed throughout the Americas and were extremely diverse. "These new societies," writes Richard Price, "ranged from tiny bands that survived less than a year to powerful states encompassing thousands of members and surviving for generations or even centuries." Marronage "did not have the same meaning in all colonies at all times." A certain style of marronage, sometimes called "petit marronage," which involved relatively short-term and generally reversible escape from the plantation, including absences "with temporary goals such as visiting a relative or lover on a neighboring plantation," was largely tolerated by planters in many societies, notably the French colony of Saint-Domingue. "It was," Price writes, "marronage on the grand scale, with individual fugitives banding together to create independent communities of their own, that struck directly at the foundations of the plantation system, presenting military and economic threats that often taxed the colonists to their very limits." In several cases in the Greater Caribbean, most notably in Jamaica and Suriname but also in Saint-Domingue, "the whites were forced to bring themselves to sue their former slaves for peace."[2]

The oldest maroon communities in the Caribbean are in Jamaica. Their roots precede the British conquest of the island. When the British invaded in 1655, the Spanish organized regiments of people of African descent, both free and enslaved, to resist the occupation. The story remains a foundational part of the history Jamaican maroons tell about themselves. The maroon Melville Curry recalled to Kenneth Bilby in 1999 how, at the time of the invasion, the Spanish "freed their slaves, and asked them to help them fight the British." These units turned out to be much more formidable enemies than the Spanish themselves, continuing to harass English forces for several years. Some of them never surrendered, taking advantage of the conflict to escape permanently from slavery. As Johnny Minott told Bilby in 1991, the Spanish had carried his ancestors to Jamaica from the "Guinea Coast," but after the British takeover, "a body of them say, 'well, boy, me naa work no more a slaving, you know' . . . because they did not want to work anymore as slave under de Englishman." As the English consolidated their control over Jamaica, many, according to Melville Curry, went "to the hills" and "formed themselves into their tribes that they belonged to, from Africa." Realizing they would not survive long if they stayed in their disparate groups, the leaders of different bands gathered under a "mango tree"— and made a pact declaring "that we are one family, we are kin, so let us join together and put our resources together, and fight the British. Because we are from one place, we are the same people, we are kin, and we are free."[3]

The early maroon communities in Jamaica were, therefore, in some sense never subjects of England, instead fighting and negotiating from the start with those who considered themselves masters of the island and who made themselves masters of the hundreds of thousands of African captives they brought into the colony in the seventeenth and eighteenth centuries. Some of these newly arrived captives escaped from the plantations and joined the maroon communities in the hills, which grew in the late seventeenth century as slavery did, living in the high mountains whose topography helped repel the invasion of the sugar and coffee economy that transformed the island. By the eighteenth century, Jamaica was one of the most profitable colonies in the Americas, overshadowed only by French Saint-Domingue, and its ruling class included many of the richest men in the British Atlantic in the eighteenth century. Yet, in 1739, the governors of Jamaica signed a treaty with one maroon community guaranteeing the maroons their freedom from enslavement. In return, though, the maroons promised not to greet new escapees and promised to capture and return any who came into their territory.[4]

How did the maroons win? Maroons today, Kenneth Bilby writes, "credit the ultimate victory of the first-time people in their war for survival to the ingenious methods and strategies, both offensive and defensive, that they used." Maroons "swam up rivers to mask their scent from the hounds" that were sent to track them and disguised themselves in elaborate costumes made up of greenery from the forest, a skill kept alive and still demonstrated today in "annual commemorative festivities" in maroon communities. They used psychological warfare, such as wiping out units of soldiers but leaving one alive to go back and tell the story to their enemies. Maroons also recall the importance of spiritual strength—"We fight and sing our song, de old [songs], and blow our war horn, that us on to strength," one maroon woman explained in the 1950s—and the spiritual powers exhibited by their leaders, notably Nanny. The same was true in Suriname, where, as Richard Price writes: "Saramakas, recounting to me their ancestors' battles with colonial troops, made quite clear that as far as they were concerned, it was their gods and obeahs that spelled the ultimate difference between victory and defeat."[5]

In one powerful statement, the Jamaican maroon Mann Rowe summarized to Kenneth Bilby how the maroon struggle, led by leaders Nanny and Kojo, had created a new people:

> We are de skin of de island. De skin of de island. We, de Maroons, we are Israelites. And we are Africans. We are warlike and peaceful people. It was the English people dem proclaim war on us, and Kojo retaliated back to dem. And we fought, and gain victory. So is God's Kojo and Lady Queen Nanny that gives us our freedom. And God, I must say, was with us—we, de only nations that flog de English at War.[6]

The treaties signed in 1739 by some (though not all) maroons were the result of military prowess and survival on the part of these groups, who exhausted the British. But peace came with a cost. In return for an end to the war and a guarantee of freedom for their community, the maroons allowed British representatives to interfere with some aspects of their community life and agreed to return new fugitives from the plantations. Maroons generally fulfilled the agreement by returning escaped slaves who came into their territory. In 1796, however, some maroons participated in an uprising in Jamaica and several hundred were deported as a result, ending up in Newfoundland and eventually in Sierra Leone.

Over the years, many have criticized the Jamaican maroons for having turned their backs on other enslaved people. At times, the deeply romantic portrait of the maroons as freedom fighters has been countered with an equally stark vision of them as turncoats who fought only for themselves and not for a larger cause. The story, of course, is more complicated. Marronage was often linked with the lives and actions of those who remained enslaved. In fact, many maroons stayed relatively close to plantations, writes Michael Craton, "because of ties of kinship as well as for the purposes of supply and intelligence." "The provision grounds and slave quarters were the meeting places, crossing points," between enslaved on the plantations and those who had fled. The decision faced by the maroons in 1739 was an extremely difficult and a contested one. Some members of the communities argued against the treaty, and at least one left in anger after it was signed, heading higher into the mountains. Still, contemporary maroons continue to set themselves apart from other members of Jamaican society. While many Jamaicans have come to embrace the image of the maroons as enemies of colonialism and as national heroes, maroons also feel themselves to be apart in many ways from other Jamaicans. They continue to draw on their history as independent people in attempts to preserve their land and their autonomy. Maroons today, Bilby writes, argue that they "have not only the right to exist, but the right to *persist*, as they have done to the present, against all odds."[7]

In this sense the struggle of various groups of maroons condenses the larger process through which the enslaved were able to imagine, and ultimately call into being, a different kind of social and economic reality for themselves. That is, ultimately, the core story in the history of the abolition of slavery, the story that best helps us understand too the broader postemancipation history of the cultures and societies of the Caribbean. Like the construction of the plantation world itself, the process of emancipation stretched out for hundreds of years. It began with the origins of plantation slavery, with the self-emancipation carried out by maroons, and through the actions of enslaved men and women who worked and bargained, as well as escaped, their way to freedom. Sometimes they were emancipated by masters, sometimes they purchased their freedom (at times with funds accumulated working for people other than their owner, a portion of which they were permitted to keep), and sometimes they earned it through military service. Such freedom was rarely a purely individual pursuit, for family members and friends, both enslaved and free, often participated in and propelled the pursuit of individual freedom. Once slaves became free, they struggled to find a place in colonial societies, frequently challenging the boundaries of the racial and social order even as they also often served to buttress and protect it. They remained connected with communities of the enslaved, whose own attempts to access and make use of plots of land in the creation of their own spheres of autonomy were a critical part of life on the plantations and in the colonial towns.

These various strands of action helped to shape what happened in the Caribbean in the second half of the eighteenth century when a sustained series of attacks on the plantation system led to the first mass emancipation in the region in French Saint-Domingue in 1793. As a movement, abolitionism was remarkable for the reach of its networks and its ability to mobilize people across regions, faiths, and social situations. Indeed, abolitionism in many ways helped create the vocabulary and strategies of much modern political activism, blending arresting visual and literary propaganda with the force of mass meetings, petition campaigns, and at times violent resistance. When historians write about abolitionism, they are generally referring to free people who fought against slavery. But there were also many powerful enslaved abolitionists, whose concerted action was both strategically and ideologically a central part of the struggle for emancipation. That is why, though it is not usually considered as such, the Haitian Revolution, an event driven by the actions of enslaved insurgents, was clearly the largest and certainly the most immediately successful abolitionist movement in modern history, securing the immediate and universal abolition of slavery in the thriving French colony of Saint-Domingue within two years from its beginning in 1791.

For decades, scholars have furiously debated the causes of Atlantic emancipation, largely through a focus on the British Empire. Much of this conversation has spiraled around the 1944 work of Trinidadian scholar Eric Williams, *Capitalism and Slavery*. Williams's argument that it was the declining significance of the Caribbean sugar economy, rather than the action of abolitionists, that led to the abolition of slavery has generated decades of debate. The story told by Williams was based on what he saw as a wonderful irony: the slave system that lay the foundation for the Industrial Revolution in England ultimately was destroyed by the consequences of that revolution. For Williams, the capital generated by Caribbean slavery in the eighteenth century allowed English capitalists to invest in new industries, notably by building factories for the production of textiles. The expropriation of the land of the English peasantry during the late eighteenth and especially early nineteenth centuries in England, he argued, provided an increasingly large pool of cheap labor within the country itself that could be used to propel the expansion of industries there. This expansion in England, in turn, enabled its expansion into new colonial territories, notably India, whose local production of sugar provided competition for Caribbean sugar. Indian sugar had several advantages, primarily the fact that it was produced outside of British control, which meant that in contrast to the Caribbean, whose colonies required military protection from both external enemies and the internal threat of slave revolt, it required little in the way of additional costs. The plantation system of the Caribbean, once extremely profitable for England, thus gradually became less important. As India increasingly provided an alternative source for sugar, Caribbean planters increasingly lobbied for tariffs that would protect their industry. Such demands were increasingly at odds with the liberal economic ideology put forth by Adam Smith and other thinkers, and increasingly embraced by members of the English elite. The planters got themselves into a curious ideological and political bind, seeking to protect their own colonial order in a way that put them on a collision course with leaders in England.[8]

Williams downplayed the importance of antislavery ideology in the larger course of abolition. For him, it was the broader structural changes as well as the advance of liberal economic ideology that explained the increasing unpopularity of slavery. Though he did not deny the courage and foresight of the leading British abolitionists, he contested the idea that the abolition of slavery in the British Empire was the result of the triumph of abolitionist ideals. His striking thesis, driven at least partly by a desire to contest a self-satisfied and congratulatory vision of British abolitionism that he had encountered as a student, incited a profound and ongoing response by scholars committed to showing that the political and ideological efforts of the abolitionists in fact played a crucial role in ensuring the end of slavery. The result of the debate has been a flourishing of rich work both on the economies of slavery and on the ideologies of abolitionism. Many of Williams's claims, notably about the declining profitability of slavery in the mid-nineteenth century, have been strongly critiqued. Yet to a large extent the broad contours of his argument remain strikingly convincing as a way of grappling with the long-term trajectory and contradictions of slavery and emancipation.[9]

Williams himself did center the role of the enslaved in the history of abolitionism in a final chapter of the book, "The Slaves and Slavery." He highlighted the ways enslaved people often mobilized in the Caribbean around rumors of emancipation. A few years earlier, another Trinidadian scholar, C. L. R. James, had established in his 1938 *The Black Jacobins* that enslaved insurgents in Saint-Domingue had brilliantly fought their way to freedom. In the half-century since these two works were published, an outpouring of scholarship has variously challenged, buttressed, and revised their central claims. Even as many scholars, notably Robin Blackburn, have convincingly championed the role of the enslaved in securing their own liberty, others have expressed wariness at the impulse to romanticize and simplify slave action and insisted on the centrality played by abolitionist ideology and action in the metropole in the unmaking of the slave system. The difficult question of how to balance the influence of these forces has been taken up most recently by David Brion Davis. In his work *Inhuman Bondage*, Davis analyzes the interplay between abolitionism and enslaved action and insurrection, notably through a comparison of slave uprisings in the early nineteenth-century U.S. South with those in the British Caribbean during the same decades.[10]

Antislavery thought, like antislavery action among the enslaved, is essentially as old as the institution itself, even if outright rejection of the institution altogether and under all circumstances was rare. By the mid-sixteenth century, the famous Dominican priest Bartolomé de las Casas came to the conclusion that the African-Atlantic slave trade and indeed the thriving, if ever-volatile, plantation society in Santo Domingo then were morally abominable, and he repented his former complicity in both. Within Catholicism there was an ongoing tradition of antislavery thought. In the late seventeenth century, for instance, an obscure man named Lourenço da Silva de Mendouça secured a statement from the papacy condemning slavery. Born in Brazil (probably into slavery), Silva appeared in the papal court in the early 1680s to protest against slavery on behalf of an organized community in Lisbon (where he played a leadership role in a black confraternity) and, more broadly, on behalf of those kept in bondage in the Catholic world. He based his protest on a sixteenth-century papal decree outlawing the slavery of indigenous Americans, whose existence he had carefully noted on a piece of paper that he brought with him to Rome. The piece of paper illuminates a broader tradition of antislavery thought and discussion within the black communities of the Portuguese Atlantic as well.

Silva's petition succeeded in convincing the papacy to condemn the African-Atlantic slave trade and to order the royal governments of Spain and Portugal to take steps to end it. This command was rejected and ignored but remains, in the words of historian Richard Gray, "among the most notable statements on human rights ever to have been published by the papacy."[11]

In the early eighteenth century, religiously driven protests against slavery began to multiply among Protestant groups as well. A Quaker named Benjamin Lay who lived in Barbados for a time in the early 1700s before moving to Philadelphia developed an intense hatred of the institution and carried out a series of creative and bold protests among the slave owning Quakers of Philadelphia in the 1730s. He also published a rambling antislavery tract provocatively titled *All Slave-Keepers That Keep the Innocent in Bondage, Apostates.* Lay was marginal at the time, but by the 1760s many of his arguments against slavery were taken up by prominent Quaker leaders on both sides of the Atlantic. During the same decades, some Enlightenment intellectuals in France also issued critiques of slavery, though only a few called for abolition, and those who did so imagined a very slow and gradual process moving from slavery to freedom, generally through a process that didn't free any slaves outright, only children born to them after a certain date.

Until the last decades of the eighteenth century, such antislavery protests, though not uncommon, were also mostly ineffectual. Their impact was relatively contained, and the institution of slavery was broadly accepted as moral among elites in Europe and the Americas. Many critiques of slavery, going back to ancient times, took aim at certain kinds of "unjust" and illegal slavery but generally allowed for slavery in cases where people were taken as prisoners of war (though their children's enslavement was somehow also accepted as legitimate), provided they were not part of an in-group excluded from enslavement regardless. Defenders of African-Atlantic slavery could take advantage of such arguments, asserting that the slaves purchased on the African coast would have been executed otherwise as prisoners in wars between African groups and thus their enslavement was morally acceptable. There were moral as well as legal justifications proffered for this as well: that the enslaved gained something by being exposed to Christianity, or else that they were so racially or culturally inferior that they were incapable of living as free people without harming themselves and the societies in which they lived.

The turn against slavery was a radical moral transformation, one of the most striking in history. There were profound ideological and economic factors at work, but at the heart of the transformation was also slave resistance, the costs and the threats of it, the difficulty of maintaining a society with a large part of it, indeed in the Caribbean often the vast majority, enslaved. This reality, of course, could hardly have been made clearer than by the Haitian Revolution. And a series of major slave rebellions in the early 1800s in the Caribbean added, for some at least, to that clarity. After the 1831 revolt in Jamaica that came to be known as the "Baptist War," one abolitionist in the English House of Lords sought to invoke this specter: "The slave was prepared to take [his freedom], if their Lordships were not prepared to give it." It would be wise to give "that which they could no longer withhold." Similarly in Cuba, the demands of the enslaved who joined the independence war (1868–80) pushed Spain toward ending slavery, even while the independence movement failed to eject overseas rule.[12]

Essential to the moral revolution against slavery, like probably all revolutions, was the creation of new coalitions and alliances opposed to the old order for however diverse and even contradictory reasons. Both free and enslaved people now argued in multiple direct and indirect ways (as we will see) against the institution of slavery, to a degree that never had occurred before. This process reflected and enabled an escalating change, of the kind that is probably at the base of all major political transformations. It generated a change in the sense of what was possible—slavery seemed less and less inevitable and its end increasingly so—and that in turn facilitated a change in the sense of what was morally acceptable. Crucially, too, this process helped to generate and anchor new, but often contradictory, ideas about precisely what freedom was and about what it should look like that would continue to play out after the end of slavery and in some ways continue to shape the cultures of the Caribbean to the present day.

Rumors of Emancipation

In August of 1789, enslaved people in and around St. Pierre, Martinique, began sharing stirring news: freedom was coming. Some gathered for mass, expecting that Father Jean-Baptiste, the Capuchin *curé des nègres* (the priest who oversaw the spiritual needs of the enslaved), was going to announce that the slaves had been freed. Jean-Baptiste, however, apparently did not make the announcement and, with an order for his arrest issued, fled to nearby Dominica. Meanwhile, however, several enslaved men—described in one account as "black doctors"—spread the word that the king of France, encouraged by some of the slaves' distinguished friends in Paris, had abolished slavery. They added that the slave owners of Martinique were determined to resist the royal decision. It was therefore up to the slaves themselves to force the recalcitrant local leaders to accept the royal decree of emancipation.[13]

Shortly after these meetings, the governor of the island wrote that rebellious slaves, "armed with the instruments they use to cut sugarcane, refused to work, saying loudly that they were free." The local militia crushed the brewing revolt, executing several rebel leaders and hunting down maroons suspected of having helped them. The governor then received two threatening letters. The first, signed "We, the Negroes," claimed: "We know that we are free and that you are aware that rebellious people are resisting the orders of the King. . . . We want to die for this liberty; for we want it and plan to get it at whatever price, even through the use of mortars, cannons, and rifles." The second read, in part:

> The entire Nation of the Black Slaves united together has a single
> wish, a single desire for independence, and all slaves with one
> unanimous voice send out only one cry, one clamor to reclaim
> the liberty they have gained through centuries of suffering and
> ignominious servitude. This is no longer a Nation that is blinded by
> ignorance and that trembles at the threat of the lightest punishments;
> its suffering has enlightened it and has determined it to spill to its
> last drop of blood rather than support the yoke of slavery, a horrible
> yoke attacked by the laws, by humanity and by all of nature, by
> the Divinity and by our good King Louis XVI. We hope it will be
> condemned by the illustrious [Governor] Vioménil. Your response,
> Grand Général, will decide our destiny and that of the colony.[14]

The revolt and composition of these letters took place *before* the news of the revolutionary events that had shaken Paris in July of 1789 arrived in Martinique. Still, the convening of the Estates General and of the Marquis de Condorcet's early 1789 attempt to put slave emancipation on the agenda of that body were known in Martinique, as was the existence of the abolitionist Société des Amis des Noirs, founded the year before. Some of the Société's publications had arrived in the colony, and slaves had been seen gathering in the towns to hear them read aloud. When the governor had arrived in July of 1789 and, following the spirit of recent royal edicts on the colonies, sought to gather information about excessive cruelties committed against slaves, he was seen by some as an envoy of the abolitionists. Certain slaves expected him to announce emancipation at a ceremony honoring his arrival, and when he didn't, a rumor circulated that he was complicit with local slave owners who were determined to resist the king. The governor, in turn, blamed the revolt of August on the fact that slaves knew slavery was being discussed in Paris. He accused slaves in metropolitan France of passing on this information to those in the colonies.[15]

The events in Martinique in 1789 took place in the midst of a unique transatlantic revolutionary context. They were, however, part of a long tradition of slave uprisings inspired by rumors of imminent emancipation. Between the 1730s, when the scale of slave resistance expanded visibly throughout the Caribbean and North America, and the ending of slavery in the British Caribbean during the 1830s, such rumors appeared again and again within slave communities. They consistently took the form of the rumors present in Martinique in 1789, in which slaves told one another that local administrators were resisting orders from the metropole—sometimes directly from the king, sometimes from elected bodies of government—to reform or abolish slavery. It was a potent form of rumor, one with many parallels in the history of other regions and times.

The form these rumors took made them perfect vehicles for political mobilization. By accusing local administrators and slave owners of hiding the truth, and pointing to very believable motivations they might have for quashing news of emancipation, the rumors created a situation in which any denials on the part of those the rumors accused of dishonesty only confirmed their truth. The content of these rumors could serve as a potent source of inspiration for slave insurgents facing the daunting possibility of retributive repression. The slaves, those who spoke the rumors suggested, already had powerful allies. Freedom was already won and simply had to be wrested from local authorities. By calling on the highest political authority in this way, slaves passing on rumors turned local authorities, rather than the slaves, into "rebellious people" and presented the insurgents themselves as allies of the metropole. These rumors made powerful claims upon metropolitan governments. They did so by identifying and intervening in existing political conflicts between local administrators and metropolitan officials over who should have the right to shape the legal order of the colonies. They therefore provide us with fragmentary traces of the ways slaves viewed and responded to the fundamental juridical and political issues surrounding the structures of imperial governance.

The example of Martinique in 1789 is just one of a striking series of Caribbean uprisings in which rumors of imminent emancipation helped to express and crystallize demands for emancipation on the part of the enslaved in ways that, at least in certain cases, were quite politically effective. In their celebration and circulation of news from the metropole, these rumors acted simultaneously as predictions and, through the particular context into which they issued their predictions, as prophetic calls for mobilization in pursuit of a better future. Rumors of imminent freedom consistently invoked the possibility of alliances between slaves and metropolitan officials. In the French and British Caribbean, some insurgents who mobilized around such rumors actually succeeded in calling such alliances into existence, and in the process contributed in crucial ways to dismantling the system of slavery in which they lived. These rumors, then, played an important role in bringing about the emancipation they claimed had already occurred.

Studying rumors of emancipation allows us explore how the enslaved interpreted and transformed the political possibilities of their world. It simultaneously shows how their struggles were tied to the evolution of abolitionist thought and action in Europe and vice versa. In the pivotal moments that led to emancipation in the French Caribbean in the 1790s and in the British Caribbean in the 1820s and 1830s, enslaved communities played a central role: by directly creating the context for emancipation in Saint-Domingue in 1793, in the first case, and by heightening tensions in the colonies and precipitating metropolitan decisions as a result, in the second.

Rumors of emancipation emerged from, and made sense within, the political and economic structuring of two powerful Atlantic empires. The rumors traveled along and exposed the sinews through which that power was exercised, in the process generating new collusions and ultimately a new order. They also represent a point of intersection between abolitionist activity and slave activity and are therefore a particularly valuable source for writing a broader history of antislavery that integrates events on all sides of the Atlantic. Such an approach allows us to see how various actors (enslaved and free, of African and European descent [or of both], literate and illiterate, living and acting in the towns and plantations of Jamaica, Barbados, Saint-Domingue, and Martinique, and in the salons and parliaments of Paris or London) participated in and related to one another through the broad field of antislavery action. It is crucial to understand these actors in all their specificity and locate them in their social and discursive landscapes with as much precision as possible. It is also crucial that we start from a basic assumption that all of these actors—including the enslaved, even if they could not read—were not only strategists but also thinkers, interpreters, and generators of political discourse and political culture.[16]

This also means broadening our sense of *who* the abolitionists of the late eighteenth and early nineteenth centuries were. Although this exclusion is rarely explicit, it is generally the case that when scholars refer to "abolitionists," they refer to people who were *not* enslaved and who fought against slavery. When scholars use the term "black abolitionists," they are referring to free people of African descent who joined the abolitionist cause. This assumption about who is to be described as an abolitionist makes it possible to argue, as many have done, that the French abolitionist movement was weaker and more elitist than the British abolitionist movement. This is true only if one neglects the Haitian Revolution. If this revolution is rarely conceived as part of the history of abolitionism, it is, we would argue, mainly because its chief theorists and protagonists were enslaved people. If we think differently about what constituted abolitionist thought and action, such exclusions can cede to a fuller understanding of the intellectual history of the Atlantic world.

As many scholars have shown, slave revolts played an important role in defining the structures of control within slave societies throughout the Americas. Even when conspiracies were discovered before they began or when revolts were quickly defeated, they spread fear among administrators and slave owners and often resulted in changes in patterns of slave importation and in the regimes of slave control. The repression of these revolts tell us a great deal about the fears and strategies of the planter class, but they also offer us traces of the political visions and projects that influenced slave insurgents.[17]

There is a permanent irony in writing the history of slave revolts. The success of such revolts depended precisely on the ability of insurgents to avoid the discovery of their plans. It was, however, through the discovery and often disruption of plans for conspiracy that the written documents on which historians depend were usually created. Because of this, there is generally more documentation of the planning of failed slave revolts than there is of successful ones. The records containing the richest material about the organization and political vision of insurgents are usually those produced by local officials as they interrogated slaves and in so doing defused their revolts. These sources, of course, pose important questions of interpretation, both because slaves, facing torture and threatened with death, may well have lied to protect themselves or been coerced into "confessing" to crimes they had not committed, and because the testimonies and confessions themselves were reported by whites who were themselves invested in certain interpretations of the events. This means that it remains possible to propose that certain slave conspiracies were in fact nothing more than phantoms invented by paranoid whites watching slave practices they did not understand. It also means that the largest and most successful revolts, those whose existence is undeniable, provide us with relatively fewer details about their organization. The slave rebels of the 1791 insurrection in Saint-Domingue, for instance, were never put on trial for the simple reason that their revolt succeeded. Though there were some interrogations of insurgents, notably in the days before the insurrection took place, and some correspondence between insurgents and administrators, no lengthy trial transcripts exist that might have created detailed information about the way they planned and executed this unique revolt.[18]

The complexities surrounding the sources available about slave insurrections make rumor a particularly important source for the study of their political ideology. The importance of rumor as a tool of political mobilization within and among slave communities is famously explored in Julius Scott's study of the "currents" of communication during the period of the Haitian Revolution, which traced out the ways in which news traveled through the "Greater Caribbean" (the region encompassing Charleston and Savannah to Caracas and Cayenne, passing through New Orleans and St. Augustine) within networks that connected Afro-American communities. Scott was among the first to identify the important role of sailors, often slaves or ex-slaves, in this process. Scott's meticulous work highlights the ways in which the circulation of information across long distances and between very different slave communities created and sustained revolutionary political visions within these communities.[19]

Scott's work also emphasizes the need to consider the particularities of the circulation of information in the Atlantic world of the eighteenth and early nineteenth centuries. The spatial dimensions of this world, a place in which journeys from metropole to colony generally took several months, created a context particularly rich in its possibilities for multiple interpretations of events in the metropole. This was, in fact, a world in which the line between "news" and "rumor" was very thin, indeed often nonexistent. Like slaves, slave owners, plantation managers, merchants, and administrators depended on a variety of sources of information, many of them oral and often fairly unreliable. The most legitimate source of information about government policy, directives sent directly to local officials, was often insufficient to provide a consistent sense of the direction of debates in the metropole, especially in times of rapid change. Within the Caribbean, official circuits of information could be slower than unofficial ones, and an administrator might learn about events on other islands after many others in his colony already had. Much of what the newspapers printed came from passengers on arriving ships or from extracts from personal letters, and they frequently provided distorted or erroneous information about the situation across the Atlantic or elsewhere in the Americas. In times of war, some colonies found themselves learning of events in their metropoles through the newspapers of their enemies, which created complicated problems of interpretation and further possibilities for misunderstanding. All this confusion also created situations ripe for improvisation.[20]

How did rumors begin and spread within slave communities? The action of passing on rumors, Ranajit Guha argues, "brings people together" and creates solidarity within a community, and this "socializing process" helps explain the "phenomenal speed" with which rumor travels. Because the source of a rumor is rarely identified, it also collapses the distinction between the "teller" and the "hearer." In such a context, improvisation is particularly common. Like other means of transmission, rumor has "the dual function of informing and mobilizing at the same time," providing news in a way that makes those who hear it participate in the events the rumor both describes and propels. As Steven Hahn has noted, rumors among ex-slaves after the U.S. Civil War became "a field and form of political struggle." These scholars, then, suggest that rumor can be usefully thought of as news that carries with it a kind of promise. Through the collusion between teller and hearer that it engenders, a rumor can produce communities of hope that can lead to something otherwise unthinkable. In the Caribbean in the late eighteenth and early nineteenth centuries, rumors often condensed expectations and hope as they claimed freedom had already arrived. In the process, they repeatedly helped to create forms of political mobilization that made it possible for the enslaved to make happen what the rumors claimed had already happened. By claiming freedom was imminent, enslaved people helped to create the conditions that brought freedom about.[21]

The conversations of slave owners and local officials, who were themselves uncertain and anxious about events overseas, often played a crucial role in providing information to the enslaved. As they spoke of their concerns about antislavery activity, and the potential for reform it carried, they offered their own domestic slaves portraits of potential allies. Furthermore, slave owning whites often exaggerated the power of antislavery forces and in so doing unwittingly provided inspiration to slaves.

This pattern was quite visible during the 1730s when a wave of slave revolts and conspiracies swept through the Americas. In addition to revolts in North America, particularly at Stono in 1739 and New York in 1741, there was the early (and for a time quite successful) revolt on the Danish colony of St. John in 1734 and revolts that led to the constitution of long-lasting maroon bands in Jamaica, Saint-Domingue, and Suriname. In his classic study of an unsuccessful 1736 conspiracy in Antigua, Barry Gaspar examines the complex interactions between enslaved people from Africa, members of the Akan group, and Creoles born in the colony in the planning of the revolt. As part of launching their conspiracy, the leaders held a huge feast in the presence of two thousand slaves along with white planters and overseers. What seemed to some white observers as nothing but a harmless performance of a "coronation" of one of the enslaved as a king was, Gaspar argues, an Akan martial dance that was "a formal declaration of war," announcing to those present who understood the cultural codes that a revolt against the whites would soon begin. The Akan language and forms of dance, performance, and dress made it possible "to communicate with and mobilize slaves who knew what was going on" in full view of whites who had no idea of what was being shared and planned in front of their eyes. In Antigua as elsewhere, dance, music, and ritual were all part of laying the foundation for imagining a world without and beyond slavery. "Religion," Gaspar writes, "was at the core of their vision to affect reality, to create a new existence, a new world."[22]

Insurgents in many places came to understand that, facing great odds, they needed to try to turn imperial conflict to their advantage. Repeatedly, enslaved insurgents saw the monarchs who sat at the head of the empires in which they found themselves enslaved as a potential source of support. In 1749, slaves organized a revolt in Caracas around rumors spread by Juan de Cádiz, "a free black recently arrived from Spain, who circulated news that the king had decreed that all the Spanish slaves in the Indies be liberated." In the French colonies, too, an early version of rumors that would later become much more important surfaced in 1775, when news was circulated that the government was planning to free all slaves. The source of the rumor was, at least according to the minister of the colonies and administrators in Bordeaux, the community of blacks, both slave and free, living in France's port towns. In 1768, a different type of rumor—which declared that "a powerful African king had arrived, had purchased from the colonial government all the slaves on the island, and that they could soon expect to board vessels to return to Africa"—had circulated in Martinique, and several slaves were whipped for passing it on.[23]

By the late 1780s, the abolitionist movement was expanding substantially in Europe, and rumors and conflicts over an always impending freedom in the Americas abounded. The European metropoles, which in principle had a clear—if consistently tested and contested—power over their Caribbean colonies, also served as a clear source of antislavery ideology. The rumors that circulated within slave communities during this period show a widening understanding within these communities of the possibilities opened up by the expansion of new political ideologies. In Venezuela in 1789, the arrival of the Spanish king's *cédula*, or decree, whose contents were in principle to be kept secret, sparked what Julius Scott calls "powerful rumors heralding an impending end to slavery." Slaves discussed the *cédula*, and, as Scott writes, "asserted—quite accurately—that the new regulations called for a short work day with 'hours of rest.'" The continuing official silence about the reforms contained in the *cédula* prompted the production of menacing posters demanding an end to the document's suppression, which accompanied text with "a rough drawing of a dark-skinned man wielding a raised machete apparently about to cut the throat of a white man." One overseer was killed by slaves convinced that the new document had granted them freedom. In the British Caribbean, meanwhile, on the island of Tortola, a revolt was organized in 1790 around a rumor that abolition had been declared in England but that its application had been "suppressed" by the local colonists.[24]

In part because of reforms in the law of slavery he instituted in 1787, the French king was evoked in several such rumors in the late 1780s. This was the case in Martinique in 1789 as well as in Saint-Domingue in the same year. As one planter wrote: "Many [slaves] imagine that the king has granted them their freedom and that it is their master who does not want to consent to it." Rumors of emancipation repeatedly appeared during the following years. In 1790, on a plantation in Guiana, "all the slaves gathered and told their master that they knew that they had been declared free in France and that they wanted to take advantage of their freedom." In January 1791, a man in St. Lucia wrote that the slaves and free coloreds in Martinique who were fighting with royalist forces on the island were doing so because they interpreted it "as a war that was being carried out to give them freedom by the order of the King of France." Another observer noted that when he left Saint-Domingue in March of 1791, "it was said that, according to a number of letters arriving from France, liberty was going to be granted to the slaves, and the whites were very worried about this."[25]

In April of 1790 in Guadeloupe, such rumors inspired a plot organized by several domestic slaves in the neighboring towns of Petit-Bourg and Goyave, who seem to have concluded from overheard conversations among their masters that their liberty had been decreed. As one administrator reported, "some miserable domestics who had so often heard the word 'liberty' pronounced in the [local] assemblies, thought that they were in fact free, and persuaded the field slaves that they were too, but that the whites were carefully hiding the news that they had received from France in this regard." On the night of Sunday, April 11, all the domestics involved in the plot were to kill their masters, set fire to their plantations, and then spread out, "with their flag unfurled," to nearby plantations and the towns, seeking weapons and gathering other followers. The leaders, however, were denounced, and thirty-three slaves, along with a white soldier who had deserted from a local regiment, were arrested. Under questioning, some field slaves declared that the domestics had persuaded them that "the French having dethroned their king, they [the slaves] were authorized to overthrow their yoke and defend themselves from their masters." Five domestic slaves were executed, their corpses burned, and their ashes scattered to the wind. The governor of Guadeloupe hoped he had also scattered all thoughts of imminent liberation: "If the philanthropists seek, again to delude the slaves with a false idea of liberty, I think they will have a hard time finding converts."[26]

In Saint-Domingue, over the course of 1791, enslaved people began meeting and planning a slave revolt. In August, a group of conspirators developed plans for a massive slave insurrection. As they met, a man read a statement announcing that the king and the National Assembly had passed a decree aimed at improving slave conditions. The decree abolished the use of the whip by masters and provided slaves three free days a week instead of two. Local masters and authorities, he went on, were refusing to apply the new decree. But troops were on their way to the colony to enforce its application. Although some of those at the meeting argued that they should wait for the troops to arrive before taking any action, others insisted that they should begin their attack right away. In the end, a date for revolt was chosen for the following week. Once the insurrection began, some insurgents fought under banners decorated with the royal fleur-de-lys and called themselves *gens du roi* ("supporters of the King"). And an insurgent leader in the southern province, Romaine la Rivière, rallied slaves around himself by telling them that the king had abolished slavery but that their masters were refusing to apply the decision.[27]

Other slave rebels focused on another, perhaps more potent, source of power: the Declaration of the Rights of Man and Citizen. As one planter in Martinique wrote:

> Since we have learned here of the Declaration . . . there are none among us who do not want to participate in the great benefits which it promises us, but there is also no one who does not shudder at the idea that a slave or even a free *homme de couleur* [man of color] might say, "I am a man as well, so I also have rights, and those rights are equal for all." This declaration is certainly something very dangerous to promulgate in the colonies.[28]

The insight of this planter turned out to be correct. If the king had been an effective focus for hopes of emancipation, the Declaration of the Rights of Man and Citizen, whose language plainly spoke of equality and could easily be applied with radical implications to the world of the Caribbean, was an even better one. Days before the insurrection began in Saint-Domingue, some interrogated slaves declared that "they wanted to enjoy the liberty they are entitled to by the Rights of Man." According to another account, after the insurrection began, "an innumerable troop of negroes presented themselves almost underneath the batteries of Le Cap, asking for the rights of man."[29]

A few months earlier in Guadeloupe, a rumor spread through the thriving plantation belt surrounding St. Anne. A man described by officials as a *mulâtre* (mulatto) and likely not himself a slave claimed that the governor of the island "had received a declaration from the National Assembly declaring all slaves free," but that he was refusing to proclaim it in the island until he had been able to sell his own human property. The man used the rumor to organize an insurrection, telling local slaves that "since they were the stronger party," they should "claim their freedom themselves." A small group of rebels, gathered together on the 15th of May, was intercepted and disarmed by a troop of local whites, and the revolt was prevented.[30]

Two years later, the same region in Guadeloupe erupted into a much larger and initially more successful revolt, which again occurred in reaction to the spread of a rumor regarding a metropolitan political decision. It was organized by two free men of color, Auguste dit Bonretour and André Mane. They had heard that a law had been passed in Paris giving illegitimate children the same inheritance rights as legitimate children. But they had also heard that the governor of Guadeloupe had decided not to apply the law in the colony and was in fact seeking to stifle any news of its existence. Such a law would have had immense significance for the community of *gens de couleur* (free people of color), many of whom were the illegitimate children of white planters and as such were denied any inheritance. Bonretour and Mane returned to St. Anne and began organizing a revolt to force the recalcitrant governor to apply the law. They decided to mobilize slaves in support of the project, telling them, "March with us. All the negroes are free," and in doing so mobilized over a thousand "Africans" who attacked several houses, taking weapons and ammunition, and demanding "The Law! The Law!" With slaves joining in large numbers, the demands of the insurrection quickly expanded into a call for the end of slavery, as well as the right to equal paternal inheritance not only for freed slaves but for all people on the island. The revolt was eventually suppressed, in part because of the division between the *gens de couleur* leaders and the slave insurgents.[31]

The rumors spread by the leaders who began the insurrection in St. Anne, like those spread in Martinique in 1789, were based on actual events in the metropole. A few months before, laws had in fact been passed in Paris granting equal inheritance rights to legitimate and illegitimate children, though these laws were never really put into effect. In St. Anne, leaders who heard some echo of these decisions applied them to a colonial situation, pushing the possibilities opened up by the revolutionary changes in metropolitan France in new and as yet unimagined directions. Those slaves who joined the insurrection in turn pushed its demands further toward a demand for an end to slavery. These events, then, illustrate in a microcosm a broader process through which certain revolutionary debates and laws could take on new dimensions and directions in the Caribbean.[32]

After 1791, when the slave revolt in Saint-Domingue destroyed many of the rich sugar cane plantations in the north of the island, the debates about slavery in both France and the French Caribbean began to change radically. In the next years, the colonial society of Saint-Domingue was fundamentally transformed. White planters increasingly turned away from the French Republic, which many blamed for the slave insurrection, and even made overtures to the English to come and take over the colony of Saint-Domingue. The slave insurgents, meanwhile, consolidated their strength and fought off all the attempts by the badly divided colonial world to defeat them. A paradigmatic example of how this process worked can be seen in the 1793 revolt in Trois-Rivières, Guadeloupe. Slave insurgents stated their intention to be part of the French Republic when they rose up and killed their masters, presenting the fait accompli to local white administrators as a necessary defense against royalist conspirators. "We have come to save you," they boldly declared to the white troops sent to repress the revolt; "we want to fight for the Republic, the law, the nation, and order." Instead of punishing them, local officials initiated an investigation that drew on slave testimony to support the accusations already made by the slave insurgents and effectively condoned the punishment the insurgents had already meted out against these enemies of the Republic. Local white Republicans had already suffered a major defeat when the island had briefly been taken over by royalists a few months before, and they were receptive to their new allies. Within a few months, the example of these insurgents helped propel a call on the part of local Jacobins, both white and free-colored, that they should free slaves in order to form a Republican legion for the island's defense.[33]

On a broader, more dramatic scale, the same thing happened in Saint-Domingue. In June of 1793, the radical Republican commissioner Léger Félicité Sonthonax, threatened by anti-Republican whites on the island, made overtures to a small group of slave insurgents camped outside of Le Cap. In return for their support, he would grant them freedom. They agreed and stormed the city, quickly routing the commissioner's enemies. Once the process began, it was difficult to stop. More and more slave insurgents joined the Republican side, and within a few months Sonthonax had expanded his call into a general emancipation of all slaves in the north of Saint-Domingue. Similar decrees were soon applied in the rest of the colony. In very real terms, then, it was an alliance between a metropolitan administrator and local slave insurgents, against the white planters of the colony, which brought slavery tumbling down. The story of this alliance, powerfully presented in Paris by a group of three representatives elected in Saint-Domingue (one of whom, Jean-Baptiste Belley, was African born), brought about the National Convention's abolition of slavery in February of 1794.[34]

The alliance imagined in the various rumors that had circulated in the French Caribbean during the early 1790s had become a reality. The way this had happened, however, in a sense reversed the narrative presented by the rumor. It was in fact slave insurgents, inspired in part by rumors of metropolitan action on their behalf, who propelled metropolitan attacks against slavery that would not otherwise have been taken. They created a situation in which they were necessary allies and in so doing pushed metropolitan policy in unforeseen directions. Slave insurgents had brought on immediate and universal emancipation. The rumors that encouraged them to mobilize were productive of a new political reality of emancipation and racial equality. French Republican armies of ex-slaves battled the British and the

Spanish with emancipation as their most powerful weapon, allying themselves with slaves in the British colonies and taking over the island of St. Lucia. The French regime helped inspire further rebellions in other empires, notably in 1795 in Coro, on the coast of Venezuela. There, slaves once again rose up to demand the full application of the Spanish king's *cédula* as they had a few years earlier. This time, however, they rallied around the French tricolor in the hopes of finding support in their struggle for emancipation. And for a time, the French allied with the Black Caribs of St. Vincent in a final struggle of the indigenous Caribbean to retain autonomy and sovereignty.[35]

Emancipation in the British Caribbean

The broader impact of the Haitian Revolution on the course of emancipation is widely debated. The destruction of colonial Saint-Domingue, reborn as Haiti in 1804 after a brutal war between local armies and French troops sent by Napoleon, propelled the expansion of other plantation areas in the Caribbean, notably in Cuba. In some ways, it was a setback for abolitionists, who would from that moment on always be saddled with the specter that antislavery activity would lead to the types of massacres of whites that European and North American writers focused on in their descriptions of the events in Saint-Domingue. At the same time, the Haitian Revolution emboldened and inspired slaves and encouraged administrators and masters to consider reform throughout the Caribbean. In 1807, the abolitionist movement in Britain, remarkable for its effective mobilization of large numbers of citizens through evangelical churches and petition drives, succeeded in ending the British slave trade. Although it took decades for this ban to spread to France, and even longer for it to be effectively policed, this was a major shift. It reinforced the idea that the king of Britain was a friend of the slaves.[36]

Already in 1807, the governor of Jamaica reported that slaves understood the abolition of the slave trade as "nothing less than their general emancipation." In the next decades, three significant revolts broke out in the British Caribbean, each of them inspired by rumors of emancipation. In each case, debates and/or reforms passed in Britain were interpreted by slaves as signs of imminent emancipation. As Eric Williams wrote in *Capitalism and Slavery*: "The consensus of opinion among the slaves, whenever each new discussion arose or each new policy was announced, was that emancipation had been passed in England but was withheld by their masters. . . .

So deeply was the idea embedded in the minds of the slaves that some great benefit was intended for them by the home government in opposition to their masters that they eagerly seized upon every trifling circumstance as a confirmation."[37]

In 1815, a bill was passed in Britain calling for the registration of all slaves. Slave owners in the British Caribbean were furious, and formal statements by the assembly in Barbados were published claiming that the bill was in fact part of a plan for emancipation. One pamphlet criticizing the bill also warned that it might lead to a slave insurrection like that which had taken place in Haiti, arguing that "the first step which the Imperial Parliament shall take, opposing, and as it were, superseding the colonial legislatures in matters of slave regulation within the colonies, will be the signal for commencing a convulsion similar to that which eventually severed from France its greatest and most valuable colony." Rumors began spreading among the slave community of Barbados that this was in fact the case. According to one report, the "opinion" among "these misguided people"—the slaves—was that their "emancipation was decreed by the British parliament." The idea, the report added, "seems to have been conveyed by mischievous persons, and the indiscreet conversation of Individuals." A domestic slave named Nanny Grigg, who was literate and frequently informed other slaves of what she learned from reading local and British papers, told other slaves that they were all to be freed on New Year's Day of 1816. She noted that "her master was very uneasy about it," and told slaves "that they were all damn fools to work, for that she would not, as freedom they were sure to get." As New Year's approached, however, she began telling others that they were to be freed on Easter, but that "the only way to get it was to fight for it, otherwise they would not get it; and the way they were to do, was to set fire, as that was the way they did it in Saint Domingo." In Easter of 1816, a revolt did erupt in Barbados when slaves on up to seventy plantations burned cane fields and buildings. It was quickly suppressed, with hundreds of slaves either killed during the fighting or executed and deported afterward. While Barbadian planters blamed the revolt on Wilberforce's actions in Britain, Wilberforce argued that the planters were the ones who had inspired the slaves to rebel by claiming that the reforms he proposed were equivalent to emancipation. The slaves' vision of Wilberforce was linked not only to his abolitionist activity in Britain but also to his connections with King Christophe in Haiti. Evocations of Haiti appeared repeatedly during the slave revolt, and some rebels seem to have hoped for support from that country.[38]

Slaves elsewhere in the British Caribbean also interpreted the Registry Bill as a move toward emancipation. The governor of Jamaica wrote that the slaves thought the bill "contemplates some dispositions in their favor which the Assembly here supported by the inhabitants generally are desirous to withhold." One visitor to Jamaica in 1816 heard a "slave ditty" that included the words "Oh me good friend, Mr. Wilberforce, make we free! . . . Buckra in this country no make we free! What negro for to do? What negro for to do? Take force with force! Take force with force!"[39]

The revolt in 1816 seems to have actually retarded abolitionist efforts in Britain, but two later revolts in fact directly contributed to the eventual dismantling of slavery. The first of these, the Demerara revolt of 1823, provides some of the most compelling evidence about the way rumors circulated and inspired action in the Caribbean. As was the case in earlier cases, these rumors developed as a result of the passage of new laws in Britain. In March of 1823, Thomas Fowell Buxton, an antislavery leader, presented a motion to the House of Commons intending to extend the protection of British law to slaves and to begin the process of emancipation in the colonies. There was stiff opposition to the proposition, but a series of proposals for the amelioration of slave conditions were approved and forwarded to the colonies. Slaves throughout the British Caribbean heard echoes of these reforms; in Barbados one was overheard asking, "Why Bacchra [the whites] no do King bid him?" In Demerara, news of the arrival of the "new laws" quickly interested many slaves and became "voices in the air" that helped propel slave revolt. A servant named Joe Simpson overheard his master talking about the measures. He rushed to tell a slave named Quamina, a leader in the Christian community on one of the plantations, and was asked for more details. He promised to search his master's papers in order to learn more. Eventually, Simpson reported that according to what he had seen in his master's papers, freedom was coming, along with a new governor, thanks to the actions of Wilberforce in London. Although it is difficult to know exactly what Simpson read, it seems likely that some worried words about Wilberforce and the unavoidability of freedom on the part of the governor were read as a statement of fact.[40]

Others contributed to the talk of imminent freedom. One man, John Hamilton, told his slave Susanna that he would not buy her freedom because this would be like "throwing money in the trench," since all the slaves were soon to be free. Susanna reported this to other slaves and continued to report Hamilton's statements in the next days. Hamilton said at one point that the slaves would probably not be freed by the governor "unless all the sensible people went by force about it," and added that the governor and masters were doing what they could to prevent the decree of freedom. He later said that if the slaves were not "a parcel of cowards" they would already have been free, "for it had been ordered for some time." An overseer flogging a slave inadvertently fed the rumors when he shouted: "Because you are to be free, you will not do any work, nor wait till your freedom is given you, but wish to take it yourself." A slave named Jack Gladstone, the son of Quamina and also a respected member of the community, asked the governor's servant, a man named Daniel, to look into the rumors. Daniel, who admitted that he frequently read the governor's papers, later told Jack that he had seen a paper declaring that the slaves were to get not freedom but three free days. Jack and other slaves continued to pursue the rumor. Masters and overseers, meanwhile, contributed to slave hopes as they responded to the possibility of emancipation by openly hoping for more limited reforms. One overseer told two slaves that "all the great men at home had agreed" to give the slaves freedom "except their masters," who would rather give them three days a week off work. Another slave overheard one master criticizing the king for being so "foolish" as to give the slaves freedom instead of three days a week to work for themselves. Slaves, overseers, and masters all participated in an intensive exchange in which the fears of some propelled the hopes of others. The passing on of knowledge about imminent policy decisions was structured by master-slave relations, a fact illustrated most clearly by the information passed on by an overseer punishing a slave, even as it held out the promise that these relations were about to change.[41]

Soon Jack Gladstone moved from collecting information to circulating it, having decided that it was necessary to confront the governor in order to force him to apply the orders he had received. He sent a slave to recruit slaves on one plantation by telling them that the king "had sent out their freedom but the white people did not want to give it to them." Another slave went to different plantations speaking about the "good news." There was confusion about whether the "new laws" were for freedom or for three days of freedom. The promise of the latter was itself quite attractive for slaves, as it would have allowed them to increase what they produced for their own accounts. Ultimately a carefully conceived plan was put into motion. Slaves, speaking of rights, "of laws coming out from England," of "the King, of Wilberforce, and of 'the powerful men of England,'" rose up and captured their overseers and masters. Except in rare cases, they did not kill them, but rather placed them in the stocks where the overseers and masters themselves had placed so many slaves, reversing the hierarchy for a moment. The insurrection was remarkably nonviolent—except on the part of the whites, who ultimately gunned down and executed several hundred slaves as they repressed the revolt. The insurgents, it seems, believed powerfully that by placing pressure on the local administration, they would force the administrators to apply the decree of freedom they were seeking to hide away. The revolt had major ramifications in the debate over slavery in Britain, notably because of the well-publicized trial of one missionary who was accused of having encouraged the slaves to revolt. It helped sharpen the lines between pro- and antislavery forces in Britain and in so doing helped propel the struggle for emancipation.[42]

Within a decade, another major revolt erupted in the British Caribbean, this time in Jamaica. By this time, the antislavery movement in Britain was very powerful, having launched a campaign for the immediate abolition of slavery in April 1831. Once again, as news of this spread to the colonies, whites mobilized in strident opposition to any plan for emancipation. There were protest meetings throughout Jamaica, and some advocated seeking assistance from the United States in pursuit of armed revolt against the British government. There was also a plan to create a representative body independent of the crown. Slaves talked about these events, circulating news about what various masters had said. It was rumored that one well-known magistrate, expressing his fears that talk of emancipation would lead to bloodshed, and inadvertently contributing to such an outcome, had said: "The king is going to give black people free: but he hopes that all his friends will be of his mind and spill our blood first." As in Demerara, masters and overseers confirmed slave suspicions; one slave told a Baptist minister that when overseers flogged the slaves, they shouted at them that they were to be free but that before freedom came "they would get it out of us." One of the major leaders of the revolt was Samuel Sharpe, a domestic slave who was a member of a Baptist church, who followed the debates in Britain closely and came to believe that the slaves needed to rise up in pursuit of their freedom. One focus of attention on the part of slaves was the pastor of the church to which Sharpe belonged, who had left the colony but who, it was rumored, was to return at Christmas with "free papers." Pastors sought to dissuade slaves from rising up, with one telling them that the story that the king had made them free was not true and asking them to "go to your work as usual." The power the rumor had gained by then, however, was such that many slaves reacted angrily to this advice, blaming the missionaries for colluding with the authorities. During the revolt, one group of slaves apparently shouted at an overseer: "We free now, we free now!"[43]

The Jamaican revolt of 1831, sometimes called "the Baptist War" because of the important role in it of Baptist slaves such as Sharpe, had a significant effect on the course of antislavery. As Mary Turner has written, it strengthened "the case for immediate abolition" because "the black insurrection engendered a white insurrection directed, ultimately, against the authority of the British government, but whose immediate objects of attack were the missionaries, unofficial agents of the imperial reform program." Planters destroyed fourteen chapels and imprisoned missionaries. "This onslaught massively confirmed the established image of the slave as victim of an anti-Christian regime." Thomas Buxton, a parliamentary leader in favor of abolition, noted in 1832 that missionaries "might more safely pursue their sacred vocation among cannibals than among their white brethren in the West Indies." White attacks on missionaries also sent spokesmen and allies of the enslaved to England, where several who had been driven from the colony began speaking in favor of abolition to large crowds in England, becoming part of a final and powerful push for emancipation. The successful abolition campaign of 1832 "focused on the star missionary eye witnesses that the whites' rebellion had, providentially, supplied." As speakers, the missionaries had legitimacy because of their "expert knowledge" of the situation in Jamaica and the "moral kudos derived from lives dedicated to the betterment of the slaves." They served, Turner writes, "as spokesmen for the rebel slaves" and threatened that "further delay" in emancipation "might promote further rebellion." Buxton mused about the unintended consequences of white resistance to abolition, appreciating "the overriding hand of Providence which had turned the intolerance of the system to its own destruction."[44]

Slaves, meanwhile, waited expectantly for emancipation to arrive. When a new governor arrived in Jamaica in 1832, a large group of slaves gathered around him at a review near Kingston, believing that he had "come out with emancipation in his pocket." The next year, the arrival of a new governor in Barbados led to desertions by slaves who traveled from distant plantations to the capital "to ascertain if the Governor had brought out freedom, or not." Some slaves again apparently thought that the local authorities were repressing news of emancipation and that if they rose up the king's troops would not fire.[45]

Emancipation was finally decreed in 1833 by the British Parliament, with the revolt of 1831 cited as one of the major reasons for the decision. As

Thomas Holt suggests, the revolt had mobilized the increasingly strong antislavery opposition in London and "transformed the very terms of the debate over abolition" by convincing many legislators of the necessity of immediate rather than gradual abolition. In this sense, it helped to propel the complicated process of emancipation, apprenticeship, and political transformation that Holt explores in his work. The rumors of imminent emancipation, heightened by the knowledge gained of debates through newspaper reports, pinpointed the set of power relations that were crucial in the onset of abolition, and allowed slaves to intervene in and shape the conflict between metropolitan abolitionists who influenced the British government's actions and the planters of the West Indies. The slave rebels in Jamaica, like those before them in Demerara, helped crystallize this conflict and deepen the struggle between the two sides in Britain, and highlighted the urgency of emancipation by reminding observers that the slaves would not wait forever. Here, as was the case during the Haitian Revolution and in Guadeloupe, rumors of emancipation helped propel emancipation.[46]

The destruction of slavery in the late eighteenth and the first half of the nineteenth centuries required the assertion of metropolitan political authority in colonial areas. The rumors of imminent emancipation that were a crucial part of this broader process evoked the possibility of this kind of assertion of power and in several cases propelled its application. They circulated in imperial contexts in which slave insurgents could effectively lay claim on distant metropoles in the struggle for freedom, and reached their peak in the struggles for emancipation in the French and British Caribbean between 1789 and 1848, when slavery was finally abolished in the French Caribbean. Even in this final emancipation, decreed from Paris because of the intervention of the abolitionist Victor Schoelcher, slaves who heard news of the imminent arrival of emancipation rose up and forced its application earlier than originally intended by the government. It was in part by calling upon the centers of imperial powers that the enslaved fought against slavery. Through their successes they achieved a new kind of "universalization" of their laws and principles of governance within their empires. This, in turn, opened up new possibilities for claims by the colonized on the rights proclaimed by the metropolitan governments. In this way, the rumors that animated slave resistance became part of a broader transformation in the legal and political order of the Atlantic world. The place of rumor in the history of abolition is a reminder of the central place slave insurgents played in shaping the political realities of this world, by making claims on metropolitan governments that ultimately could not be ignored, using the particularly potent weapon of hope.

Rooting Freedom: Family Land

The passage to freedom and the brutalities it put an end to were long remembered among the descendants of slaves. In the late twentieth century, Eugene Norris, a resident of the village of Granville, in Jamaica's Trelawny Parish, recalled to the anthropologist Jean Besson how his great-grandmother, who was a "slave child" at emancipation, told him about a song sung at the time. It said that "everybody tie them head with a red hand-kerchief for delivery from slavery, and they sang it all around the place beating drum, like Jonkunno: 'And they starve us, they beat us, but One above will punish them.'"[47]

In the nearby village of Refuge (once called Wilberforce), several descendants of an enslaved woman who had been brought to Jamaica from Africa recalled their ancestor's passages through slavery. One recalled how her grandmother, "Queen" Elizabeth Bell-Merchant, or Queenie, had a "mark on her knee" put there by her mother, who seems to have been carrying on African traditions of scarification taught her by her mother. She also heard stories of a "Freedom Dinner" cooked to celebrate emancipation. Another grandchild of Queenie recalled being told by "the old people" how "in the days of slavery, they slaves lived in little huts, and in the mornings they are called up in the big yard, they call it big pen, like how you gather up animals, and you are taken out to work, by a task master." Such ongoing memories helped to define the distance traveled and helped to contextualize ongoing struggles for autonomy and dignity.[48]

But what was freedom? What did it look, feel, and taste like? From the moment of emancipation, the formerly enslaved set about concretizing and rooting freedom through the creation of a new institution: family land. This institution was rooted in older practices of cultivating provision grounds and plots on the plantations, but it expanded in critical ways as people moved away from the plantations when they could, or else found ways to gain access and control over former plantation land. The goal, however, wasn't just to gain immediate access to land, but rather to create a system of land use and ownership that would sustain a radically different future, one in which people's backs were turned firmly away from slavery, their eyes focused on securing a space of autonomy and liberty for themselves and their descendants. As Sidney Mintz writes, while the story of the enslavement of millions of Africans in the Caribbean was the "most dramatic instance of forced acculturation in human history," the story of what came after, "the creation of a free and independent peasantry out of these ex-slaves," is "no less dramatic and in all ways more inspiring." Family land, according to scholars Yvonne Acosta and Jean Casimir, played a central role in creating a set of "totally new and innovative institutions" in the Caribbean by the formerly enslaved. The creation of family land effectively subtracted it from the plantation-oriented designs that had always dominated in the colonial context.[49]

In the wake of emancipation, planters and colonial officials were most of all concerned with how to continue to find a supply of cheap labor to work on the plantations. For the enslaved, however, the moment of freedom meant something much larger and more important. They, of course, wanted control over their own labor, but that was just the beginning. "Emancipation, for them, promised something more, namely the possibility of taking control of their own lives," writes O. Nigel Bolland. They wanted to "reunite families that had been broken up during slavery and to create new communities in which they developed institutions such as churches and mutual aid societies." In the process, they were developing, articulating a vision of freedom, of their society and their place within it, and finding ways to root that in a new relationship to the land. Before emancipation, notes Jean Besson, maroon communities had already established their own "recognized sovereignty over the land itself." They had transformed these spaces into "sacred landscapes" and established forms of the use and transmission of land that brought together agricultural practice, family structure, and spiritual life. Now, in the wake of emancipation, land came to signify freedom for a much larger population of formerly enslaved people. "Before emancipation the ex-slaves had been legally landless and property themselves," writes Besson. "Afterwards their newly acquired freehold land symbolized personhood and freedom."[50]

In his classic study of what he called Free Jamaica, historian Douglas Hall documented the remarkable expansion of land ownership in the years after emancipation, particularly the breakup of larger plantations into small freeholds owned by former slaves. In 1840, there were 883 plots of land smaller than ten acres owned across the island. By 1845, there were over twenty thousand. There were similar transformations in Trinidad and Guyana. While many of those who were able to purchase small plots of land continued to occasionally seek out short-term wage labor on the plantations, they did so on their own terms, privileging and foregrounding the planting, harvesting, and marketing of their own products as much as possible. The individual who owned even a small plot of land, writes Hall, was "from an economic point of view, a remarkably buoyant individual." Such individuals could vary their crops, producing food for their families and for local markets but also planting some export crops, such as ginger, arrowroot, and sometimes coffee. Though it took several years before newly planted coffee trees bore fruit, there were plots of land to be found with standing coffee trees that could be pruned and yield healthy crops. In the meantime, provisions could be planted among the coffee trees, a process that likely helped to stave off soil erosion on the slopes where most coffee trees were planted.[51]

Many among the formerly enslaved gained access to land by becoming part of newly formed villages that represented a collective project of seeking freedom and autonomy through access to land. The first independent villages in the Caribbean were established on the small island of Antigua by 1835, just two years after emancipation was proclaimed there. By 1842 there were twenty-seven village communities with 3,600 inhabitants, and by 1858 there were over 15,000 inhabitants in such villages, one of which was called Freeman's Ville. A similar process took place in all the other colonies of the British Caribbean after emancipation. Already in 1845 in St. Lucia, less than a decade after the end of slavery, there was a new village on the heights of the Soufrière, and the governor of the island noted that "cultivation might be seen creeping up the mountain in every direction." This migration into the hills is powerfully recounted in Patrick Chamoiseau's novel *Texaco*, in a section in which the memory of that journey upwards becomes a symbol of the broad aspiration and hopes of a people in motion, looking for a place to anchor and root their freedom. In time, writes Bolland, these journeys would expand into "ever increasing circles, first temporarily and then permanently, to more remote villages and lands in the hills or the interior, to other colonies or countries in the Caribbean and Central America," and ultimately in the twentieth century, the descendants of the formerly enslaved "have extended the perimeters of migration to metropolitan centers of Europe and North America."[52]

In Jamaica, in addition to settlement in the hills, there was also a remarkable movement led by various Baptist and Methodist leaders, who in the years after emancipation created "Free Villages" where the formerly enslaved settled. Plantation owners, with the support of the colonial administration, sought to force the former slaves to stay on the estates and continue working as wage laborers. The landowners and the colonial regime wished to limit the mobility of the formerly enslaved, in part by forcing them to "pay rent for access to the provision grounds and family homes, often built by themselves, that they had occupied as slaves" and had come to consider their own. Many found this intolerable, and sought out ways to get their own land. This was not easy for individuals just out of slavery, especially since the planters did everything they could to monopolize as much land as possible, not always necessarily to use it, but to keep it out of the hands of the former slaves. Still in the midst of the economic transformations caused by abolition, a certain number of plantation owners were forced to sell off land. Baptists and Methodists, who had been deeply involved in the lives of the enslaved for decades, now hit upon a new plan: buying up "ruined estates" in order to "resettle parishioners as independent peasants in *church communities*." Having purchased large tracts of land, they divided them into small plots and sold them at affordable prices to those who wished to be part of the religious community. As one reverend, who founded the village of Sturge Town, reported, he had been able to buy the property for 700 pounds and rapidly received 400 back from eighty to ninety people who were ready to purchase land. A hundred lots for houses, and an equivalent number of provision grounds, were quickly surveyed. "Small neat cottages were speedily built, and the land brought into good cultivation." One house was converted into a school, "placed in trust for the benefit of the villagers," and they built a "large booth, capable of containing 400 or 500 people" as a "temporary place of worship" and later built a church. Sturge Town was one of a series of such remarkable new settlements. Between 1838 and 1844, as many as one hundred thousand former slaves "removed themselves from the estates, bought land, and settled in free villages." Sturge Town continued to thrive. A visitor in 1850 described how each house had an acre of land, where residents cultivated pimento, provisions, and sometimes a bit of sugar cane, which was ground in small wooden mills. The free villages, he wrote, "built on the summit or slope of some fine hill, interspersed with bananas and plantains, and shaded by mangoes and breadfruit trees, have a pleasing appearance, and greatly enliven the face of nature." And by 1861, there were "more peasant proprietors in Jamaica than there were people employed in casual estate labor."[53]

Access to land also gave formerly enslaved men access to politics. While those who only owned small plots of land didn't qualify to run for seats in the Jamaica Assembly, they could vote and support candidates who they felt defended their interests against those of the planters. In 1849, a black carpenter named Charles Price was elected to the assembly thanks to the support of "mountain settlers" in St. John's Parish. Sixty percent of the assembly by 1854 was made up of people of African descent and Jewish residents, most of them elected thanks to the support of formerly enslaved small farmers. Small farmers could be elected at the parish level to the vestry, a local administrative body. In 1844, two former slaves became vestrymen in the parish of Vere, and in 1857 nine out of ten members of the vestry in St. David Parish were black, most of them former slaves. These new political voices demanded access to education and health care and protested economic policies and draconian laws that disadvantaged and punished rural farmers. The increasing political power of black Jamaicans alarmed colonial officials, and in 1855 the governor referred to one parish where black voters were the majority as "St. Domingo of Jamaica," invoking the threat of the Haitian Revolution. The ongoing conflicts between rural residents, and the political leaders who represented their interests, and the colonial government allied with the planter class culminated in the Morant Bay revolt of 1865. The colonial government brutally repressed this political movement and, in its wake, abolished the Jamaica Assembly itself, cutting off access to local politics and centralizing power in the hands of British colonial officials.[54]

Though unable to transform the political order of Jamaica, rural residents nonetheless articulated their political and social vision in their communities in the way that they took control over the land and rooted themselves and their families within it. In the process, they also developed a powerful new way of thinking about land and its meaning. The conceptual core of the practice of "family land" is the principle that it cannot be alienated, for to do so would in effect be a violation of the struggles of the ancestors who acquired the land and an act of theft from the generations to come who may need it as a sanctuary and guarantee of their own freedom in difficult times. As Edith Clarke, who wrote the earliest study of family land, describes it, land can be sold only if the entire family agrees. The family includes "besides all living members traceable through the blood or the name, wherever they may be, generations to come, who can obviously not be consulted." The sale of the land would also be "a breach of faith of the dead," whose passing on of the land was with the understanding that those who occupy it would always do so only as "trustees" for the larger family group. Family land very often houses the graves of these founding ancestors and others who have lived there since. Religious rituals are held on and around these graves, so that the loss of the land would mean not just the alienation of the bones of the ancestors but the impossibility of carrying out and carrying on spiritual practices. In this sense, notes Jean Besson, the land is intricately linked to practices that connect it "to another world, another time, another place"—back to Africa, in some ways back to the experience of slavery, but also forward into a future meant to be one of greater freedom and autonomy, or at least sanctuary from new forms of oppression. "What the existence of family land did," writes Erna Brodber, "was to give each holder a sense of origin and therefore of security."[55]

The key to family land is an innovative form of transmission from generation to generation that places no limits on who inherits the land: the land is meant to "sustain all the founder's descendants, traced through both sexes, forever." The descent lines are traced without any kind of distinction by gender and without consideration of "legitimacy" or "illegitimacy" of given children. The bloodlines are what matter. In contrast to the usual patterns of transmission of land in colonial legal codes, this was an "unrestricted system, which included all descendants regardless of sex, birth order, legitimacy or residence, and also maximized the descent ties of former slaves by creating ever-increasing and overlapping kinship lines." This "central principle," that all should be included in the inheritance, was a promise to future generations. It was "stipulated by the ancestor who established the family land and is reiterated by his or her descendants down the generations." As one man in the Jamaican village of Martha Brae told Jean Besson, his grandfather had explained: "The land should not be sold. It is for heritage going down. It must go from children to grandchildren, right down the line." It is, a woman in the same town explained, "generation land . . . not to be sold. It must go from generation to generation." "I am not free to sell it," explained one man to Edith Clarke in the 1950s. He lived on family land left to him by his grandparents, who had come to Jamaica as slaves from Africa. "The land is left to reap generations."[56]

The creation of this powerful sense of future family was a response to the conditions of plantation life, in which the enslaved were treated as "kinless," their attempts to maintain family connections always constrained and in many ways rendered impossible by the dictates of an order in which they were considered chattel. The symbolic dimensions of the land extend far beyond its immediate economic utility to those who live in it. The land "symbolized their freedom, and provided property rights, prestige, and personhood." Its power comes not from its "productive capacity of size" but from its "permanence or immortality," and a contrast is drawn between the mortality of individual family members, and generations, and the aspired-for immortality of the land itself. The "tiny plots of land" are "imbued with an unlimited capacity for sustaining ever-increasing generations of descendants forever." They "serve children's children, till every generation dead out," as one Jamaican resident explained to Jean Besson. The land is clearly never enough to sustain the entire family, especially generation after generation as the number of heirs increases. But "the short-term aspect of family land as a scarce economic resource among living kin" is ultimately "subordinated to its long-term symbolic role of serving generations." The *"entitlement"* to the land is the "crucial aspect of family land," rather than the *"activation* of such rights." The principle is that all members of the family can always return to the land, even if they have been away for a long time—and even if they were born away from the land, in the city, or in a foreign country. As one woman explained, there would always be a space on the land for the family: "If they even want stan' up under tree, is for them."[57]

The institution of family land was developed in essentially all postemancipation Caribbean societies, across different empires and legal orders. Karen Fog Olwig has studied one family in the Danish colony of St. John, which was purchased by the United States in 1917, who live in a place they call Hard Labor. As one family member described it, this was "family land" that "goes from one generation to another from my grandparents." "When we die, we got our children, and it goes to them and when they die, it goes to their children." If anyone in the extended family wanted to settle there, they could. "You could pick a piece of land to build a house. You would tell the older ones that you were going to fence off a piece and build a house or cultivate a garden, either in the hill or even around the house. You just asked the brothers for permission. They would say 'go ahead'; we were all family." As is the case throughout the Caribbean, some ancestors were buried there, under a calabash tree in the "back of the yard." For women, the access to family land could be particularly important. They often left home at the time of marriage to move onto their husband's land, but they always had a claim to the family land, giving them "independence of movement." When one woman wanted to leave her husband on the neighboring island of St. Thomas, "the family land was there for her to go when she needed a place to stay." Earlier her mother had found a space of independence on the family land. She had told a male family member she wanted to build her house right next to the sea. He had warned her not to, "because there was so much wind down there." But she had responded, "No, I want to be right by the sea." "Any place you want you can build a house," he replied. And so she did, alongside the water.[58]

Family land works as an institution to a large extent because so few members of a given family actually use it at any time. Given how small many of these plots are, they could never sustain an entire network of descendants, who in many cases are scattered in many different locations, working in other communities, or living in cities on a given island, or else farther afield in another part of the Caribbean or in North America or Europe. For those who have left, the primary value of the land is symbolic: "it is a place where they are always welcome, not an economic resource of which they actually take advantage." Those who do remain on the land often take responsibility for paying any taxes that may be due on the land. They also take care of the property, notably of any graves or burial plots there. Sometimes they send portions of their harvests from trees to relatives in the city, and those away or abroad can send gifts back, maintaining a web of kin relations. There is, in the end, a symbiotic relationship between those who remain and those who have left. "It is only because most family members leave, that the land can become a physical home for a few who stay. But it is also only because some relatives do live on the land and take care of it that it can remain a symbolic home and place of belonging for the many who are absent from the island." Family land, in fact, can be seen in many ways as a crucial jumping-off point for wide-ranging, often risky, migration journeys. For those who leave, the fact that the land is there—and will always be there for them, and even for their children who may be born far away—is a "powerful buttress against anxiety." There is a strong "sense of security" that comes from knowing the family land is there, waiting, a permanent home to return to if necessary. At the core of the practice of family land is an understanding that life will probably always be precarious for many in the family, that they will continue to live in an economic and social order that will restrict rather than sustain their own aspirations for autonomy. That is why it is so vital never to sell the land, for to do so is in effect to steal that security from future generations, who will more likely than not need it at some point.[59]

This new form of settlement, land use, and transmission represented a way of understanding, and enacting, freedom and community. It was a reorientation of the forms of production, away from an exclusive focus on export commodities produced on a large scale on plantations and toward a more mixed economy, one that combined production of certain products, such as coffee, for export with a focus on internal markets and community use. It was also based on an understanding of land as something that did much more than produce goods for a market. As Bolland notes, family land was the antithesis of slavery, an order based on "natal alienation" and the "loss of kinship ties." The plantation order, "as conceived by the masters," was "the very negation of sociality," envisioning the enslaved as "dehumanized tools who have become isolated from each other and denied their human social existence." Family land was an effort at "transcendence of slavery" and an attempt to "recover a lost birthright" as it reestablished kinship ties, knotting and rooting them anew. Family land offered "material security," but even more importantly it was a way of "creating and maintaining" the kinds of networks and connections denied within slavery. It was the "negation" of the plantation society, not in the articulation of a "liberal society of autonomous citizens" or "an aggregate of self-individuals," but rather as "a genuine community of people linked by kinship and other social ties." Family land, then, was "a symbol and potential core of a different kind of society." The very way the maintenance and transmission of land is structured makes the argument that individual autonomy "becomes achievable only in connection with others," offering a "vision of society" in which "mutuality, cooperation, and interdependence"—rather than "hierarchy, competition, and the dependency of subordinates"—are seen as "the very fabric of society itself."[60]

Family land is also, fundamentally, a form of memory, and a reminder of the links between ancestors, the living, and future generations. The fact that family are buried on the land itself is one of the most powerful guarantors against it ever being sold. Not just the bones, but also the trees planted long ago, which Besson notes are "viewed as sacred and part of the corporate estate," are understood as an inheritance that cannot be destroyed. Often, family members who do not live on the land nevertheless come and harvest fruit from the trees. "For the slaves and their descendants trees had a spiritual dimension and, like the eternal land, symbolized the continuity of kinship groups and communities." The trees, like family land itself, were a continual reminder and symbol of "the fruits of freedom."[61]

One of the favorite crops among smallholders in Jamaica, especially in highland areas, was the banana tree. It had been common in the plots of the enslaved before emancipation as well, thanks to its hardiness and productivity. "The banana," explains Thomas Holt, "is not a tree but a herbaceous plant that can grow to over twenty feet and matures in thirteen to sixteen months," and produces "a single bunch of fruit on each plant." New plants grow from "underground runners" after one stem reaches maturity. As a crop, the banana is relatively easy to sustain as well as relatively easy on the soil, and producing bananas is far less labor- and capital-intensive than producing sugar, for instance. No processing is required before bananas are consumed or exported. In the late nineteenth century, many small farmers, most of them ex-slaves, increasingly grew bananas and sold them in local markets.[62]

Banana production was one piece of a larger patchwork of local peasant production, much of it focused on growing and selling fruit. By the second half of the nineteenth century, Jamaica had seen a radical reconfiguration of its agricultural economy, driven by the collapse of the traditional plantation economy and the rise of peasant production. "In 1865," writes Holt, "traditional crops—sugar, rum, coffee—accounted altogether for more than two thirds of the island's export earnings, mostly from Britain, while nonplantation crops—fruit, pimento, ginger—accounted for only one eighth." Within a few decades, the situation had completely changed, and "fruit had become the single most important export," constituting just over 40 percent of the total in 1898–99. Along with a change in crops came a change in destinations: the United States was now "the most important trading partner in both exports and imports," with nearly 60 percent of exports heading north rather than across the Atlantic toward the United Kingdom.[63]

In the mid-nineteenth century, some North American entrepreneurs began importing Caribbean fruit, including coconut, limes, pineapples, oranges, and bananas. "They procured fruit from peasant producers, who brought it down from the hills," writes Thomas Holt, carrying the fruit in small quantities "to the seaports or to light boats plying the coast." The expansion of this export trade sent prices for fruit, notably bananas, up dramatically in the 1870s. Shipping fruit, however, was more complicated in many ways than shipping sugar, coffee, or tobacco, for the shipments were much more fragile. This is especially true of bananas. Once harvested, the fruit lasts only a maximum of three weeks before it is too ripe to be eaten. Bananas are also easily bruised if they are not carefully handled. Shipping them on sailing vessels was an unpredictable and risky endeavor. If travel took too long, importers ended up with ships full of overripe bananas. In the 1870s and early 1880s, shipments of oranges outpaced those of bananas significantly, in large part because oranges traveled better. By the 1880s, however, the growth and development of steamship travel decreased the travel time between the Caribbean and North America as well as making the journeys more predictable. Although shipping them to the United Kingdom remained very difficult, bananas could now make it in good form to the kitchens of North American consumers. Banana production, which had been primarily aimed for local consumption, became a massive export trade. Increasingly, U.S. companies took and maintained control of almost every aspect of production, from agriculture to island transport to shipping and marketing in the United States.[64]

The story of the rise of bananas is inescapably tied to the story of the rise of the company that came to be known as the United Fruit Company, whose empire ultimately extended through much of the Caribbean, Central and South America, and beyond. United Fruit had its roots in an earlier company, Boston Fruit, founded by Lorenzo D. Baker in 1884. The owner of a fishing fleet operating out of Cape Cod, Baker visited Jamaica in 1872 and soon began importing fruit on his ships. By 1882, he was already shipping 42 percent of the bananas being exported from Jamaica, and he was living on the island. In 1885, his son was appointed a consular agent in Jamaica, which provided the family with additional commercial advantages as they expanded their hold on the island economy. Baker succeeded in overcoming the challenges involved in banana export, by mastering "careful control of selection and handling and rapid shipment to market" and developing a highly effective method of organizing "purchasing and shipping." Although at first he contracted with steamship lines to ship his bananas, eventually he acquired his own fleet of vessels for the purpose. He even gained a "virtual monopoly over the carrying trade," and from there went on to "establish control over production as well." In order to do so, he needed to gain control over the price of bananas by gaining a better bargaining position in relation to local producers. He did so first by acquiring his own banana plantations in Jamaica. Though his own estates never produced more than one-sixth of what he shipped out, owning them allowed him to exert control over the prices from other suppliers. Eventually, he also expanded his banana empire into Central America, thus creating an alternative source for the fruit that made it possible for him to buy at lower prices in Jamaica.[65]

The same advances in technology that made possible the expansion of the banana industry also made possible the growth of another, parallel industry: tourism. The expansion of the two industries was tightly linked, with companies like the United Fruit Company participating directly in both. Starting in the second half of the nineteenth century, local elites had increasingly sought out ways to attract visitors to the islands in the hopes of developing a tourist industry. As early as 1861, the luxurious Royal Victorian Hotel was opened in the Bahamas, and a few decades later, in 1887, the Crane Beach Hotel was built on the east coast of Barbados. One of the pioneers in tourism in the area, the U.S.-owned United Fruit Company, by the late nineteenth century was exporting large quantities of bananas from its plantations in Jamaica on barges leaving from Port Antonio. Characteristically, the company found a way to maximize its profits by filling the barges, which were usually empty on their return journey, with tourists. Travelers spent five days on the banana boats before arriving in Port Antonio, where the company built the Titchfield Hotel. The successful hotel was not just "patronized by Americans" but also "owned by Americans, run by Americans, and staffed (from chef to waitresses) by Americans." It was a powerful symbol of the "new economic imperialism" of the United States in Jamaica. It was also an exemplary model of what economists call "vertical integration," with United Fruit controlling and profiting from both travel and accommodation, using the infrastructure it had built for banana production and export to develop another industry.[66]

In order to attract tourists to the island, local elites and companies in the British Caribbean first had to dispel reigning images of the islands as "breeding grounds for potentially fatal tropical diseases." "To many old-fashioned people" in Britain, noted one tourist guide written in 1893, the thought of the West Indies brought up images of yellow fever, hurricanes, and earthquakes, and "to book a passage to Jamaica is almost synonymous with ordering a coffin." The guide reassured readers that, in fact, insurance companies had determined that "life in Jamaica is on the average quite as healthy and prolonged as elsewhere." In order to change people's image of the Caribbean and to attract them, Caribbean elites and corporations active in the region turned to photography, producing a stream of powerful images that portrayed the islands as "tropical and picturesque tourism destinations." The United Fruit Company, busy expanding its banana empire in the region, heavily invested in tourism as well. In one brochure, the company warned tourists coming to Jamaica that they would "regret" coming without a camera, "as the island is one continuous succession of pictures."[67]

Elites in the British Caribbean also insisted that tourism was a form of development, one that would transform the societies "from colonial outposts into modern societies." The production of a certain image of the tropical Caribbean, meanwhile, had long-standing consequences for the geography of the islands themselves, for colonial elites "physically transformed areas of the islands through planting campaigns or cleanliness drives in efforts to make the islands appear as they did in photographs— orderly, picturesque, and tropical." They imported trees from other parts of the globe and created botanical gardens and verdant hotels that would fulfill the expectation visitors had built up on the basis of the photographs they had seen before arriving, making sure that they themselves left the island with the kinds of photographs they expected to harvest.[68]

Not everyone, of course, was eager to be captured in a photograph. English anthropologist and photographer Harry Johnston, who traveled through the Caribbean in 1908 and 1909, lamented that the Jamaican maroons were "insolent and disobliging, and inclined to levy blackmail on any one who passed through their villages or plantations and wished to photograph the scenery." He did manage to take at least two portraits of maroons, however, including one of a man and a woman in Nanny Town offering half-obliging smiles, perhaps doing just enough to get what Johnson had offered them to take the photograph. In another, taken in a different community, a child seems not to mind being photographed at all. In one remarkable photograph, taken from a distance of a maroon town on the banks of a river, someone washing clothes along the river bank has thrown a piece of clothing over his or her head. It was, notes Krista Thompson, perhaps a "shield from the sun," but more likely a gesture taken as protection "from the camera's intrusion."[69]

Many Jamaicans were acutely aware of the stereotypes travelers and tourists brought with them to the island. In 1901, a writer in the newspaper the *Daily Gleaner* parodied the arrival of tourists who were "clad in wonderful garments, which they fondly imagined to be ordinary tropical clothing. . . . They came ashore in the spirit of explorers and seemed quite disappointed to find we wore clothes and did not live in the jungle." The *Daily Gleaner* had a regular column entitled "How Others See Us," with commentaries on photographic exhibitions and other representations of the island. Residents were keenly aware that such representations were far from innocent and could have a significant impact on the political and economic future of the islands.[70]

The Lakou in Haiti

Over the course of the nineteenth century, Haiti also developed a powerful set of rural institutions anchored in family land. There, the main export crop was coffee. This had been a major plantation crop in the colonial period, but unlike sugar, it was also suited to production on independent, small farms. There was a significant international market for the product as well. Over the course of the nineteenth century, the port towns of Haiti became major sites for the export of coffee. Merchants from abroad, notably from Germany, settled in the country, and some married into Haitian families in order to get around an 1805 constitutional stipulation that forbade foreign-ers from owning property in the country. Coffee became the main source of external trade, alongside dyewood exports, and the primary basis for tax revenue in the country. In contrast to the banana industry in Jamaica, the production of coffee remained firmly in the hands of local farmers in Haiti, and it contributed to a thriving rural sector in the country. Throughout the nineteenth century, Haiti was in fact a magnet for migrants who arrived from the Caribbean and North America, from which two different waves of African American emigrants traveled to the country, but also Europe and the Middle East.[71]

The counter-plantation system, based on the institution of family land, was in fact quite productive on many levels. It sustained rural communi-ties that were, during the nineteenth century, almost certainly the sites of the greatest autonomy and well-being for people of African descent in the Americas. In many ways, it was most developed in Haiti itself, where it had particularly deep roots. Many landholdings were acquired by ancestors who had served in the armies of the Haitian Revolution or in the armed forces after independence and were given land grants from the government for their service. The process began earlier in Haiti than anywhere else in the Caribbean, starting in fact during the revolution in the 1790s as formerly enslaved people in many areas began to take effective control over parts of the plantations. Researching in rural communities in the area of Leogane in the early 1970s, anthropologist Serge Larose focused on a community called Cotin, named after the French planter whose sugar plantation had once occupied the land, its "ruins still visible in the midst of small peasant gardens," and another called Bois l'Etang that had been used as pasture land by two adjacent plantations in the eighteenth century. Among those acknowledged as founding ancestors in religious ceremonies, interestingly, are the original French plantation owners who are "incorporated into the genealogies of many groups." From these grants as well as other ways of acquiring portions of former plantations, families created *bitation la fanmi*, or "family land," which throughout Haiti are also known as *lakou*, from the French word *cour*, or courtyard. Larose defines the lakou as "a group of in-terrelated conjugal families, each one occupying its own dwelling-unit and sharing a common yard." This was a form of family landholding that, as was the case elsewhere in the Caribbean, tightly wound together agricul-tural production, kinship, and religious practice. The core belief about the lakou is that "the land is for all of us." To live on the family land is in a sense always to act as a trustee both for the ancestors and for future generations. It is a "provisional sharing," and in Haiti the construction of fences within the space is discouraged, seen as an indication of "factions" in the family, something that would put "stress on the group's unity and harmony."[72]

The deeply rooted religious practices of the lakou serve to negotiate and resolve such tensions. Ritual is the "cultural material through which the social relations or production are expressed," writes Larose. At the center of the lakou are often a family cemetery and a small "cult house" used for family ceremonies. The presence of the tombs and the ritual space is a reminder of the core precept that the "inherited land should stay in the family," and "any sale to an outsider would bring the wrath of the ancestors who left it all for their children to live on." Periodically, the family—both those who live on the land and those who may live farther away—gathers to hold "public rituals laid down by its founding ancestor." "The ancestor did not only leave land to his descendants; he also left them a number of ritual practices which contributed to his own achievement and whose regular performance should ensure similar success to all his descendants." The rituals are organized around a "ceremonial meal" in which the living and the ancestors are all fed, a reaffirmation of the "reciprocal relationship of dependency between the group and its protective spirits." "The food offered to the spirits is said to give them enough strength to protect their 'children,' and give them adequate material means to feed them in turn."[73]

The spirits in Haitian Vodou are known as lwa, and they take many forms. The lwa are divided into "nations," a recognition of the diversity of African roots that have been brought together in the religion. Many are known and served throughout the country, including Ogou and Ezili, linked respectively to war and to love. But these names in fact refer to "a group of related spirits," and there are as many Ogun "as there are cult groups honoring them." "They all share a common temper and a number of attributes, yet they are all individually owned and transmitted within the family." As one practitioner explained to Larose, Ogou is "a nation." "They are just like Haitians. In a sense, they are all the same, and yet, there are five million of them." In a lakou, among the lwa is also the founder of the family, the first who established the family on the land, who receives particular focus in ceremonial feasts. And the trees on the family land serve as "repositories for the family spirits." "It is strictly forbidden to cut them," and stories are told about "uncareful land surveyors" who died after cutting a tree, and stories about "trees bleeding or crying after one of their branches had been cut." The trees, the tombs, and the rituals all stand as powerful symbols "of the continuity of the family group and the domain over which, as a group, it maintains rights."[74]

The Haitian lakou, and the broader rural system of which they are a part, center women as both landowners and economic power brokers. Starting in 1793, when slavery was abolished and new regulations were put into place governing labor on the plantations, women played a lead role in pushing for more free time and autonomy. The economic system that developed in rural Haiti centered on women, who became the dominant force in the marketplaces. There is a general division of labor on the lakou in which men do most of the agricultural labor, though women do cultivate smaller gardens near the house. Women's role, however, is in the market: as one woman told Larose, "the market is a woman's garden." Participation in the markets provides women with autonomy of movement and with control of the money in a given family. In turn, the lakou system makes possible the movement necessary to participate in the market, since children can be left in the care of relatives in the lakou during journeys to markets both near and far.[75]

One family in the Cotin community recounted the family's genealogy going back to the founder of the line, a woman named Marie Jeanne Zumba, who had "come into the area with Mr. Cotin." "Marie Jeanne came from Africa with all her sacred things," the family recalled. "During the war," however—that is, during the Haitian Revolution—"the whites had forbidden these practices; they had to hide their things in the woods." "Then Dessalines threw the whites out of the country." Afterward, however, there was a time when the sacred practices were forgotten, including the dances from Africa that had been performed. One day Ti-Jeanne, Marie Jeanne's daughter, fell ill, and Marie Jeanne consulted a local priest who told her that all that was needed was to "restart the group," to gather the family around the old dance. He helped her organize the ritual, and "Ti-Jeanne was cured." This story was told in the context of the repetition of the ritual, a reminder of the roots of the family in exile and of the necessity of remembrance. Life on and within the lakou, then, is the long history of struggle, and triumph, a codification of both gratitude and defiance, a centering of a commitment to the future based on a rooting in the past.[76]

Part II **Empire and Revolution**

Histories from the Independent Caribbean

....

4 U.S. Occupations in the Independent Caribbean

• •

Traveling in Haiti in the early 1870s, the North American traveler Samuel Hazard asked residents living near the ruins of Christophe's Sans-Souci Palace, "Why do you dislike the Americans so much?" "I was invariably told that the Government had informed them the Americans wanted to come and take their lands and make them slaves and work." Hazard's response was to explain to them that America had freed its slaves. Haitians, though, might have felt justifiable suspicion at the late conversion of the United States to the cause of emancipation that Haitians had defended for more than half a century. Also, Hazard's literal interpretation of the threat of a return to slavery probably missed the point: the past here served as a metaphor helping to define kinds of imperial domination and labor control that Haitians sought to avoid. Taken in this way, their perspective on U.S. intentions was quite clear-eyed. In the coming decades, U.S. corporations and banks would gain an increasing foothold in Haiti, as well as in nearby Cuba and the Dominican Republic. And in the wake of U.S. companies would come U.S. Marines, who soon embarked on occupations that U.S. leaders declared necessary to ensure progress and order.[1]

The Caribbean had been tightly linked to North America for centuries. Early trade in provisions, rum, and molasses connected the expanding sugar colonies to the south to the mainland colonies to the north. But by the mid-to-late nineteenth century, the cast of the relationship had changed significantly. In the earlier period, the North American colonies and then the United States represented sites of trade that often undermined the control of European empires, even as they also profited those empires by sustaining growth in the Caribbean. Especially in the wake of the U.S. Civil War, however, the expanding North American power increasingly came to compete directly in the region as its own kind of empire, initially through the growing presence of corporations interested in plantation production, especially of sugar and bananas (as in Cuba and Jamaica, respectively), and ultimately through a series of direct military and political interventions that brought portions of the Caribbean under U.S. control. First came the occupation of Cuba and annexation of Puerto Rico in 1898, then the almost decade-long occupation of the Dominican Republic (1916–24) and nearly two-decade-long one of Haiti (1915–34). By the middle of the twentieth century, the United States was the dominant economic and political force in the region. Political actors in the Caribbean had to figure out how to deal with the often overbearing power of the United States and whether to embrace, negotiate, or—as the leaders of the Cuban Revolution did in the 1960s—openly reject that power.

During the nineteenth century, as the United States "expanded" by conquering, purchasing, and incorporating new peoples and territories on the mainland, a number of U.S. leaders had envisioned taking in Caribbean islands as new states in the Union. But what ultimately emerged at the end of the 1800s was a different configuration involving diverse forms of imperial governance. There was the annexation of overseas lands that would indefinitely remain "territories," or colonies. This was the case in 1898 for Puerto Rico, Guam, the Philippines, what became American Samoa, and Hawai'i (which ultimately did become a state in 1959), and for the Danish Virgin Islands after they were annexed in 1917. In other lands, U.S. military invasions and the overthrow of governments, generally followed by a period of temporary U.S. military rule and a restructuring of the state, formed a new and distinct type of empire. These imperial occupations left behind state institutions and political figures whom U.S. leaders expected to serve U.S. strategic and business interests. The countries remained independent, but their sovereignty was formally as well as informally compromised by continuing forms of U.S. control. The three large nations that constituted the independent Caribbean in the early twentieth century—Cuba, Haiti, and the Dominican Republic—would be subjected to, indeed were the birthplace of, this peculiar form of U.S. empire based on military occupations and state restructuring.

During the decades when U.S. leaders turned to this new channel for the expansion of U.S. power in the world, Cuba, Haiti, and the Dominican Republic were at a critical juncture of their own in the longer history of battles over land. Rural populations in these nations were struggling to preserve— or in the case of postemancipation Cuba, to find—opportunities for farming independently rather than having to work for others on plantations or in urban areas. But in all these countries, popular aspirations for access to land ran up against growing efforts by large landowners, in particular U.S.-owned sugar companies, to expand their holdings and production.

Long-standing practices related to land access among rural populations would both constrain and be constrained by the rise of U.S. economic and political power in the region. Expanding foreign interests in Haiti and the Dominican Republic confronted popular resistance from people struggling to maintain their traditional access to land. Foreign corporations also faced harassment by local strongmen, antigovernment rebels, and bandits. And the line between these three groups was often blurry. Armed bands in all three countries demanded funds or stole from the sugar companies. In eastern Cuba, the region where there had been the most opportunities for small-scale land ownership but also where U.S. firms moved in aggressively in the late nineteenth century, intense struggles over land took place. Within the Dominican Republic, conflicts grew in size and strength in the one region of the country in which sugar had begun taking over. This was not a coincidence. Those dispossessed and disenchanted by the transformations wrought by the sugar corporations—specifically, the end of a long history of free access to abundant lands—produced recruits for and supporters of the rebels and gangs in the area. U.S. military interventions would help ensure the victory of U.S. sugar firms in this battle for land, property, and security for their investments in Cuba and the Dominican Republic. They had far less success in Haiti.

U.S. military interventions, though, were not simply an effort to protect and further U.S. economic interests. There was a broader concern within the U.S. government about the weakness of state power and authority, especially in Haiti and the Dominican Republic. The Caribbean bordered the United States, and Cuba, Haiti, and the Dominican Republic—by far the region's largest nations—were close to U.S. shores. The U.S. government set out to ensure that neighboring states were not only willing but also able to guarantee perceived U.S. interests, both strategic and economic. U.S. leaders wanted to make sure, too, that in the future new kinds of U.S. interests, including new forms of business investment, would be protected. In the early 1900s, the Dominican and Haitian states appeared too weak to protect U.S. investments from the various local armed bands and also from feared threats and competition from European powers. These weak states and their national militaries had only limited capacity to impose public policies and enforce laws across the country. Their presidents were frequently toppled by regional leaders and popular forces resisting the authority and actions of the central state or by rivals seeking political positions and access to state revenues and contracts for themselves and their followers. These internal political dynamics worried U.S. leaders, who ultimately decided that military intervention was required in order to create a form of political stability suitable to their interests in the region.[2]

During the early twentieth century, the United States invaded all of the independent Caribbean at various moments, occupying Cuba repeatedly, the Dominican Republic for eight years, and Haiti for nineteen. Haitians and Dominicans from all classes protested and took up arms to put an end to U.S. rule over their lands. But U.S. leaders did not end the occupations until they achieved their core mission: the creation of a powerful new military both dutiful to U.S. interests and able to control society. These U.S.-created forces would remain central to the political life of these countries, under-writing dictatorial regimes friendly to the United States that ruled with unprecedented power and longevity. They remained dutiful out of fear of another U.S. invasion and as a result of ongoing training by and network-ing with U.S. military personnel. Through these new militaries, U.S. occu-pations left behind powerful states that were now seemingly beyond challenge from popular forces. The United States, in other words, formally withdrew but never really left.

At the same time, the periods of U.S. military rule, which led to the deaths of thousands of Dominican and Haitian opponents and the expansion of U.S. plantations, also stoked populist-nationalist sentiments. As a result, even the most ruthless dictatorial leaders in the independent Caribbean adopted a populist-nationalist orientation. Sometimes this was largely rhetorical, as was the case with François Duvalier in Haiti. He mobilized powerful strands of cultural nationalism that had emerged during the U.S. occupation to craft a political ideology presenting him as the defender of the country's black masses, a latter-day Dessalines, both against elites within the country and against white foreigners abroad. Yet, although in his words he celebrated the rural population, Duvalier ultimately did little in practice to support their farming and other activities. In Rafael Trujillo's Dominican Republic, on the other hand, the government created important new state policies, particularly a substantial agrarian reform and extensive rural infrastruc-ture, to benefit small and medium-sized farming both for local consump-tion and for broader markets. These agrarian policies responded to long-standing desires on the part of rural Dominicans and appear to have been well received. They help explain the capacity of this brutal and fright-ening dictator to sustain his rule for three decades with little open resis-tance and even to be remembered nostalgically by many long after his demise.[3]

U.S. occupations and hegemony in the independent Caribbean lands of the Dominican Republic, Haiti, and Cuba produced contrary political forces. On the one hand, the U.S. empire of intervention projected and institutionalized U.S. power abroad. Until the early 1950s, Trujillo would slavishly follow U.S. government positions in almost all foreign policy matters and protect U.S. business interests. On the other hand, U.S. interventions created populist-nationalist reactions. The most successful and enduring dictators in the region rode these contrary waves. Others failed to do so at their peril, as in the 1950s Fulgencio Batista would learn in Cuba.

A Peculiar Empire Is Born:
The United States and the Caribbean, 1898

In 1898, in what would be called in the United States the "Spanish-American War," the U.S. military conquered and annexed the far-flung Spanish colonies of Puerto Rico, Guam, and the Philippines. The U.S. government also unilaterally annexed the independent country of Hawai'i, despite widespread protests on the islands. This was the culmination of a process initiated five years earlier, when U.S. officials and troops facilitated a coup in Hawai'i led by elite U.S. and northern European–descended residents and backed by U.S. sugar interests that stood to benefit from annexation. There was little expectation among U.S. leaders that the lands taken in 1898 would become states and be given the constitutional rights inhering in that status. This was a stark contrast to the approach generally taken in past U.S. conquests in war or through purchases from European powers. The new territories would instead be subjected indefinitely to U.S. congressional power, as outlined in the territory clause of the U.S. Constitution: "The Congress shall have Power to dispose of and make all needful Rules and Regulations respecting the Territory or other Property belonging to the United States."[4]

Throughout U.S. history, Congress had exercised absolute authority over territories. But numerous court rulings and general public opinion had assumed congressional power to be temporary and exceptional, with territories sooner or later becoming states. This understanding allowed the undemocratic nature of territorial status to be ignored for the most part. The new forms of U.S. empire that began with the War of 1898 upended the principles that had structured, and for some justified, U.S. expansion in the past.[5]

In 1901, the legality of permanent "territories" was affirmed by the Supreme Court in a case concerning Puerto Rico's status, even though this meant the indefinite denial of self-government and constitutionally guaranteed civil rights for Puerto Ricans. The justices supporting this ruling stressed the fact that the Constitution did not lay out or require any road from territory to state. The Court's decision and the newly unveiled political reality of U.S. domination was disillusioning, perhaps even shocking, to many Puerto Ricans. Most appear to have readily accepted U.S. annexation in 1898 under the presumption that Puerto Rico would become a state and an equal part of the Union, rather than simply exchange one colonial ruler for another.

Despite the decision of the Court's majority, the establishment of permanent territories, in essence European-style colonies, was hard to accept for many in the United States—a nation born in its own anticolonial revolution. There was, in fact, deep discord among the Supreme Court justices themselves. Justice John Marshall Harlan denounced the Court's majority for seeking to "engraft upon our republican institutions a colonial system such as exists under monarchical governments. . . . The idea that this country may acquire territories anywhere upon earth, by conquest or treaty, and hold them as mere colonies . . . the people inhabiting them to enjoy only such rights as Congress chooses to accord them—is wholly inconsistent with the spirit and genius as well as with the words of the Constitution."[6]

Under pressure from activists in the territories and allies in the United States, Congress gradually doled out conditional forms of autonomy and symbolic equality to Puerto Rico and other territories over the next fifty years. This helped shroud their colonial status and mitigate the domination of the U.S. government. But the territories seized in 1898, along with the Danish Virgin Islands purchased in 1917, would continue to be subject to the complete power over them accorded to Congress in the U.S. Constitution. This included, in principle, the right to remove or overrule any measures of self-government that had already been granted. Congress even held the power to de-annex them unilaterally. To this day, 120 years after their conquest, the millions of U.S. citizens residing in Puerto Rico and the populations of the other territories that never became states have no right to vote for the president and Congress that rule over them, nor to decide whether to become states, claim independence, or insist on the status quo.[7]

In the Philippines, a nation of almost ten million people at the turn of the twentieth century, U.S. colonization followed a far bloodier course. In 1899, a major war broke out between Philippine and U.S. forces after the vast archipelago was annexed. Following the defeat of Spanish troops by a combination of U.S. and Philippine forces, Spain ceded ownership of the colony for $20 million. But Filipinos who had long been struggling for independence soon began resisting a new colonization by their erstwhile ally, the United States. The U.S. president called for 125,000 U.S. volunteers to fight with regular troops to defeat the fledgling Philippine Republic. U.S. novelist Mark Twain wrote bitterly at the time: "There must be two Americas: one that sets the captive free, and one that takes a once-captive's new freedom away from him, and . . . then kills him to get his land."[8]

U.S. troops were able to defeat the Philippine independence forces only by carrying out an extraordinarily lethal and destructive military campaign. An estimated fifty thousand Filipino soldiers perished in combat and from battle wounds and disease, as did over 4,000 U.S. troops. The toll on civilians was greater. To try to separate out independence guerrillas living among and backed by civilians, U.S. troops forcibly resettled vast numbers of Filipinos into hastily assembled reconcentration camps within garrisoned towns, where poor sanitary conditions, overcrowding, and malnourishment bred often fatal diseases. Philippine civilians also died from famines resulting from U.S. forces burning crops, livestock, food stores, and entire villages in areas they perceived as supporting the revolutionaries. Including the indirect consequences of the war, as many as 250,000 Filipino civilians are estimated to have perished. Several U.S. newspapers protested, pointing out the hypocrisy of U.S. forces having recourse to reconcentration camps and other horrors of war, tactics that had provoked widespread U.S. condemnation when carried out by Spanish troops against Cuban independence forces prior to the Spanish-American War.[9] For some 45 more years, the U.S. government would rule in the Philippines, until Philippine resistance movements and global anti-colonial ideologies finally forced the United States to reverse course.

Although Cuba's struggle for independence was the ostensible cause of the Spanish-American War, the United States did not annex this country. Here, U.S. leaders did not play what Twain called the old "European game" of colonial empire. Instead, in Cuba they developed a new mode of empire, one based on overthrowing foreign governments and militarily occupying other nations for widely varying periods of time to further U.S. interests. U.S. officials increasingly—and rather euphemistically—called these forms of overseas rule and control "intervention."[10]

As was the case in the Philippines, Cuban forces had been fighting against the Spanish before U.S. intervention. Cuban revolutionaries first began armed struggle for independence in 1868 in fighting that lasted for twelve brutal years—in the Ten Years' War and the Little War that followed until 1880. Those battles ended in a temporary defeat for the independence movement. But the revolutionaries had successfully pushed Spain to abolish slavery and thereby, Spanish leaders surely hoped, to eliminate much of the impetus for the war, particularly for the majority of rebel troops composed of escaped slaves and free people of color. In turn, though, the abolition of slavery eliminated a major reason for the collapse of the first independence war, for many conservative white troops had abandoned the first revolution when emancipation became one of its immediate objectives. So although ending slavery may have helped Spain defeat the rebels, it also would soon help spell the demise of Spanish rule. In 1895, a new independence revolution broke out. Unlike the first independence war, the insurrection spread steadily from eastern Cuba into the western sugar plantation region.[11]

By 1898, U.S. leaders expected a revolutionary victory in the near future. Spanish troops had been unable to quash the guerrillas, especially in the east. Almost a quarter of Spanish forces—over forty thousand—had died from the island's mosquito-bred illnesses and other diseases. They were also beginning to starve. "Spain's struggle in Cuba has become absolutely hopeless," the U.S. assistant secretary of state asserted. "Spain is exhausted financially and physically, while the Cubans are stronger," controlling "virtually all the territory outside the heavily garrisoned coast cities." With Spanish forces appearing to U.S. leaders to be on the verge of defeat, U.S. intervention via the Spanish-American War was not so much for them an effort to aid a rebel victory, which seemed already inevitable. Instead, it was an attempt to control the outcome of that victory. U.S. intervention served to stop the revolutionaries from taking over the state, becoming Cuba's new national army, and exerting their influence over the direction of the country's public policies. U.S. leaders saw that potential outcome as a threat to expanding U.S. economic and strategic interests in the country. U.S. military occupation and the creation of Cuba's postrevolutionary state and armed forces succeeded in guaranteeing those interests.[12]

The strength of the Cuban independence movement, however, posed a problem for the United States. Any naked form of U.S. colonization risked a long, bloody war with Cuban forces, like that which quickly broke out in the Philippines. So U.S. leaders adapted. They conceived instead a new form of empire that would entail neither the military perils nor potential legitimation crises of European-style colonial rule over territories. And they envisaged one that would not require incorporating Cuba as a new U.S. state, a move that would have made former slaves and other free people of African descent—approximately half of Cuba's population—citizens of the United States.[13]

There was a deep history to U.S. designs on Cuba. In the early 1800s, there were those who dreamed of expanding the United States to the south, into the Caribbean, as well as to the west. In fact, Cuba was among the first lands that prominent government leaders imagined for new U.S. conquest. Cuba's "addition to our confederacy is exactly what is wanting to round our power as a nation," former U.S. president Thomas Jefferson wrote to President James Monroe in 1823. Monroe's secretary of state agreed, calling for annexation of Cuba and Puerto Rico, which he described as "natural appendages to the North American continent." Jefferson had dubbed the United States' expansion through military conquest and purchase of other nations and colonies an "empire for liberty." The "liberty" envisioned here was one that coexisted with and depended on enslavement and white supremacy, excluded all women from political power, and entailed the seizure of native and foreign lands. Jefferson, then, was in no way imagining the establishment of universal freedom. Still, the logic of his phrase rested on the fact that any new lands annexed by the United States were to be added to the Union as equal states, not colonies or indefinite territories.[14]

Following the abolition of slavery and the establishment of legal racial equality in the United States, as well as the violence and corruption deployed to suppress black suffrage, Caribbean nations with large enslaved, formerly enslaved, poor, and African-descended populations were no longer seen by many white political leaders as acceptable additions to the Union. The political, and concretely electoral, impact was perceived as too harmful to dominant interests by U.S. politicians. When President Ulysses Grant submitted a treaty to Congress in the early 1870s that would have annexed the Dominican Republic to the United States, there was fierce congressional opposition based on the fact that what was perceived as a majority black population, composed mostly of economically independent peasants, would be enfranchised. The proposal was defeated. The problem with annexing "tropical countries," Senator Carl Schurz lamented to his colleagues, is that "you must admit them as states . . . upon an equal footing with the States you represent . . . not only to govern themselves, but to take part in the government of the common concerns of the Republic. Have you thought of what this means?" It would, he asserted, transform the "destinies of this Republic."[15]

This racist logic shaped attitudes toward Cuba as well. Despite the perceived commercial and strategic benefits of annexing Cuba, the prospect of enfranchising the country's massive formerly enslaved population discouraged U.S. leaders from pursuing this course. An editorial in a Philadelphia paper in 1889, presumptuously titled "Do We Want Cuba," asserted: "There is much to be said in favor of our acquiring the island [Cuba]. . . . The nation possessing her will have almost exclusive dominion over the approaches to any of the interocean waterways. . . . Her tobacco is the best in the world. She has the finest soil for growing sugarcane, and her acquisition . . . would open a great new market for all we now produce." "But," the writer asked, "what would be the result of attempts to incorporate into our political community a population such as Cuba's?" The conclusion was that annexation would be dangerous for the United States. An article in the *New York Evening Post* that same year opposed the idea of incorporating into the United States "nearly a million blacks . . . who must . . . be armed with the ballot and put on the same level politically with their former masters."[16]

Racist opposition in the United States to annexing Cuba was inseparable from economic concerns. Former slaves would likely have voted for political leaders who supported policies at odds with U.S. sugar and other major interests on the island. Their perspective on Cuba's lucrative plantation economy, after all, differed greatly from that of those who formerly held them in slavery. Freed people in Cuba, as in all postemancipation societies, sought access to their own land and alternatives to plantation work. The development of those alternatives would decrease the supply of labor and put upward pressure on wages, which would benefit those who ultimately did choose employment in the sugar industry and hurt company profits. Plantation owners, understanding this, hoped to expand their estates while preventing workers from easily acquiring land, thus keeping laborers dependent on employment as cane cutters, however poor the wages and conditions were. Any government that sought to increase people's land access and economic independence would, inevitably, do so at the expense of the sugar companies.

The independence revolution, a predominantly left-wing, transformative one in both its vision and its composition, led as well as staffed largely by people of African descent, promised just such a government. And the revolutionaries' desires for socioeconomic transformation were especially clear with regard to land. In the early 1890s, the foremost advocate of revolution, José Martí, proposed distributing the nation's uncultivated lands "to anyone desiring to work [them]." The revolutionaries' goal, wrote Martí, "is not so much a mere political change as a good, sound, and just and equitable social system." During the war, rebel commanders decreed that all lands belonging to Spain and to those who had backed the colonial government would be redistributed, and they began granting these properties to soldiers and others. This was a revolution whose goal was not just to make Cuba independent but to make freedom real for former slaves—providing them with the independence of owning their own land. "Former slaves found their legal freedom within a colonial context to be incomplete," historian Rebecca Scott writes, and this was what made them ready "candidates for recruitment to a rebellion [against Spain] that seemed to promise a new beginning."[17]

That new beginning for many Cubans in the countryside was precisely what plantation owners and many better-off Cubans most feared, for it could result in decreased or more expensive laborers as well as less available land for the sugar industry, thus impeding profits and expansion. In 1895, the Spanish prime minister had warned that "this insurrection threatens Cuba with all the evils of Haiti and Santo Domingo." This was a way of calling up a specific specter: that the plantation economy would be replaced with a rural population mostly of African descent with political rights and engaged in small-scale farming and other economically independent activities. This was an equally frightening scenario for U.S. landowners and leaders.[18]

In the summer of 1898, facing the uncertain political consequences of Cuba's independence revolution and taking advantage of popular outrage in the United States at Spain's bloody colonial war, President McKinley ordered U.S. troops to invade the island. After a quick rout of Spanish forces, with Cuban and U.S. troops fighting on the same side, U.S. military leaders took over, occupied the country, and then quickly demobilized Cuba's formidable rebel army. They founded a U.S. military government, which in turn set out to shape the character of a new Cuban military and state. The goal was to establish enduring and effective political institutions, such as the armed forces, that would protect and further perceived U.S. interests. In this way, the benefits of empire could be had without the annexation of Cuba as either a state or an indefinite U.S. territory.[19]

The U.S. military sought to reverse some of the radical implications of Cuba's independence revolution with regard to race, but with only limited success. U.S. authorities insisted that the new Cuban army limit military commanders to white Cubans. This was a starkly retrograde action, turning upside down the history of integration in the Liberation Army, as well as an insult to its foremost leader, Antonio Maceo, who was of African descent and had been killed during the war. U.S. authorities also quickly tried to restrict voting rights. Through property and literacy requirements, U.S.

authorities disenfranchised most of Cuba's popular classes. One U.S. leader celebrated this elimination from the polls of "so great a proportion of the elements which have brought ruin to Haiti and [Spanish] San Domingo." Yet many Cubans were outraged. When the United States organized a convention to draft the new constitution, the Cuban delegates insisted on universal male suffrage. Though they were virtually all elite, they understood Cuba's decades of popular and cross-racial revolutionary struggle made disenfranchisement of Cubans of color and the popular classes a virtual political impossibility.[20]

The U.S. dictatorship had greater but still ultimately mixed success imposing new property laws and land tenure arrangements. Specifically, U.S. authorities intervened in the question of who could use and own lands known as *haciendas comuneras* that were common in the east. Although more research needs to be done on this subject, the basic outline seems clear. These were large estates jointly owned by often great numbers of shareholders (with larger or smaller shares). Co-owners did not have title to a specific plot but rather possessed rights to use available land within the property (the *hacienda*). This loose land tenure arrangement worked well when land pressure was limited or desire for open range to raise animals was common. Such land use and property rights also facilitated the use of these areas by squatters, who might have seen these areas as, essentially, crown lands or public property. In time, title-less occupants might have succeeded in gaining legal rights to the land they cultivated through squatters' or "prescription" rights (a legal form in many countries across the globe at the time), which took effect following years of peaceful, uninterrupted use. In the Dominican Republic, a similar property form known as *terrenos comuneros* allowed much of the country's land to be successfully claimed by squatters there, both during the U.S. occupation and, above all, under the Trujillo regime.[21]

In Cuba in 1902, though, U.S. authorities explicitly rejected the rights of squatters to use and over time gain title to land in *haciendas comuneras*. This move effectively undermined the rights and interests of large numbers of landless occupants and others who had hoped to become small farmers, many of whom had been galvanized by and fought for independence. The U.S. authorities, furthermore, did not fulfill the promises for land distributions to soldiers and residents that had been made by the Liberation Army. As a result, an unresolved war between title-less occupants and titleholders continued to smolder in the east, one that Fidel Castro's rebel fighters would find still raging in the 1950s. In essence, the U.S. occupation undid the independence revolution's promise of agrarian reform.[22]

As the U.S. regime short-circuited any potential agrarian reform, U.S. sugar companies, many of which had begun investing in Cuban sugar in the late 1800s, expanded their operations. During the war, Cuban insurgents had destroyed sugar plantations as part of their military strategy. Afterward, U.S. investors were able to buy many of the damaged and distressed properties. And in the east, a new U.S. sugar empire spread into what had been an undeveloped land frontier, where U.S.-owned corporations now purchased shares to *comunera* lands and then enclosed areas with fences to claim rights to them. U.S. firms soon were responsible for almost half of all Cuba's skyrocketing sugar production. This placed U.S. investments in the middle of what would be unending land battles in the east.[23]

The U.S. military government also put in place a political structure intended to ensure the continuation of its economic policies following the end of the U.S. occupation of the island. As a condition for withdrawal, which would occur in 1902, U.S. authorities demanded that Cubans approve a constitution that included what became known as the Platt Amendment. This amendment formally yielded part of Cuba's sovereignty to the United States. It decreed that "all Acts of the United States in Cuba during its military occupancy . . . and all lawful rights acquired thereunder shall be maintained and protected." It put the U.S. government in control of the island's foreign treaties and public debt. It obliged Cuba to cede territory to the United States for military bases on the island, and a massive base was in time established at Guantánamo Bay, a choice location because of its formidable deepwater harbor and its location on the channel between Cuba and Haiti. The constitution also stipulated that Cuba's neighboring Isle of Pines would remain a U.S. territory. Last, and perhaps most profoundly, it granted the U.S. military the right to reoccupy Cuba whenever the U.S. government decided that such action was needed. In fact, U.S. forces would intervene repeatedly in the decades to come.[24]

The Platt Amendment provoked widespread opposition in Cuba among political leaders, in the press, and in the streets. But Cuban leaders, faced with what they saw as a choice between limited sovereignty or no sovereignty at all, gave in. This was not the "independence we had dreamed about," one former Cuban independence revolutionary leader, the Dominican-born Máximo Gómez, lamented. The Platt Amendment was ultimately repealed after a popular uprising in Cuba in 1933. But even afterward, the peculiar U.S. empire of intervention continued de facto in Cuba. And it would serve as a model for U.S. interventions both in other parts of the Caribbean and across the globe in the long twentieth century.[25]

Rural Autonomy and Statelessness
in the Dominican Republic and Haiti

In 1904, Hugh Kelly, the American owner of a major sugar corporation, wrote to U.S. president Theodore Roosevelt urging him to "Cubaize" (Cuba-ize) the Dominican Republic. Kelly's company owned plantations in the southeastern coastal regions of the country, known in the Dominican Republic as the East, and his properties were being attacked by antigovernment rebels and armed gangs called *gavilleros* (bandits). Kelly warned Roosevelt that U.S. investments of supposedly "vast economic importance" were "at the mercy of hordes of untrained and unintelligent mobs led by opposing political leaders . . . likely at any moment to commit outrage upon person and property." Kelly also objected to a European blockade of Dominican ports designed to press European creditors' claims on the country's revenue for outstanding loan payments. Finally, Kelly asked the secretary of state to act to prevent the Dominican government from reestablishing taxes on sugar exports.[26]

Kelly was not the only U.S. business owner imploring the U.S. government to reshape its relationship with the Dominican Republic to support his and other U.S. investments. A year earlier, W. L. Bass, owner of the largest sugar plantations in the Dominican Republic, had also called on the U.S. government to find a way to dominate the country in a fashion parallel to what it had already done in Cuba: "Although there is no Platt amendment [in the Dominican Republic] . . . modern industries must be allowed to continue to operate and life and property respected," Bass wrote. Already, Cuba had become a model and metaphor for U.S. overseas domination in other parts of the Caribbean.[27]

The dreams of U.S. investors to have the Dominican Republic Cuba-ized by the United States would come true in 1916, when the U.S. military invaded the country. A year earlier, the United States had occupied Haiti. In combination with the continued domination of Cuba, this meant that the three largest nations of the Caribbean were all under some form of U.S. military or political control during the early twentieth century. In Haiti and the Dominican Republic, this military control produced extensive armed opposition, and thousands of lives were lost fighting to end U.S. military occupation. In both countries, U.S. rule also had major repercussions for future generations. It would ultimately give rise to dictatorships, that of Trujillo in the Dominican Republic and François Duvalier in Haiti. And even after those dictatorships fell, efforts to consolidate a liberal state—one with democratic elections, civil rights, and the rule of law—would repeatedly founder.

At the start of the twentieth century, Haiti and the Dominican Republic shared a great deal. The population of both countries descended mostly from escaped or revolutionary slaves who had successfully battled for independence against colonial rulers and had forged economically independent lives. Although various forms of racism operated in both countries (in particular, colorism and denigration of cultural practices associated with Africa), they were governed mostly—or entirely in Haiti's case—by presidents of African descent, a rarity in the Americas at the time.

There were also deep similarities in the organization of rural areas in both countries and in the centrality of independent farmers in their economy and society. Most Dominicans lived by farming and by hunting and raising animals on the open range, enjoying free access to still vast areas of uncleared and unenclosed lands. Into the twentieth century, the Dominican Republic was, in the words of poet Pedro Mir, a place where land had "belonged to no one like the wind like the rain like the nights like life and death." In Haiti, most rural areas—notably those of the Central Plateau, which bordered on the Dominican Republic and would become one of the heartlands of the resistance to the U.S. occupation—were also populated by people engaged in various kinds of small farming.[28]

Thanks to the collapse of sugar plantations and emigration after the Haitian Revolution, an open frontier for cultivation appears to have prevailed for generations in Haiti. Most people had free access to the land they farmed, though there was some sharecropping. By the middle of the nineteenth century, Haitian leaders had begrudgingly abandoned their efforts to rebuild the plantation system. Acquiescing to people's determination to farm and own their own land, the government even distributed or sold small parcels of state land. Few plantations remained, but rather a nation of small farmers prevailed with plots averaging perhaps two or three acres. As the population increased during the 1800s, new generations simply cleared and exploited available idle areas. With ample land, small farmers successfully grew a mix of subsistence, cash, and export crops, particularly coffee. There were thriving markets throughout rural areas in Haiti, and zones of commerce connected eleven ports in the country through which coffee, dyewood, and other goods were sold internationally. This system sustained a strongly autonomous life for rural Haitians, one that they had developed and anchored in the landscape over several generations since winning independence in 1804. It also sustained the nation's per capita income. During the second half of the nineteenth century, annual coffee exports matched those of the prerevolutionary period.[29]

The rural Haitian population was, then, clearly drawn to the market and successfully produced a surplus in the 1800s. In 1915, the prominent U.S. intellectual W. E. B. Du Bois wrote that Haiti had "succeeded in placing on their own little farms the happiest and most contented peasantry in the world." He criticized the political class in Haiti but declared hopefully that if "the best elements of Hayti secure permanent political leadership the triumph of the revolution will be complete." Du Bois's interest in conditions in Haiti was to some extent personal. His father had been born and lived in mid-nineteenth-century Haiti before coming to the United States.[30]

The existing political class in Haiti, though, remained at odds with that "contented peasantry." The happiness of the rural majority therefore depended on weak central states, as was the case also in the Dominican Republic. The rural populations in both of the island's nations were widely dispersed, armed, and difficult for state officials to control. Both central governments opposed rural autonomy and attempted to thwart it in various ways, whether by trying to restrict free access to land, requiring that livestock be enclosed, abusively executing vagrancy laws, or establishing onerous new taxes. Those included tariffs on trade between Haiti and the Dominican Republic and forced (corvée) labor to build roads and infrastructure. Under such political conditions, the rural population proved to be especially fertile ground for recruitment by armed groups seeking to resist or usurp the national government's power and authority. These groups encompassed gangs, known as *gavilleros* in the Dominican Republic and *cacos* in Haiti, and regional strongmen able to marshal local forces to challenge and topple state leaders.[31]

Rebels and other local armed groups had numerous and differing goals that can variously be seen as political or criminal: informal resistance to new state attempts at control; demands for government positions, contracts, or revenues; and extortion from and raids on plantations and customhouses (where external taxes were collected). The success of all these informal armed groups both reflected and contributed to the weakness of the central state and to tense peasant-state relations. Neither Haiti nor the Dominican Republic had an effective central army or police that could control the island's armed bands or consolidate the national state's power over local strongmen and regional leaders. In the Dominican Republic, a central military had existed almost in name only. National conscription laws existed on paper, but recruitment and service were mostly a local affair.[32]

These conditions were anathema to capitalist enterprise, which suffered losses from extortion and raids. Furthermore, the independence enjoyed by people in the countryside limited their readiness to work for low wages, making laborers scarce or more expensive. Nonetheless, taking advantage of the fact that property rights remained unclear and land abundant, Cuban and then U.S. sugar entrepreneurs began growing their businesses in the Dominican Republic at the end of the nineteenth century. They purchased inexpensive *comunero* titles—that is, shares in a jointly owned estate or *comunero* "site" (similar to *haciendas comuneras* in Cuba)—paying occupants for their "improvements," or they simply enclosed vast areas without any title or purchase at all. Given the poor wages and conditions these companies offered and the independent subsistence readily available to most Dominicans, the future sugar giant had to depend almost entirely on immigrant Caribbean laborers, mostly from the British colonies and, as we will see, subsequently from Haiti.[33]

When the sugar companies first began investing in the Dominican East, many title-less occupants from the area had been willing to leave where they were farming in return for a small payment for their cultivated crops, as initially open-range land and forest remained available nearby. Over the course of three or four decades, however, what had seemed an endless land frontier in the southeast was exhausted. Plantations staked out claims to hundreds of thousands of acres primarily in this region. As they did, many residents on these lands began to refuse to leave, claimed title based on long-term use ("prescription"), and became embattled squatters. Individuals with *comunero* titles and competing claims to fairly large areas also began to wage both legal and armed battles with the sugar companies. These relatively privileged individuals joined and, in some instances, led movements by growing numbers of locals who refused to recognize the authority of the national state, particularly to adjudicate property, and attacked its symbols and representatives.[34]

The new sugar corporations accumulating lands across the collectively exploited woods and plains of the Dominican East quickly fell prey to a mixture of theft, requisitions, and demands for protection money, especially from local armed gangs. Like the customhouses near the border with Haiti, the sugar companies were attacked frequently by *gavilleros* because that's where the money was. Sugar companies also faced these threats, though, because their expansion was undermining the way of life in the region by swallowing up the once seemingly endless woods and pasture that had been collectively exploited until then. Those who experienced dispossession and were negatively affected by the massive spread of plantations in their lands often joined or supported the *gavilleros*.

A similar process unfolded in rural Haiti in areas where U.S. companies made incursions. Here, though, even prior to difficulties arising from foreign interests, the challenges for the peasantry were more widespread than in the Dominican Republic. In Haiti, because of the steady growth of the population, the frontier of open land was shrinking by the start of the twentieth century. Little arable land remained that was neither cultivated nor claimed, economist Matts Lundahl contends, and plots would have to decrease in size if new generations sought to continue to farm their own land. State support for agriculture—irrigation, roads, loans, less burdensome taxation, and so forth—might have made farming more productive and profitable even on smaller plots, but none was forthcoming. As a result of these conditions, sharecropping became more common over the twentieth century.[35]

Foreign investment soon compounded the stress on rural Haitians. In 1910, for instance, a U.S. investor named James McDonald gained a concession from the Haitian government to build railroads in the country. He was given access not just to the land for the line but to a swath twelve miles wide on either side where he planned to develop banana plantations. Starting in 1911, local residents—many of whom did not have titles to the land where they lived and farmed—were kicked out. Some displaced residents took up arms, attacking the buildings of McDonald's company, smashing tools and pressuring Haitian workers to refuse to work on the railroad construction. The loss of land also expanded the ranks of various *caco* bands operating in the country, many of whom became part of armed movements that propelled a string of new leaders to power in Port-au-Prince in the years before the occupation began. U.S. companies' incursions into the countryside, then, contributed to the political instability that ultimately became the justification for occupation in 1915. As historian Roger Gaillard puts it, during these years the United States helped to "ripen" political conflict in the country until it was ready to pick the fruit.[36]

In both Haiti and the Dominican Republic, rural residents overall had contradictory attitudes toward the local armed bands who played, in fact, contradictory roles in their lives. On the one hand, many "men from the woods," as most people in the Dominican countryside called them, requisitioned food, coerced young men into becoming recruits, and at times subjected women to sexual exploitation and violence. To some, the armed conflicts and threats "presented a fearsome spectacle," historian Julie

Franks writes. On the other hand, local armed groups were available allies against an ominous national state supportive of foreign investors and threatening the traditional rural economy. As Franks explains, writing about the Dominican Republic, "the armed bands did not wreck wanton violence on rural populations. They targeted representatives of national authority." In doing so, they doubtless gained some sympathy locally, as those representatives in, for instance, the Dominican Republic—land surveyors, judges, and police—tended to favor the interests of the new sugar giant in the region over those who had previously and often still exploited the lands it now claimed. Similarly in Haiti, historian Marvin Chochotte writes, "peasants complained about vigilantism, banditry, and other forms of popular violence that were linked to an armed and insurrectional society," even if the state's power to coerce the labor of rural communities was constrained by that very political violence. "To be sure," Chochotte writes, "revolutions were not entirely virtuous."[37]

Both the Dominican and Haitian states proved vulnerable to regional strongmen and local armed bands. In Haiti, the local armies often overthrew unpopular central governments, though once they came into power their leaders rarely delivered on promises for change made to recruit participants. In the Dominican Republic, when governments sought to impose central authority across the country, they met strong pushback and were overthrown with relative ease. The police and army were often too weak to intervene to protect the government or the sugar companies when they were pressed to pay protection money to local leaders and bands or else be torched or plundered. Indeed, the police and army themselves were under siege. Gangs sacked police stations and army posts in the Dominican Republic at the same time that they harassed and attacked U.S. sugar plantations.[38]

Starting in the first years of the twentieth century, U.S. sugar company executives like Hugh Kelly began protesting to the U.S. State Department about their subjection to armed gangs and antigovernment rebels in the Dominican Republic. The Central Ansonia Sugar Company wrote in 1904 to the secretary of state: "Mr. Secretary, surely it cannot be the purpose of the United States to abandon its citizens and their interests much longer to such a condition as exists in Santo Domingo!" Other businesses also complained. The Central Dominican Railroad Company of New Jersey wrote that same year that armed gangs were taking apart its tracks and had forced it to stop service. Another major U.S. investor requested that the State Department inform him when "the time has arrived when American capital can, with reasonable assurance of protection, be justified in embarking in the development of the natural resources of Santo Domingo." U.S. investors in the Dominican Republic were demanding the same thing that overseas investors in general were demanding at the time: that, in the *New York Times*'s words, their operations "be protected if need be by the power of the United States."[39]

Notwithstanding Hugh Kelly's claims of their "vast economic importance," U.S. investments on Hispaniola were minuscule relative to the U.S. economy as a whole in 1915. U.S. investments in the Dominican Republic and Haiti were a tiny part of even U.S. overseas capital. These were not countries like Cuba or Mexico with substantial U.S. investments and domestic markets for U.S. goods. U.S. investments in Haiti were only 0.32 percent of those just in Latin America. And the amount of U.S. overseas capital at large remained small relative to U.S. domestic investments. It seems unlikely, then, that these economic involvements were seen by U.S. government leaders as in and of themselves sufficient to drive a U.S. invasion and long-term occupation of the island's nations.[40]

At the same time, given the political access and leverage of its wealthy and well-connected investors, the presence of U.S. capital on the island ultimately had political significance. And U.S. policy makers may have perceived overseas investments and markets as, in some ways, all of a piece and in need of protection from unfavorable precedents anywhere. Finally, there were the imagined possibilities for future investments in and commerce with the Caribbean. If through intervention the U.S. government was able to "Cubaize" the island in terms of U.S. political control—and thus make it a safer and more lucrative space for U.S. investments—perhaps U.S. companies could "Cubaize" it economically as well. If so, they might help expand the then modest role the island was playing in what Eric Williams called the "American Sugar Kingdom," the vast empire of U.S. sugar corporations with plantations in Hawai'i, Puerto Rico, the Philippines, and, above all, Cuba.[41]

Perhaps most importantly, the protests of U.S. corporations spoke to broader strategic concerns that helped fire the U.S. imperial imagination at the turn of the twentieth century. Neither the Dominican Republic nor Haiti was the type of state that U.S. leaders wanted on its Caribbean borders. The complaints of U.S. corporate executives made clear that the central governments on the island still had minimal control over their own populations. This meant also that they were in no position to prevent intervention into their political or economic affairs—or waters—by powerful U.S.

rivals. U.S. leaders were particularly concerned about the prospect that Germany would find a strategic foothold in the region. They were worried about the presence of a small but influential German merchant community in Haiti, especially since the German navy had occasionally been dispatched to extract indemnity payments from Haitian governments—to pay back property losses suffered by German merchants during political conflicts—and interfered directly in some of these conflicts. Some raised the specter of a German state seeking to establish a submarine presence in the region, to secure a military base in Haiti, or to acquire the Danish West Indies (a prospect the U.S. government preempted by annexing them itself in 1917).[42]

The extent of German ambitions in the Caribbean was less than some U.S. officials suggested at the time. And these concerns might have been overstated as an excuse for expanding U.S. power in the region. Yet whether or not Germany posed a threat, and even if U.S. leaders believed it did not, the real power in expressing these concerns was that they called up the anxiety about a type of vulnerability that might become an issue in the future. Even if the Haitian and Dominican governments were ready and willing to support U.S. strategic as well as economic interests, they were seen as unable to guarantee them against either internal or external forces. Historian Hans Schmidt argues that U.S. authorities ultimately came "to the conclusion that . . . Haitian guarantees were insufficient . . . to eliminate the threat of European encroachment," something they also believed for the Dominican Republic. Strategic rivalry and ambition abroad thus contributed to U.S. leaders' wishes to project U.S. empire into the neighboring Caribbean Sea and to assure obedient lands and friendly waters on its borders.[43]

The U.S. government had at its disposal increasing military power and wealth, along with a sense of entitlement and superiority. These were the foundations for its bold project of building more potent and dutiful states across the independent Caribbean. In 1912, the U.S. minister in Santo Domingo proposed that the best course of action was "complete control by our Government" of the Dominican Republic. There was, though, intense hostility in the Dominican Republic and in Haiti to the United States' gaining financial and military control, let alone to its entirely taking over the two nations' governments, whether de jure or de facto. This was the case even among numerous officials and intellectuals in the Dominican Republic and Haiti who had positive views of the United States and who longed for a stronger central state—and with it, they hoped, the realization of their particular visions of "progress." They hoped that U.S. investment and support could help them in that project, but they did not envision a full U.S. takeover. The generally positive view of the United States among elites is one reason why, when the United States sent troops into both countries, there was little initial resistance. Many seem to have believed these interventions were temporary, and necessary to reestablish order, but would not ultimately become full military occupations. They were wrong. The arrival of U.S. Marines in Haiti in 1915 and in the Dominican Republic in 1916 was the beginning of a long process of seizing, ruling, and reshaping the Caribbean's second-largest island.[44]

Occupation in the Dominican Republic and Haiti

In November of 1915, U.S. president Woodrow Wilson issued three demands to the Dominican government that made clear his administration's intentions. First, he demanded that Dominican president Juan Isidro Jimenes accept a U.S. financial adviser who would have full control over the formulation and execution of the Dominican government's budget; second, that another U.S. official oversee public works; and third, that a new national army and police force be organized under U.S. command. An effective central army forged by and linked to U.S. military leaders could protect both U.S. investments and the government in power from bandits and rebellious regional leaders. And control over the nation's public works could mean the pursuit of particular infrastructure projects (major roads, bridges, and possibly rail lines) that would expand the national military's reach and mobility as well as facilitate commerce. Wilson's demands would have left only a façade of self-government, and Dominican leaders refused to cooperate.[45]

The diplomatic stalemate between the two nations coincided with tensions within the Dominican Republic. A number of military officers and others in the government opposed President Jimenes, including the secretary of war, Desiderio Arias, who was one of the country's most powerful regional military and political leaders. In the spring of 1916, Arias rebelled and sought to oust Jimenes. U.S. leaders saw an opportunity and pressured President Jimenes to request assistance. When he refused, U.S. forces invaded anyway under the pretense of protecting the U.S. Legation amid fighting in the capital. Over the next two months, the U.S. Marines took control of the entire country. They faced snipers but little else. The U.S. commander demanded that Arias surrender, and Arias withdrew his forces from the capital. He fought one battle against the Marines on his home turf in the northwest but was defeated. It seemed obvious to Dominican leaders that, at least in open battle, they did not stand a chance against the Marines. U.S. troops were able to take over the country practically unscathed.

The U.S. military takeover was even smoother across the border in Haiti, where U.S. Marines who had disembarked in 1915 had encountered almost no immediate resistance. Only one U.S. soldier was killed, mistakenly, by his own troops during the nighttime advance into Port-au-Prince, and one lone Haitian sentry also died. The initial ease of occupation, however, was ultimately deceptive: in time, in both the Dominican Republic and Haiti, the Marines would encounter intense and ongoing resistance in rural areas.[46]

Attempting to legitimate the invasion of the Dominican Republic as an act of benevolence, the U.S. minister reportedly declared that the United States had "as its objective the well-being of the Dominican people." The Dominican minister scoffed at such justification: "For nations, as for individuals, material well-being is not sufficient; honor comes before everything and the supreme good for every state is based on the full enjoyment of its sovereignty." "The Dominican people," one Dominican nationalist group protested, "neither needs nor accepts guardianship." And the Dominican government invoked Wilson's proclaimed support for national self-determination: "President Wilson, who has repeatedly declared himself to be the defender of the principle of equality among nations and of respect for the sovereignty of weak states, cannot sustain, with regard to the Dominican Republic, a position that contradicts these same values."[47]

U.S. authorities ignored such protests and inaugurated the U.S. Military Government in the Dominican Republic on November 29, 1916. The outlines of this occupation, which paralleled that already underway in Haiti, had been planned for some time. Existing laws would continue in effect unless superseded by executive orders from the new military government.

In Haiti, many high-level politicians sought to collaborate with the United States, though in time a number of them would pull away from such a stance. Their ongoing collaboration reflected hope among the upper classes that the occupation would bring a stronger national state, an end to *caco* rebellions and abuses, and economic development. Political Scientist David Nicholls argues, too, that some "saw in the occupation a chance to re-establish the political hegemony of the mulatto elite which had been gradually eroded in the preceding decades." Certainly, a good number of distinguished Haitians balked at the idea of openly cooperating with U.S. rulers. But U.S. leaders were soon able to secure a figurehead president and place him in office through a sham legislative election. This put a self-described puppet in charge of the Haitian government, Philippe Sudre Dartiguenave, rather than Rosalvo Bobo, a popular, highly educated, and well-respected politician and obvious successor to the presidency. Bobo, however, had been critical of the McDonald railroad concession. He had also strongly opposed handing over customs receipts to U.S. authorities (the main source of government revenues), a takeover U.S. leaders had continually insisted on to no avail and that had been earlier secured in the Dominican Republic. Bobo was unlikely to be as subservient a leader as the U.S. government sought.[48]

In the Dominican Republic, elite resistance to U.S. occupation was swifter and more universal than in Haiti. The Dominican cabinet immediately resigned in protest, and the president went into exile in Cuba. As senators abandoned their posts, the U.S. Military Government indefinitely suspended the Dominican Congress. The secretary of the U.S. Navy appointed a military governor, who would rule over both the old civil government and a parallel new military one.[49] No puppet president would ever be put in place, unlike in Haiti.

Thus the military dictatorship imposed on the Dominican Republic would be de jure as well as de facto. There would be no pretense of democracy, self-government, elections, or political representation. Instead a foreign government backed by a foreign army ruled by fiat. And the occupation government imposed strict censorship laws restricting speech as well as publications "unfavorable to the government of the United States of America or to the military government in Santo Domingo." Even references to "freedom of speech," "freedom of thought," and in certain contexts "national" and "rebellion" were censored by the regime.[50]

The U.S. Military Government also immediately criminalized gun ownership for all but a small number of Dominicans who were issued permits. In the face of fierce opposition from people refusing to surrender their arms voluntarily, U.S. troops carried out a massive, brutal disarmament campaign. They forced their way into homes and searched for and seized weapons. Guns were for many Dominicans an everyday tool relied on for subsistence (hunting). They were also a means and an emblem of political independence, needed to resist a national government seen as oppressive and threatening. Some Dominicans managed to hide their weapons. But a year after the occupation began, supposedly fifty thousand firearms and two hundred thousand rounds of ammunition, along with thousands of knives, had been seized by the U.S. regime. Such numbers are striking for a poor country with a small population. Disarmament was essential to realizing the U.S. government's basic objective for the occupation—the strengthening of state control over society. On the other hand, the Marines reported, forcible disarmament intensified the already intense popular opposition to U.S. occupation. And, as we will see, disarmament would not prevent the development of an effective regional insurgency against U.S. rule.[51]

Dominican hostility to the U.S. occupation reached across society. "I have never seen such hatred displayed by one people for another as I notice and feel here," the head of U.S. forces confessed. "We positively have not a friend in the land." Resistance to the occupation grew on two separate fronts, one nonviolent and one armed. Nonviolent opposition was mobilized primarily by the better-off and more urban classes: professionals, former politicians, merchants, members of the clergy, and prominent intellectuals. Especially during the early years, they confronted tight restrictions on free speech and assembly. But Dominican exiles, many living in Cuba and the United States, had more freedom. Across the Americas and Europe, they mounted a public relations campaign to demand the restoration of their national sovereignty and to denounce U.S. war crimes on the island.[52]

The exiles' public relations campaign succeeded in triggering protests throughout Latin America as well as securing financial support from Cuban nationalists, who in 1917 were themselves protesting U.S. military intervention in their home country—the third U.S. intervention in fifteen years. A leading U.S. State Department official recalled: "Protests both informal and formal, emanating from Latin American Governments, prominent publicists in South America, and from associations throughout the continent, were being addressed continually . . . to President Wilson, urging the termination of the occupation." And in Spain, political leaders of all stripes signed petitions to Wilson condemning the U.S. takeover of the Dominican Republic. Critical articles and editorials also appeared in the mainstream U.S. press, and the president of the American Federation of Labor wrote a letter of protest on behalf of the Dominican Republic to Wilson. European governments also criticized the U.S. occupation of Haiti, and in the United States, African American activists including James Weldon Johnson campaigned for withdrawal, publicizing the atrocities carried out by U.S. Marines against insurgents. This international opposition, which highlighted the hypocrisy of Wilson's policy in the Caribbean even as he championed the sovereignty of "great and small states alike" in other contexts, made military intervention a vexed question within the United States.[53]

There was armed resistance to the United States in Haiti in rural areas from the beginning of the occupation, as a number of Haitian military officers rebelled against the figurehead government and some *caco* bands refused to put down their weapons. Both groups soon joined a nationalist guerrilla force made up also of peasants, better-off farmers, market women, teachers, and others. One rebel Haitian military officer, Benoît Rameau, invoked the history of the Haitian Revolution and accused the United States of attempting "to re-establish slavery" when he protested to the U.S. consul in Port-au-Prince: "For almost 112 years, we have been a free and independent people. Our sweat and our courage gave us our independence. In that time, we have never been governed by a head of state chosen by a foreign power." However, at this time, at least, the rebels were not widespread enough to be any match for the U.S. Marines, nor could they win a war fought with older rifles and pistols, along with machetes and pikes, against machine guns. U.S. soldiers in Haiti who had earlier fought in the Philippine-American War deployed some of the same strategies against the guerrillas in Haiti. U.S. troops burned down countless homes and entire villages in areas believed to be friendly to the rebels. The insurgents were forced to disband within a few months.[54]

But U.S. rulers' reliance on corvée labor starting in 1916—in which residents were rounded up and forced to work building roads—soon helped mobilize a new and more widespread round of popular armed resistance. Oppressively burdensome as this work was—based on an old Haitian law for payment of taxes by laboring for the state—it was the abusive, sometimes even lethal, ways the Marines executed it that especially horrified and outraged people. It is no surprise that both Haitian and U.S. observers compared the practice to slavery, given that gangs of workers were roped together and forced to carry out backbreaking labor in the hot sun without adequate water, food, or rest. Some of the recruits, both men and women, perished from dehydration and disease; others were shot trying to escape.[55]

It was by means of this gruesome forced labor that the occupation ultimately achieved its main claim to fame, reportedly a thousand miles of roads, including a 170-mile highway linking Cap-Haïtien and Port-au-Prince. This achievement served well one of the U.S. occupation's key objectives. The new roads would permit more rapid troop movements and a greater state presence in areas of conflict, hence the complaints of some leading Haitians that roads were being built only in areas of unrest, not in stable ones. Yet this U.S. military strategy of new roads had contradictory effects given its reliance on forced labor. While it boosted the state and armed forces' control over the country, it also galvanized widespread hatred toward it. That outrage helped fuel a new and more resilient independence rebellion.

This new uprising commenced with a major attack in late 1917, but the rebellion really took off the following year when the well-educated and charismatic former officer Charlemagne Péralte took charge. He eventually mobilized several thousand troops, some gained by freeing corvée laborers, most small and medium farmers driven to resistance by the Marines' abuses and denial of self-government. Different groups of rebel forces were relatively autonomous. But through Péralte's leadership and inspiration, they coordinated their efforts in important ways. In 1919, Péralte announced a provisional government: "We demand our rights, unrecognized and flouted by unscrupulous Americans who, by destroying our institutions, deprive the Haitian people of all their resources. . . . With cruelty and injustice, the Yankees have for four years cast ruin and destruction on our territory. . . . We are prepared to make any sacrifice to liberate Haitian territory." In Port-au-Prince, posters went up everywhere. One read: "Let us chase away these savage men" and "Long live independence!"[56]

The uprising in Haiti coincided with rebellion against U.S. occupation on the other side of the island, where a Dominican guerrilla war for independence erupted in the countryside soon after the start of the occupation, primarily in the eastern sugar zones. Some six hundred regular Dominican troops were in "open insurrection," the Marines reported in 1918, and there were many more part-time soldiers who could be called upon by the movement's dozen or so main leaders. Insurgent camps comprised as many as one hundred or more soldiers each. And, alarmingly for the United States, the rebels in Haiti and the Dominican Republic worked together across the border, providing each other with weapons, provisions, and troops when needed in their struggles to expel the occupiers. Diverse Dominican and Haitian antistate forces in the frontier areas, from smugglers and bandits to insurgents, had always collaborated across what was a de facto open border to gather arms and to take refuge, as well as to trade free of taxation—practices prior Dominican governments and U.S. officials had sought in vain to stop. Now there were broader forces firing this transnational collaboration and pulling the entire independent Caribbean together: common subjection and resistance to U.S. occupation.[57]

Both the form taken by resistance to the United States and the ultimate impact of U.S. occupation policies were shaped and constrained by the demography and person-to-land ratio of the two countries. In Haiti, U.S. companies were unable to gain a major foothold due in part to the relative lack of available idle land as well as to Haitians' readiness to resist all efforts at dispossession. That there was no large land frontier in Haiti, as there was in the Dominican Republic, meant that land acquisitions to develop large-scale agriculture entailed uprooting families who usually had a long-standing claim to the land. Although the independence rebellion in Haiti had been crushed relatively easily, the insurgents' intense armed resistance made clear the perils of igniting another and perhaps even greater rebellion. In that light, U.S. authorities were generally less ready, it seems, to use their power and authority, whether through state coercion or legal maneuvering, to effect widespread dispossession.

U.S. rulers' other efforts in Haiti to promote plantation agriculture and foreign investment, including the removal of a constitutional provision that barred foreigners from owning property and ceding land to foreign companies, were largely ineffective. Two U.S.-owned companies did develop their holdings during the occupation, the Haitian American Sugar Company (HASCO) and the Dauphin sisal plantation. And they dispossessed large numbers in the northern regions of the country, perhaps tens of thousands. Devastating as these evictions were, though, they were exceptional within Haiti at large. It is also not clear even how much of the state land conceded to foreign companies was ever actually claimed or used, but it appears to have been a slim portion. According to Mats Lundahl, only "perhaps 28,000 hectares of American-owned plantations . . . [were established] between 1915 and 1927." Haiti began to grow sugar again under the U.S. occupation, but the industry remained small.[58]

In stark contrast to what occurred in the Dominican Republic, the United States also never followed through with any major legislative or legal steps to settle the country's murky system of ownership without clear land titles. In the late 1920s, U.S. authorities did take aerial photographs of Haiti to begin surveying landholdings as a first step to determining and issuing definitive titles and to facilitating land commerce. But the office where the photographic survey was filed burned down in what was perhaps an act of arson. Soon the U.S. military authorities abandoned efforts at surveying as well as new land legislation. One U.S. official warned against trying to push forward with these projects for fear it would antagonize "the mass of the Haitian people." Many rural Haitians surely anticipated that without surveyors, judges, and a government overall committed to helping small farmers, the settlement of inherently ambiguous questions of land ownership was not likely to favor them. Broadly speaking, the counter-plantation system in Haiti defeated the U.S. occupation dream of rebuilding a plantation economy in the country.[59]

Perhaps recognizing this, U.S. president Calvin Coolidge "advised Secretary of State Frank Kellogg on the imprudence of developing latifundia [giant estates]. He preferred that the 'natives' keep the land," recounts historian Brenda Gayle Plummer. But U.S. rulers were not going to offer support for small farmers. Had the U.S. occupation provided new irrigation, loans, and other infrastructural assistance, it could certainly have made small-scale agriculture more profitable, even if it were constrained by an increasingly high person-to-land ratio over time. But the occupation government failed to focus on rural needs and public works designed to boost agriculture among small farmers. Instead, it just collected onerous taxes from them more effectively than past governments had been able to.[60]

U.S. rulers did, though, oversee a different economic transition: the large-scale emigration of Haitian laborers to U.S. plantations elsewhere in the American Sugar Kingdom. Although some Haitians had migrated to Cuba before the occupation, between 1916 and 1930 the numbers skyrocketed, ranging between five thousand and thirty-five thousand per year (and unofficial migration added another perhaps 30 percent). In a system known then as "the slave trade," U.S. sugar corporations, particularly the colossal United Fruit Company, recruited inexpensive laborers in Haiti to take to their plantations in Cuba. This helped fuel the astonishing postslavery sugar expansion there during the first three decades of the twentieth century—from roughly one million to six million short tons. But Cuba was not the only place Haitian emigrants went. Haitian migration to the Dominican Republic, relatively small prior to the U.S. occupation, grew rapidly in the late 1910s and 1920s. Tens of thousands of Haitians traveled across the border in these years for work in the Dominican cane fields.[61]

Migration did not necessarily reflect a choice to abandon small farming for wage labor. Perhaps most saw plantation work abroad as a means, long-term, of maintaining or expanding family farms through temporary employment elsewhere. Wages were five times as high in Cuba as in Haiti, and many sent remittances home. Return migrants often used their earnings to purchase or lease land. The fact that labor conditions were abysmal helps explain, too, why a large portion of the emigrants to Cuba—almost all men—decided to return home. (Many others would be forcibly deported by the Cuban government after the Cuban economy went into decline in the late 1920s.)[62]

Certainly some Haitian migrants left home after being pushed off their land. But, Matthew Casey contends, we should not overstate this particular grievance. The primary regions of out-migration were not in areas where evictions took place, but rather areas of the South, including some where idle land remained. The U.S. occupation did, though, disrupt rural life in ways that exacerbated conditions in the countryside, spread insecurity, and helped push many Haitians to embrace the risks, sacrifices, and hopes of movement away from home. U.S. authorities more effectively enforced agricultural taxes, particularly taxes on goods bought and sold in local markets, adding to the burden of small farmers who had long, directly or indirectly, provided the lion's share of the country's internal revenues while getting virtually nothing in return from the state. And numerous Haitian writers at the time expressed fear that foreign land concessions and peasant evictions were the start of a process that would eventually transform a nation of small farmers into one of impoverished laborers and emigrants.[63]

In the short term, too, political leaders in Haiti were happy to make profits off migrants, especially since conditions in Haiti turned out to be resistant to plantation agriculture and foreign investment. Under U.S. rule, the government charged private recruiters of Haitian laborers a stiff licensing fee and imposed a tax on individuals leaving the country. This was a major source of revenue for the Haitian treasury during the U.S. occupation—and yet another way the rural poor were "footing the bill," in Michel-Rolph Trouillot's words, for a state that did nothing for them.[64]

Substantial emigration out of the Dominican Republic did not begin until the 1960s, and even without it, rural-urban migration remained modest into the 1950s. This difference corresponded with a deeper contrast between Haiti and the Dominican Republic overall. Most people in the Dominican countryside still had free access to ample land during the period of the U.S. occupation. The fact that such free and secure land access continued to prevail in much of the country may help account for the unwillingness of Dominicans at large to risk their lives and livelihood in an armed battle against the formidable U.S. regime. In the Dominican Republic's East, however, things were different. Here, U.S. sugar firms were able to expand under the occupation. And here the dispossessed, disaffected, and proletarianized were more ready to fight, even against terrible odds. The insurgents in the Dominican Republic thrived primarily in this region, and some 1,500 Marines were dispatched there to try to crush these guerrillas or "bandits," as U.S. officials generally identified them. Nationalist animosity to U.S. rule in the area drew on the preexisting war between a central state that had facilitated the expansion of the plantations and peasants accustomed to exploiting land and wildlife freely, a war that intensified as the policies and actions of the U.S. Military Government helped U.S. planters solidify their claims. Most of the rebels were "voluntary recruits from the riff-raff among the unemployed," one Marine reported, "those who were being forced from their lands, where they had lived for years, by the expansion of the Sugar Estates."[65]

In 1916, the basis for determining land ownership remained a deeply contested and momentous question in the Dominican Republic, and the property titles that did exist were often fraudulent. As had been the case in Cuba's east at the time of the first U.S. occupation there, probably most land ownership in the Dominican Republic was still based not on clear titles to a specific plot but rather on use rights to raise animals, hunt, farm, and fence off any unenclosed areas within a generally vast jointly owned, or *comunero*, estate. Furthermore, the large unoccupied areas within *comunero* estates were generally freely used by those without any titles at all. In the years just before the occupation, battles—both armed and in court—had been heating up between the sugar corporations and local squatters and landholders. The overseas U.S. rulers sought to intervene in this squatter war and to settle the profound question of what constituted the basis for legal ownership of land. But the actions taken by the U.S. Military Government regarding land rights and access in the eastern sugar region ended up fueling more armed resistance.[66]

From the onset, the U.S. occupation government sought to solidify a system of private property and begin the long process of clearing land titles in a newly created Superior Land Court. What the U.S. regime would fail to accomplish in Haiti would be its only major public policy reform in the Dominican Republic. The new land laws involved a sweeping set of changes: the establishment of a new property regime, including legislation that provided criteria and mechanisms for determining and firmly establishing land ownership. In 1920, Executive Order No. 511 effected a dramatic reversal of the prevailing bias in favor of *comunero* (joint) title owners over occupants in property adjudications and affirmed instead squatter or "prescription" rights—that is, property rights based solely on long-term, uninterrupted possession. This was a departure from the position taken by the U.S. government in Cuba, where such prescription rights were rejected in 1902.[67]

The U.S.-established property regime in the Dominican Republic had, at least at first, the potential to further the interests of the rural majority, many of whom occupied land to which they did not have titles. "It is the desire of the [U.S. Military] Government," the new legislation asserted, that the new property laws would benefit "above all . . . those small-scale independent possessors who are dedicated to productive labor, and strongly tied to their native soil." In fact, in 1917, the U.S. military governor reported to the U.S. secretary of the navy: "I am far from convinced that the large business corporations that are in Santo Domingo are of very great value to the Dominican people." He also objected to the fact that the sugar companies appeared to believe that the U.S. Military Government's "principal duty was to further the interests of Americans here."[68]

Yet despite such populist impulses among some within the U.S. Military Government, when it was time to write the laws for the new property regime, U.S. officials turned to the sugar companies' lawyers for help. And these lawyers reshaped the potentially equitable aspects of this legislation into policies that instead advanced the interests of their clients. The new law managed to privilege the land claims of U.S. sugar corporations—themselves rooted in putative long-term "possession"—over both everyday people exploiting the land without any formal titles to it and those who possessed *comunero* titles. That was because, while the majority of rural residents there were exploiting land without any formal titles, giant sugar companies were also technically squatters who possessed but did not formally own their land. And the definition of "possession" in the 1920 act favored the sugar companies over peasant claims, because it recognized almost any type of enclosure or land survey as constituting possession. These forms of possession were often the product of corrupt and abusive surveyors and notaries, a fact many Dominicans denounced and even U.S. administrators acknowledged. Enclosing and surveying land also required resources that peasants could scarcely afford.[69]

The majority of the peasantry, furthermore, had not been tied to any one plot of land for sufficient time to claim legal ownership on the basis of squatters' rights. The 1920 legislation did not provide the social equity it promised because most rural Dominicans still practiced shifting agriculture coupled with hunting and raising animals unenclosed on the open range, a practice one U.S. official described as an "unquestionable evil," though one with "many advocates" among Dominicans. So while Dominicans rarely had held the same plot long enough to claim property via prescription, the sugar companies could make such claims on the basis of enclosures that, ironically, encircled vast areas that they were not cultivating. Within these enclosures large numbers of Dominicans were still farming and raising animals. Not surprisingly, then, the law was seen, the U.S. Legation later reported, as "merely a Yankee trick to despoil the small landholders for the benefit of the sugar estates and other American interests."[70]

The sugar companies' consolidation of property rights had a seismic impact in the East, closing the land frontier in that region and dispossessing and displacing thousands of people during and after the U.S. occupation. With greater power and authority in their hands after 1920, sugar companies increasingly resorted to terror to eject people from lands the companies had claimed and now, more and more often, owned. In several infamous incidents, corporations set fire to entire villages in order to evict residents. In one town, the houses of reportedly four hundred residents were burned to push occupants off the land. An official from the U.S.-owned South Porto Rico Sugar Company was arrested for ordering the burning of two other villages where 150 families resided in 1921 after notifying residents that they had twenty-four hours to evacuate the area. Despite his arrest, the occupants were never allowed to return.[71]

One of the triggers for the U.S. government's invasion of the Dominican Republic had been threats to U.S. investments from armed bands and other forms of statelessness seen as perilous to U.S. economic and strategic interests. Yet the violent monopolization of land by the sugar companies in the East and the state violence deployed by U.S. rulers generated more and more recruits for antistate armed groups. These rebels gained popular appeal as residents watched the U.S.-owned sugar industry steadily enclose and evict occupants from the once vast untamed frontier and open range that had previously been theirs for the exploiting. Opposition to the Marine invasion transformed long-standing antistate bands into nationalist "patriots." Whatever ambivalence Dominicans at large may have had about the armed bands, they were increasingly accepted as "revolutionaries" who were part of the anti-U.S. occupation alliance. One Marine officer in 1917 reported that all Dominicans—including the rural authorities—"hate us so that they will not give us information of any value" about the rebels. In one battle with the Americans in 1918, the insurgents cried out that they were not bandits, or *gavilleros*, but rather "revolutionists."[72]

In the face of covert civilian support for the guerrillas, U.S. troops' tactics and actions became more brutal and arbitrary. Marines often fired at anyone who appeared to be fleeing from them, even at those who were unarmed. "People who are not bandits do not flee at the approach of Marines," declared one officer to rationalize these attacks. Another officer warned their soldiers only that they should "exercise extreme caution in firing on fleeing parties which contain women and children." One Marine protested to his commander in 1918 because his captain was ordering arrests "indiscriminately": "His policy sooner or later would have found nearly everyone in jail." U.S. troops also burned the homes of suspected "bandit families" and destroyed their *conucos*, or small farms. At one point, the Marines required hundreds of residents in guerrilla-active areas to abandon their homes and move into U.S.-controlled military camps—much like those U.S. soldiers had established in the Philippines and the Spanish had in Cuba following the 1895 independence revolution. Insufficient food made life in the camps precarious, and many fled despite the dangers of doing so.[73]

U.S. troops also turned to torture in their efforts to defeat guerrilla opponents of the occupation. These activities exceeded official U.S. policy, and some U.S. officers and soldiers were arrested by the U.S. Military Government for regularly torturing both prisoners and civilians. Government records detail U.S. military personnel beating, maiming, and killing their victims. Reports of such practices led to a Senate investigation in 1921. It revealed cases in which individuals were subjected to "water torture," during which liquid was forced continuously down their throats until they were on the verge of drowning. Marines were also found to have deployed sexual abuse and humiliation and engaged in other atrocities, such as that experienced by one eighty-year-old man who was reportedly tied to a horse's tail and dragged around at full speed. Those subjected to torture were prisoners and civilians suspected of aiding the rebels, possessing information about them, or refusing to turn over weapons. Some soldiers were found guilty and punished by the military courts, and at times commanders ordered their subordinates to cease practices such as letting prisoners escape so as to have an excuse to shoot them. In many other cases, charges of torture and other forms of abuse were dismissed without investigation or punishment.[74]

The U.S. Marines deployed similar tactics across the border in Haiti, terrorizing the population in the U.S. war against the *cacos*. Many villages were burned to the ground, and civilians suspected of sympathizing with the rebels were beaten and killed by Marines, including market women. "Practically indiscriminate killing of the natives," one Marine explained, or "open season," prevailed in areas where guerrillas were believed to be living amid the population at large. In Port-au-Prince, where a curfew was imposed, orders were given to shoot "on sight" anyone "out of doors after nine o'clock, whose behavior makes him seem like a sympathizer with *Caco* rebels," a shockingly open-ended rubric for permission to kill. Also, prisoners of war were summarily shot. That was "ordinary routine," a commander reported, in part to limit the problem of overcrowded jails. The Marines produced monthly casualty reports, which for one eight-month period between 1919 and 1920 registered a staggering 3,071 Haitians killed by U.S. soldiers. These figures reflect both the strength of popular Haitian resistance to the occupation and the enormous human cost of U.S. military rule. Referring sarcastically to U.S. "approaches to 'civilization,'" the French vice-consul reported on numerous acts of torture, murder, and other atrocities by the United States against those suspected of hiding knowledge about the rebels' whereabouts or even for petty crimes. "It is not surprising" under these conditions that "the peasants would rather die fighting than submit."[75]

Despite hearing detailed testimony of Marine atrocities given by Haitian and Dominican witnesses, the Senate evidently accepted the soldiers' defense that their actions were a legitimate and necessary response to the supposed brutality and backwardness of Haitians and Dominicans. U.S. officials also dismissed Dominican charges against the Marines within an overall framework of white supremacy that they brought with them to the island. When a U.S. soldier was accused by a Dominican of killing several men, for instance, the complainant's testimony was rejected because it came from "an individual of a different race . . . who has no conception of honor as we understand it." According to the U.S. investigator, the "negro race" could not be trusted because it had "a totally different conception of right and wrong." U.S. officials also dismissed charges of rape in racist fashion. "Rape, I believe, implies a lack of consent," one official in Haiti stated, but "I never heard of a case where consent was lacking in Haiti's black belt." Haitians, of course, saw things differently. The violation and abuse of women in Haiti by the U.S. Marines remained a salient part of historical memory of the occupation. Marines also often referred to Dominicans as "the niggers." Dominicans recognized these racialized fault lines and frequently referred to U.S. occupiers as "the whites." "Eradicate the White Blood of [from] the Republic," Dominicans shouted at a 1921 anti-occupation protest. In the 1990s, many in the East still recalled the occupation as when "the whites invaded."[76]

In the Dominican Republic, resistance continued, despite—and in some ways because of—the intense U.S. military repression. In fact, independence rebels were acting with ever-greater boldness, U.S. authorities reported. The role of the Marines' repression in sustaining and animating the resistance was stressed by Julio Peynado, an elite Dominican closely tied to the sugar industry: "When someone . . . was killed, his brother joined the *gavilleros*, to get revenge on the Marines. . . . Some joined the ranks inspired by patriotism, but most of them joined the ranks inspired by hate, fear, or revenge." Peynado made an analogous argument about the U.S. reconcentration camps boosting the insurgency because of the widespread civilian suffering and resentment they caused. And in both Haiti and the Dominican Republic, rural armed resistance, and the violence used to suppress it, helped to nourish increasing protests in urban areas. "The people as a whole, are against the Military Government," U.S. military leaders in Santo Domingo reported in 1921. Protests were breaking out openly condemning the U.S. occupation.[77]

In the Dominican Republic, support among the population at large for the rebels grew across the country, and for the first time an alliance formed, however tacit and uneasy, between the guerrillas and the urban "nationalist" movement. At first, urban anti-occupation activists had cast the armed rebels as antistate strongmen and gangs and disavowed armed resistance. In time, however, some began supporting the guerrillas financially. They also supplied arms, provided cover, and offered intelligence. At the same time, rural insurgents made their political character more explicit. They circulated political programs, demanded unqualified independence from the United States, and outlined policy goals, such as the expansion of public education.[78]

At this point, over a thousand Dominican troops and civilians had been killed or wounded in the East, with a reported hundred U.S. casualties. Large numbers of U.S. troops had been dispatched, the local population had been herded off and concentrated in military encampments, and practically every resident in large areas of the East had been arrested and held for questioning. As they had in Haiti earlier, U.S. forces had also brought in an air squadron with 139 men and six bombers. A few rebels were killed when they ventured out into open terrain, and the sounds of the bombers must have been frightening to the population below, but the squadron was unable to locate, and thereby attack, guerrillas in the hills and woods. So, despite concerted U.S. efforts, the occupation forces and the rebels remained at a stalemate in 1921. The U.S. military was also unable to stop guerrilla activity or raids on the sugar companies. Attacks on the plantations continued to yield thousands of dollars that the insurgents could use in their war against the "whites" who had invaded their land. U.S. surveyors mapping out territory claimed by the sugar companies were also attacked. In 1921, one of the few former Dominican officials who had initially backed the occupation nonetheless described U.S. rule as "five years of failure."[79]

Together with armed resistance, the international diplomatic and press campaign spearheaded by Dominican exiles succeeded in pressuring U.S.

leaders to begin negotiations for a withdrawal. In 1921, Washington entered into discussion with nationalist leaders to orchestrate an end to the occupation, provided certain U.S. objectives could be achieved first. This was a seismic shift from just two years earlier when the U.S. military governor had announced that he expected the occupation to continue indefinitely. With the promise of U.S. withdrawal now on the table, the guerrillas too were ready to negotiate. Doing so was no longer a surrender to foreign rule. When the U.S. military regime offered amnesty to rebels and even sought to secure jobs for them, insurgents began to lay down their arms. In 1922, Dominican and U.S. leaders agreed to establish a provisional Dominican government that would organize elections to be held in 1924. Once the elected government was in place, U.S. troops would end their rule over the country. But the U.S. government retained significant power over the Dominican government: for another nearly twenty years, it continued to appropriate the majority of the Dominican state's chief source of revenue, tariffs—earmarked for servicing the country's external debt—as well as to control tariff levels and the contraction of any new foreign loans.[80]

The U.S. withdrawal was a victory for the anti-occupation rebel forces in the Dominican Republic. In the final months of the U.S. occupation, elections were held, and Horacio Vásquez was freely and democratically elected for a term that was supposed to last four years without the possibility of reelection. On July 12, 1924, the U.S. military dictatorship ended with great public celebration. For the fourth time in its history, the Dominican Republic became independent from a foreign power. Cuban troops traveled to the Dominican Republic to participate in the festivities.[81]

This was a contrast to what happened in Haiti, which would remain occupied until 1934. Here Marines had been able to crush most of the resistance fourteen years earlier, in large part by recruiting a native armed force called the Gendarmerie, commanded by U.S. Marine officers. Joining the Gendarmerie offered poorer Haitian men without sufficient land an alternative to plantation labor in Haiti or emigration to Cuba or the Dominican Republic—however unpalatable it might be to serve U.S. officers occupying one's country or potentially to face in combat friends and even relatives who were rebels. Already by 1916, this new national military had recruited 1,500 men, and its numbers would rise to 2,153 by 1931. Their service proved pivotal in suppressing the rural insurrection. In 1919, two Marines together with several Haitian *gendarmes* managed to disguise themselves as rebels and sneak into Péralte's headquarters, where one of the Marines shot the rebel leader at point-blank range. The rebellion continued nonetheless, but the following year Péralte's successor was also killed, and the leaderless rebellion was crushed soon after.[82]

Although the guerrilla war ended in 1920, Haitians continued their opposition to U.S. rule. Taking inspiration from the rural uprising, urban anti-occupation movements celebrated the slain Péralte as a martyr to the cause of the Haitian nation. A mass protest movement in 1929 triggered by a student strike and encompassing a wide spectrum of society spelled the beginning of the end. The strike coincided with demonstrations by some 1,500 small farmers and others near the southwestern town of Les Cayes. Many were small-scale sugar producers with grievances against HASCO. Others had grievances against the occupation government and its lack of support for small coffee and sugar farmers' interests. As they headed toward Les Cayes, a Marine detachment took objection to the peaceful protesters and opened fire on them, killing at least twelve, perhaps as many as twenty-five, and wounding many more. The massacre drew international condemnation and sowed doubts in the United States as well about U.S. rule, especially amid this clear show of cross-class opposition—from elite students to small farmers. "[When] will you give us back our government?" a Haitian journalist asked members of a U.S. investigative committee sent to the island the following year.[83]

In the face of political and continuing economic costs, U.S. leaders were convinced it was time to end their overseas rule and to accept Haiti's "second independence," as Haitian leaders now referred to it. The successful creation of the new armed forces, renamed the Garde d'Haiti in 1927—now able to maintain control without the Marines' support—was the necessary, though evidently not sufficient, condition for U.S. withdrawal. The Garde created a permanent conduit for continuing U.S. influence in the political realm in Haiti. It would be the single enduring institutional legacy of the occupation, and it would mark the end to the century-old stalemate between the central state and the rural nation.[84]

In the Dominican Republic, U.S. authorities had also created a new armed body similarly named the Dominican National Guard—the Guardia—to replace the existing Dominican military forces. Although established in 1917, as long as the occupation appeared indefinite, U.S. authorities had been unwilling or unable to develop fully the Dominican force and instead continued to rely on U.S. troops. Brigadier General Harry Lee scoffed in 1921 that still the Guardia's "value as a military force was nil," given its poor training and organization. But once they had decided to withdraw, U.S. leaders got to work "organizing a native constabulary in order to ensure peace and order."[85]

Prior to the agreement for a U.S. withdrawal, the Guardia had remained small. Nothing close to the authorized numbers for troops was ever reached, and a significant portion of those who enlisted soon deserted. Recruitment was stymied by the widespread opposition to U.S. rule among Dominicans at large. Those who joined the force were seen by many others as traitors to the nation and had to bear insults such as being called "Americans" or "pimps." Furthermore, while some Dominicans were enticed by the promise of upward mobility, they were barred from officer positions, at least those above second lieutenant. U.S. officers in Santo Domingo were dead-set against working with Dominican officers, and the U.S. minister and the State Department similarly insisted that the military be commanded by "white officers and not Dominicans." This refusal all but guaranteed that the Guardia would not be able to recruit better-off Dominicans. The troops were made up almost exclusively instead of those from the lower-class majority (including immigrants working on U.S. sugar plantations). For them, the Guardia represented one of few options for decent work and possible advancement, and for those who stuck it out until a U.S. withdrawal, perhaps movement up the officer ranks.[86]

As the end of the occupation approached, the U.S. military leadership in the Dominican Republic was "given unofficial instructions to 'lighten' the Guardia a little," because the army "was a little too black." The implicit goals of the order were probably both to gain elite Dominican acceptance of the Guardia and to leave in place officers who, on the basis of their race and color, were imagined to be more likely to abide by U.S. interests. Given the small number of people who were not of color in the Dominican Republic, the U.S. goal here may have been to advance lighter-skinned persons of African descent, if not people of entirely European lineage.[87]

But U.S. efforts to whiten the Guardia and put it in more elite hands ran up against the structures established during its first five years, as well as the demographic reality of the Dominican Republic. When the U.S. Marines were forced by their anticipated departure to open up officer positions to Dominicans, this in fact provided the space for men from the popular classes—generally persons of African descent without much means or education—to occupy even high leadership positions. The Dominican elite was a small and modest white upper class that had sought for centuries largely in vain to control an independent peasantry mostly of African descent. It remained one of the weakest and poorest in Latin America and the

Caribbean. Now the elite suffered a new blow. The most powerful and structurally sound institution in place after the U.S. occupation, the Guardia, was not in upper-class hands. The most dramatic manifestation of military control falling out of elite hands—almost immediately after the occupation—was the rise of the country's future dictator Rafael Trujillo. He was a literate but little-educated, lower-middle-class man of partial African descent. He joined the Guardia in 1919 as a second lieutenant, became a company commander in 1924, and became the Dominican military's commander-in-chief three years later. In 1930, he seized control of the country to embark on three decades of despotic rule.[88]

After Occupation: A State beyond Challenge

The U.S. government had achieved its primary objective in Haiti and the Dominican Republic: the consolidation of powerful U.S-built and -linked armed forces. The scale of weaponry, training, organization, and centralization in both countries were a far cry from the weak and regionally divided forces that prevailed prior to the occupations. The Haitian and Dominican states would never again be overpowered by regional strongmen and rebels—a stark contrast to the almost annual changes of government they produced in the pre-U.S.-occupation years. Both governments were now as capable as they were willing to advance U.S. strategic and business interests on their territory. The other nations that U.S. forces occupied for prolonged periods in the early twentieth century—namely, Nicaragua and Cuba—would see similar outcomes in this respect. All of these states would remain vulnerable only to overthrow by means of the military itself or to the most doubtful of developments: large-scale revolution reaching deep across society and political divides.[89]

In the Dominican Republic, two related factors boosted the military's new power over society following U.S. rule. First, the nation's military no longer faced a highly armed population. Second, the country's military might was expanded through the development of national infrastructure. Prior to U.S. rule, there had been few roads in the countryside suitable for cars. Travel was possible by foot, horse, or mule. Nor had there been any real "telephone, telegraph, radio or other field communications," as one U.S. commander complained in 1921. The U.S. Military Government had constructed highways and developed telecommunication. As was the case in Haiti, hundreds of miles of roads had been built with international loans and on the backs of the rural poor, who, lacking funds to pay the road tax demanded by the U.S.

regime, had been compelled to meet the obligation through public labor. The Dominican countryside was linked to Santo Domingo as never before through the development of three main highways to the north, the south, and the east—doubling their length in just five years and reducing transportation times to a fraction of what they had been. The new infrastructure permitted rapid troop movement and almost instantaneous military communication. All this greatly augmented state knowledge and reach across the country and into spaces whose isolation had until then facilitated local power. It also increased the potential for commercial agriculture and for the imagining of a national as opposed to regional community.[90]

On the economic front, the impact of occupation was less obvious. As we saw, despite twenty years of occupation, U.S. rulers had for the most part not succeeded in implanting new plantations in Haiti except for a few companies. The depth of rural resistance, anchored in the ongoing counter-plantation system, had stymied such projects even in the face of military and political domination. In the Dominican Republic, foreign-owned sugar plantations had already made significant inroads prior to the occupation and then grew further under the U.S. military regime's land policies. Between 1905 and 1926, production soared sixfold from fifty-three thousand to four hundred thousand short tons. But sugar cultivation was still limited mostly to one eastern province, and the country's output remained far smaller than the plantation economies found in other parts of the far-flung and expanding U.S. sugar empire. Even though it was five times the size of Puerto Rico, the Dominican Republic produced substantially less sugar. By 1929 only an estimated sixth of the country's area had been surveyed by the state, and less still had completed the process of title adjudication. The process of determining property rights had hardly begun outside the sugar zones. Even in 1940, sugar would be grown on less than one-tenth of the country's cultivated land. The heart of the U.S. sugar empire remained Cuba, which produced almost six million short tons in 1925.[91]

But politically, occupation transformed nations in the U.S. empire in ways that were made crystal clear, when, in 1930, the head of the new U.S.-made army, Rafael Trujillo, stole a presidential election through military intimidation and violence. At the time, Trujillo lacked any independent political base and derived his power solely from command of the powerful U.S.-created army. The U.S. foreign minister, Charles Curtis, worried now about what the United States had created through its occupation, "a well-drilled standing army" whose goal was to "be a firm support for the President and prevent uprising against him." But General Trujillo had understood "the power which laid in his hands," and was now instead deploying "it for the purpose of putting himself in the Presidency." Curtis warned the U.S. secretary of state presciently: "If General Trujillo succeeds in his desire to be President, it seems likely that the Dominican Republic will have to endure a prolonged military dictatorship." The acting U.S. secretary of state, however, made clear to Curtis that the U.S. government would recognize a President Trujillo and "maintain the most friendly relations with him and his government." They would "recognize Trujillo even were the elections palpably fraudulent or the result due to intimidation by the military forces," because, he added without recognizing the irony, "the Department desires to avoid as much as possible the possibility of any intervention or interference in Dominican affairs."[92]

Curtis continued to question this State Department plan, denouncing Trujillo for "violating the liberties of the Dominican people with a weapon forged by the Military Occupation." This was, though, seen in Washington as no more than tolerable collateral damage for the political stability and submission that U.S. leaders sought in the independent Caribbean. At the same time, the British foreign minister reported that U.S. corporations were "supporting General Trujillo" and "using influence in Washington" on his behalf. U.S. Marines and Navy officers were also backing Trujillo. This support was built around personal connections. Major Thomas Watson was in Santo Domingo in the fall of 1930. Since training Trujillo during the occupation, Watson had maintained a close relationship with the new Dominican ruler and was now lunching with him every day. This was precisely how U.S. occupations and their military-building projects were intended to work, forging enduring institutional networks between the U.S. and Dominican armed forces so as to maintain U.S. influence.[93]

After the election, President Trujillo quickly imposed "order" by repressing rebellion and dissent, at the cost of many lives. Several opponents took to the hills to mobilize for armed struggle against the new dictator, much as they had done in the past, but they were soon crushed by Trujillo's new and vastly more powerful armed forces. Trujillo also ordered the assassination of hundreds of his opponents during the first year of his rule. Despite these horrors, Curtis now fell in line with the State Department's position and praised the dictatorship for maintaining "the strictest order" throughout "the length and breadth of the country."[94]

The stated reason for Washington's immediate backing of Trujillo had been President Herbert Hoover's newly proclaimed policy of "nonintervention" in Latin American affairs. There was also no commercial or strategic reason for U.S. intervention in the Dominican Republic at the time. And in any case, the U.S. government could always intervene in practice via its behind-the-scenes influence over the U.S.-created militaries. The rise of Trujillo made powerfully clear that the U.S. occupations had established an effective apparatus of indirect overseas power.[95]

The power of this new configuration was also made clear in Cuba in 1933. In that year, a popular uprising began demanding better wages and improved labor conditions. Workers found common cause not only with students and other groups but also with disaffected soldiers in the Cuban army. Junior officers had been demanding, to no avail, higher wages and more opportunities for advancement into what was still an elite white club of commissioned officers. Together, these forces carried out a joint civil-military coup and formed a new self-described "revolutionary" government. The new administration immediately revoked the despised Platt Amendment, ending the island's protectorate status imposed under U.S. occupation in 1902. The government also moved quickly to limit the workday, establish a minimum wage, reduce utility rates, and extend suffrage rights to women. And it promised agrarian reform through the distribution of public lands.[96]

These reforms were similar to ones then being enacted in the United States under President Franklin Roosevelt, and they transpired in the supposed new era of "nonintervention," which Roosevelt named for his administration the "good neighbor policy." Yet in contrast to its rapid recognition of Trujillo, Washington refused to recognize the new government and instead quickly began conspiring to overthrow its leadership, which Assistant Secretary of State Sumner Welles denounced as "communistic." That these U.S. machinations coincided with a policy of supposed "nonintervention" suggests how narrow the room for maneuver was for independent Caribbean nations.[97]

Cuba's new military leadership, headed by Fulgencio Batista, quickly turned on its civilian allies and toppled the postcoup civilian government. Batista took control of the state and would retain it for most of the next twenty-five years under one guise or another: first as an increasingly reformist military ruler, briefly as a quasi-democratic president in the early 1940s, and finally as a dictator with increasingly few backers in the 1950s.[98]

Like Batista's first incarnation, during which he would eventually ally with the Cuban Communist party, other Caribbean dictators who arose out of histories of U.S. intervention and domination were often more populist and even nationalistic than might be assumed. The Trujillo regime, for instance, was a product not only of the U.S.-made Guardia but, paradoxi-cally, of a postoccupation nationalist-populist wing of the lettered class that had grown in hostile reaction to U.S. hegemony and sugar plantations. Although cane fields dominated only a small part of the Dominican Repub-lic, their spread had fueled a reaction among political figures, civil ser-vants, and intellectuals against any further expansion of the mostly U.S.-owned sugar industry. The title of a 1927 editorial in one of the coun-try's leading newspapers condensed the sentiment: "The Alarming Menace of the Sugar Mills: The Dominican Republic and Haiti, Once Two Sovereign States, Are Becoming Two Yankee Colonies." Another journalist warned that measures needed to be taken so that "the octopus of conquest cannot penetrate in the guise of foreign capital." Many of the nationalist-populist figures from the country's best and brightest were recruited by Trujillo, al-beit often by force, into the state during the early years of Trujillo's reign. Once there, they helped shape the new regime's policies.[99]

Under the guidance of such advisers and seeking popular backing to strengthen his rule, Trujillo orchestrated a massive land distribution pro-gram. His regime also facilitated the awarding of property titles to land re-cipients and others based on "prescription" or "squatter" rights. This benefited a substantial portion of the rural population. The state also built local roads and irrigation supporting small farming and blanketed the coun-try in a discourse of "respect" for "hard-working" rural folk.[100]

Trujillo's agrarian reforms were of significant benefit to most rural Do-minicans relative to the alternatives they faced in 1930s. But these reforms also represented a profound compromise for most. The country's vast un-tamed and uncultivated areas (*los montes*) had for centuries provided much economic freedom and subsistence security through small, generally itin-erant, farming, hunting, and raising of animals on the open range. Now, though, expanding commercial agriculture and the issuing of definitive land titles in the eastern sugar regions threatened ominous changes in land use across the country. Trujillo offered to those most hurt, or potentially hurt, by these changes a compromise: continued access to land, but on a single, sedentary plot, without the collective pasture or hunting of the past, and with a push, where possible, to surplus production. If not at first, distributed lands would become the recipients' property over time if they continued to cultivate it, often on the basis of prescription rights. Typically, distrib-uted land did not have to be expropriated from anyone with clear titles, given that the majority of the country was still *comunero* or state land. But in areas where the government built irrigation, it did seize much private (or privately claimed) land, taking a fourth of all cultivated and half of all idle areas served by new state canals. Vast areas of excellent land thus became available for redistribution.[101]

Trujillo's government promised, in effect, to mediate rural transformations through a focus on small farming. This approach led to impressive growth in agricultural production beyond sugar. And the Dominican Republic continued to meet most of its own food needs.[102] The benefits of the regime's policies were available to those who acquiesced to Trujillo's domination, while those who resisted faced possibly lethal repression. The result was a three-decade-long authoritarian regime with little open opposition until its twilight.

Despite the significant degree of popular acceptance Trujillo gained through his rural policies, he simultaneously terrified the population with the regime's extreme violence and widespread surveillance. Hundreds were killed for resisting the regime's dictates, for purported links to dissenters, or even for being connected by friendship or family to a supposed enemy of the state. Trujillo also constantly sexually coerced and violated women from all classes of society, whether from families of modest means in rural towns or those of important Dominican officials. By far the most massive and infamous act of state violence under Trujillo—and in all Dominican and Haitian history since the era of European conquest—occurred in 1937, when Trujillo commanded the Dominican military to massacre all Haitians and Dominicans of Haitian descent living in the northern frontier provinces. Around fifteen thousand people, whose families had been living peacefully in this region for generations, were slaughtered over the course of a few days, while large numbers of refugees fled for their lives across the border. As a result of this genocide, Trujillo destroyed a frontier world and local communities formed by generations of Haitian and Dominican integration and movement back-and-forth across the border—a world that had once facilitated, for instance, the cross-border collaboration between Haitian and Dominican opponents of the U.S. occupation on the two sides of the island. In fact, the state's inability to control and tax the ongoing movement of goods, people, arms, and revolutionaries across this porous border and throughout this bicultural and transnational frontier was one of the forces driving the massacre. The regime no longer had to tolerate such spaces of statelessness, thanks to the powerful new Dominican military.[103]

In every country that the U.S. government occupied for long periods in this era, a new military was built that remained a key political force. And in the Dominican Republic and Cuba, as well as Nicaragua, leaders of the

U.S.-created armed forces used their power to seize the presidency and become extremely powerful and enduring tyrants. Postoccupation Haiti, though, was somewhat different. Here, a mixture of authoritarianism and democracy characterized the two decades after U.S. withdrawal, with an increasingly interventionist military determining who the president would, would not, or would no longer be. But Haiti's comparable long-ruling tyrant, François Duvalier, would not rise up through the military. Rather, he was a professional, respected both for his work as a doctor in the countryside and as an intellectual, who ran for president in 1957. Duvalier was, though, the preferred candidate of the military, which forced an opposing popular leftist candidate into exile and killed hundreds of his followers. Continued close links between the Haitian and U.S. militaries meant that Duvalier also had the open support of the U.S. Embassy. After winning the election, decisively defeating the candidate of the elite—with probably some voter fraud—Duvalier quickly turned to violence to repress his perceived opponents. He gradually abandoned all pretense of democracy and in 1964 established a new constitution that made him president-for-life. He and then his son would rule Haiti for a total of twenty-nine years.[104]

Much like Trujillo, Duvalier cast himself as a populist who was deeply committed to helping the rural masses of Haiti and representing them in the national government. He spoke of improving the lives of small farmers through land distribution, public irrigation, and tax relief. He broadcast a discourse of "social justice" and the reduction of regional and class inequality. Yet he never carried out a significant land reform policy or developed an agricultural policy that helped the rural population in substantial ways, as Trujillo did. Duvalier was constrained by land scarcity, lacking the highly favorable conditions for agrarian reform—large areas of uncultivated land and woods with no clear ownership—that the Trujillo regime had in the Dominican Republic. There was, though, still much that could have been done, certainly attempted, to support most Haitians' aspirations to live as independent farmers. But Duvalier, like the governments before him, including the U.S. occupation regime, did nothing to change or to improve conditions for small farming (nor for the economy overall). Instead, in contrast to the Trujillo years in the Dominican Republic, Haiti's total GNP dropped under Duvalier. And coffee production declined by almost a third by 1967.[105]

The Duvalier years in Haiti were more similar to the Trujillo era in the Dominican Republic in terms of state terror. All Haitians lived under the threat of imprisonment, torture, or death for criticizing the regime or even failing to laud it when and where that was expected. Some estimate that thousands or perhaps even tens of thousands were killed for political reasons during the Duvalier dynasty. Duvalierist violence seems also to have been, in some cases, deliberately random to inspire greater terror: "A tally of its casualties would count more scapegoats, more victims of sheer arbitrariness, of accidents of birth, or of presence at inopportune times and places than opponents who represented any real menace to the regime," writes Trouillot. No groups were immune to the violence—not religious clerics, not children. This included a seemingly limitless range of torture and terror, including rape, sexual humiliation, and coercive sexual relationships.[106]

Unlike other long post-U.S. occupation dictators, Duvalier's control rested less on the U.S.-made military than on newly created paramilitary forces. In Haiti, the dictator organized a mass civilian militia that became far larger than the army. He also established a secret police force. The two bodies overlapped, and members of both were popularly known as Tonton Makouts (named after a menacing figure in Haitian folklore who steals children in his *makout*, or bag), even though this term was used at other times to refer solely to the secret police. Both forces enjoyed status and power that placed them above the law. With tens of thousands of members, the mass militia served as an effective counterbalance to the army; much to the chagrin of U.S. officials and, of course, the traditional military leadership, which, although still powerful under Duvalier, had lost its monopoly on the means of state violence.[107]

According to historian Marvin Chochotte, Makouts or *milisyen* (militia members) functioned both to forestall potential threats to Duvalier from the U.S.-linked army and to control the population. Following orders from above, the mass militia was responsible for crushing a number of rural rebellions. Makouts received no direct compensation but were endowed with local power and authority, including the ability to extort, steal from, and abuse fellow members of their community with relative impunity. The dictator essentially created a vast network of local bosses beholden to him, who used their status largely at their own discretion and for their own ends. Although Makouts typically used their power for repressive purposes, some also threw their weight behind popular and progressive ones at times—for instance fighting dispossession of squatters or assisting workers on strike.[108]

Duvalier's mass militia was open to all, without regard to education, income, gender, or age. It offered a perverse form of upward mobility to ordinary Haitians that helps explain its successful recruitment of vast numbers—a type of democratization of the terror apparatus. Perhaps having no fiscal or other resources for carrying out promised populist policies of rural "social justice," Chochotte hypothesizes, Duvalier saw the paramilitary forces as a form of populism—however perverse—and the only political base within reach. Trouillot similarly explains: "Many among the urban and rural poor joined . . . not just because it was a 'genuine [economic] elevation' . . . but also because for the first time they were becoming citizens—acknowledged members of the nation." The increasingly miserable rural economy under Duvalier added to the desperation to be elevated and to become "citizens" in this way.[109]

A few years after Duvalier was elected in Haiti, Trujillo's regime began to crumble. At this point, Trujillo was no longer the rural populist figure he had been in his first decades of rule. In the 1950s, the dictator himself forcibly bought out most of the U.S. sugar companies in the Dominican Republic and expanded the cane fields into new areas of the country, to the great harm of many exploiting these lands. Some also considered that he had gone "mad," even violently attacking members of his regime's erstwhile strong ally the Catholic Church and by 1960 arresting hundreds of mostly middle-class opponents in the cities and large towns. As opposition and outrage spread, a group led by a disgruntled out-of-favor military leader and the secretary of the armed forces began to conspire against Trujillo, sharing their plans with the U.S. Consulate and the CIA. In 1961, following an ambush of his unaccompanied Chevrolet and a dramatic gun battle with the sixty-nine-year-old dictator and his chauffeur, Trujillo was assassinated.[110]

The regime's leaders tried to maintain power under the command of the figurehead president, Joaquín Balaguer, and the dictator's eldest son, Ramfis. They succeeded for six months, for the army overall, at first, remained loyal to the Trujillo family. But soon a group of military leaders rebelled, and the Trujillos and Balaguer were forced into exile. The resistance to the regime also now included the U.S. government, significant elements of the armed forces, and much of civil society. Democratic elections were scheduled for the following year.[111]

Two years earlier, U.S. leaders had seen the unprecedented happen in Cuba: a guerrilla uprising had managed to defeat the U.S.-created, -trained, and -armed military and the long U.S.-supported dictator Fulgencio Batista in that relatively large Caribbean nation. Over the course of the next three years, the victors of this revolution would establish a new socialist regime sharply at odds with U.S. business and subsequently strategic interests. U.S.

officials now hoped to forestall a similar outcome in the Dominican Republic by ending Trujillo's out-of-control rule before it produced a similar large-scale rebellion. U.S. leaders had analogous fears about the Duvalier regime generating revolution and began aiding a group of Haitian exiles who had vowed, however improbably, to topple both Duvalier and Castro. However, after Duvalier promised to support U.S. positions in international bodies, including the 1962 swing vote expelling Cuba from the Organization of American States, the United States reversed course and began sending additional aid to Duvalier.[112]

How had the unprecedented happened in Cuba, a revolution overthrowing the most powerful state in the overseas U.S. empire, one saturated with U.S. economic interests, aid, and political influence? How had this been achieved by a small number of revolutionaries within just a few years? And how and why did the new revolutionary regime become a radically socialist one just ninety miles from the United States—a seismic change comparable only to the Haitian Revolution in the Caribbean?

We turn now to the remarkable story of the Cuban insurrection and of the powerful forces leading to almost lightning-fast change after the revolution's triumph. Lying at the center of this history is, here too, popular resistance to the plantation economy as well as U.S. control, popular desires to farm one's own land, and popular demands for better wages and conditions if and when obliged to labor in the cane fields. We will see, too, those same forces at work in the Dominican Republic and Haiti after the triumph of the Cuban Revolution and the collapse of the Trujillo and Duvalier regimes. The struggle over plantation agriculture, agrarian reform, and U.S. empire would continue to play a key role in violent political dramas in the independent Caribbean.

5   The Making of the Cuban Revolution

··

The rebel camp was hidden in the midst of a dense tangle of century-old *marabú* trees. It sat just a quarter mile from an army garrison. The trees, however, created a refuge, so that the insurgents inside could not be seen. The *marabú* tree had been brought to Cuba from Africa in the nineteenth century as a way to create living fences to surround cattle. It is covered in thorns, sticking out "from the trunk, the branches, and even . . . the tree's exposed roots." A thicket of such trees is called a *marabuzal*. It was the genius of the rebel leader Celia Sánchez, from the mill town of Pilón in the eastern province of Oriente, to understand that a *marabuzal*, when formed by mature tall trees, was the perfect place to train recruits in secret and to prepare to send them to the nearby mountains, the Sierra Maestra. There they would join rebels fighting to overthrow the dictatorship of Fulgencio Batista and to create a new society. The rebels were able to gain a foothold in the mountains of eastern Cuba in 1956 thanks to leaders like Sánchez, people who knew the terrain and who knew who could be trusted, and people who were themselves trusted by small farmers and squatters living in the region. Sánchez in particular not only helped link the urban fighters, who always made up a large part of the rebel forces, with the guerrillas in the mountains. She also helped connect those rural guerrillas to the local population, many of whom quickly came to see the rebel group as a vehicle for their own aspirations. It was that alliance that ultimately made the Cuban Revolution possible.[1]

This revolution was the most dramatic event in the twentieth-century Caribbean and probably the most radical challenge to the social and economic order in the region since the Haitian Revolution. It had deep roots, stretching back to Cuba's struggles for independence and long-standing battles over land. But the insurgency began in a less-than-triumphant fashion when, on July 26, 1953, a small, lightly armed rebel group led by a young lawyer named Fidel Castro Ruz attacked the second-largest military barracks in Cuba, the Moncada in Santiago de Cuba. The rebels hoped to seize weapons and distribute them to insurgents, and in the process win a symbolic victory that demonstrated the vulnerability of the Batista dictatorship.

Above all, Castro said afterward, they hoped to inspire popular support for resistance and rebellion, even if they failed in their military mission. And fail they did. They were discovered before they attacked the barracks and were quickly defeated, with several killed and the rest forced to retreat. Over the next few days, some seventy rebels were taken prisoner, tortured, and executed. As word of the killings spread, the bishop of Santiago and other notables from Oriente Province demanded an end to the slaughter of the prisoners. When a small remaining group of rebels, including Castro, was captured in the mountains, the bishop successfully intervened to prevent their execution. Unlike so many of his followers—mostly men from the working class—Castro was incarcerated and his life was spared.[2]

Castro's story could well have ended here: a reckless leader had attempted a seemingly futile act of armed struggle, was swiftly captured, and was imprisoned indefinitely. Yet the spectacular failure at the Moncada ended up contributing to a revolutionary process that six years later culminated in the collapse of a powerful dictatorship backed by a proportionally huge military and by the U.S. government. Although the Moncada attack had been almost destined to fail as a military action against the state, it generated excitement among some of Batista's opponents, who may have been encouraged by signs of such intense resistance to the regime. That group included Celia Sánchez, who, writes historian Lorraine Bayard de Volo, was "inspired by Moncada" and worked with her sister after the attack "writing messages of support on small pieces of paper and inserting them into cigarettes to be delivered to the imprisoned rebels."[3]

Within a short period, opponents of Batista would form a revolutionary movement that would triumph, seemingly against all odds. Its leaders would then transform the basic socioeconomic structures of Cuban society and reverse its Cold War alliance with the United States, inspiring and terrifying people around the globe with new socialist visions and possibilities. After the revolution, Castro would promise a "true democracy" serving majority interests and improving the material well-being of most Cubans, a promise that would be realized in key ways during the first thirty years after the revolution's triumph. But Cuba's revolutionary leaders also refused to establish or even espouse electoral democracy, the one clear goal that both right- and left-wing opponents of Batista had expressed in the 1950s, and instead perpetuated authoritarian rule on the island.[4]

This chapter explores the development of the 1950s revolutionary movement, its leaders and goals, and how it triumphed both against Batista's army and over competing resistance forces and opposition leaders. This history explains how the Batista regime steadily corroded and lost all support over the course of the revolution and thus ultimately fell to Castro's small army. It emphasizes the contingencies and context of the struggle, including the ways in which rural guerrillas found support and were able to root themselves in eastern Cuba specifically because they connected their movement with a longer history of struggles over land and in opposition to the actions of U.S. companies in the region. This story sheds light more broadly on the inchoate and irreducible ideological character and complexity of revolutions at large. The aspirations of revolutionary leaders were often strikingly open ended and contingent. This may have been a political necessity, since successful revolutions depend on alliances among groups with contradictory interests and goals, alliances facilitated by ambiguity and compromise. But understanding the evolving visions and programs of the insurgents also illustrates the ways political consciousness often develops through, not necessarily before, revolutionary struggle. Political aims shift in response to changing perceptions of the possible, to perceived political opportunities, constraints, and alternatives—at least for leaders who wish to succeed.

The Roots of Radicalism

Until the Moncada attack, Fidel Castro was a young lawyer with political aspirations who had led a bourgeois life. His father, Ángel Castro y Argiz, was an immigrant from Spain who had joined a large migration to Cuba and settled in the eastern Oriente Province. In time, he was able to make enough money to lease land from the U.S.-owned United Fruit Company, where he grew sugar. He expanded these holdings until he operated a giant plantation, some of the land purchased but most of it leased indefinitely from the mills for harvesting sugar, a common arrangement then for what were known as *colonos*. Castro's mother, Lina Ruz González, was a domestic worker who was employed by his father. The two were married after Fidel was born. For high school, Castro was sent to Havana to attend the country's best Jesuit school, Belén, where he was renowned for both his debating skills and athletic prowess.[5]

Castro studied law at the University of Havana, where he became politically engaged. Castro also joined a student association supporting Puerto Rican nationalists' demands for independence from the United States. And in 1947, Castro postponed his law exams in order to participate in an armed expedition being assembled to overthrow the long-ruling dictator, Rafael

Trujillo Molina, in the Dominican Republic. The organizers of this expedition built on a long tradition of Caribbean revolutionary links and collaboration by seeking to bring together Dominican exiles and volunteers from Cuba and elsewhere in the Caribbean. It was an open secret that they had the support of the Cuban government and armed forces. Initially the United States did not object since post–World War II U.S. leaders were brimming with anti-dictatorship sentiments and at odds with the Trujillo regime. Support for democratic change in the Caribbean, though, quickly vanished with the start of the U.S.-Soviet Cold War around this time, and U.S. leaders once again sought to shore up their despotic ally in Santo Domingo. Pressure from the U.S. government compelled Cuban president Ramón Grau San Martín to switch sides and to arrest most of the participants in the anti-Trujillo expedition, some 1,200 men. A small number escaped, including Castro.[6]

That same year Castro joined the Orthodox Party, which was focused on exposing state corruption and demanding honesty in government. The party brandished the slogan "Decency [*Vergüenza*] over Money." "To moralize [*moralizar*] the state and the government" was the party's main goal, according to its founder, Eduardo Chibás. In principle, Cuba had had a liberal democracy since the end of the first U.S. occupation in 1902, and many of the island's leaders had been democratically elected. But for fifty years, the liberal state had also failed in fundamental ways. Periodic military coups, high levels of political and criminal violence, and corruption were endemic. During the democratic 1940s, the state was shot through with bribery and extortion. The president and other officials embezzled millions of dollars from the national treasury. Rival armed gangs with links to the governing Authentic Party, student leaders, the police, and other authorities engaged in criminal operations almost with impunity. They fought with each other for spoils, turf, and revenge in Havana's streets and at the university. And political leaders continually promised the Cuban majority major socioeconomic reforms that never came. The Orthodox Party's goal of finally establishing a legitimate and well-functioning liberal democratic state, "an accountable, representative government," might be viewed as a "radical" aspiration in this context, as historian Lillian Guerra suggests. For some, such institutional transformation may have also held out the promise of substantive social democratic change in pursuit of a more egalitarian society and greater life chances for most Cubans.[7]

After the failed anti-Trujillo expedition, Castro worked hard to become one of the prominent faces of the Orthodox Party. In 1952, he ran for Congress on the Orthodox ticket, which promised less a new program than simply an end to corrupt leadership. Castro was projected to be the winner for a seat in Havana. But his bid for office was cut short when then senator Batista, a candidate for president who was running behind in the polls, carried out a coup. He toppled Cuba's democratically elected government with the army's assistance and took over the presidency. This was a return to power for Batista, who began his career as a dictator back in 1934. In the late 1930s, Batista became an increasingly reformist ruler, even allying with the Communist party, which followed the Soviet directive since 1935 to forge broad alliances in a "popular front." In this spirit, and however ironically, both the Communist party and Batista played a role in the creation of Cuba's formidable 1940 democratic constitution. Batista's reformist politics and alliances helped lead to his victory in the 1940 presidential election, albeit with military intimidation ensuring that outcome. When in 1944 Batista peacefully turned over the presidency to the winning candidate from the opposition party, the 1933 revolutionary leader Ramón Grau San Martín, Batista set what appeared to be a democratic milestone in Cuba. Democracy, however, and Batista's commitment to it, did not last long.[8]

In the days after Batista's 1952 coup, university students and faculty rallied against Batista's seizure of power. Defying a police order against demonstrations, hundreds staged a theatrical funeral for the 1940 Constitution. Faculty at the University of Havana also denounced the rule of "any government that does not achieve power through election." Students continued protesting Batista's tyranny, as did some members of the Orthodox Party, including Castro, who exhorted "courageous Cubans to sacrifice and fight back!" The Orthodox Party was particularly successful at mobilizing women. Out of their ranks came many who would play a critical role in the overthrow of Batista, including Celia Sánchez, who had been active in a local chapter of the party in Eastern Cuba since the 1940s.[9]

Still, in the early 1950s, the opposition was fragmented, with some holding out mistaken hope that Batista would keep to his word, hold free elections, and allow politics to return at least to their traditional patterns. Castro, though, saw hope for resisting the dictatorship and—as he would soon stress—for attacking socioeconomic inequality through armed struggle. The year after Batista's coup, Castro launched his spectacular attack on the Moncada barracks. Other opposition parties denounced Castro's action. The Communist party, which had played a largely reformist role in Cuban politics during the previous years, condemned the "heroism" of the Moncada attack as "false and sterile." But the action ended up magnifying the anti-Batista movement, largely because of the brutal reaction to it. Gruesome tales and photographs of the army's torture and slaughter of the captured rebels circulated in the press. This publicity raised Castro's national profile and thrust the idea of armed civilian resistance into the popular imagination. Although most of the opposition leaders remained averse to an armed struggle, some people argued that a regime that carried out such atrocities could only be confronted with force.[10]

Castro was put on trial in October 1953 for insurrection against the government. In court, when called on to present his defense, he seized the opportunity to deliver a powerful political speech. The trial was closed to the public, but Castro was able to smuggle out of his prison cell a reconstructed and probably expanded version of the speech. Eventually thousands of copies of Castro's speech were printed and distributed the following year under the title *History Will Absolve Me*. In this important and often stirring work, Castro displayed extensive knowledge both of Cuban society and of intellectual history at large. Castro did not defend himself from the charge of insurrection or petition for the court's leniency. Instead, he denounced Batista's regime, claimed the right to rebel against tyranny, and laid out a "revolutionary" alternative both to Batista's dictatorship and to the socioeconomic status quo. Castro lamented the deplorable and difficult conditions under which a large part of the population lived: landlessness, limited access to health care, inadequate housing, rural illiteracy, and lack of educational opportunities. Noteworthy for its absence, however, was any discussion of racial inequality.[11]

In *History Will Absolve Me*, Castro also provided an outline of the revolutionary goals that animated the Moncada attack, which he hoped would galvanize the population behind the rebel movement. As he wrote from prison to one of his fellow revolutionaries, the speech contained "our platform and ideology." "We must . . . make our ideas known, and win the support of the masses," he insisted. At the heart of Castro's ideas were a series of "revolutionary laws" or decrees that would become the law of the land as soon as the new revolutionary government triumphed. Put into practice, these proposed laws promised a massive redistribution of wealth. They also would usher in a profound transformation in the way land was owned and used. First, farmers who were renting, sharecropping, or squatting on lands of up to 165 acres would be granted ownership to their plots. The former owners were to receive compensation equivalent to ten years of rent. This would have given land to about one hundred thousand Cubans. Second, the farmers known as *colonos*, who worked under contracts to deliver sugar to mill owners, would be guaranteed the right to 55 percent of their crop. Third, all properties determined to have been acquired corruptly and all profits obtained by fraud were to be appropriated by the government. Fourth, 30 percent of the profits made by all "large" firms were to be distributed to employees—other than agricultural firms, which would be subject instead to other new laws. Finally, all rents were to be cut in half.[12]

Other laws would follow, including the nationalization of the U.S.-owned Utility Trust and Telephone Trust, and, most importantly, a more far-reaching agrarian reform. Castro strongly condemned the fact that half of Cuba's fertile lands were in the hands of foreigners, much of it lying idle rather than being cultivated. To change this, he proposed enacting a policy that was a part of Cuba's 1940 Constitution but had never been put into effect: placing a limit on the permissible size of landholdings in different agricultural sectors to free up land that could be redistributed. Such a reform would inevitably break up Cuba's great sugar and cattle estates, including the expropriation of a vast amount of U.S. property.[13]

Castro's state program entailed a radical redistribution of wealth, but it nonetheless would have left most of the economy in private hands and subject to market forces. In that sense, it was not socialist. The fact that Castro's first revolutionary law declared that the 1940 democratic constitution was to be the "supreme law" of the land also suggests his recognition of widespread desires for political democracy. Yet Castro did not call for the immediate establishment of liberal democracy. Instead, his plan entailed a revolutionary leadership ruling at first "with all the attributions necessary to proceed with the effective implantation of popular will and true justice"— that is, the revolutionary laws that Castro had laid out earlier in the speech. This new revolutionary government would take over the judicial system and purge it of those who had "dishonorably capitulated" to the Batista regime. Until the reform of the courts was complete, all legislative control would also be placed in the hands of the revolutionary government. In this way, Castro explained, old corrupt institutions and officials would not be able to stand in the way of popular reforms.[14]

Under Castro's plan, the revolutionary leadership would also not have to face, at first, the constraints on reform inhering in liberal democracy; that is, both the slow-moving system of checks and balances capable of impeding any major transformation and the disproportionate political weight exerted by those with greater economic means, whether legal or corrupt. If liberal democracy had been established right away after the revolution, Castro's proposed revolutionary laws might have faced formidable challenges in court, however much the legislation was backed by most Cubans. That would have slowed, if not altogether quashed, core parts of the revolutionary agenda such as agrarian reform. On the other hand, by establishing Cuba's liberal 1940 Constitution after revolutionary legislation was implemented, as Castro proposed, any subsequent government "would have to respect" the new socioeconomic order, because once the people had obtained something they had been seeking "for generations," there would be "no force in the world capable of tearing it away from them." Then, the slow, self-limiting character of liberal democracy could help sustain rather than impede the new revolutionary laws. Castro, however, broached neither how realistic it was to expect an initial revolutionary government to give up power nor the antidemocratic perils his plan might entail.[15]

Castro concluded his speech to the Supreme Court with ironic magnanimity by offering, rather than requesting, mercy: "I know that the President of this tribunal, a decent man [de limpia vida], can hardly disguise his repugnance for the reigning state of affairs that forces him to pronounce an unjust sentence." But Castro famously boasted: "Condemn me, it does not matter. History will absolve me." Castro's expansive sense of his own place in history was striking for a twenty-seven-year-old with no real accomplishments to his name who was about to be sentenced to fifteen years in jail. At that time, many observers might have thought it was doubtful that history would even remember Castro, let alone absolve him. They would, however, be proven wrong.[16]

As was the case for numerous intellectual and political figures in the twentieth century—from Antonio Gramsci to Malcolm X—Castro's years in prison were an intellectually productive time. In solitary confinement, he took refuge in the works of Dostoevsky, Balzac, Hugo, and Marx. "Prison is a terrific classroom!" he wrote in December 1953. "I can shape my view of the world in here, and . . . I feel my belief in sacrifice and struggle getting stronger." He found inspiration in world-historical struggles against slavery, colonialism, and poverty, notably including the Haitian Revolution:

> I love the magnificent spectacle offered by the great revolutions of history: they have always meant the victory of the huge majority's aspirations for a decent life and happiness over the interests of a small group. Do you know what I consider very moving? The revolt of the black slaves in Haiti. . . . What a small place in history is given to the rebelling African slaves who established a free republic by routing Napoleon's best generals! . . . I am always thinking about

these things because I would honestly love to revolutionize this country from one end to the other!

But he showed equal respect for great reformers—and his wonkish side—in his laudatory discussion of U.S. president Franklin Roosevelt's agricultural policies:

> I want to find out as much as I can about Roosevelt and his policies: in the agricultural sector, raising the prices of farm products . . . increasing the fertility of the soil, ways of providing credit, canceling debts, expanding national and international markets; in the area of social programs, more jobs, reducing the workweek, raising salaries, social benefits for the unemployed, the aged, and the sick; and . . . new tax systems. . . . Roosevelt actually did some wonderful things, and some of his countrymen have never forgiven him for doing them.

Castro's prison writings suggest an openness to diverse political goals, as long as they were on the side of the powerless and the oppressed, "the unredeemed masses, to whom all make promises and whom all deceive and betray," as he declared at the trial. As Cuba's revered revolutionary and antislavery intellectual from the nineteenth-century wars of independence, José Martí, wrote about himself, Castro sought to "cast his lot" with the "poor of the earth."[17]

City and Countryside in 1950s Cuba

In the 1950s, Cuba, and particularly Havana, was wealthy by Latin American standards. Per capita income and literacy rates were among the highest in the region, and the recorded infant mortality rate was the lowest. There was a sizable middle class in the country. Yet there was also widespread poverty. Cuba was, in fact, one of the most unequal societies in Latin America in terms of income distribution, health, literacy, and the rural-urban divide. The country's labor force was composed primarily of sugar workers, who numbered almost half a million. Most were cane cutters who earned low wages for backbreaking work and were unemployed half the year during the "dead season" in between planting and harvesting, when there was little work to be done on the plantations. In the countryside, most of the population had access to only minimal health care and education, and few had running water or electricity. The rural illiteracy rate for adults was over 40 percent, nearly four times that of urban residents. About Cuba the World Bank lamented in 1951, "it is impossible to be optimistic."[18]

Unlike Haiti and the Dominican Republic, Cuba was not a country predominantly of small- and medium-scale farmers. But there was one region that was an exception to this pattern: Oriente ("the East"). There, a large number of farmers without title to the land they cultivated—squatters—had for decades been battling large landowners backed by state and private armed forces trying to dispossess them. They often faced off against U.S. companies that, starting in the late nineteenth century, had been moving into the area to create plantations to grow sugar and other crops. The goal of this regional peasantry was to secure landholdings and individual property. They would play a pivotal role in the Cuban Revolution, linking their aspirations for access to land to Castro's movement and joining with revolutionary forces who promised to help them realize their long-standing goals. The same kinds of small-farming practices and focus on free land access that shaped the politics of the rural populations of Haiti and the Dominican Republic played a key part in the region's most important twentieth-century revolution.[19]

Cuba's rural poverty contrasted sharply with the prosperity and glamour of 1950s Havana. Yet the residents of Havana also had reasons for discontent. The city had been a prominent and thriving port in the Atlantic world from the sixteenth to the twentieth century, with a rich architectural heritage and cultural identity. During the early 1900s, it was transformed into a major center for tourism from the United States, a lucrative development but one whose evolving character ultimately hurt national sensibilities and pride. Tourism first took off at the beginning of World War I when U.S. tourism to Europe was suddenly interrupted and U.S. promoters saw an opening in the Caribbean instead. Especially after 1919, the year Prohibition went into effect, U.S. tourists had a powerful reason to go. Cuba offered a haven for those who wanted to keep drinking in public, as well as for barmen put out of business. Between 1920 and 1940, a total of two million U.S. tourists visited the island. And tourism continued to grow in the 1950s. In just the year 1957, a total of 356,000 U.S. citizens descended on Havana.[20]

During these years, Batista built up the tourism industry not only through tax and loan incentives but also by promoting gigantic gambling and sex industries run largely by U.S. organized crime leaders. As a result, not only the volume but also the character of tourism had profound consequences for the lives of Cubans themselves, in ways that many found disconcerting.

What made Cuba successfully stand out from other tourist destinations in the Caribbean, including Puerto Rico, was its reputation as the "vice capital of the world." Many foreign spectators and visitors constructed Cubans in racist fashion as inherently sexual and Cuba as a site of fantasy and escape. Marijuana and cocaine were readily available. Journalist Jay Mallin described "the air" in Cuba as "a heavy, aphrodisiacal wine that dissolves the inhibitions and dissipates restraint." The famous English novelist Graham Greene repeatedly visited Havana, "an extraordinary city, where every vice was permissible and every trade possible," he recalled. "I liked the idea that one could obtain anything at will, whether drugs, women or goats."[21]

There were approximately two hundred thousand employees in the tourism and gambling industries, and in Havana alone an estimated 11,500 sex workers. For thousands of Cuban women and some men, labor in the sex industry represented one of few, if any, job opportunities, however perilous and degrading it might be. The industry also spread into residential spaces. Sex work took place frequently in people's homes, leading neighbors, fed up by knocks on the door, to put up signs reading, "Don't Bother [Us]; Family House." Cubans wrote despairingly at the time about the transformation of Havana into a glittery underworld of sex labor, commercialized vice, and organized crime. Was tourism, Luis Conte Agüero asked rhetorically, "worth paying the high price of imported gangsterism, the demoralization of our customs, and the disrepute of the name of Cuba?" The Cuban press in the mid-1950s bemoaned the portrait of Havana "as a city where virtue does not exist," while many Havana residents appeared to hunger for a state that would protect national dignity and pride.[22]

In 1958, the revolutionary leader Enrique Oltuski would argue that "the increase in gambling and prostitution" was contributing to discontent among Havana residents and their sympathy and support for the movement against Batista. The prominent Cuban intellectual Roberto Fernández Retamar similarly recalled decades later: "Havana was the most corrupted city I have seen in my life . . . the mafia . . . gambling . . . prostitution. I do think this is one of the most important sources of the Cuban Revolution, the outrage of a people who didn't want the humiliation of being the bordello of America."[23]

Havana's perceived degradation by U.S. and other tourists dovetailed with U.S. government backing of Batista's corrupt dictatorship to pique nationalist resentment. In 1954, a few months after Batista sought to legitimate his rule through farcical elections, U.S. vice president Richard Nixon traveled to Havana and gave the dictatorship his stamp of approval. Nixon was soon followed by the director of the Central Intelligence Agency (CIA), who came to ensure that Batista formed an effective repressive body to counter any possible threats from the now-outlawed Communist party. U.S. business interests in Cuba were also solidly behind Batista and his pro-business policies. The following year, when all the legal opposition parties came together to meet with Batista and demand new and fair elections, he was confident enough of his control to reject their proposals. This was, it turned out, the last opportunity for a nonrevolutionary transition out of Batista's dictatorship.[24]

Che Guevara and "Valuable Lessons"

In May 1955, as part of a new amnesty law announced on Mother's Day, Batista released Castro and eighteen of his followers from prison. Batista's reasoning is unclear: he may simply have been overconfident, or else planned on having Castro killed once he was free. Continually harassed by police after his release and hearing rumors of a planned assassination, Castro headed into exile in Mexico. He left behind in Cuba the nucleus of what would soon be called the 26th of July Movement, referring to the date of the Moncada attack. That group included new allies, such as Frank País, a schoolteacher organizing armed resistance to Batista in Santiago, as well as old left-wing friends. It also included Vilma Espín, Haydée Santamaría, and soon Celia Sánchez, adding to the important role of women in the movement at this time. These leaders forged the forces that would remain outside the mountains—in the cities and the plains—and would play a key role in revolutionary developments and the 26th of July Movement's ultimate victory.[25]

Life as an exile was not what Castro planned for himself. He quickly began organizing an invasion of Cuba by a small expeditionary group, hoping they could start a revolution against Batista. He attracted participants where he could and acquired funding from former Cuban president Carlos Prío Socarrás and Venezuela's once and future president, Rómulo Betancourt. Most of those recruited were Cuban. But one soon-to-be-famous new member of the group was not: an Argentine named Ernesto Guevara. He was nicknamed "Che" by Cuban exiles from the Moncada attack who had met him in Guatemala. "Che" was a common Argentine expression that Guevara frequently used. It means something akin to "hey" or "hey, man," depending on the context.[26]

Guevara was a twenty-seven-year-old recently minted physician from a prominent but downwardly mobile family of Spanish and some Irish descent. During his early twenties, he had glided from bourgeois medical student to bohemian traveler to a militant seeker of social justice. Guevara had traveled across Latin America, visiting a copper mine in Chile and, at another time, working in leper colonies in Peru and Venezuela. He spoke vaguely of his dreams of "being sacrificed" to the cause of "authentic revolution" and becoming a "soldier of the Americas." He had, though, no specific plans, at least that we know of.[27]

In 1953, having heard that Guatemala was "the place to see," he traveled there. At the time, the democratically elected president, Jacobo Árbenz, was carrying out a peaceful revolution aimed at both economic development and a redistribution of wealth by means of a sweeping agrarian reform. That reform expropriated a sizable chunk of the lands owned by the United Fruit Company in Guatemala. Guevara greatly admired Árbenz's policy, having earlier expressed outrage at the "dominions of the United Fruit," describing the company as a conglomerate of "capitalist octopuses" that should be "annihilated." In a letter to his mother, Guevara described Guatemala as an "authentic democracy" and soon applied for authorization to stay in the country and practice medicine.[28]

Soon afterward, however, Guevara watched as the dream of peaceful transformation to a more equitable order was shattered. In June 1954, a ragtag band of some five hundred CIA-organized rebels overthrew Árbenz. The Guatemalan military capitulated to the outmanned and out-armed band of insurgents for fear that a U.S. invasion would follow if the rebels were defeated. Árbenz was then forced into exile. The U.S.-sponsored overthrow of democracy in Guatemala would usher in decades of horrendous civil war with an unparalleled death toll in modern Latin American history. It also profoundly marked Che Guevara's political view of the U.S. role in the region and of the process of reform and revolution.[29]

U.S. intervention in Guatemala was driven by hostility to Árbenz's sweeping agrarian reform and its impact on United Fruit. It was also a product of unfounded and convenient paranoia about Communist influence in the country. Árbenz's domestic policies, objective, and ideology were capitalist: the goal was the creation of a nation of small property-owning farmers. But Árbenz had included members of the Guatemalan Communist party in his circle of advisers and the government bureaucracy that helped organize the agrarian reform. When he was confronted about their presence in the government by Guatemalan army officers fearful of a U.S. attack, Árbenz responded: "I am not now, nor will I be, a communist." But, he added critically, "neither am I, nor will I be, an anticommunist." "There are communists in the agrarian reform department," he acknowledged, "but they are the best workers and the most honest." They were following, not reshaping, what traditional Communists would consider a bourgeois agrarian reform. Árbenz either did not fully grasp the realities of U.S. power, the Cold War, and the stark rivalry between the Soviet Union and the United States or else refused to abide by them as a matter of principle. For the United States, firm anti-Communist rhetoric and the exclusion of Communist party members from the government, however reformist and capitalist their actual politics may have been, were required.[30]

The lesson for Guevara was clear: egalitarian socioeconomic reforms, even when carried out at a moderate pace by a democratically elected government, would meet with unflinching resistance from the United States. If governments in the region were unable to stand up to U.S. threats and intervention, their egalitarian economic efforts would fail. Looking back in 1960, Guevara referred to Árbenz's regime as a "democracy that perished" in order to offer others "valuable lessons." One of the most critical lessons came from seeing a democratic president's inability to maintain control over a military opposed to the president's socioeconomic reforms and fearful of U.S. hostility. Just two weeks after the coup, Guevara wrote to his mother that "once again we see confirmed that saying which dictates the elimination of the army as the true beginning of democracy (if the saying does not exist, I have now invented it)."[31]

After Árbenz's fall, Guevara continued his wanderings. In 1955, he headed to Mexico, where he met Fidel Castro and decided to join Castro's group of Cuban revolutionaries. Guevara appreciated Castro's commitment to armed struggle rather than to what seemed now to Guevara a doomed electoral path for the Left in Latin America. But it was also in some ways a deeper endeavor for Guevara. As he wrote to his mother: "The concept of 'I' has been replaced by the concept of 'us.' . . . Really it was (and is) beautiful to be able to feel that removal of 'I.'"[32]

Although Guevara took from Guatemala the lesson that the U.S. government would never tolerate egalitarian reforms that hurt U.S. capital, it was not clear how that lesson might be applied in Cuba. It was, objectively speaking, nearly impossible to imagine Cuba surviving a break with the United States given Cuba's extreme economic dependence on the colossus to the north and the likelihood of a U.S. attack to maintain control over its strategically valuable neighbor. However, Castro's optimism about the possibilities for transformation in Cuba seems to have drawn Guevara in. In Mexico, Castro studied how Lázaro Cárdenas had achieved sweeping agrarian reform and the nationalization of foreign oil companies in the

1930s. Both of these actions hit U.S. interests hard, and yet tensions between Cárdenas and the United States were resolved in a few years. Perhaps Castro hoped, despite having seen what happened to Árbenz, to replicate Cárdenas's exceptional achievement.[33]

A few weeks into his stay, Castro issued a new manifesto for radical capitalist reform that he hoped to smuggle into Cuba. The sweeping document called for "distribution of the land among peasant families. . . . The right of the worker to broad participation in the profits of all the large industrial, commercial, and mining enterprises . . . decrease in all rents . . . decent housing to shelter the 400,000 families crowded into filthy single rooms, huts, shacks, and tenements. . . . Extension of electricity to . . . our rural and suburban sectors who have none. . . . Nationalization of public services: telephone, electricity, and gas. . . . Extension of education to the farthest corner of the country. . . . General reform of the tax system . . . measures in education and legislation to put an end to every vestige of discrimination for reasons of race or sex which regrettably still exists in our social and economic life." The inclusion of measures to combat racial and gender discrimination, which were not present in his earlier statements, was one notable addition to Castro's program.[34]

There was an arguably paternalistic-authoritarian quality to Castro's vision at this time, as he repeatedly stressed what "the Revolution" will "give" to "the people." In a lengthy missive written in 1955, Castro asserted that "Cuba wants a radical change in its entire public and social life. The people must be given more than an abstract ideal of freedom and democracy; every Cuban must be able to live a decent existence." Castro continued to emphasize "radical change" and socioeconomic transformation, not electoral democracy. "Those who have had to suffer and still suffer the indignities of a miserable existence . . . expect nothing from the political parties. They expect to get everything from the Revolution, and they will get it!"[35]

With Guevara on board, Castro had picked up a devoted revolutionary who would become a powerful military leader. But their path was uncertain. Their alliance made it no clearer how the impossible could be achieved. How could a small band of revolutionaries with almost no military experience bring about the surrender of Cuba's forty thousand well-armed troops, soldiers backed by continuing support from the U.S. government? And even if the revolutionaries succeeded, where would the financial resources for the pursuit of the egalitarian goals articulated in Castro's manifesto come from? And how would the inevitable resistance of the powerful U.S. interests be faced and overcome?

From Squatter to Guerrilla War in Oriente

The attack on the Moncada barracks in 1953 had been a quixotic attempt by a small rebel group acting like a conventional army. By the time Castro arrived in Mexico he understood he needed a different military tactic. For help, he sought out Alberto Bayo, the son of a Spanish officer and a Cuban mother, who carried remarkable military credentials. Bayo had fought for eleven years with the Spanish army to suppress independence forces in Morocco. Those forces relied on guerrilla warfare, *guerrilla* meaning "little war" in Spanish and referring to small battles, ambushes, and hit-and-run attacks typically carried out by irregular or civilian forces with less firepower than traditional militaries. At military schools in Spain, Bayo had studied guerrilla warfare and later taught classes on the topic.[36]

Bayo was also a veteran of the Spanish Civil War, in which he battled on the side of the democratically elected government, the Republicans, against an ultimately successful rebellion by the Spanish army that established the long right-wing dictatorship of General Francisco Franco. After being exiled from Spain to Mexico, he became a strong proponent of the potential of guerrilla warfare against dictatorships. When Castro presented his plan of action to Bayo, however, and asked him to commit to teach "guerrilla tactics to his future soldiers," Bayo laughed. As Bayo later recounted: "The young man was telling me that he expected to defeat Batista . . . with men 'when I have them,' and with vessels 'when I have the money to buy them,' . . . Come now, I thought, this young man wants to move mountains with one hand." Bayo nonetheless consented to work with Castro. "What did it cost me to please him?" he said.[37]

In his training, Bayo emphasized that "the guerrilla is invincible when he can rely on the support of the peasants." Bayo explained further that for a guerrilla movement to thrive it needed the support of the local population, among whom the guerrillas could hide from the state's gaze and recruit growing numbers of troops, rather than be turned in by the population to state authorities. To secure that support, the guerrillas had to be fighting for popular goals. These goals, in turn, could contribute to attrition and even capitulation among government troops, who were, after all, connected to the rest of society through friends, family, public discourse, and history. Castro heard this advice and made it key to his strategy.[38]

Even with Bayo's training, the odds seemed stacked against a guerrilla group overcoming Batista's forces. Castro, however, boldly ignored this ostensible reality. In November of 1956, Castro and a small band of followers, eighty-two in number, all men, including several who had participated in the earlier Moncada attack, embarked for Oriente, Cuba. They traveled on a tightly packed old motor yacht named *Granma* that Castro purchased from a U.S. resident in Mexico City. The plan was to capture arms from an isolated rural garrison in Niquero, Oriente, and then to escape into the mountains, the Sierra Maestra. This was the region of Cuba where decades of peasant land struggles and a veritable squatter war continued at a fever pitch. The Sierra Maestra was also home to the country's highest mountains, some of its thickest woods, and almost inaccessible rain forest. Politically and geographically, it was therefore the ideal place from which to launch a guerrilla resistance movement. The troops could not be seen by Batista's air force in the jungle, and the steep inclines would compel the Cuban army to fight on foot. Meanwhile Castro would hold the high ground. With the support of the local population, Castro hoped to begin organizing a regional guerrilla war against Batista that could tap into growing animosity toward the regime and ultimately spark a nationwide mass revolution.[39]

The terrain had been prepared by members of the urban 26th of July Movement in Santiago under Frank País. One of the pivotal organizers on the ground was Celia Sánchez, who lived in a small town, Pilón, close to the Sierra Maestra. After Batista's coup, Sánchez helped mobilize fellow Orthodox Party members in this region against the regime. And in early 1956, she began working with País. Knowing of her extensive connections in the countryside, País gave her the mission, writes Sánchez's biographer Nancy Stout, "to figure out how to get them [Castro's fighters] away from the coast and into the mountains" after they made it to Cuban shores. Sánchez would draw on the many contacts she had as the daughter of a prominent country doctor and leader of a regional charity to create a network of rural residents ready to help Castro reach and move through the hills.[40]

Sánchez's work began by enlisting the collaboration of Guillermo García, a rancher with contacts around the coastal area Castro had chosen for his landing. García evidently had no love for the sugar planters, the abusive local military, or the Batista regime and was ready to help. García later recalled that a few days before Castro's anticipated arrival, "we sent out patrols to organize the peasants and tell them that they should give protection to any armed men who might show up." Sánchez also reached out to Crescencio Pérez, a truck driver for the Central Niquero sugar plantation. Pérez was also a leader, along with some of his children (reportedly in the dozens), of hundreds of armed squatters battling against eviction by sugar companies, coffee planters, and other large landholders. Pérez immediately signed on after meeting with Sánchez and became a key organizer in the fledgling rural underground preparing to assist the guerrillas. Pérez brought with him a community of resisters, relatives, and neighbors in the lower reaches of the Sierra Maestra that complemented the networks of Sánchez and García on the coast.[41]

The plan was for the rebels coming from Mexico to begin operations at the home of Ramón (Mongo) Pérez, Crescencio Pérez's brother. Unfortunately for the would-be insurgents, things did not go as planned. In fact, the landing was a disaster. Castro's overcrowded yacht arrived several days late and did not come ashore at the designated site, so no one was there to assist them. The rebels headed for the Sierra Maestra, but it was still sixty miles away. En route, they encountered Batista's troops and fled in every direction. Within a few days, the army had tracked down and executed or imprisoned all but about twenty of the insurgents. Castro, his brother, and Guevara managed to escape. But the once-slim odds of success had now gotten even smaller, with just twenty or so rebels against forty thousand government soldiers.[42]

On the other hand, the guerrillas were never really only twenty. Celia Sánchez had forged an impressive movement in the region, a type of unarmed rural militia ready to assist the rebels. And it was this militia and members of its communities who found Castro's few surviving fighters before Batista's army did and ushered them to safety at Mongo Pérez's farm. From there, the 26th of July Movement's local supporters helped the guerrillas scale the Sierra Maestra.[43]

It was not only Sánchez's savvy political networking that helped secure local assistance for the guerrillas. Social conditions in the area where Castro's movement had chosen to begin its operations were also key. The rebels had landed in the region with the largest proportion of squatters in the nation. The squatters were under siege, and they appeared ready to embrace the 26th of July Movement as an ally in their ongoing war. Rather than starting a movement in the Sierra Maestra, Castro had found an existing one there to lead. To understand Cuba's guerrilla revolution and its ultimate success, we need to recognize the soil in which it took root: the decades-old struggle, going back to the Cuban War of Independence, for land on the part of the population of the region.[44]

The Sierra Maestra was, in fact, unique within Cuba: it was the only region of the country in which squatters made up a major portion of the farming population. Almost one-tenth of farmers in Cuba overall were classified as squatters. In the eastern province of Oriente, however, they made up nearly a quarter of the farm population, in the Sierra Maestra about half of it, and in the region of Niquero a stunning over four-fifths of rural residents. And these occupants were in continual conflict with landowners seeking to evict them, at times by means of a court order enforced by soldiers or local police and at other times simply through violence and arson carried out by landowners' private guards.[45]

When Castro's rebel soldiers arrived in Oriente and specifically the areas around the Sierra Maestra and Sierra Cristal, they were, in a sense, taking up the work of the Liberation Army of 1895–98, which had fought to secure land for the peasantry. Castro's troops offered small farmers a means of finally tipping the balance against plantation owners and authorities seeking their eviction. Castro quickly issued a revolutionary edict that promised both squatters' and tenants' rights to the land they used. In return, peasant support helped Castro's minuscule band of rebels to survive, grow, and thrive. With the help of the rural underground, Castro and Guevara were able to move their force into the Sierra Maestra and regroup. This support contrasted sharply with what happened in Trujillo's Dominican Republic when revolutionary exiles landed there. Trujillo's regime had distributed land and offered property rights to large numbers who had been exploiting lands without title to them, and in many cases substantial agricultural assistance was provided. And there the exiles were denounced by the peasantry and quickly captured. The squatter war in Eastern Cuba became a war against the Batista regime because that state had continued to empower rather than stop private overseers and local authorities who attacked squatters. There was no reform or other assistance for the peasantry under Batista. Local police and soldiers instead assisted in the removal of those without property titles from their land.[46]

Castro also cultivated good relations with the local population by reportedly paying double the going rate for food rather than requisitioning it for free. In contrast to the traditional behavior of soldiers, bandits, and other armed figures in isolated rural zones, Castro harshly punished any acts of abuse and theft by his troops. These respectful practices continued even as the region's traditional armed men, accustomed to such banditry, were integrated into the revolutionary movement.[47]

The guerrillas' first successful attack was an assault on a small garrison at La Plata in January, almost two months after their landing. The rebel forces—now strengthened with thirty-two peasant recruits but arms for only twenty-two—outnumbered and surprised the government's troops. Batista's men at this rural outpost were killed, wounded, and taken prisoner in the attack, though some managed to escape. The rebels suffered no casualties and seized the ample arms and supplies at the post. Castro let the captured troops go free as a way of making clear that the soldiers themselves were not the enemy, but rather people to be won over to the cause. On the other hand, Raúl Castro wrote in his diary then that "the fate of any land company overseer who falls into our hands . . . is summary execution, the only way to deal with those thugs." This violence was strategic. The rebels' attack on the landowners' muscle demonstrated the loyalties of the 26th of July Movement and surely helped mobilize popular rural support for it.[48]

Three months after the tiny armed band of exiles made it from Cuba's shores into the mountains, a *New York Times* senior editor, Herbert Matthews, visited their hideout. Matthews had been invited to the Sierra Maestra by Castro, who was seeking a foreign journalist to write an uncensored report on the guerrilla movement. Celia Sánchez organized the visit, mobilizing a group of activists who managed to bring Matthews from Havana into the Sierra Maestra, even though the area had been cordoned off by government troops. Though the move was risky for the rebels, the payoff was favorable publicity. Castro had always understood that spearheading a revolution against Batista would depend more on political maneuvering than military might, and he was able to work the media to a remarkable degree. The interview was in part a work of theater to impress Matthews with the size of the movement: Fidel's brother Raúl marched repeatedly into the camp with what appeared to be different platoons but were actually the same group of men marching in, then back into the woods and changing clothes, and back again.[49]

Matthews's article, which ran on the front page of the *New York Times*, painted a heroic portrait of Castro and his movement. In it, Castro declared: "A dictatorship must show that it is omnipotent or it will fall; we are showing that it is impotent." Guerrillas do not have to defeat the government's army to appear strong; they gain prestige by the sheer act of survival, especially if that survival is well broadcast, as Sánchez and the 26th of July Movement had now ensured. "President Fulgencio Batista has the cream of his Army around the area," Matthews reported, "but the Army men are fighting a thus-far losing battle to destroy" the guerrillas, for "thousands of men and women are heart and soul with Fidel Castro." The journalist praised Castro in his article: "The personality of the man is overpowering . . . an educated, dedicated fanatic, a man of ideals, of courage and of remarkable qualities of leadership. . . . One got a feeling that he is now invincible. Perhaps he isn't, but that is the faith he inspires in his followers."[50]

By late May of 1957, the number of guerrillas directly under Castro's command had risen thanks to a stream of peasants from the area seeking to join the rebels. Decades later, one rebel and soon treasurer of the movement, María Antonia Figueroa, recalled her time in the hills: "mostly I talked a lot with the *guajiros* [small farmers], so that they joined the Rebel Army." Although they were still a far smaller number than Matthews had perceived, the rebels would continue to gain new rural recruits and soon extensive armed allies from the area, all of whom were intimately familiar with the geographic and social terrain. And the urban wing of the 26th of July Movement sent weapons, supplies, and new fighters, often individuals seeking refuge after being identified as opponents by the government. State repression against Castro sympathizers, as well as in the continuing squatter war in the area, contributed to the growth of the movement.[51]

At the same time, Castro continued to show his flair for public relations. CBS broadcast an interview with him filmed by Robert Taber at the summit of Pico Turquino (6,500 feet above sea level), standing before a statue of the founder of the Cuban independence revolution, José Martí. Celia Sánchez, who had installed this bust herself the year after Batista's coup, also appeared in the film with a bouquet of mariposa lilies pinned to her uniform. Mariposas had been worn by women who supported the independence wars at the end of the nineteenth century and were sometimes used to carry messages rolled up inside their stems, as many Cuban viewers would have known. Through this potent symbol, Sánchez was likely insisting on the link between their revolution and that of an earlier generation of insurgents, just as Castro did by speaking from in front of a statue of Martí. At the same time, Sánchez was reminding viewers, and probably the guerrillas themselves, that women had always been part of Cuba's revolutionary movements, including in armed combat. In New York City, over six hundred Cuban expatriates watched the broadcast during a rally against Batista and called for a U.S. embargo against Cuba.[52]

Six months after losing all but twenty of his landing force, Castro had gathered some 150 local recruits, established supply lines from Santiago, secured much regional support, and gained favorable publicity in the most respected channels of the U.S. press. In late May, the rebels captured an important rural garrison, El Uvero, which was staffed by over fifty government soldiers, and took the post's arms and supplies. The guerrillas released all the prisoners: treating captives well and freeing them contributed to good public relations and could eventually facilitate military defections. Castro's forces were embarrassing the regime and inspiring civilians. One student remarked at the time: "He has given us heart and courage to fight and, even if he is killed now, this fight will go [on]."[53]

As a counterinsurgency measure, Batista ordered the army to evacuate people from the Sierra Maestra and to relocate them to detention camps in Santiago and Bayamo. All who remained in the wooded hills would be considered enemies of the government. Batista declared the Sierra Maestra a "free fire zone," and the air force began to drop bombs indiscriminately in the mountain jungles in what was dubbed a "campaign of extermination." Some two thousand people were driven from their homes and farms in mid-1957. But the measures backfired. Landowners seized the opportunity to secure the military's help in attacking squatters. This played into Castro's hands by making the link between the peasants' war against the landowners and the guerrilla war against the Batista state even clearer. Many peasants resisted relocation into detention camps and fled into the jungle, where they supported the 26th of July Movement. This was a classic example of counterinsurgent state violence only mobilizing more resistance. Batista was forced to recognize his strategic error and to suspend resettlement and "extermination" efforts.[54]

Rebellion in the Cities

Batista's regime also faced a growing rebellion in the cities. At the start of 1957, armed resistance escalated in Santiago, Havana, and other cities. The urban wing of the 26th of July Movement set off bombs on a weekly basis. Instead of arresting and trying suspected rebels, the police and army shot suspects and political opponents on the spot. All constitutional guarantees were suspended, as Batista's forces arrested, tortured, and killed not only suspected revolutionaries but also critics in the two main political parties, the Authentic and Orthodox Parties. Batista's violent repression only spurred further protest. In early January 1957, more than five hundred self-described "Cuban mothers" dressed in black marched through Santiago brandishing the banner "Stop the murders of our children!" The march was led by a woman whose teenage son, William Soler, had been tortured and murdered by police who suspected him of working with the 26th of July Movement. This was one of many marches and other protests in which women played a central role, deploying what Michelle Chase has called a "creative repertoire of dissent" that included "phone chains and rumor campaigns, collective 'stay at home' days, 'flash' protests, patriotic street theater," and boycotts. These actions played a pivotal role in mobilizing and broadcasting the anti-Batista sentiments that the 26th of July Movement was channeling into an armed revolutionary campaign.[55]

Overall women represented a large part of the urban resistance, both violent and nonviolent. They transported weapons, troops, and messages to the guerrillas in the mountains. They also carried out espionage against the Batista regime, for instance, when telephone operators listened in on regime officials or sex workers discovered information from clients linked to the regime. Women distributed revolutionary leaflets, provided safe houses for rebels, and collected money for the resistance. They also built and detonated bombs. In response, the regime cracked down increasingly hard, subjecting women, like men, to beatings and torture, even when women were peacefully protesting police killings or mourning in funeral processions. This repression, in turn, generated further popular outrage against the regime.[56]

As state violence and the country overall appeared increasingly out of control, new groups began to support overthrowing Batista through armed struggle. The professional classes, particularly the old Orthodox Party members, came more and more to accept Castro. One of the Orthodox Party's former leaders, Raúl Chibás (the brother of the party's founder, Eduardo Chibás), founded the Civic Resistance in Havana in early 1957, which was made up of middle- and upper-class individuals opposed to the regime. The Civic Resistance began collaborating with the more radical 26th of July Movement, sending it supplies and money and expanding its base of support.[57]

The most ambitious action in early 1957 was carried out by the Revolutionary Directorate, a group formed the year before by university students in Havana and driven by young middle-class opponents of the Batista regime. The Directorate's founder, José Antonio Echeverría, had earlier expressed hope that overthrowing Batista would lead not only to a democratic government but to "a profound transformation in our political, social, and economic reality . . . that will solve the problem of the unemployed, the landless peasants, the exploited workers, and the [educated and professional] youth condemned to economic exile." The Directorate, though, did not articulate a particular policy or political agenda and focused its efforts largely on political assassinations. In March 1957, the Directorate organized an impressive attack aimed at assassinating Batista. Many in an eighty-person mission managed to penetrate the Presidential Palace, but almost all who did were soon killed by the police. Batista's response was brutal.

An estimated four hundred opposition members were arrested, tortured, and executed without trial, including some who had no connection to the assault, such as the former senator and leader of the Orthodox Party Pelayo Cuervo. This murder made it clear that the lives of all those who opposed Batista or resisted the regime were at risk, however peaceful and elite they might have been. Cuervo's son went to the courts to demand an investigation of the murder. After his calls for justice were dismissed, he journeyed to the Sierra Maestra to join the guerrilla force.[58]

The regime's decimation of the Revolutionary Directorate during the failed palace attack did not stop armed resistance in the cities. Bombs continued to be targeted at police, soldiers, infrastructure, certain commercial establishments, and sugar mills. The aim was to weaken the economy and the regime while avoiding civilian casualties, though inevitably—given these tactics—some civilians were wounded or killed. The police responded with arbitrary arrests and summary executions. "The police continued to kill men but each death created ten new supporters of the revolt," writes historian Hugh Thomas with probably little exaggeration. This was certainly true of friends and family of those who were executed by the state. Some members of the Communist party, which had opposed armed resistance, began to support the 26th of July Movement. And opposition began to grow even among elite Cubans. The Cuban National Medical Association protested to the country's Supreme Court in October of 1957 that regime forces were attacking hospitals, killing wounded patients, and murdering doctors who were simply following the ethical dictates of their profession by helping the injured.[59]

In the countryside, rebels struck at the economic heart of Cuba's agriculture by setting fire to vast cane fields and finding other ways to sabotage sugar production. Batista was clearly no longer able to maintain order and protect the property of plantation owners and business people, and began to lose their support as well. In 1957, Julio Lobo, the largest Cuban sugar magnate, with more than ten mills and roughly one million acres of land, donated $50,000 to various opposition groups. Havana's staunchly conservative newspaper *Diario de la Marina* protested Batista's extraconstitutional practices and called for immediate elections. The Catholic Church never formally condemned Batista's regime, but numerous priests gave support to the rebels. Members of the military would soon begin defecting. And another group of important players was becoming increasingly concerned about the situation in Cuba: the U.S. State Department and the CIA.[60]

A Revolution's Uneasy Allies

It is not easy to explain the relative ease with which many in the better-off classes suddenly accepted rather than feared the 26th of July Movement. As we have seen, Castro had promised in his famous 1953 speech, "History Will Absolve Me," both a deep redistribution of wealth through major socioeconomic reforms and an authoritarian mechanism for imposing them: the creation of a revolutionary government and the decree of revolutionary laws prior to putting the democratic 1940 Constitution into effect. These laws promised to benefit the lower classes at the expense of Cuban and U.S. landowners, landlords, and business owners. These groups, however, probably assumed that Castro's promises would never be realized. After all, they had heard similar rhetoric before from earlier leaders—such as Grau, who was elected in 1944—and their proposals had never come to be. Moderates also doubtless hoped to prevail over Castro once Batista was deposed, when former allies would compete for control over the subsequent course of the revolution.

Moderate opponents of Batista who sought democratization but not egalitarian economic reforms had other reasons to be confident that things would not go too far. Wouldn't the Cuban armed forces and U.S. government be able to force whoever came into office to follow a moderate line or be overthrown militarily? There were simply too many powerful forces ready to resist any radical transformation of Cuba to see Castro's promises as anything more than politically opportunistic and ultimately empty rhetoric. Without even taking overt or covert military action, the U.S. government could easily destroy the Cuban economy: in addition to the massive direct investment in Cuba, almost two-thirds of the country's export earnings came from trade with the United States, which had made a political choice to purchase sugar from Cuba at preferential prices rather than from other eager suppliers.[61]

As in all successful revolutions, then, the Cuban Revolution brought together multiple constituencies with diverse and even contradictory political visions. Peasant squatters facing eviction did not share interests or goals with plantation owners and sugar magnates, such as Julio Lobo, though they both supported armed opposition groups seeking to overthrow Batista. Lobo could hardly have appreciated it when in late 1957 Castro's branch of the revolutionary struggle torched upwards of ten thousand acres of his cane fields in an effort to hold the sugar economy hostage until Batista was toppled. The university students in the Revolutionary Directorate did not oppose agrarian reform, but they were not focused on the dreams of squatters and other peasants of securing their own land. The professional classes engaged in armed struggle against Batista sought to end state terror, not to redistribute wealth. Even within the 26th of July Movement, all did not share the same precise political goals.[62]

Recognizing that "the enemy of my enemy can be my friend," at least at certain moments in a revolution, Castro reached out to new potential allies. In July 1957, he met with Felipe Pazos and Raúl Chibás in the Sierra Maestra. Pazos was the titular head at that time of the Orthodox Party and one of Cuba's foremost economists, who had previously worked at the International Monetary Fund and as the first director of Cuba's Central Bank. Chibás was the leader of the Civic Resistance, a middle- and upper-class organization. Together, the three leaders hammered out a jointly signed document that came to be known as the Sierra Manifesto. This was clearly a profound compromise for Castro. Agrarian reform was the only major public policy included in the Sierra Manifesto, which envisaged "the distribution of barren lands" along with the conversion "into proprietors [of] all the lessee-planters, partners and squatters who possess small parcels of land, be it property of the state or of private persons, with prior indemnification to the former owners." This might have been an important agrarian reform, if fully implemented. But it remained safely ambiguous regarding what would count as idle land and how precisely it would be obtained and distributed.[63] The document also promised immediate democracy, something to which Castro had previously been opposed.

Castro had been committed to, and doubtless still hoped for, a more radical revolutionary outcome than that laid out in the Sierra Manifesto but signed on nonetheless to get liberal democrats and left-wingers on board. In a sense, this was deceptive. Yet the programs and even visions of successful revolutionary leaders are inevitably shaped and reshaped by the twists and turns of the struggle itself and evolving perceptions of what is possible. At this point in time, Guevara made clear to his fellow revolutionaries that he suspected little would be possible in Cuba beyond what he saw as a "bourgeois" revolution. But even he, though hoping for something radical and socialist, was nonetheless willing to risk his life for a more moderate transformation.[64]

It seems that both Guevara and Castro understood that the possibilities for profound socioeconomic change would depend in large part on whether the hopes mobilized by the revolutionary process ended up creating a powerful enough constituency to make that change happen. That Castro recognized this political reality, and that the revolutionary process itself had a radicalizing potential, is suggested in a missive he wrote to Frank País in July 1957: "given a choice between a victory of days from . . . our landing, or victory one year later, without hesitation I would prefer the victory that is brewing through this fantastic awakening of the Cuban nation."[65]

The Politics of Revolution

Over the course of 1957 and 1958, the leaders of the 26th of July Movement continued to pursue a two-pronged strategy for a revolutionary triumph: guerrilla warfare in the countryside and bombings and sabotage in the cities. They hoped that the latter would create, in the words of one urban leader, an atmosphere of "insurrection . . . [and] abnormality" that would lead to a sense of opportunity, to a general strike, and to the crumbling of the regime. While urban rebels carrying out these attacks (and others) were paying a high price—hundreds, probably thousands, were arrested, tortured, and murdered—national infrastructure was hit hard. And in rural areas many plantations were torched in late 1957 and early 1958.[66]

In the hills of Oriente, the revolutionaries continued to pile up guerrilla victories. The attacks were often small, but they were adding up to something larger. The number of regular troops in the Sierra Maestra had expanded to some three hundred, mostly men, by the end of 1957. This did not include the forces of local strongmen who supported the rebels and who would soon play a major part in the insurgency. Popular rural support of the movement helped the guerrillas enormously. Geography also worked to the rebels' advantage. The Cuban military's advantages in numbers and weapons did little to help the air force's bombs find guerrillas in the jungles. And the army's tanks were useless in the mountains. When government troops searched for rebels in the hills or were baited to pursue them there, they suffered substantial losses in ambushes and soon retreated. The Cuban forces remained unable to penetrate the rebels' stronghold in the Sierra Maestra. After continued losses, the Cuban military decided in February 1958 to withdraw, leaving Castro to control the entire western half of the region.[67]

The guerrillas declared the areas that they controlled "liberated territory" and implemented a de facto land reform. Area residents were protected from evictions, and their rights to the lands they were using were recognized. This was one of several ways the rebels favorably contrasted their embryonic and potential future government with that of Batista. Their criminal justice measures were another way. These reportedly won residents over, particularly women, due to the strict punishment meted out to men for sexual assault—execution—while rape by Batista's forces drove some survivors to join the insurgency. Indeed, Celia Sánchez had made helping rural victims of sexual violence a priority even before the *Granma*'s arrival in Oriente.[68]

The rebels' criminal justice system, though, also involved repression and human rights violations. To prevent information about the rebels falling into the hands of Batista's forces, the rebel leadership made this passage of information punishable by death, and some were executed without ample evidence of their guilt or the extent of their crime. About one such case in 1957 Guevara admitted: "Today we wonder if he was really so guilty as to deserve the death penalty and if his life should not have been saved . . . War is difficult and tough, and while the enemy's combativeness is on the rise, one cannot allow for even a hint of betrayal . . . Months later, because of our relatively greater strength, his life might perhaps have been saved." Dozens of alleged informants were executed.[69]

The rebel government, though, effectively paired such repression with policies aimed at winning the population's support. The guerrillas secured adherents by providing free health care to all, with rudimentary hospitals and a medical staff perhaps ultimately numbering in the hundreds. Furthermore, the new revolutionary state developed literacy programs and schools and collected taxes from large landowners. In return for these new government services, small farmers provided food for the rebels and helped build military structures for them. Also, with the help of the local population supplies were delivered into the mountains from the plains below. There was also, though, growing self-sufficiency in the "liberated territory," with the development of crafts, animal husbandry, and even weapons factories.[70]

Many of the key services that the new rebel state provided—health care and education especially—depended on women's labor, and women played a critical role in gaining support for the insurgency. Women remained, though, generally barred from engaging in armed combat, because this was opposed by most of the men. Later on, a small female platoon would be established and named after Antonio Maceo's mother, Mariana Grajales.[71]

The withdrawal of Batista's military from the region allowed Castro to consolidate his control and mastery of Oriente's difficult terrain. The guerrillas now spread out into multiple columns and fronts across the entire mountainous zone. In early March, Castro's brother Raúl was sent to the

Sierra Cristal in northeastern Oriente with roughly sixty-five Sierra Maestra veterans to help develop a second front. Just a month or two later, Raúl Castro reported that he was already leading one thousand "rebels" there. Those forces comprised not just several hundred new recruits fully under his command but preexisting rebel groups in the area and those he identified as *escopeteros* ("musketeers" or irregular troops), farmers and squatters armed with hunting guns who were ready to fight on the side of the guerrillas.[72]

The broader 26th of July Movement now claimed some thirty thousand members, including over one thousand carrying out armed resistance in the urban underground. As the rural army was consolidating political control across the Sierra Maestra, sabotage by urban guerrillas was reaching a fever pitch. Rebels set fire to four hundred thousand gallons of fuel at the U.S.-owned Esso oil refinery. They also took over the National Bank of Cuba and burned all its checks and drafts. And they kidnapped the international race-car champion Juan Manuel Fangio the day before he was set to race in the Gran Premio de Cuba, a major tourist attraction. Fangio was released the next day and referred to the rebels as his "friends the kidnappers." "If my capture can serve a good purpose, as an Argentine, I support it," he stated publicly. The episode, according to the U.S. Embassy, "cast the government in a bad light as incapable of maintaining order in its own house." Rebel attacks on railways stopped trains from running. And most of the nation's schools and universities were closed because of the escalating state and guerrilla violence rocking the country.[73]

The regime was looking increasingly precarious, its last pillars of support beginning to crumble and opposition mobilized against it from all sides. In March, the sugar planters' national association made clear that it no longer supported the regime, apparently in response to Batista's inability to stop the torching of plantations and escalating sabotage against company infrastructure. On the other side of the political spectrum, the Communist party reversed its previous position and embraced both a nationwide general strike planned by the 26th of July Movement and armed struggle against the dictatorship. This decision was driven by the brutal repression party members were suffering then at the hands of their once-close ally, Batista. The dictator apparently hoped these attacks would ingratiate him with U.S. leaders by demonstrating just how loyally anti-Communist he was.[74]

The U.S. government, however, increasingly distanced itself from a regime that was starting to look like a lost cause. In March 1958, U.S. president Dwight Eisenhower halted U.S. arms shipments to Batista, stating that contrary to legal stipulations they were being used for internal security matters rather than hemispheric defense. This suspension was, on the one hand, inconsequential: the regime already had ample arms that the U.S. government had provided over the last six years. And close relations continued to prevail between U.S. officials and the Cuban government after the arms suspension. Ambassador Earl Smith's horror at government repression in July 1957 had been supplanted by growing apprehension of a Castro-led revolution, and Smith appeared closer than ever to Batista. Still, the arms cutoff was a symbolic blow for the regime, showing cracks in the erstwhile unqualified U.S. government support Batista had depended on for most of his rule. And the waning of U.S. support for Batista further discredited and weakened the regime. Even the military's support for Batista was growing shaky. By the start of 1958, growing numbers of government soldiers were refusing to fight Castro's forces, and some even switched sides.[75]

In April 1958, the 26th of July Movement organized a general strike that was meant to paralyze the country. The strike, though, was a failure. It did not garner sufficient support from workers and shopkeepers in the city, and Batista used it as an opportunity to decimate the urban rebel organizations. Afterward, urban sabotage was reduced to a relatively small problem for the regime. Hundreds of urban revolutionaries in Santiago now fled to the hills to join the rural guerrillas. The momentum of the entire 26th of July Movement took a serious blow. But the collapse of the urban underground would be Castro's chance to assume fuller command and have the movement concentrate its efforts, weapons, and strategy solely on the rebel army under his command in the countryside. Castro and the rural guerrillas became the last, best hope for ousting Batista.[76]

Revolution and the Disappearing State

Across Oriente's mountain ranges, the rebels had established a state-within-a-state subject to their military and political control. But their now world-famous troops were still too small in number and did not have enough armaments to pose any direct military threat to Batista's rule. The regime was not compelled, therefore, to launch a major new counterinsurgency campaign. In May 1958, however, Batista ordered one anyway. This decision may have been the result of elevated confidence following the defeat of the "general strike" the month before, or perhaps Batista feared that Castro's forces and popularity would continue to grow the longer they thrived in Oriente. The existence of this revolutionary state-within-a-state was clearly a slap in the face to Batista's power and authority. So, two years after the insurrection had begun, Batista decided on an all-out assault against the rebel army to reconquer the territory it controlled. Ironically, it was this decision by Batista that would fuel the revolution's ultimate success. When Batista ordered Operation End-of-Fidel (as he called it), the insurgents were ready. During a year and a half of only limited attacks by the Cuban army, the rebels had been able to master skills in guerrilla warfare, familiarize themselves with obscure jungle terrain, and build popular support. This last accomplishment resulted in superior combat intelligence. Dickey Chapelle, a senior U.S. war correspondent who camped out with the rebels for a month, reported that "Batista's forces could not go a yard without a perspiring runner arriving a few minutes later to tell Castro of it." Castro's headquarters, established on the high ground at the summit of the Sierra Maestra, La Plata, were hidden in the woods underneath thick branches. They were nonetheless supplied with electric generators, telephone wires, storage facilities, a field hospital, and even an airstrip for small planes.[77]

Batista did not send his entire army to Oriente, which would have left his regime vulnerable in the rest of the country. But he did dispatch a giant force, more than twelve thousand troops, to hunt down Castro's forces on land while the air force and navy bombed them from air and sea. The Cuban army focused on the rebel troops in the Sierra Maestra rather than those to the northeast in the Sierra Cristal. Batista officials reported that in the Sierra Maestra Castro commanded "between 1,000 and 2,000 first-class combatants, very well armed." But a leading Cuban rebel, Carlos Franqui, later recalled that Castro in fact had only three hundred regulars at that time, along with some one thousand "musketeers," with Raúl Castro commanding about the same number of troops in the Sierra Cristal.[78]

Batista's troops began scaling the Sierra Maestra in late May 1958. Most did not have training in guerrilla warfare, and they advanced with difficulty through the jungle terrain. Government soldiers also triggered hidden mines and were ambushed by rebel forces. The first major engagement occurred after over a month of unsuccessful and exhausting pursuit of the guerrillas. In one three-day battle, some eight hundred soldiers were trounced, and many troops deserted, escaping into the woods. Subsequent battles went the same way. On July 21, after a sustained fight, Major José Quevedo surrendered his battalion, one of the army's fourteen, to rebels. Quevedo was a former law school classmate of Castro's, and the major would later join the insurgency.[79]

Practically speaking, it would not have been possible for the guerrillas to detain and control prisoners of war, so they had to release them. But returning them unharmed also had the benefit of spreading word of the prisoners' humane treatment. This gave Castro an honorable image in contrast to Batista's history of torturing opponents. And it also likely enticed government troops to surrender given the prospect of safe and quick release. Reporting on the Cuban military's "very low" morale, General Eulogio Cantillo noted the efficacy of Castro's tactic. Soldiers, he reported, were discouraged by the "major setbacks" in recent battles and, knowing "that they do not treat harshly those who turn themselves in," had come to understand that "their problems end when they are taken prisoner." Cantillo also described another form of informal military resistance: "The number of losses due to self-inflicted wounds is extraordinarily large." Most dramatically, "entire combat units . . . [have] refused to advance" into new positions against the rebels. The weak commitment of Batista's soldiers to the war may have reflected the fact that seven thousand of the twelve thousand troops dispatched to Oriente were conscripts, forcibly drafted and quickly trained. But it also stemmed from widespread opposition to Batista's rule. Ultimately, the collapse of Operation End-of-Fidel reflected Batista's political weakness as much as military challenges. Neither troops nor society was committed enough to the regime to sustain the heavy casualties required for an effective counterinsurgency campaign against the guerrillas.[80]

The rebels were now riding high. Ever attuned to the power of the media, they broadcast their triumphs across Cuba and abroad from Rebel Radio, the shortwave radio station they had set up on a mountain peak. During the campaign, Castro's forces had also captured an impressive arsenal of weapons that made them a more formidable army than they had been at the start of Batista's "summer offensive." These included two tanks and as many as two hundred submachine guns. Rebel troops did suffer casualties when they moved out of the mountains in pursuit of government forces, but not as many as did the Cuban army. After three months, when Batista's soldiers went home, reportedly around a thousand had been killed, captured, or wounded, while the rebels had lost roughly a hundred fighters. Guevara boasted in an interview in December that the campaign had been "humiliatingly lost by the dictatorship's army."[81]

Following the defeat in Oriente, one Cuban officer expressed his frustration that the troops were being demoralized by "Fidel Castro's radio station," which was making it "appear as if we were paralyzed by some atomic ray inflicted on us by the *guajiritos escopeteros* [little peasant musketeers]." Batista's big military push and defeat had made the rebels both militarily and politically more powerful than they had been beforehand. David was actually defeating Goliath. And if Castro had bested Batista's army in the Sierra Maestra, perhaps he could somehow win across the nation. Almost all of the opposition bodies now allied with Castro in a formal statement of unity, the Pact of Caracas, signed on July 20. Operation End-of-Fidel appeared now more like Operation End-of-Batista, or self-destruction by the regime.[82]

The Communist party had been excluded from the pact. But in early June, Carlos Rafael Rodríguez, a long-standing leader of the party, made a trek into the Sierra Maestra and Sierra Cristal seeking to join the bandwagon. The 26th of July Movement had been envisaging some kind of alliance with the party since the failure of the April general strike. The movement's leaders realized then that without backing from the vast population of sugar workers and other wage laborers on the island, the revolution could probably not succeed. And if they did win, they would need support from a mass constituency to successfully carry out major socioeconomic reforms, a constituency that the Communist party, with a long history of leadership in the unions dating back to the 1930s, could deliver. From the Communist party's point of view, an alliance with Castro also made strategic sense. If an alliance was formed and the 26th of July Movement prevailed, the alliance could help the party regain its leadership role in the labor unions and perhaps some of the political significance it had enjoyed in the 1938–44 period, when it was allied with the old reformist Batista of that era.[83]

With new allies, and perceiving the Batista regime's political and military weakness, Castro shifted military strategy. Despite the fact that his troops were overwhelmingly outnumbered and outgunned, he decided to head out of his inaccessible regional stronghold and to engage government forces on the lowlands in more conventional battles. Castro's rebel army had grown. Its confidence-building victories had attracted new volunteers, and it had integrated other rebel groups. Still, the size of Castro's forces was never impressive. If they were to survive a march on Havana, government troops would have to refuse not only to risk dying for the regime but even to kill for it. They would have to no longer be able to see the enemy as the enemy. The triumph of the revolution would have to be a political victory. It required winning over Batista's troops.

Castro's new plan to topple the regime was to surround and take the city of Santiago in Oriente. Castro dispatched several hundred troops in two columns, one under Guevara and the other under Camilo Cienfuegos (a member of the original *Granma* crew), to the Escambray Mountains in Las Villas Province. They were to pursue the approach taken in the Sierra Maestra and implement an agrarian reform benefiting the peasantry, as part of a larger plan to establish a strong foothold in the area. If they could take and hold Las Villas Province in the middle of the island, they could destroy its infrastructure and impede the movement of troops and supplies from the country's military headquarters in Havana to Oriente, where the rebels were. This would reduce the government's military superiority and make a rebel siege of Santiago more feasible. The fact that there were already hundreds of rebels operating in the region, largely from the remnants of the Revolutionary Directorate who had moved there after their failed palace attack in Havana, would facilitate the effort.[84]

As Guevara and Cienfuegos made the three-hundred-mile, seven-week trek from the Sierra Maestra to the Escambray across much difficult terrain, they were subjected to attack from the sky. They managed to evade the bombs by escaping into the woods and marshes. But the real key to their success was political. Some Cuban officers and government troops refused to engage the rebels in combat. The units of thousands of soldiers deployed to stop them suffered desertion, defection, and various forms of informal insubordination. A September 21 military report in Camagüey noted that even some officers refused to fight.[85]

As they had in the Sierra Maestra, the rebels in the Escambray began acting with the authority of a government. Small farmers were granted, at least for the time being, free access to land on which they had been paying rent. In October, Castro issued a vague agrarian reform edict for the areas under the rebel army's control. All those with less than 150 acres would be entitled to keep their land. But large estates would be subject to expropriation, at least of idle areas, and owners would be compensated for their lost property. State lands would also be made available for distribution. Batista himself owned properties in the area, which were to be taken over and distributed to peasants.[86]

In an interview on Rebel Radio two months after arriving in the Sierra del Escambray, Guevara spoke at length about agrarian reform. "The Agrarian Reform Law," he explained, "has as a basis the elimination of the latifundia, distributing small parcels of land so that the peasant can live a dignified life; we should also give him easy credit terms and the necessary technical aid which, of course, we cannot now offer as a revolutionary army. That will follow later. The peasants will pay nothing for the land." But

Guevara did not engage a critical question. Would all of the vast areas taken from sugar plantations and ranches be distributed to squatters, tenants, and small farmers, or would these also become the locus of state enterprise? Guevara's emphasis at this time was on the small farmer.[87]

The 26th of July Movement in Las Villas focused not only on the peasantry but also on the large number of workers in the province's multiple sugar mills and plantations. Just as the movement's leaders had superimposed themselves on preexisting squatter struggles in Oriente, they now built on an active movement of sugar and textile workers in Las Villas, many of whom were part of Communist and other independent unions and labor opposition groups. With the help of Communist party members, Cienfuegos organized a series of meetings with laborers from the region's numerous sugar mills. At each meeting, hundreds gathered to share their grievances and hopes for change. Cienfuegos promised that the rebel army would help them in their struggles with the owners of plantations and mills.[88]

At this time, a rough consensus was forming within the U.S. State Department and the intelligence community that Batista was doomed, and that the only way to prevent the 26th of July Movement from triumphing was by cultivating a moderate "third force," some kind of military group that could replace Batista and stop Castro from taking power. But U.S. government intervention to thwart a Castro-led revolution came surprisingly late. Why did U.S. leaders wait until the eleventh hour to begin searching for ways to stop the Cuban Revolution? Although Castro had long been at odds with the Communist party and formed alliances with moderate groups that spoke of a liberal political rather than a left-wing socioeconomic revolution, he himself had always shown an obvious commitment to a sweeping agrarian reform and other major redistributionist programs.[89]

The failure to perceive Castro as a potential leader of a radical revolution was, above all perhaps, a failure to perceive the potential for radical revolution in Cuba, regardless of its leadership. This complacency of U.S. officials stemmed from a confidence in U.S. hegemony in the country. In late 1958, the U.S. Embassy reported on political developments with only modest concern: "It is improbable that a Government actively unfriendly to the United States could exist for any length of time." Cuba's economy was simply too dependent on trade with the United States. Furthermore, if a Cuban government were to go astray of U.S. interests, the U.S.-built Cuban army would be there to defend those interests and overthrow such a government if necessary. In fact, many U.S. leaders saw Cuba as belonging to the United States almost as much as Puerto Rico and other U.S. territories.[90]

Well aware of these realities, some members of the 26th of July Movement expressed strong desires for greater Cuban autonomy from the United States while optimistically hoping that this could be reconciled with a continuing alliance and good working relationship with the U.S. government. As an official 26th of July Movement pamphlet from 1957 explained: "Through a new treatment of *constructive friendship,* Cuba could truly be, as is advisable for many geographical, economic, and even political reasons, a loyal ally of the great country of the North, and at the same time safely preserve the capacity to determine its own destiny."[91]

Probably most U.S. leaders assumed that the U.S. government could ultimately impose its will on Cuba if necessary, whether through economic pressure, covert operations, or traditional acts or threats of U.S. military intervention (as in both the 1898 and 1933 revolutions). The U.S. military itself was at the doorstep and could easily deploy overwhelming military force. And the CIA had managed without great effort or expense to overthrow covertly the governments of Guatemala in 1954 and faraway Iran in 1953. This seemed even easier to carry out in next-door Cuba. Wayne Smith, a member of the U.S. Embassy between 1959 and 1961, later explained: "The United States . . . didn't really take [threats in] Latin America very seriously. It certainly didn't take Central America and Caribbean countries seriously. These were little countries that we wanted to do what we wanted them to do and if they didn't, well, we would get something going like the operation in Guatemala and that would take care of it."[92]

But there was a fundamental difference between Guatemala in 1954 and Cuba in 1958. The 26th of July Movement and other rebel groups had created an armed revolution in both the city and the countryside, and it was that which was on the verge of bringing about great change rather than a democratic election. Not only were these resistance forces that had inspired widespread hopes across the country for deep reforms to government and society. Years of rural insurgency had also built a new army that could replace the existing Cuban military linked to the old regime. The revolution in Cuba had what Árbenz did not: a new military to defend a truly transformative government. Castro had already made clear that the rebel army intended first to defeat and then to supersede the old Cuban army on which the U.S. government had counted to sustain its interests since the turn of the century.[93]

In December 1958, the U.S. government forced Batista to make plans to go into exile, but it was already too late to oversee the transition to a new government that could forestall the victory of Castro's now powerful revolutionary movement. There was no longer any strong leader among the moderate opponents, one with the kind of public support or even name recognition to have any chance of capturing the revolutionary momentum against Batista and stealing Castro's thunder. As the U.S. deputy secretary of defense told President Eisenhower on December 23, "there was no 'third force' . . . to support," only Batista or Castro.[94]

The Cuban army leadership understood this and scrambled to find a way to stave off a total defeat. Before Batista resigned, his senior military officers sought behind his back to try to cut a deal with Castro that would have kept the military leadership and structure in place. The top brass sent a representative to meet with a member of Castro's urban underground in Havana on December 23 and proposed that the Cuban and rebel armies together invade the western provinces and then Havana. Batista would be removed from power and a mixed civilian and military junta established. Castro was offered the power to choose its civilian members, and his already announced presidential choice for the provisional government, Manuel Urrutia, would stand. But Castro refused. He could almost taste victory, and he was not going to ally with the army and thus sacrifice, for an easier more certain triumph, his key postrevolutionary strategy of supplanting the Cuban military. He knew that it would be impossible to make radical popular reforms without changing the old military institutions and leadership. There was not just the example of Guatemala as a warning, but also that of the 1933 Cuban Revolution, when the leadership of a left-wing uprising allied with elements in the military. Together, they carried out a coup only for the new "revolutionary" government to be overthrown through U.S. pressure and mediation by that same military within a year. The result was the first Batista dictatorship.[95]

On December 29, Guevara launched the largest battle of the revolution by far, the battle for Santa Clara. With several hundred troops and strong support from the civilian population, the rebel troops faced an army in the thousands. Nonetheless, they were able to capture an armored train filled with hundreds of government soldiers and a vast store of weaponry sent to shore up Santa Clara's defenses. The government soldiers on board surrendered and handed over all their weapons to Guevara. Meanwhile, back in Havana, Batista threw a New Year's Eve party. The effort at forced gaiety quickly ended, though, when Batista announced his resignation and immediate flight from the country along with those of his close collaborators who could fit on the available planes.[96]

The U.S. government was not willing to take in its loyal client. So Batista headed for the Dominican Republic, hoping the dictator Rafael Trujillo would welcome him. Trujillo was reportedly aghast at Batista's capitulation, seeing in Fidel Castro's revolution an enemy next door. (Castro, in fact, would sponsor a failed Dominican exile invasion to overthrow Trujillo just six months after victory in January.) Nonetheless, Trujillo permitted Batista's entourage to land. But he insisted that the fleeing strongman pay him a chunk of the hundreds of millions he had spirited out of Cuba, reportedly as repayment for past Dominican military aid. With no other government yet willing to grant him a visa, Batista was compelled to offer up millions of dollars to his hostile Dominican host. "Batista's presence here is repugnant," the state-controlled Dominican media declared after he took asylum in the country. "Contact with him disgusts and shames us."[97]

After Batista's flight from Cuba, a military junta led by General Cantillo, the army chief of Oriente, took charge and attempted to pick up the pieces. But the military leadership no longer had any power or authority. The soldiers of Santa Clara refused orders to continue fighting and instead surrendered to Guevara. After the rebels took Santa Clara, Castro ordered Guevara and Cienfuegos to advance to Havana. Castro's troops, meanwhile, entered Santiago and demanded the unconditional surrender of its garrison, which he received without a shot being fired. Rebel Radio announced proudly that this revolution would not end the way the Cuban War of Independence had.[98]

On January 2, Castro called a nationwide strike to demonstrate the strength of the revolutionary movement and to intimidate the Cuban military. When Cienfuegos arrived in Havana on January 2, 1959, he marched directly to the military headquarters, Camp Columbia. The rebel leader Carlos Franqui recalled the ironic and even surreal scene he found at Camp Columbia two days later: "On the one hand the bearded rebels with Camilo [Cienfuegos], no more than five hundred of them, and on the other hand, twenty thousand army soldiers intact—generals, colonels, majors, captains, corporals, sergeants, and privates. When they saw us walk by, they stood at attention. It was enough to make you burst out laughing. In the commandant's office was Camilo, . . . his boots thrown on the floor and his feet up on the table, as he received his excellency the ambassador of the United States."[99]

The Cuban Revolution had no great military battles and comparatively few deaths in the field. It was a profound political victory rather than a magical military one. But this was far from a velvet revolution. Large numbers in the resistance died to make it happen, fighting for disparate causes and goals: for sweeping agrarian and other radical redistributionist reforms, for political liberalization and an end to police abuses, for redeeming Havana's dignity from perceived foreign humiliation and commercialized vice, or because a family member or friend had been tortured or murdered by the regime. Through armed and other forms of resistance, Castro and his diverse allies and rivals galvanized popular, cross-class support for a revolution against Batista's regime. The regime lost even the kind of minority support that comes from a powerful social group perceiving benefits in the political status quo and that has enabled many brutal dictatorships to endure. In this context, there were no longer enough government soldiers willing to die or to kill for it. And under Castro's charismatic leadership in the Sierra Maestra, the left wing of the revolutionary forces had survived and thrived seemingly against all odds. The result was that it was these forces who were the main rebel body still standing and fighting when the Batista regime imploded, still growing, captivating public attention, and ready to take control of the state. The 26th of July Movement thus prevailed not only over the Batista regime but also over its revolutionary rivals, as well as over any moderate anti-Batista alternative envisaged by the U.S. and elite Cuban groups that might have forestalled revolution and kept the old military in place.[100]

Yet despite Castro's standing as the leader of a wildly popular insurgency, he could not now simply dictate the course of the revolution. Whatever Castro's and other leaders' ideas were, however redistributionist Castro's vision had been since the start of the 26th of July Movement, it was still an open question whether the revolution would end more radically or more conservatively. That would depend on Cuba's overall political realities. The Cuban population had been mobilized as never before. And that revolutionary mobilization, as well as the actions of elite Cuban groups and U.S. government leaders, would now trigger massive political forces, both transformative and reactionary. Castro could help direct these competing forces, but ultimately he would have to ride a continuing revolutionary wave if the radical transformation of Cuban society that he and the left wing of the insurrection were imagining was to come to be.

6 Revolution and Intervention in Cuba and the Dominican Republic

. . . .

"The Revolution will not be an easy task," Fidel Castro told a cheering crowd gathered in the middle of the night on January 2, 1959, to welcome him into Santiago. His forces had seized control of the city, the country's second largest; the dictatorship of Fulgencio Batista was crumbling; and Cuban troops were surrendering to rebel soldiers across the country. Castro, until recently a "hunted young man" leading a small guerrilla rebellion, was suddenly the nation's towering political figure. But Castro warned the crowd that victory was not yet at hand. There were battles still to be fought, and much was still up for grabs. "The Revolution will be a difficult undertaking, filled with risks."[1]

Cuba's previous revolutions, Castro reminded his listeners, had ultimately been stalled and reversed. And yet he exuded confidence that this new revolution would triumph. "Fortunately for Cuba, this time the Revolution will truly come to power. It will not be like 95 [the 1895 independence revolution], when the Americans came and took over and intervened at the last moment." "It will not be like 33 [the 1933 revolution]," Castro went on, "when after the people began to believe that a revolution was taking place, Batista seized power and instituted a dictatorship." "It will not be like 44 [the 1944 democratic election]," he continued, "when the multitudes were ecstatic, believing that the people had come to power, at last, but it was the thieves who came to power." This time would be different, Castro promised. "Neither thieves nor traitors, nor interventionists would control the fate of Cuba. This time, it is truly the Revolution." Castro was anticipating, correctly, that there would be powerful resistance to his plans for change. But, infused with the surprising confidence that had characterized his political life since the Moncada attack, he also declared that this resistance would be overcome and a new Cuba would be born.[2]

Yet the shape of this revolution in Cuba would inevitably depend on more than the will of its leaders or even the majority of its population. Outcomes would be conditioned also by what was politically possible, nationally and internationally. What would unfold would inevitably be a dialectic between the popular hopes, demands, and fears inspired by the revolution; the ambitions of its leaders; and a set of harsh international constraints imposed by U.S. reactions to change in Cuba.

Not only would Cuban history be forever transformed by the outcome of this dialectic. It would also have far-reaching consequences beyond the island, variously inspiring hopes and fears of social and economic transformation in other nations—of "another Cuba" as well as of possible U.S. intervention. Those hopes and fears guided forces for change in other Caribbean countries as they carved out their own paths to popular socioeconomic reforms, particularly in the Dominican Republic, Jamaica, Grenada, and Haiti. Though the projects for transformation in each of these nations would be far more moderate than the Cuban Revolution, they all nonetheless faced U.S. hostility and a debilitating mix of domestic elite and foreign opposition.

This chapter explores, first, the unfolding of the Cuban Revolution as it was shaped by a radicalizing dynamic between a mass "constituency for change" and escalating U.S. intervention to forestall it.[3] Second, it illuminates comparable political dynamics of reform, revolution, and intervention in the neighboring independent Caribbean nation of the Dominican Republic. In 1963, despite efforts to heed lessons from the experience of the Cuban Revolution, the social democratic government of Juan Bosch in the Dominican Republic would be stopped in its tracks by a military coup and then, after Dominicans eventually rose up to restore Bosch to office, a U.S. military invasion of the island. In both Cuba and the Dominican Republic, the U.S. government turned to armed force to quash a popular Caribbean revolution that U.S. leaders did not see as being in U.S. interests. And in both cases, U.S. intervention had dreadful consequences.

Cuba's "Vast Constituency for Radical Change"

The Cuban Revolution essentially smashed the old state, starting with its military. This opened up both opportunities and risks: there was now space for an exceptionally wide range of outcomes. A "vast constituency for radical change," writes historian Louis Pérez, seized the moment in the hopes of realizing many and varied aspirations. The revolution itself had done something that few had imagined was possible a few years earlier. In the process, popular demands expanded, and the possibility of great changes at great speed appeared on the horizon. Hundreds of thousands of expectant citizens turned out for Castro's hours-long speeches, surely hopeful that the revolution would live up to their dreams.[4]

By Pérez's calculation, the "constituency for change" comprised some two million people out of a total population of approximately six million. First and foremost there were 1.1 million wage laborers and between some perhaps 400,000 and 665,000 unemployed workers, the number depending on the time of year given seasonal unemployment in the sugar and tourist industries. These workers rapidly mobilized to make the revolution their own. Strikes, hunger strikes, slowdowns, walkouts, and demonstrations spread like wildfire. Unions demanded a 20 percent increase in wages. Large numbers of laborers dismissed back in 1957 insisted that they be reinstated. Electric company employees, railway workers, paper mill laborers, nickel miners, restaurant workers, construction laborers, and sugar workers all demanded job security and a higher standard of living. Cane cutters, the largest and probably worst-off labor sector, halted the harvest at twenty-one major sugar plantations, demanding wage increases from their companies.[5]

There were also over two hundred thousand small farming families, most of whom lived in poor conditions as squatters, tenants, and holders of small plots. This population, specifically the landless and sharecropping inhabitants of Oriente, had been central to developing and anchoring Castro's guerrilla movement in the Sierra Maestra. Like wage laborers, those seeking land were not willing to wait for change from above. They sought to exploit the breakdown of the old state and the promises of "the Revolution" to pursue dramatic advancements for themselves. In the countryside, poor farmers were taking over idle lands, reversing the prerevolutionary pattern of small-farming squatters being pushed off their holdings. Tenants also refused to pay their rents. Concerned, the new government passed a law in February threatening those who took such actions with disqualification from a future agrarian reform. But this did not stop instances of direct action in Oriente and elsewhere.[6]

Finally, from the first days following the revolution's triumph, there were also demands made by Cubans of African descent to make racial justice central to the revolutionary program. They constituted between a quarter and a third of the country and comprised a disproportionately large part of the rural and urban lower classes. The politics of racial equality had been at the center of the War of Independence in the 1890s, but subsequent Cuban regimes had rarely addressed the question. The 26th of July Movement itself had been slow to call for antidiscrimination measures. During the early months after Castro's victory, however, popular demands for change put questions of race and racism on the revolutionary agenda.[7]

Castro knew his political future depended on his being seen as responsive to popular demands. As a leader, he had to live up to the rhetoric of "the revolution." He would succeed at doing so only by riding the waves of popular mobilization. The population now demanded real socioeconomic change, as Castro had long promised, not just political liberalization and civil rights. It remained to be seen how much of that change could and would be accomplished through state intervention within a capitalist system based overwhelmingly on the private sector and in a country so deeply tied economically and strategically to the United States. It also remained to be seen whether Castro's erstwhile promises for a transition from an authoritarian to a democratic regime, even if not immediate, would be fulfilled.[8]

Some of those who had participated in the resistance to Batista were fighting for an essentially political revolution—the elimination of the dictatorship—but not a socioeconomic one. Castro, on the other hand, had called for a radical redistribution of wealth, though not a fully socialist order or a break with the United States. But when Castro faced insuperable U.S. opposition to popular radical reforms, both economic warfare and armed intervention, he mobilized nationalist support for just such a break and steered the country in a new geopolitical and ideological direction that was not rooted in either Castro's long-standing ideals or popular political visions. That new direction involved a deferential alliance with the Soviet Union and a turn toward Communism, with an almost fully state-run economy and a smothering set of official national ideas. Until the fall of the Soviet Union around 1990, Cuban Communism would disprove both its apologists and its detractors, creating a series of contradictory outcomes for many Cubans, both profoundly welcomed forms of egalitarian change and deeply resented state repression.

Revolutionary Reforms

Before Castro could institute the redistributive reforms that he had laid out in his 1953 speech, "History Will Absolve Me," and that now fired the popular imagination in Cuba, he had to establish a new government and refashion the state. As had been planned by the 26th of July Movement and agreed to by other opposition groups, Castro appointed Judge Manuel Urrutia provisional president. The new prime minister was José Miró Cardona, the president of the Havana Bar Association who, like Urrutia, had been a centrist opponent of Batista. These appointments gave the provisional government a moderate image, and it was immediately recognized by the United States. The creation of a new "ministry for revolutionary laws," however, hinted that some of the revolutionary laws decreeing dramatic redistribution of wealth outlined in *History Will Absolve Me* might be on their way.[9]

Castro, meanwhile, was appointed the nation's new commander-in-chief. It was unclear how much real control Urrutia and Miró could exercise in the shadow of this fantastically popular figure. *New York Times* correspondent Herbert Matthews wrote that Castro was now, in fact, "the chief power in Cuba." Urrutia's swearing in had been almost a nonevent, eclipsed by a dramatic march by Castro and his troops five hundred miles across the island from the east, where the insurgency had raged, to the capital after the triumph of the revolution. Castro drove slowly atop a tank from Santiago, delivering long speeches to jubilant crowds as if he were campaigning for office. Castro's political skills were on full display. He could have taken a plane to Havana. Instead he turned the voyage to Havana into a week-long triumphant procession. Castro was drawing the population into the revolutionary struggle, directly and through mass media. In Havana, he was welcomed with a mass rally. An awed British ambassador described the image Castro projected as a "mixture of José Martí, Robin Hood, Garibaldi, and Jesus Christ."[10]

Despite the moderate and respectable image lent to the new government by its president and prime minister, it immediately swung open the doors to deep socioeconomic transformation in two key ways. First, all agreed that elections would not take place for eighteen months. Until that time, the unelected government could exercise absolute authority, with the cabinet endowed with legislative power. "Revolution first, elections later" was the official slogan.[11]

Elections appeared to be of little popular concern as well. President Urrutia noted how the audience booed when Castro mentioned government elections in one of his speeches, and this phenomenon was echoed at future rallies. Repeated promises to reduce poverty and inequality by democratically elected presidents in the past had never been fulfilled. They were unable or unwilling to overcome opposition by powerful groups to popular socioeconomic reforms. And Cuba's at least nominally liberal state had long been characterized by massive graft and embezzlement, political violence, government neglect, and often authoritarian rule. Perhaps elections simply were not a priority for most Cubans in this context or not a serious concern given Castro's popularity and widespread optimism about the future of the revolution. Furthermore, liberal democracy is slow by design while revolutionary change is fast by definition. Many perhaps instinctively understood this and longed for the latter. The government's absolute rule was solidified when in mid-February Prime Minister Miró resigned and recommended that Castro take over his position. It was clear that Castro was the real power behind the throne anyway. "I resigned. Cuba did not protest; it accepted, it applauded," Miró noted.[12]

The second and perhaps most important step taken by the new government to facilitate revolutionary change was the immediate elimination of the old Cuban military structure. On January 13, it was announced that the Cuban military would be replaced by a new one organized by Castro. In the place of armed forces with deep ties to the U.S. government, Castro established a military that was ideologically committed to the revolution even in the face of possible threats of U.S. intervention. The most effective means U.S. leaders and powerful Cuban groups had for guaranteeing policies favorable to their interests in the Cuban republic suddenly vanished before their eyes.[13]

The new regime also swiftly set up tribunals to try members of the old armed forces alleged to have committed war crimes and atrocities. Hundreds, probably thousands, of Cubans had been tortured and killed by the armed forces and security organizations during the 1950s. Now hundreds of Batista's military, police, and security forces were found guilty of capital crimes and executed in the early months of 1959. The decision to sentence to death many from the regime's repressive apparatus was popular in Cuba. According to one independent survey, 93 percent of those polled supported the executions. Accounts of the trials suggest that in most cases there was some facsimile of legality that made these more than pure theater but far short of due process. Most observers, though, including critics of the trials, concluded that the defendants were probably guilty as charged.[14]

With the old army gone and the foundations for a new state in place, Castro began making good on the redistributionist reforms he had envisioned six years earlier in *History Will Absolve Me*. Even without the promised elections, Castro appears to have sustained his popularity with these reforms. The first step was the Urban Reform Law of March 1959. As promised, all rents were reduced by between 30 and 50 percent (depending on their cost). The law also required that all vacant urban lots be sold to anyone prepared to build a home or to the government so they could be used to construct low-income public housing. Unsurprisingly, the Urban Reform Law was a popular measure. Other similar measures followed at a fever pitch. By April, Hugh Thomas contends, "national income had been seriously and visibly redistributed." It was a "remarkable political achievement" that gave "a large section of the populace a big stake in the Revolution." Utility rates, bus fares, and medicine prices were all reduced. As a result of labor activism and the presence of a pro-labor government, wages began rising substantially across the board, including a 15 percent increase in wages for all cane cutters. Government employees' salaries were also raised. New schools and hospitals were built at a dizzying rate from the first months of the new regime, expanding the availability of public health care and education across the country. Needless to say, these dramatic improvements in the standard of living of the popular classes, and the reduction in income inequality, came at the expense of landlords, employers, and large landowners. They voiced vehement opposition to a government many of them now labeled "Communist." The U.S.-owned telephone and electric companies also protested the government's required rate reductions.[15]

The "Revolutionary Government," as it called itself, also sought to challenge the country's structures of racial discrimination and de facto segregation. In March 1959, Castro devoted a major part of one of his speeches to condemning racism in Cuba. Until this time, Cubans of African descent had been excluded from many private schools, social clubs, restaurants, nightclubs, hotels, and even parts of public parks and other public spaces. They were effectively barred from employment in certain branches of the economy, such as retail stores and banking, and in companies where hiring practices were determined by nepotistic white-only unions. Racial prejudice and exclusion in social networks were present not just among elite white Cubans but across class. Railway and electrical workers, for instance, had clubs that banned Cubans of African descent. Earlier legal changes had not stopped these practices: the 1940 Constitution explicitly banned racial discrimination, and subsequent government decrees had affirmed this principle.[16]

The new Cuban regime took immediate and effective steps to counter discrimination, first in recreational spaces, soon afterward in education, and then in the realm of employment. Town parks that had been informally segregated were rebuilt so that their "traditional, racially significant layouts" were wiped out. In one case, historian Alejandro de la Fuente explains, "the old flowerpots that had divided the white and black areas were removed and replaced with an undivided walkway." The country's beaches had previously been segregated, with the most desirable ones in private hands, owned by "openly discriminatory" social clubs or luxury hotels. Castro resolved the issue in one simple decree that made all beach property public. He also instituted measures to end racist practices in hotels, restaurants, and other public spaces. The "racial integration of previously white social spaces marked one of the starkest distinctions between pre- and post-1959 Cuba," writes historian Devyn Spence Benson. Castro had rarely spoken about racism during the insurrection. But in the immediate aftermath of the revolution's triumph, Afro-Cuban leaders demanded forceful anti-racist measures that help explain the Cuban government's immediate attention to race. That included "a fruitful and unprecedented public debate," in de la Fuente's words, over how to address the problem of racism in Cuba. People of color were roughly 30 percent of the population, and Castro acted to mobilize this demographic as part of the revolution and its base of support.[17]

Yet there was also strong white resistance to these revolutionary efforts to end racial segregation and discrimination. Some white Cubans expressed opposition even to sitting next to Cubans of color in public transportation, walking in the park in the same zones, being in the same labor clubs, and having their children attend the same schools. Given Castro's popularity at the time, it was a sign of the severity of racial inequality and prejudice in Cuba that he encountered many antagonistic responses among white Cubans to his March 1959 speech against racism. One better-off white Cuban recalled that "Many people left Cuba because they did not want to mix with [Cubans of color]." Opponents of the perceived radicalization of the revolution publicly brandished the racist slogan "Neither Black nor Red."[18]

It would take many years before quality of life and life chances across race began to equalize in Cuba, and the disappearance of some forms of racism would not mean the end of others. Antiblack prejudice continued among whites in, for instance, the criminal justice system. Also after the initial years of the revolution, critiques of racism would be smothered by an official discourse of supposed revolutionary triumph over racial discrimination and prejudice. Race-based organizations and expressions of black consciousness were repressed, even though, in contrast to white-only institutions, black organizations' aim had always been to help end, provide refuge from, and triumph over racism. In these ways, some of the government's own policies helped certain forms of racism continue to prevail, even as racial inequality and discrimination were dramatically reduced in key spheres—health, education, and access to the professions—over the next two decades.[19]

In the aftermath of the revolution, the new government also sought to implement a national agrarian reform. Since its beginnings, the 26th of July

Movement had made the promise of agrarian reform a centerpiece of its political platform. The movement had depended on the support of squatters, tenants, and other small farmers in Oriente, who had helped shape the practice and ideology of the guerrilla forces during their years in the Sierra Maestra and Sierra del Cristal. Now that they were in power, the revolutionary leaders were determined to do what they had said they would.

On May 17, the regime announced its agrarian reform law, which prohibited property holdings in excess of 1,000 acres or beyond 3,333 acres for sugar, rice, or cattle estates that were being productively exploited. Compared with other agrarian reform policies, such as that in Puerto Rico in 1941 and Guatemala in 1952, these property limits were actually high and far from radical. But given the tremendous magnitude and overall dimensions of Cuba's sugar and cattle estates, the law would have an enormous impact. The gargantuan fifty-thousand-acre, U.S.-owned Pingree Ranch in Oriente would be almost entirely taken over by the government. And altogether an estimated 2.5 million acres of ranch land and 1.5 million acres from U.S. sugar estates were targeted for expropriation in the months after the law went into effect. Ultimately the law would subject three million acres of U.S. sugar properties and two million acres of Cuban-owned estates to expropriation and potential redistribution.[20]

The agrarian reform also banned sharecropping. All those farming on land belonging to others (or the state) were to be given the area that they were already cultivating, provided it was no more than sixty-seven acres. Furthermore, confiscated property could be distributed to individual farmers in plots up to sixty-seven acres. Among the beneficiaries who were to receive individual land, priority was to be given first to landless peasants in the area where the land was expropriated, second to wage laborers in the area, third to peasants from other parts of the country, and fourth to workers in other areas.[21]

The agrarian reform law promised land not only to sharecroppers and landless peasants and workers but also to some of Cuba's farmers known as *colonos*. Much sugar production in Cuba took place under a system dating back to the 1880s in which *colonos* produced cane on land generally leased or granted to them by foreign and Cuban corporate sugar refiners and under contract to sell the cane to those refiners at agreed-upon terms. (*Colonos*, though, comprised not only small- to medium-scale farmers on a mill's land but also large planters who might own their own estate.) One year after the new law's promulgation, lands held or leased by *colonos*, but legally belonging to the refiners were expropriated and given to the *colonos* themselves. Areas expropriated from the mills might also be redistributed to squatters, sharecroppers, and tenants on the property. Finally, the agrarian reform law placed limits on foreign land purchases in the future.[22]

The agrarian reform law also included a major provision that went in a different direction. The law provided for the use of confiscated land for the formation of "agricultural cooperatives" under state direction. The term "cooperative" was misleading. The workers there would be employed by the state and a manager appointed to oversee their labor. This formal employment represented an improvement for workers, most of whom had previously labored as cane cutters and were laid off half the year during sugar's dead season. Now, they would be employed year-round. But although in theory workers were to receive a cut of any profits made, the vast majority of the cooperatives' earnings were to go to the state to develop roads, schools, and housing. One observer aptly called these new institutions "pseudo cooperatives," and soon they would be formally turned into state farms.[23]

Castro explained the decision to use confiscated land to create cooperatives, rather than giving it to individuals to set up farms, to the U.S. ambassador. "Distribution of land into very small parcels," he explained, "would be ruinous to production and government aimed rather at establishment of cooperatives of reasonable economic size." Neither sugar cultivation nor cattle raising lends itself to profitable small farming, so if production in these areas was to be maintained, there had to be a way of preserving large landholdings. The advantages to the new state were clear, since revenues from the cooperatives flowed into their coffers directly. Ultimately, the "agricultural cooperatives" were a profound, unanticipated, and controversial innovation that would move Cuba in a state socialist direction, with the government playing a major new role in agricultural production. Nearly 160,000 rural families—certainly a substantial number—did gain either full title or free access to land thanks to the agrarian reform. But overall the government sustained the plantation structure after the revolution, though now with a large portion of the country's plantations under state control.[24]

The shape given to this land reform meant that the number of agricultural laborers who had the opportunity to become independent farmers was far more limited than it might have been. The government at the time justified this by arguing that there was no great desire for land among Cuba's wage laborers and that the state-run cooperatives in fact offered an attractive alternative to low-income jobs, underemployment, and unemployment. For many, this may have been the case given the potential challenges of switching to new work, possible relocation, and a somewhat different way of life. But for others the autonomy of small farming was an appealing prospect. And despite the limited availability of land for wage laborers, some were able to make the choice to become independent farmers through the reform. Data from eleven rural areas show a substantial drop in the number of agricultural laborers and a notable jump in the number of farmers between 1957 and 1966. This suggests desire among a significant group to access land as a way of opting for independent farming rather than wage labor, even under the improved conditions offered by the government.[25]

The agrarian reform was controversial within Cuba, particularly because it hurt large landowners in the country. Still, it appears to have been quite popular. A public opinion poll in June 1959, after the law had been promulgated, indicated that Castro had a nearly 80 percent approval rating (though there was some fretting in his cabinet that this was down from around 90 percent in February). In August the U.S. ambassador explained, "The Castro regime seems to have sprung from a deep and widespread dissatisfaction with social and economic conditions," responding "to an overwhelming demand for change and reform." "The universal support it has received from the humble and the lower middle classes" is evidence of this. Acknowledgment of popular backing for the government, though, did not cause U.S. leaders to question their implacable opposition to it or to consider compromise. The agrarian reform policy, in particular, had an immediate international effect, provoking an escalating and ultimately insuperable conflict between the island and the superpower ninety miles away.[26]

Agrarian Reform and the United States: "The Rubicon"

In the spring of 1959, Castro set out to tackle an urgent issue: how the United States would react to his new regime. Always attentive to the importance of media representations, in April he took an "unofficial" trip to the United States hosted by the American Society of Newspaper Editors. He hoped to get the U.S. public on his side and to offset a growing hostility from U.S. investors and the foreign policy establishment toward the Cuban government's escalating populist and nationalist policies. Although the U.S. State Department was divided on its policy toward Cuba in the immediate months after the revolution, as early as March 1959 some officials began calling for action against the "Communist" regime and the dangerous precedent it was supposedly setting for other nations in the hemisphere. Castro's trip was a charm offensive. He delivered long speeches to cheering crowds. An estimated ten thousand appeared at his Harvard University speech and around thirty-five thousand in New York City's Central Park. He gave interviews on the Sunday television talk shows, including *Meet the Press*. "It seems obvious," the *New York Times* wrote about his visit, "that Americans feel better about Fidel Castro than they did before."[27]

It was probably no coincidence that Castro's trip to the United States preceded the Cuban government's announcement of its agrarian reform. Given the severity of rural inequality in Cuba, the reform inevitably involved a major redistribution of property, including that held by vast U.S. estates. While U.S. firms were less dominant in the sugar industry than they had been in the 1930s, they still controlled 40 percent of the production, including seven out of the ten largest estates. This was an immense U.S. investment, accounting for almost half of all U.S. agricultural interests in Latin America. Cuba had more per capita U.S. investment than any other country in the region. U.S. investors were predictably enraged by the agrarian reform. Unfortunately, Castro's efforts to win over portions of the U.S. public did nothing to dissuade U.S. business interests and the U.S. government from forcefully opposing the new policy.[28]

The agrarian reform law affirmed the "constitutional right of owners affected by this Law to receive compensation for their expropriated properties." That compensation would be based on the 1958 assessed tax value of the land, as well as the buildings and other improvements on it. Given the Cuban government's financial constraints, however, the compensation would come in the form of twenty-year government bonds earning an annual interest rate of up to 4.5 percent, a competitive rate at the time. This was similar compensation to that granted in agrarian reforms elsewhere, such as that carried out by the United States in Japan after World War II.[29]

Just two weeks after the agrarian reform law had been announced in mid-May, a senior U.S. State Department official asked the U.S. ambassador in Havana, Philip Bonsal, to share its objections to the law with Castro. U.S. investors were being "unfavorably affected" by "compensation provisions" that were "inadequate" both in terms of the "valuation" of property and how the compensation was to be paid out. The State Department also immediately issued an open statement to the Cuban government. While it "recognize[d]" Cuba's "right to take property within its jurisdiction for public purposes," it emphasized there was a "corresponding obligation" for compensation that was "prompt" and "adequate." Castro met with the U.S. ambassador the next day and stood his ground. Cuba was "not disposed to quibble over 20, 30 or 40 million pesos," he explained, and was "confident difficulties could be negotiated" regarding compensation. But, he made clear, the "government lacked resources to pay promptly in cash." And "land reform could not wait." It was "a matter of life or death."[30]

The U.S. government's insistence on immediate cash payments for appropriated lands was, in a way, disingenuous. U.S. leaders were demanding from the Cuban state something that it could not deliver, and they probably understood this. The real target, it seems, was the policy of agrarian reform itself. At seemingly every opportunity, U.S. leaders made clear to Cuban officials that the reform—the extent of it and the terms of compensation—had crossed a red line that the U.S. government would not accept from its erstwhile dutiful, investment-friendly, and controllable ally next door. Fifty years later Raúl Castro would note, "The 1959 land reform was the Rubicon of our revolution—a death sentence for our U.S. relations."[31]

U.S. overseas investors protested the agrarian reform law ever more forcefully and deemed it a menacing example of Communism. They took advantage of impressive political access and found much sympathy among Washington's leaders. They provided them, too, with a Cold War narrative to justify actions on behalf of corporate self-interest. After the Texas cattle rancher Robert Kleberg had his property taken from him by the Cuban government, he protested to U.S. Senate majority leader Lyndon Johnson. The agrarian reform was a "Communist effort to block the flow of American capital to all Latin-America, create eventual chaos and soften the hemisphere for Communism." Kleberg proposed that the United States retaliate by suspending Cuba's sugar quota, thereby strangling the island economically, until either the agrarian reform was revoked or Castro's government fell. Kleberg well understood the economic power the U.S. government had over Cuba. The U.S. system of sugar quotas offered preferential and protected prices up to a certain level of imports. Almost three-quarters of the United States' entire foreign sugar quota was granted to Cuba. The sugar industry in Cuba employed approximately one-third of all Cuba's wage laborers, roughly half a million, and constituted 80 percent of Cuban export earnings. So Cuba was utterly dependent on the United States purchasing its sugar, with an economy highly dependent on foreign trade. In mid-1959, government leaders in the United States considered ending importation of Cuban sugar too aggressive a step, understanding that it would make it virtually impossible to return to normal relations. But the lobbying by U.S. companies laid the groundwork for what was to come.[32]

The U.S. government also had significant strategic concerns about the hemispheric, and global, implications of the Cuban Revolution. It had triumphed at a pivotal moment in the development of the Cold War, which made the stakes involved in the U.S.-Cuba relationship seem particularly significant to many in the United States. Members of the U.S. Congress reported that they were put into a state of "shock" when they heard that the new Cuban government "planned to be neutral" in the Cold War. As early as January 13, 1959, Castro had proclaimed Cuba's nonalignment in the conflict between the United States and the Soviet Union. Like Árbenz in Guatemala five years earlier, Castro embraced a position of being neither pro- nor anti-Communist. Membership in the Communist party would be neither illegal nor grounds for exclusion from jobs and positions in the government. This went against the demands the United States was making of Cuba and other countries in Latin America in this period.[33]

Cuba's Communist party had functioned for decades in Cuba as a reformist and pragmatic left-wing organization seeking, for the time being, broad political and labor alliances rather than a revolution to establish a one-party state in the name of socialism (notwithstanding the Cuban Communist party's links to a totalitarian, anticapitalist state—the Soviet Union). That orientation helps explain the party's alliance in the late 1930s and early 1940s with the then also reformist Batista. But that was a very different time in U.S.-Soviet relations, and the United States was now imposing new Cold War rules. At the time of the Cuban Revolution, the Soviet Union was becoming more aggressive globally. Countries throughout Africa, Asia, and the Caribbean were moving toward decolonization in the 1950s and 1960s. And the rival powers of the United States, the Soviet Union, and China were now all competing for influence, standing, and alliances in these newly independent countries—what people had begun calling the "Third World." A neutral Cuba had always been unacceptable to U.S. leaders, but was even more so in the context of the Cold War and the perilous superpower rivalry for dutiful allies. Cuba's sudden move toward nonalignment and its alarming independence in the international arena were quickly on display. In 1959, the Cuban representative at the United Nations voted at odds with the United States thirty-nine times.[34]

U.S. attacks on Cuba and its agrarian reform had a divisive and ultimately radicalizing impact on the revolution. What remained of the alliance between the more conservative and more left-wing revolutionaries was torn apart. It is revealing that this split did not happen at the time the agrarian reform was passed, but rather two months later, following the official protest by the U.S. government. Many centrist revolutionaries had been ambivalent about the agrarian reform as a domestic policy to begin with. But now that the reform clearly had potentially devastating consequences for Cuban trade and relations with the United States, centrists were even less willing to support it and to remain in the government. Within just six months the Cuban Revolution had been transformed, at once leaving behind and being abandoned by its conservative wing.

Still, the future course of Cuban history remained far from clear. The Cuban Revolution had not issued an attack against the principle of private property or promoted a broad program of state ownership of the means of production. At the time Cuba also had no formal diplomatic relations with the Soviet Union. The Cuban Revolution still appeared to many to be closer to the Mexican Revolution under Lázaro Cárdenas in the 1930s—with its sweeping agrarian and nationalist, but capitalist, reforms—than to the Russian and Chinese revolutions. A major egalitarian transformation of the economy and society had already taken place in Cuba. It had hurt the upper and upper-middle classes, the landowners, the landlords, and employers in general. Nonetheless, private enterprise remained a major part of the economy, enough so that some well-off Cubans were still willing to make peace with the revolution, given the hope and excitement it had inspired among Cubans at large, including some of their children.[35]

The U.S. government, though, was not willing to make peace. This was the U.S. quasi-colony of Cuba during the Cold War administration of Dwight Eisenhower, not the far more formidable and independent nation of Mexico amid the transformative Depression-era presidency of Franklin Roosevelt. The situation in Cuba at this time found more parallels with soon-to-be-overthrown Guatemala in 1954. In October 1959, Assistant Secretary Rubottom wrote up a policy statement representing the views of the State Department leadership regarding the need for "a change in the Cuban regime." As he later recalled, as early as June 1959, "we had reached the decision that it was not possible to achieve our objectives with Castro in power," and by July and August, the State Department was "busy drawing up a program to replace" him. Cuba's economic policies were unacceptable, for they were "directly affecting adversely the rights of United States investors in Cuba." Furthermore, they had "a distinctly statist and nationalist orientation which, if also adopted by other Latin American countries, would seriously undermine our economic policies and objectives with respect to the Latin American region." Rubottom recognized that Castro retained "a great popular following in Cuba" because of the way he had "tapped and crystalized the more humble Cuban's aspirations." He therefore advocated against open U.S. intervention to force a "change in the Cuban Government." U.S. opposition would instead be channeled toward covert support for Cuban exiles and others willing to fight against the Cuban government.[36]

The CIA began to organize a covert paramilitary Cuban exile force to invade the island and, it was initially hoped, to spearhead an armed movement to overthrow the Cuban government. To do so, CIA officials turned to a community of antigovernment Cuban exiles in the United States, including members of Batista's old repressive apparatus. They had been the first to leave Cuba for South Florida, but they were soon followed by large numbers from the business and landowning classes along with professionals and skilled workers—typically white, well educated, high income, and urban. Miami was familiar to many of these migrants from before the time of the revolution. Over the first few years after the 1959 revolution, tens of thousands—around 135,000 by April 1961 and nearly 250,000 by October 1962—arrived in Miami not to frolic or relax, as before, but as migrants. That was not how they saw themselves, however. Many imagined that the Castro regime would soon be overthrown with the help of the U.S. government and that they would then be able to return, reclaim their property, and resume their old lives.[37]

Popular Support for the Revolution

The exodus of those groups that were most hurt or threatened by the revolutionary transformation of Cuba provided opportunities to organize a movement and launch armed attacks from abroad to try to undermine the new government. But it also significantly reduced the size of the minority within Cuba that was opposed to the government. That said, there was nonetheless notable resistance on the island from the beginning. Some of the cycle of political repression and violent resistance that had shaped Cuban politics for the previous years began again, though now with opposing parties playing reversed roles. Denied the democratic means of a free press, civil rights, and elections by the government, making it no different from the Batista dictatorship in this respect, the minority that opposed the government turned to armed resistance. An estimated one thousand urban guerrillas organized acts of sabotage against mass transportation, infrastructure, commercial stores, plantations, and oil refineries. Political opponents of the new regime were subject to brutal repression. U.S. officials guessed that "anywhere between 4,000 and 8,000" opponents were imprisoned by April 1960.[38]

In 1960, there were also between 1,000 and 1,200 rural rebels who had taken up arms in the region of Escambray. Many of these opponents were not initially counterrevolutionary, but they now feared that the emphasis on cooperatives in the agrarian reform would take precedence over awarding property to small farmers, former squatters, tenants, and *colonos*. But, as the CIA wrote in February 1961, the Escambray guerrillas were "unable to conduct effective operations" and were not a significant threat to the regime. Later in 1963, the regime would also have to suppress a serious rural rebellion in Matanzas led by prosperous farmers driven by fears of state expropriation of their properties—seizures demanded by some of their workers and justified by owners' putative counterrevolutionary collaboration. The central government itself denounced local officials' "despotism" against landowners at that time.[39]

Throughout its early years, then, the regime faced opponents, but they were far outnumbered by those then backing the government. CIA analysts and the U.S. ambassador recognized this political reality. In 1960, the CIA estimated that some two-thirds of the population remained behind Castro. His charismatic leadership played a role in this. But historical and structural factors were key. The political institutions of the old, ever-failing liberal state, with governing parties and a press seen as corrupt and ineffective, had little popular standing that could serve as a counterpoint to the drive for rapid social and economic change. Furthermore, Cuba's social structure was such that there were few large groups predisposed to resist the increasingly socialist economy. In contrast to the Dominican Republic, this was not a land predominantly of small and medium-sized farmers with long-standing traditions of and attachments to individual property in land, but rather a nation of low-income wage laborers. (Escambray's comparatively high numbers of small property owners made it exceptional.) It's certain that most of the some 160,000 squatting, sharecropping, and tenant farmers and their families, who now had secured free legal access to the land that they were using through the agrarian reform, felt some loyalty to the revolutionary government. Thanks to other economic reforms, Cubans also now paid no rents (only amortization), owed half as much for phone and utilities rates, and received higher wages. This was indeed a welcome revolution for many, albeit not for others.[40]

The revolution also had transformative dimensions for many of the individuals involved, who felt they were part of something larger than themselves. It excited youthful hopes for a new and better world finally replacing an old and unregenerate one, a sense that "we can do the impossible."

A massive literacy campaign in 1961, for instance, mobilized hundreds of thousands of idealistic students and other volunteers and was remarkably successful. The campaign brought literacy to as many as seven hundred thousand Cubans, and by 1962, Cuba claimed that already 96 percent of the population was functionally literate. The campaign's impact was felt by teachers as well as students. Most of the teachers were white, from Havana, and often relatively well off. On the other hand, most who were taught lived in Oriente, where literacy was abysmally low, poverty widespread, and the population mostly of African descent.[41]

Over half of the participants in the literacy campaign were female, and a large number were teenagers. The months of teaching literacy in unknown parts of the country were a new experience for many. For female participants, it was an exceptional opportunity to participate equally with male Cubans in "a monumental change," as one then sixteen-year-old later recalled. Although far more modestly than in terms of class and race, the revolution was disrupting traditional gender norms, perhaps most obviously through the incorporation of women into the country's mass militia, as Bayard de Volo writes, "dressed like men and carrying guns."[42]

By the early 1960s, the left wing of the Cuban Revolution had prevailed within the new government, and Castro's regime was carrying out a major redistribution of wealth of the kind promised in his 1953 programmatic speech "History Will Absolve Me." But the promise of liberal democracy after that transformation was in place fell by the wayside. In a May Day speech in 1960, Castro offered, instead, a different vision of "democracy," one defined by socioeconomic rights, material well-being, and racial and gender equality. "*This* is democracy, where you, worker, are guaranteed the right to work, so that you cannot be thrown out on the streets to go hungry." A real democracy, Castro argued, was a place where students, whether rich or poor, all "have the opportunity to win a university degree," where the children of workers, farmers, or "any other humble family" had "a school where you can be taught," and where the elderly "have sustenance guaranteed." It was a place "where you, Black Cuban, have the right to work without anybody being able to deprive you of that right because of stupid prejudice," and one "where the women acquire rights equal to those of all other citizens and have a right even to bear arms alongside the men to defend the country." "Democracy," Castro insisted, "is that form of government in which the interests of the majority are defended."[43]

In his speech on democracy, Castro did not explain why a government that defended the interests of the majority, that is, one for the people, could not also be by the people. He did not explain why he was not going to hold elections and run for office himself, even though he surely would have won and doing so would have helped legitimate his rule. We can, though, assume that Castro did not want to share or limit his power or lose it at some point in the future. He also no doubt feared that the checks and balances between different branches of government that characterize liberal systems would have made the changes he promised difficult to enact quickly, or possibly to enact at all. Even if they were supported by the majority of Cubans, reforms would also have to overcome the disproportionate political influence of the wealthy.

Meanwhile, the Cuban population overall was not clamoring for elections. This surely stemmed in part from the widespread enthusiasm for the government's policies and perhaps vague expectations that at some point in the future there would be elections. But there were other possible factors at work. Cuba's past democratically elected leaders—prior to Batista's 1950s dictatorship—had been either unwilling or unable to follow through on promised socioeconomic reforms, even during the 1940s presidency of the once revolutionary leader Ramón Grau San Martín. It is understandable if this history had engendered considerable cynicism about electoral democracy's prospects. Cubans doubtless also suspected that these failures were, in part, tied to imperial constraints imposed by the superpower to the north, which had helped shape Cuban governments that, even if elected, were somewhat divorced from their own people. Castro's speech on democracy surely gave voice to ordinary Cubans' popular frustrations with the past failures and limitations of liberal democracy on their island and their desire to overcome them.

Castro also seemed to discount civil rights in this speech: "They spoke to you of civil rights," he told his audience. "In that situation of civil rights your child could die of hunger before the unconcerned glance of the government. Your child could be left without learning to read or write a single letter." He almost suggested here that Cubans had to make a choice between emphasizing new substantive rights, such as good health care and education for all, and traditional civil rights guaranteeing freedom of speech, religion, and so forth, matters of particular concern to political or social minorities. Castro did not acknowledge or try to forestall any of the perils of not choosing a liberal democratic path; that is, threats to and oppression of intellectual, economic, sexual, and other minorities. At this point, it was most obvious to large property owners that their rights were under attack. But the perils of Castro's illiberal system would soon become a reality also for a growing number of people who did not conform to the norms of the majority or loudly applaud those of the revolution.[44]

Cuba, the United States, and the Soviet Union

Castro had quashed the potential for liberal democracy in Cuba after the revolution, and he managed to do so without losing the loyalty of the majority of Cubans at the time. Liberal democracy would thus not impose any constraints either upon rapid socioeconomic transformation or to the regime's continuing rule. But U.S. opposition to Cuba's domestic policy reforms, along with Cuba's "neutralist" foreign policy, now threatened the new regime, most obviously its economy. At any time the U.S. government could stop importing Cuban sugar; trade on which the Cuban economy entirely depended. There was no alternative market for Cuba's sugar, and without one, Cuba would remain hopelessly vulnerable to U.S. economic warfare.

In the summer of 1959, serving as Cuba's commercial attaché, Ernesto (Che) Guevara began informal discussions with several Soviet ambassadors around the world, lobbying for the possibility of Soviet trade and aid. These discussions had a clear goal: to lay the groundwork for a potential Cuban countermove in its brewing conflict with the U.S. government. If the United States did decide to curtail its sugar purchases from and exports to Cuba in retaliation for the agrarian reform, the U.S.S.R. could buy Cuba's cane and thus prevent an otherwise seemingly unsustainable blow to the island's economy. Of course, to take such a step would deepen the conflict with the United States.[45]

Aware of its military vulnerability to the United States, the Cuban government also acted to boost its defense capabilities, reaching out to European nations to purchase arms. But the U.S. government had exerted pressure on Western European nations not to sell weapons to Havana. So it was welcome news to the Cuban government when, after much hesitation among Soviet officials, Premier Nikita Khrushchev decided in late September 1959 to let Poland secretly sell a small amount of arms to Cuba. This was a first, significant gesture of support for this exciting but still politically inscrutable revolution from the Russians. A Soviet official, Aleksandr Alekseev, was sent to Havana in October to gather information about the regime. As he later recalled, Moscow at that time had no sense of "what kind of revolution this was . . . [or] where it was going."[46]

In early 1960, bombing raids on the island by Cuban exiles were escalating. Four or five times a week, their planes flew over the island and dropped incendiary bombs throughout the country. Meanwhile, Vice President Richard Nixon warned Castro that harm to U.S. investments in Cuba might provoke an end to U.S. sugar imports from the island. In this context, Castro expressed his fears to Soviet officials that the U.S. government could strangle the revolution economically at any time. When Soviet minister Anastas Mikoyan visited Cuba in February offering a trade deal between the two nations, Castro accepted the deal even though it meant selling Cuban sugar at only half the price at which it was then being purchased by the United States. Despite its poor terms, the trade deal sent a powerful message to Washington: Cuba might have a trump card to play if the United States cut off the sugar quota or escalated military aggression. According to CIA chief Allen Dulles, when Mikoyan delivered a speech on the virtues of the new trade deal to Cuban farmers, the audience called for Soviet "guns and planes too." On March 3, Castro asked Alekseev, the Soviet intelligence officer in Havana, whether Cuba could secure "the help of the USSR with supplies of goods and weapons in case of a blockade or intervention" by the United States. Although Castro was looking for a Soviet backstop and potential support that would be unique in that empire's relations with Latin America and the Caribbean, the possibility may have appeared plausible given the escalating Cold War rivalry in that moment. What, though, would Cuba be locked into in return? At this point, Cuban agency in shaping the revolution was more limited than Castro would have ever wanted to admit.[47]

On March 4, a French freighter, *La Coubre*, bringing Belgian arms to Cuba exploded in Havana's harbor, killing the crew members along with seventy-five Cuban dockworkers. Another roughly two hundred were injured. It is still unknown whether this was an accident or the result of sabotage or bombing and, if it was the latter, whether there was a link to U.S. covert operations. But Castro immediately blamed the United States for the explosion. This seemed to many Cubans a reasonable conclusion, given the ongoing attacks on the island by Cuban exiles who were being sponsored by the U.S. government as well as the U.S. demands on allied nations not to ship arms to Cuba. In any case, the explosion made clear how vulnerable a position Cuba was in. At the funeral for the hundreds who died in this tragedy, Castro gave what international observers felt was a deeply moving as well as combative speech: Neither "war nor famine," he contended, could conquer Cuba. A few days after the funeral, Soviet intelligence officer Alekseev reported to Moscow that Castro had made clear that he now saw socialism as the path forward. On March 15, Moscow agreed to let

Czechoslovakia sell weapons to Cuba and opened the door to direct sales from the Soviet Union if required.[48]

Prior to *La Coubre*'s explosion in Havana's harbor, Eisenhower had already approved a plan for "a program of positive action to re-establish a stable, friendly, non-communist government in Cuba" through covert action. Eisenhower stressed that the plan had to remain hidden from the public: "Everyone must be prepared to swear that he has not heard of it." Nonetheless, it seems, word soon got out. At a May Day rally, Castro thundered against the "invasion plots" sponsored by the United States. One week later, Cuba and the Soviet Union formally resumed the diplomatic relations that Batista had broken off in the 1950s.[49]

From here, events unfolded in a seemingly mechanistic series of anticipated actions and reactions. The U.S. government now turned openly to economic retaliation, though first through oil rather than sugar. Earlier that year, the treasury secretary had envisaged a cutoff of U.S. oil exports, arguing that this would cripple the Cuban economy within about a month. Castro had anticipated this move and had taken action to reduce Cuban dependence on U.S. oil. As an outgrowth of the February trade deal with Cuba, the Soviet Union began exporting crude oil to the island in April. Though this protected the island somewhat, Cuba still depended on U.S. companies to refine oil, and the U.S. Treasury and State Departments effectively pressured those companies to refuse to process Soviet crude oil. The Cuban government responded by taking over the U.S.-owned refineries.[50]

The U.S. government quickly retaliated in early July by ending all imports of Cuban sugar. Cuba responded by authorizing nationalizations of U.S. properties, now offering essentially no compensation, in contrast to what had been offered earlier through the agrarian reform law. The United States had thus sacrificed almost $1 billion of U.S. investments in its economic war against the Cuban government.[51]

At this point, the Soviet Union promised to purchase all the sugar that the island had formerly sold to the United States, though not on generous terms, and to provide military aid to the Cuban government over the next year. These were ominous developments from the point of view of U.S. strategic concerns. Cuba had moved immediately after the revolution to become part of the nonaligned world. But now it was becoming tied directly to the Soviet empire and was importing Soviet weaponry virtually on U.S. borders.[52]

Washington had pushed the Cuban government against the wall, hoping for the regime's surrender. Instead, Cuba had secured an escape hatch, though one that was an imperial trap of its own: the Soviet Union. In a July 19 radio interview, Castro asked rhetorically about U.S. leaders: "What did they expect? . . . For us to kneel down and wait to be killed? For us to renounce all help in this world, so we will remain alone, without a [sugar] quota, and easy victims of aggression. What do they want? For us to place our necks under the Yankee axe and tell our mighty northern neighbor: 'You can go ahead now, and let the axe fall'?"[53]

Of course, the alliance with the Soviet Union did not secure a proud independence for Cuba. The island was trading one nearby empire for another more distant one. But because of its plantation economy, the Cuban government had little room to maneuver. Unless someone bought its sugar, the island would collapse economically, at least in the short-term. Did Cuba have an economic alternative? Though it would not have happened easily, the Cuban government might have taken a different course, launching a transition away from the island's hyperdependence on sugar by diversifying its exports, developing new trading partners, and furthering its economic self-sufficiency. But the transitional years may have produced scarcities and sacrifices that could have been politically unsustainable. The Cuban government stuck instead with the sugar economy. This required either capitulation to U.S. demands or the rapid opening of a massive new market, one that the Communist world was suddenly willing to provide.

The last predictable chess moves now played out in the once unimaginable schism between Cuba and the United States. The dialectical unfolding of this conflict not only pushed Cuba closer to the Soviet Union but dramatically expanded state ownership of the economy. On August 5, most of the still-vast U.S. investments on the island were seized: the great sugar mills, the large utility companies, and the oil refineries. More takeovers would follow, including that of U.S. banks. The Eisenhower administration soon decreed a ban on virtually all exports to Cuba. This was another devastating blow given that over three-fourths of Cuba's imports came from the United States. Cuba then turned desperately to the Communist world. In December, the United States broke off diplomatic relations with Cuba.[54]

The Soviet Union and, to a lesser extent, China could forestall Cuban economic catastrophe, but they could not make up for the loss of U.S. trade— for the thriving, massive market and supplier next door, the minimal transportation costs and times, the appropriate spare parts, and so forth.

During the next two years, buses, trains, and tractors all began grinding to a halt on the island. To make things worse, nearly one-fourth of the nation's technicians and professionals had abandoned the island after the revolution. It was economic folly to integrate Cuba with a Soviet market and economy seven thousand miles away rather than with its giant, prosperous neighbor. Cuba had been, until then, economically "an extension of . . . the U.S. world," writes Carlos Franqui—a Cuban exile and former rebel leader who had been a prominent journalist in Cuba during the early 1960s. Looking back, however, he explained the dilemma as the Cuban leadership saw it: "To break with that world would mean going back to square one." Yet "to accommodate ourselves to it would mean giving up any chance for reform."[55]

In the fall of 1960, the Cuban government took over major domestic as well as foreign businesses. Under the terms of a second Urban Reform Law, rental properties were also expropriated. Renters were now able to acquire the properties by paying modest installments to the government over a period between five and twenty years. In essence, tenants became the owners of the properties they had rented—a great boon for lessees but a catastrophe for the erstwhile landlords.[56]

Cuba's revolutionary government had been an authoritarian regime from the start. Its leaders had openly dismissed the value of liberal democracy and nonetheless found overwhelming support in the early years. Since at least 1953, Castro had also openly called for a dramatic redistribution of wealth and major government-supported reforms to promote equality in education, health care, and overall material well-being for even the poorest members of society. But as the revolution developed, it was never clear how Castro and others envisaged gathering the resources for these egalitarian goals, whether through taxation or through profits from state enterprise, including the appropriation of private firms. The 1959 agrarian reform expanded the state sector substantially in socialist style. But the greatest move and momentum in the direction of socialism came from Cuban appropriations of U.S. sugar and oil companies, which were carried out in a response to U.S. economic attacks.

More clearly still, the actions of the U.S. government pushed, and would continue to push, the Cuban regime into something it did not initially seek, something that was part of neither popular desires nor the Cuban leadership's wishes: a new dependence on and, as would be increasingly clear, dutiful alliance with the Soviet Union. Neither a complete break with the United States nor such a relationship with the Soviet Union was anything anyone concerned with Cuba would have wanted, for it brought a host of practical disadvantages. It was also a compromise of Cuban nationalism, of Castro's announced nonaligned position after the revolution, and of the increased national pride the revolution had brought, as well as a radical historical reorientation from the deep commercial, political, and cultural logic of shared U.S.-Cuban history. The accelerated events of these short years would create a strange structure of economic and political relations, linking the Soviet Union and Cuba, Eurasia and the Caribbean, and instituting a policy of hostility and isolation between the United States and Cuba that would last for six decades, perhaps more. The event that fully cemented this painful reconfiguration was, ironically, an attempt by the United States to overthrow the Cuban government.

The Bay of Pigs Invasion

When John Kennedy was inaugurated as the new U.S. president in January 1961, Fidel Castro expressed readiness "to begin anew." In early March 1961, he raised the possibility of negotiations over compensation for nationalized properties formerly owned by U.S. investors that might lead to a deal for renewed U.S. sugar purchases. Instead, though, Kennedy proceeded with his predecessor Dwight Eisenhower's plans, which had been initiated in the fall of 1959, for a covert military operation to topple Cuba's revolutionary government.[57]

Kennedy did so despite his administration's serious doubts about the CIA's plan. The plan entailed some one thousand exiles-turned-soldiers invading the island under the direction of the agency. Yet how could they defeat the new Cuban armed forces, which totaled thirty-two thousand troops, and a popular militia with at least two hundred thousand? When the CIA briefed the incoming secretary of state, they offered two different prospects for success. In plan A, the landing of Cuban exiles would "cause the revolt of large segments of the Cuban Army and Militia" and "precipitate a general uprising." There was, however, no empirical or analytical reason to suspect this might happen given the absence of any evidence of widespread opposition among Cubans at large or the military leadership. The CIA also presented a somewhat more realistic plan B: "The lodgement established by our force can be used as the site for establishment of a provisional government which can be recognized by the US, and hopefully by other American states, and given overt military assistance. The way will then be paved for United States military intervention."[58]

The new administration was not reassured. The assistant secretary of state for inter-American affairs, Thomas Mann, immediately dismissed the likelihood of an uprising against the government, central to plan A, and Kennedy himself rejected the idea of "U.S. military intervention," key to plan B. These objections, though, did not dissuade the CIA from pushing ahead. Arthur Schlesinger Jr. would later attempt to explain its seemingly irrational behavior. The CIA "did not believe" that the president would not send in U.S. troops even though he stated this both privately and publicly. Richard Bissell, who had been in charge of the operation, himself later affirmed that he had "felt that when the chips were down—when the crisis arose in reality, any action required for success would be authorized, rather than permit the enterprise to fail." Schlesinger had also earlier warned the president that the "real belief" of Miami's exiles was certainly "that the logic of the situation will require the US to send in Marines to make the invasion a success."[59] Why Kennedy agreed, then, to move ahead with the plan is difficult to discern. Perhaps the president was simply overtaken by events and by the confidence of the CIA leadership that, despite what it seemed, this plan was going to work even without U.S. military intervention.

On April 15, 1961, U.S. fighter planes painted with Cuban markers took off from Nicaragua—then under the Somoza dictatorship, a U.S. ally—and began bombing Cuban military bases to try to destroy as much as possible of the country's military aircraft and runways. Two days later, some 1,400 Cuban exiles descended on the island at the Bay of Pigs, most by ships escorted by the U.S. Navy. The majority hailed from Cuba's professional middle and upper classes, and some were members of Batista's regime, including a few of its old henchmen. The following day, the CIA reported, "six friendly B-26s, two of them flown by Americans, inflicted heavy damage on the Castro column" heading toward the bay, "using napalm, bombs, rockets, and machine gun fire to destroy several tanks and 20 troop-laden trucks." Despite suffering significant casualties, the Cuban militia and regular army continued marching forward. They appeared willing to fight what must have seemed against all odds—against what they likely assumed was the beginning of a full-fledged U.S. invasion.[60]

U.S. troops, though, never came. Less surprisingly, there was no uprising in support of the invaders and against the government. Instead, the invasion inspired an outpouring of nationalism and widespread mobilization among the population at large to defend the homeland. However, it also provoked a massive wave of repression against those the government perceived as potential opponents, including critics on the left. Security forces rounded up tens of thousands suspected of discontent in makeshift detention centers, a portion of whom would remain imprisoned even long after the operation was over. Cuban victory came swiftly on the battlefield. Already by April 18, the day after the exile troops landed, thousands of Cuban troops surrounded the CIA-trained exiles, and the exiles soon surrendered. They had hoped for further U.S. air strikes on the Cuban military. Had this happened, it might have allowed them to hold their ground in the thick Zapata Swamp a bit longer, but they still would have had no prayer, on their own, against the army and popular militia.[61]

When the exile brigade was surrounded by Cuban troops, Kennedy's national security adviser raised the issue that had shadowed the operation from the beginning: "The real question is whether to reopen the possibility of further intervention." But Kennedy, to the surprise of the CIA leadership, stuck to his earlier position and refused to go in with U.S. troops, even once it was clear that the expedition was headed for a humiliating defeat. The president proved willing to suffer a symbolic and real loss in Cuba, even in this tense moment of rivalry in the Cold War between the United States and the Soviet Union.

Kennedy recognized that a successful U.S. invasion would likely require, in his words, "a fucking slaughter" if it lacked popular backing. Kennedy also had to consider the Cold War rivalry between the United States and the U.S.S.R. in a broader context. The day after the exile troops landed on the beaches at the Bay of Pigs, Khrushchev telegrammed Kennedy and indicated that any expanded intervention in Cuba by the United States could provoke Soviet action elsewhere in places where things had been, for the moment at least, "settled" between the superpowers. By proposing possible Soviet action in response to any U.S. intervention in Cuba, Khrushchev was most likely implying a military move on West Berlin, which was perhaps the most pivotal Cold War concern that Kennedy faced when he was inaugurated in January. For Moscow, a U.S. invasion of Cuba could serve perversely to legitimate Soviet demands for control over West Berlin— occupied by the United States, France, and England after World War II— and distract from possible aggressive moves on the city vulnerably situated in the heart of Communist East Germany. Kennedy tried to assure Khrushchev that "the United States intends no military intervention in Cuba."[62]

The CIA's loss was Castro's gain. David had, once again, defeated Goliath. In this moment of strength, the Cuban government reached out to the United States. Guevara, now serving as minister of economics and the most prominent revolutionary figure after Castro, contacted a White House aide at an inter-American conference in Uruguay, Richard Goodwin. "Guevara began by saying," Goodwin reported, that the Cuban government intended "to build a Socialist state, and the revolution which they have begun is irreversible." But, Guevara went on, "they would like a modus vivendi" with the United States. Toward this end, Guevara's government would be willing to pay for nationalized properties "in trade" (sugar sales presumably); refrain from "any political alliances with the East," that is, the Communist bloc and confer with the U.S. government about "the activities of the Cuban revolution in other countries." Perhaps Guevara hoped that U.S. leaders now recognized how difficult it would be to overthrow the Cuban government and would therefore consider a compromise that was preferable for both sides to the status quo. (The status quo would lead, for instance, to the Cuban missile crisis the following year.) The Kennedy administration, though, was unwilling, or unable politically, to accept this compromise that would have respected Cuba's domestic autonomy in return for constraints on the island's foreign policy.[63]

With every reason now to expect a U.S. invasion might follow the failed Bay of Pigs attack, the Cuban government also sought to maximize Cuba's military wherewithal and security. To that end, it requested large amounts of Soviet military assistance, which until then had remained relatively modest. And the Cuban government's growing ties to the Soviet Union were accompanied by further movement toward a fully state-run socialist economy and, soon, a ubiquitous official Communist ideology. By 1961, one-third of agriculture, half of retail commerce, and higher levels of the other sectors of the economy were already in state hands. From there the government moved rapidly toward an even greater takeover of the economy. In 1963, the limit on landholding was cut drastically from 1,000 to 166 acres, with the state providing compensation to owners of expropriated land over a ten-year period. Private land was thus reduced from about two-thirds to roughly one-third of all agricultural property. There was also a second wave of socialization of property in 1968. Most of the remaining nonagricultural parts of the economy were taken over by the state, particularly retail trade, at this time as well. This stimulated another exodus of Cubans, bringing the total number of emigrants following the revolution to almost a million by 1970.[64]

State ownership of the means of production, including two-thirds of the country's land, foreclosed some revolutionary possibilities surrounding agriculture in Cuba. In the Sierra Maestra, a great number of people did gain land and realized many of their hopes. And in the country as a whole, the Cuban government kept its promise to make property holders out of the large population of sharecroppers, tenants, and squatters. But the plantation economy driven by cane cutters, the country's core, remained intact. The country was also as dependent on a single foreign purchaser and a single export as ever—and thus as vulnerable to Soviet dictates as it had previously been to the U.S. government.[65]

Might it have been possible to create a different agricultural model—to break up the sugar plantations, diversify agriculture, and provide vast opportunities for small farmers; to forge a new rural order with greater individual and national autonomy? Might that even have allowed the island to avoid having to accept either U.S. or Soviet dependence and hegemony? The space of possibility opened up by the revolution for a counter-plantation restructuring was shut down so rapidly by Castro in the 1959 agrarian reform, and then by the turn to Soviet trade and growing aid on the basis of sugar exports, that these questions remain unanswered.

The sugar industry did modernize in ways that would be beneficial for workers as well as the country. By the 1980s, the vast majority of the industry was mechanized, and labor became less physically arduous. The terms of employment improved. And the number of workers declined—at one point to less than a third of pre-1959 levels—with no reduction in output, an impressive feat even with Soviet aid. Many then found preferable employment outside of the sugar fields and agriculture altogether. And cane cutters, like others, had access to newly established rights, most dramatically universal health care, which over time would reach the level of high-income nations such as the United States. In terms of the workforce, labor conditions, and the socioeconomic quality of life, Cuba was no longer the same kind of plantation society it had been for the past nearly two hundred years.[66]

Politically, however, there was no silver lining for the population at large. After the Bay of Pigs invasion in 1961, the Cuban Revolution consolidated a regime of widespread surveillance, rigid control, and political conformity. And socialism made the dictatorship all the more powerful, for now the government controlled the means of employment as well as repression. Furthermore, with the turn toward Communism, official ideology became increasingly doctrinaire and repetitive, constraining the life of the mind and surely a people's spirit.

Even when the leadership of the Cuban Revolution enjoyed much support among the majority of the population early on, its leaders insisted on an environment of strict and far-reaching political intolerance and repression, denying people free speech, assembly, and other civil and political rights. The writer Virgilio Piñera pressed Castro in late 1961 to think about the oppressive and constraining aspects of the revolution from the perspective of intellectuals: "Have you ever asked yourself why any writer should [have to] be afraid of the Revolution?" he asked, and "Why [is] the Revolution . . . so afraid of writers?" The revolutionary government was repressive, too, in social domains. The government viciously repressed, for instance, those perceived as homosexual or gender nonconforming, most infamously in the late 1960s and early 1970s. In these years, many people thought to be gay were sent to forced labor camps, excluded from the university, and fired from their jobs. Harsh government repression was also reflected in the extraordinarily high number of political prisoners, especially during the 1960s and in the 1970s as well.[67]

The way the Cuban Revolution had played out, and particularly the fact that it had led to a radical break with the United States, conditioned political visions and possibilities throughout the region. In the Dominican Republic, another Caribbean leader, Juan Bosch, who had witnessed the radicalization of the Cuban Revolution, sought to find a different path. Committed to the consolidation of a non-plantation order and social democracy, he hoped that he could work with the United States to pursue these goals. He was to discover, however, that land reform and any refusal to cater to U.S. strategic concerns would still be seen as intolerable, by both U.S. and local elite interests, even when they were carried out through a liberal democratic process and without any links to the Communist world. The results, in fact, of the Bosch-era social-democratic and nationalist-populist blip in the Dominican Republic would be bloody and stormy, ushering in a military coup, a revolutionary uprising against it, and a U.S. military invasion to help put down that uprising.

"Revolutionary Democracy" in the Dominican Republic

In December of 1962, fair elections were held in the Dominican Republic for the first time in almost four decades and only the second time in the country's history. The overthrow the year before of the dictator Rafael Trujillo Molina, who had ruled with an iron fist for over three decades, unleashed powerful forces of change. While some Dominicans focused only on democratization, others dreamed of carrying out dramatic socioeconomic reforms. Among the latter was Juan Bosch Gaviño, a longtime anti-Trujillo exile from a fairly modest rural background, who ran in 1962 for the country's highest office as the candidate of the Dominican Revolutionary

Party. Bosch had helped found this party in 1939 in Cuba while in exile from Trujillo's regime. He campaigned on a populist platform, promising agrarian and other reforms and to govern for the people rather than the powerful. In addition to land redistribution, Bosch called for expanding public education and health care and a rise in the minimum wage. He won a landslide election, receiving 59 percent of the vote.[68]

This was a moment of great hope in the Dominican Republic. With a popular mandate for change, Bosch was ready to take the country peacefully away from a despotic past and toward greater equity as well as freedom. His philosophy was that of a "revolutionary democracy," he proclaimed in Washington shortly after his election: "revolutionary" because he sought rapid socioeconomic reforms, "democracy" because he sought to achieve them in the context of self-government and guaranteed civil liberties. Bosch promised meaningful social change within a liberal democratic order—in contrast to neighboring Cuba—and with it, he hoped, continued good relations with the United States. To that end, Bosch frequently expressed staunch opposition to Communism. In a speech given several weeks after his inauguration, he proclaimed: "There is only one dilemma and it is quite clear: either democracy or communism. And communism means death, war, destruction, and the loss of all our possessions."[69]

Yet despite every effort to steer a course for social change that could not be compared to Castro or Communism, Bosch quickly provoked the anger of U.S. government leaders, as well as the wealthy and powerful in Santo Domingo, and would be overthrown by a military coup less than one year later. That, in turn, would eventually provoke an urban uprising demanding the restoration of Bosch's government. And, in response, the U.S. military invaded and occupied the Dominican Republic to help the Dominican military put down the uprising. For the next thirteen years, the Dominican state would remain under authoritarian rule, characterized by corrupt elections and brutal repression overseen by a president whom U.S. leaders helped put in office, Joaquín Balaguer, Trujillo's former right-hand man. The history of the short-lived Bosch government and its unsuccessful struggle to realize popular reforms dramatizes the tremendous challenges facing any attempt at socioeconomic change in the twentieth-century Caribbean. U.S. opposition to change in Caribbean nations was couched in the rhetoric of anti-Communism, but it reflected a pattern dating back to long before the Cold War: U.S. intervention to ensure in the strategically important neighboring Caribbean region allies who both dutifully and effectively supported U.S. international positions and economic interests.

As was the case in Cuba, the center of Bosch's promised transformation was a major new agrarian reform. Over the violent objections of its opponents, in 1963 his government passed a new constitution that prohibited latifundia, stipulating that limits on the size of landholdings were to be determined by future legislation. Bosch also spoke of the possibility of putting state sugar mills "in the hands of the workers and administered through cooperatives." Bosch promised, too, new public hospitals, schools, housing, and public works jobs to reduce unemployment and build new infrastructure. For such projects to succeed in this low-income nation, the Bosch administration would have to find funds to support them and property for land redistribution, all the while not mobilizing elite resistance and losing U.S. support. This was challenging given that Bosch sought measures that inevitably would come at some expense to powerful domestic groups as well as U.S. interests.[70]

Bosch had reason to hope, though, stemming from political developments in the United States. President John Kennedy, prior to his election, had expressed support for governments such as Bosch's. In March 1962, Kennedy delivered a speech in which he declared that "those who possess wealth and power in poor nations must accept their own responsibilities" to help the country. "Those who make peaceful revolution impossible," he warned, "will make violent revolution inevitable." Clearly the Cuban Revolution had awoken U.S. leaders to the dangers of inequality and dictatorship producing radical ferment.[71]

Bosch sought to take advantage of the rhetoric surrounding what became known as Kennedy's Alliance for Progress. He praised the United States for no longer considering any government that did not conform to the policy preferences of the U.S. government "communist, or pro-communist." Bosch was, in a way, trying to remind U.S. officials of their own new stance as a way of protecting himself, by petitioning them proactively not to cast his presidency as Communist and unacceptable if and when it took measures that were not perceived as ideal for U.S. interests. He clearly understood that he had to negotiate carefully with the United States during his hoped-for "revolutionary democracy." Soon after his election, Bosch decided to rescind a contract signed between the previous government and U.S.-owned Standard Oil, whose terms he considered unfair. He discussed this directly in a meeting with Kennedy, and at the same time offered to cooperate with the United States, in alliance with other democratic Latin American countries, to support opposition within Cuba. Bosch was convincing: Kennedy concluded the meeting stating that the democratic experiment in the

Dominican Republic, if successful, would represent a blow to Communism. Similarly, *New York Times* reporter Tad Szulc would write that Bosch's "success could dramatize for Latin America the possibility of . . . a system of freedom and material improvement . . . [while] failure would strengthen the claim of Fidel Castro that violent revolution and Communism indeed offer Latin America's only road to economic development and human justice."[72]

Yet Bosch faced intense opposition from better-off Dominicans, who condemned the new constitution and lashed out at Bosch for supposedly giving in to workers' demands and discouraging foreign investment. U.S. investment interests in the Dominican Republic also began to attack him as a Communist. At first, the threat posed to Bosch by his powerful opponents remained relatively small, because U.S. officials manifested support for the government and commitment to democracy in the Dominican Republic. Understanding that U.S. approval was vital, Bosch continually shared his policy plans, particularly those about agrarian reform, with the U.S. ambassador John Bartlow Martin. Bosch had seen how the 1952 and 1959 land reforms in Guatemala and Cuba had helped lead to U.S. covert operations that aimed to topple their governments. He might have found some comfort in the fact that those reforms profoundly affected U.S. direct investments in ways that changes in the Dominican Republic would not. In the 1950s, Trujillo had harassed most U.S. sugar companies into selling their properties to the government, and to Trujillo himself. As a result, U.S. investments in the country were now only a modest $105 million. Still, Bosch worked to sell the agrarian reform to the United States in Kennedy-like fashion. On May 27, he told the *Miami Herald* that the best way to ensure that Communism did not win over hearts and minds in Latin America was with policies proving that democratic systems could effectively address the social and economic hardships of the region.[73]

Although they refrained from labeling his regime as Communist, U.S. officials still protested the efforts by Bosch that they saw as being disadvantageous for U.S. business interests. U.S. officials were also unhappy with Bosch's attempts to obtain private land to distribute to small farmers through a policy that levied a 20 percent tax on acreage in excess of certain limits, to be paid in land. "The U.S. press, already deeply suspicious, would scream that it was Cuba all over again," the U.S. assistant secretary of state for Latin America predicted, and Bosch would then "be denied all U.S. aid." Bosch was, in fact, receiving barely any aid at the time, but the threat of losing U.S. support was nonetheless dangerous symbolically, for it might make him more vulnerable to his opponents at home. "There's going to be trouble on that little island for a long time" if Bosch went ahead with a tax on land, Secretary of State Dean Rusk remarked ominously in late June.[74]

Bosch, though, was committed to agrarian reform, and he envisioned not only this tax but also other measures designed to facilitate state confiscation of land for distribution. He planned to send to Congress a law that would require owners to give a portion of their land to the government in return for new public improvements, particularly for irrigation. He also sought legislation defining precisely what constituted excessive land ownership (latifundia), as called for in the constitution, to help obtain land that could be redistributed to those in need. Finally, from the start of his administration, Bosch set out to redistribute the immense landholdings that had been in the hands of the Trujillos and their close associates. Some five hundred thousand acres had reportedly been confiscated by the state after the dictator's assassination. But here Bosch faced legal, fiscal, and practical obstacles on the domestic front. The majority of the Trujillo family's properties were sugar plantations or timberland, neither of which was seen as readily suitable and comparatively profitable for small-scale farming. Breaking up the sugar estates might therefore reduce the nation's collective wealth, at least at first. And the state sugar industry was critical for government revenue. There were strong pressures, therefore, to leave these estates intact. Bosch gave in to these forces, following a long tradition of even the most profound of the Caribbean's revolutionaries—Toussaint Louverture and Fidel Castro—who refused to break up large plantations in order to constitute an alternative economic program built around a different model of production and different kinds of products.[75]

Still, the government had hoped to grant to small farmers almost half of the confiscated properties, which was close to 250,000 acres, a vast amount of land in the Dominican Republic. Yet many of these areas, too, faced obstacles to redistribution. Under the prior transition government, numerous individuals, claiming that the Trujillo state had wrongfully seized their properties, took possession of them again. Many of these individuals were now challenging the Bosch government's right to the confiscated land. The previous administration had also quickly sold or leased a part of them.

Concretely, this all meant that a great deal of land that might have been controlled by the state and redistributed to small farmers was going instead to better-off and wealthy citizens. Bosch argued publicly that many of the claims being made to return confiscated lands were based on fraud and clever manipulation of the courts, as a result of which "the Dominican people are in danger of seeing all the confiscated properties" lost and even returned to indirect representatives of the Trujillo family and others, many of whom were "people accused of having made fortunes, under the protection of the tyranny, with the bones and the blood of the Dominican people." A new law, Bosch declared, was needed that would allow Congress to intervene in property disputes over confiscated lands in order to keep injustices from occurring and to let the agrarian reform move forward. Unsurprisingly, Bosch's introduction of this law to the legislature earned him many powerful enemies. U.S. ambassador Martin explained afterward: "It hit a nerve—the money nerve," and in the process "galvanized the bitter enmity of the propertied classes." The nation's business associations joined together to condemn Bosch's proposed law as unconstitutional. Bosch fought back, promoting his approach as the only way to preempt a revolution. His law was needed to "forestall the popular explosion that may be [otherwise] provoked here," he claimed.[76]

Amid these growing tensions with the nation's powerful, Bosch also began losing support from his needed ally, the United States. Although U.S. officials' formal relations with and public statements about the still clearly democratic Bosch remained nominally supportive, informally some began to make clear they were, in fact, intensely opposed to his administration. Military advisers, those working at the Agency for International Development, and others were "talking at cocktail parties" now "about the danger of communism in the Republic."[77]

The weakness of the U.S. commitment to Bosch was only partly attributable to concerns about investment. Bosch sustained an independent stance regarding foreign as well as domestic policy, something virtually unprecedented in Dominican history and in the independent Caribbean at large until the Cuban Revolution. Significantly, Bosch rejected U.S. calls to publicly denounce Cuba. U.S. officials were similarly unhappy with Bosch for refusing to ban the country's two small Communist parties and take action against its members. Only a tiny number of Dominicans were members of either one of the two, each of which had membership only in the hundreds (negligible numbers in a nation of three million). Despite the insignificance of Communism in the Dominican Republic, Kennedy wrote to Ambassador Martin about Bosch: "I'm wondering if the day might not come when he'd like to get rid of some of the left. Tell him we respect his judgement . . . but the time may come when he'll want to deport thirty or fifty people. . . . I suppose he'd have to catch them in something." Bosch protested in a public speech that to arrest and deport people because of their political ideas would make us "begin to resemble the thing we hate." U.S. leaders also fretted over Bosch's refusal to ban travel to Cuba. Bosch responded to their pressures by proudly insisting that his administration would "kneel neither to Moscow, nor to Washington." "I wrap myself in the Dominican flag, and I will not wrap any other around me, alive or dead."[78]

The growing U.S. antagonism toward Bosch emboldened the opposition within the Dominican Republic, and some in the military began to plan a coup. Bosch made a reluctant last effort to save the dream of the "revolutionary democracy" when he requested that a U.S. aircraft carrier be sent to Santo Domingo to signal to his opponents that he still had U.S. support. On September 24, 1963, the Kennedy administration refused Bosch's request. It also took no steps through diplomatic intervention or pressure to stop the plotting of a coup. Given the intimacy of U.S. officials with the country's military and key players, and the leverage the U.S. government had over them, such dissuasion would not have been difficult. But the State Department explained to Ambassador Martin that the U.S. government had decided it would not "save Bosch in view of his past performance," including his refusal to follow the ambassador's directions on how "to govern effectively." The U.S. government would certainly not "intervene militarily unless a Communist takeover were threatened." It would not, that is, act against a pro-U.S. military takeover, even one overthrowing a democratically elected government that had staunchly defended civil liberties.[79]

In the absence of contrary U.S. pressure, conservative forces in the Dominican Republic made their move against Bosch's "democratic revolution" seven months after it began, with no explanation or justification other than policy differences. On September 25, 1963, one day after Kennedy ignored Bosch's plea for a show of support, the military staged a coup, took Bosch prisoner, and forced him into exile in Puerto Rico. Forty-five minutes after Bosch's arrest, Ambassador Martin sent a recommendation to Washington that advocated rejecting Bosch's vice president as a possible successor to the president. This makes clear how readily the U.S. ambassador accepted the coup as a fait accompli and presumed the U.S. government would have leverage, if needed, in choosing the makeup of the new regime. But while Martin would have preferred a pseudo-constitutional resolution, with the president of the Senate appointed as president, the military chose a civilian triumvirate led by Donald Reid Cabral, a wealthy entrepreneur from one of the country's leading families and a member of the conservative Civic Union Party. Reid Cabral had been a vice president in the pre-Bosch regime and an opponent of Bosch's administration. He was also a U.S. favorite.[80]

"I take it we don't want Bosch back," Kennedy said to Martin a few days after the coup, seeming to presume it was, to some extent, up to him. "No, Mr. President," the ambassador replied. U.S. leaders could not count on Bosch to be a pliable ally, certainly, in the present or for whatever future contingency might arise. Still, the United States did not immediately recognize the new government imposed by the military. "The easiest course to follow here is recognition after considerable delay and hard bargaining," Martin explained to the secretary of state two days after the coup. The delay provided the U.S. government with leverage and would also insulate it from domestic and international criticism. After all, a democratically elected government—its president, legislature, and constitution—had been overthrown by a coup without any legal pretext or procedure, and Kennedy had continued until the end to support Bosch's government publicly. Still, recognition came soon enough. In December, the new U.S. president following Kennedy's assassination, Lyndon Johnson, quickly resumed normal diplomatic relations with the Dominican Republic and began sending economic aid and military assistance.[81]

The 1963 Constitution that had been Bosch's signal accomplishment was immediately abrogated and replaced by the previous one. Some one thousand perceived opponents were arrested in the first two days after the coup, although about half were released after a brief detention. Following State Department wishes, Communist organizations were banned and political undesirables prohibited from entering the country, including any Dominican citizen who had traveled to a Communist nation. The new state leaders, Martin reported with satisfaction two days after the coup, were pro-U.S. and would turn to him "personally."[82]

The new Reid Cabral regime was neither popular nor stable. It had overturned a social democratic leader who had gained office with the backing of two-thirds of the electorate. The new government, following dictates by the International Monetary Fund (IMF), cut back spending on public works and social services. Unemployment rose, and there was little assistance available to the population. Opposition developed quickly, and the state arrested, wounded, and killed hundreds in response to increasing numbers of protests and strikes.[83]

By early 1965, a CIA poll indicated only 5 percent of Dominicans supported the government. Despite the virtual unanimity with which the high-ranking military officers had supported the coup against Bosch, this lack of any social base for the new regime may help explain why numerous officers began now to conspire against it, building secret alliances with

Bosch to overthrow the Triumvirate. From Puerto Rico, Bosch organized a movement involving soldiers at the lower ranks. Those who opposed Reid Cabral called themselves "Constitutionalists," rallying around their desires to restore democratic rule and Bosch's 1963 Constitution.[84]

On April 24, 1965, a segment of the military rebelled, with much backing— or at least acceptance—among high-ranking officers. Massive crowds took to the streets in Santo Domingo and other cities cheering "We want Juan Bosch!" and expressing their support "for the honest military fighting for the Constitution." The demonstrators were unarmed and peaceful, and there was no immediate resistance to them by the armed forces. Recognizing that he had as little backing among civilians as he had within the military that had originally helped put him in power, Reid Cabral quickly resigned and left the government in the hands of a military junta. Hopeful that they would soon be returned to office, the Constitutionalists appointed a provisional president, José Rafael Molina Ureña, on April 25. Molina Ureña had been president of the Dominican legislature's Chamber of Deputies during Bosch's aborted presidency. This placed him next in the line of constitutional succession after the vice president and president of the Senate, who were also in exile. He agreed to govern "until Professor Juan Bosch, the constitutional president, returns to his native soil."[85]

Democratic Revolution and U.S. Intervention

This Constitutionalist movement had not begun in revolutionary fashion. The goal was to return the office of the presidency to the person who had been elected, Juan Bosch, and to oust the dictatorial government that a military coup d'état had ushered in nineteen months back. Bosch was a proven democrat and reformist, and a leader who had continually reached out to the U.S. ambassador during his brief presidency. The moderate character of his government helps explain the substantial military support for the counter-coup to restore him to office. Eight of the original twenty-five officers who had officially backed the removal of Bosch in the 1963 coup now advocated Bosch's return, with only six still supporting the Reid Cabral government.[86]

U.S. officials, including the relatively new president Lyndon Johnson, responded to events unfolding in the Dominican Republic with concern. "Failure to resolve the dissension among the military," the State Department reported to Johnson, "would cause a dangerous situation." Their immediate focus was on resolving the crisis in a way that left the existing army intact. As we have seen, the creation of a powerful new military linked to the United States had been one of the main objectives and certainly a lasting legacy of the U.S. occupation of the Dominican Republic between 1916 and 1924, as it had also been of the occupations of Haiti, Cuba, and Nicaragua in the early twentieth century. An armed rebellion with popular support and the government's display of far greater independence from U.S. wishes than before, whether in domestic reforms or foreign affairs, could open the door to the military's replacement. The creation of a new army in Cuba after its 1959 revolution had changed everything.[87]

The initial reaction of the Dominican military leadership to the counter-coup was not to defend Reid Cabral's government, but rather to try to find a modus vivendi with his opponents. The military leaders immediately entered into negotiations with the rebelling Constitutionalist military officers and proposed that a military junta replace the Triumvirate. This, however, was not acceptable to the leaders of the counter-coup, who insisted on Bosch's return to the presidency. In the midst of potentially successful negotiations over this dispute, U.S. officials exhorted the military leaders who had not openly supported the coup to act decisively now to stop a possible "communist takeover," even if this ended up involving much "bloodshed." Swayed by U.S. pressure, those who would now call themselves the Loyalists withdrew from negotiations. The air force then bombed the Presidential Palace where those negotiations had been taking place, as well as areas of the city supporting the Constitutionalists. Rapidly, the situation escalated into civil war between the Loyalist army establishment and the Constitutionalist soldiers, who soon began arming civilian supporters. The reaction of the U.S. government thus helped turn a relatively conservative civil-military coup that looked like it had a chance of restoring a democratically elected government into a mass uprising and the beginning of long, bloody battles that would leave an estimated six thousand Dominicans killed or wounded.[88]

Johnson made clear to one of his key advisers, Assistant Secretary of State for Inter-American Affairs Thomas Mann, that he wanted to take control of the ongoing process of change. "We're going to have to really set up that government down there and run it and stabilize it some way or other," Johnson told Mann in a recorded phone call. "This Bosch is no good." Mann agreed: "He was, he is no good at all. . . . The man to get back, I think, is Balaguer," meaning Joaquín Balaguer, the former puppet president under

Trujillo and current leader of the Reformist Party. Johnson then instructed Mann: "That's what you're gonna do, so that's your problem. . . . You'd better figure it out. . . . Do it some way or other." Johnson essentially ordered Mann "some way or other" to take control over who the next president of the Dominican Republic would be. The independent Caribbean was clearly the U.S. Caribbean in Johnson's eyes.[89]

"We will not consent to Bosch's return," U.S. Embassy officials told the leaders of Bosch's party the following day. The issue for U.S. leaders seemed to be the restoration of Bosch's presidency in and of itself, whether or not there was a perceived Communist threat. U.S. officials had found Bosch too resistant to U.S. demands for their liking in the past, and now, in the wake of a mass uprising, Bosch's administration would have more political capital to carry out his program and sustain his political principles. Furthermore, if Bosch were restored on the backs of a popular revolution, a number of military leaders who had opposed it would no doubt be removed, reducing the possibilities for a new reactionary coup against Bosch if he acted too independently from elite Dominican and U.S. wishes. As Piero Gleijeses writes, "there would have been more urgency for, and less resistance to, social reforms"—reforms U.S. leaders had opposed in 1963—and the dream of "revolutionary democracy" that had fueled Bosch's landslide election might be realized.[90]

What the Constitutionalist leaders had initially hoped would be a bloodless coup had turned into a civil war. The Loyalists supporting the military junta had the military momentum at first and the potentially overwhelming armed forces of the United States on their side. Some Constitutionalist leaders abandoned the struggle and secured asylum in foreign embassies. But the chief military leaders and the supporters of the Constitutionalist cause continued to fight with the support of thousands of soldiers and civilians. Urban residents in Santo Domingo, particularly in working-class and poor neighborhoods, joined the armed struggle in large numbers. Some helped set up barricades, while others provided food and tended to the wounded. They resisted Loyalist attempts to take control of the capital, at a cost of a great many lives. The Constitutionalists, gaining more and more ground, planned an assault on the country's army headquarters, San Isidro. The uprising represented something unprecedented in Dominican history. Whereas traditionally insurrections had started in rural areas and sometimes invaded the capital, this time the urban working class had risen up, fighting for a state that represented them and was responsive to their needs.[91]

"To Prevent Another Cuba"

Both the United States and the Dominican military junta now insisted that U.S. intervention was needed. The military asked for "unlimited and immediate military assistance" from the United States. As it became clear that the military junta was losing control, the U.S. ambassador panicked and advised Washington: "[T]ime has come to land the Marines." His justification: "All indications point to the fact that if present efforts of forces . . . [of] the government fail, power will be assumed by groups clearly identified with the Communist Party. . . . [We] should intervene to prevent another Cuba from arising out of the ashes of this uncontrollable situation."[92]

The claim made by the U.S. ambassador and the junta of the leading role of the Communist party in the uprising was a profound distortion of reality. Communist and far-left parties were only marginal players both in the Constitutionalist movement and in the country overall. The two minuscule Dominican Communist parties had a combined membership of only eight hundred to a thousand people. Somewhat larger and more relevant, but still small and weak, was the 14th of June Movement. Originally an anti-Trujillista party, the movement had moved increasingly to the left after 1962, and some members, though not others, supported state-socialist economic approaches. After Bosch's overthrow in 1963, the movement, unlike the larger political parties, had supported armed struggle against the military regime, and a small number of its members had traveled to Cuba to receive guerrilla training. None of these parties, though, played a role in planning or leading the counter-coup. In fact, it took them by surprise. They did not even back it at first, though they did join in after the counter-coup gave rise to a popular uprising supporting Bosch's return to the presidency.[93]

The claim that the Constitutionalists posed a Communist threat nonetheless served as a powerful rationalization for U.S. intervention, one that resonated in Washington. We do not know the precise brew of ignorance and cynicism in the baseless assertions of a Communist threat. U.S. officials were not wrong, though, that the revolution involved a measure of uncertainty. By sending U.S. troops into Santo Domingo, U.S. leaders would put themselves in a position to control the process of change and to ensure that it moved in a direction serving what they saw as U.S. interests.

Johnson revealed another part of his own motivation when he expressed concerns that a victory by the side that the U.S. government opposed in the Dominican Republic could represent a second major embarrassment for U.S. power in just a few years—another Bay of Pigs. As he told Mann, he simply didn't "want the rebels to win; he had just about lived down the Bay of Pigs," and he did not want to end up "in another spot like that." Johnson was determined to demonstrate U.S. strength and resolve, especially in the independent Caribbean, which U.S. presidents had long considered to be their turf. A swift military victory in the Dominican Republic looked feasible, and it would serve as a reassertion of U.S. overseas power. Johnson also considered his action in the Dominican crisis as part of a global Cold War chessboard. The administration began major deployments of U.S. forces to Vietnam in April 1965, the same month as the U.S. invasion of the Dominican Republic. Johnson's advisers recalled him voicing concern that no one "could believe his determination in Indochina if he appeared weak in the Caribbean."[94] The logic, though, of invading the Dominican Republic in part to make a statement to the Vietnamese would prove as ineffective in Asia as it was imperialist in the Caribbean.

Just four days after the launch of the counter-coup to reinstate Bosch, forty years after the Marines had withdrawn from their first Dominican occupation, the U.S. military invaded the Dominican Republic a second time. U.S. deployments rapidly escalated until they reached twenty-three thousand troops, a large number for a country with just over three million inhabitants. From Johnson's point of view, overwhelming military force ensured that the Dominican crisis would not lead to anything seen as a humiliating defeat for the United States like the Bay of Pigs, but rather would demonstrate continuing U.S. power in the region and beyond. From Dominicans' point of view, this was something very different: a second U.S. trampling on their nation's sovereignty and imposition of U.S. political wishes on their country, just four decades after Dominicans had last fought for independence from U.S. rule.[95]

Immediately after the invasion was launched, the CIA began searching for evidence of a Communist threat within the Constitutionalist movement. CIA director Admiral William Raborn asserted that three Constitutionalist leaders were Communists, that eight "hard-core, Castro-*trained* guerrillas" had "knocked the Bosch people out" of the picture and seized "command of the city," and that the uprising in support of Bosch was, in fact, a "struggle *mounted by* Mr. Castro." The numbers of "Castro-trained guerrillas" that U.S. leaders claimed were part of the uprising quickly ballooned. The next day, Johnson spoke to his aides of a list of forty-five "Castro-trained, Castro-operated" Dominican rebels.[96]

The list of these forty-five supposed "Castro-trained, Castro-operated" rebels was quickly discredited by journalists, and the CIA's claims were rejected even by several key Johnson aides. National Security Adviser Mc-George Bundy sought to be a voice of reason or, at least, slightly plausible rhetoric. He cautioned the president against making anti-Communism the stated rationale in his television remarks when there was no evidence for it. Bundy pointed out that the Constitutionalist leadership was made up of "military that are with Bosch that nobody says are Communists. . . . They're just Dominican colonels trained under Trujillo, every one of them."[97]

"There were not enough Communists in my country to run a good hotel, let alone the country," Bosch wrote from his continuing exile in Puerto Rico, mocking U.S. assertions of Communism. When Assistant Secretary of State for Inter-American Affairs Mann argued that in Cuba "there were only 12 people in the beginning, and yet they took it over," Bosch pointed out that unlike the minuscule and divided Communist parties in the Dominican Republic, the Cuban Communist party "was the only efficient, organized political force in Cuba at the end of 1958." By contrast, the Dominican Republic was characterized at the time by strong liberal parties and weak far-left organizations—and especially weak Communist parties.[98]

Bosch might also have emphasized the political-sociological differences between the Dominican Republic and Cuba. Despite a growing urban population that was behind the Constitutionalist movement, the Dominican Republic was still a nation of small farmers and of tenants and squatters seeking to be independent property owners who would have been hostile to any state effort to impose socialism and take away their private property or their hopes for it. This contrasted sharply with Cuba, where most of the rural and urban populations were wage laborers at the time of the revolution's triumph. Furthermore, the road to Communism became politically feasible among Cubans only in a multistep process when the seismic but still capitalist Cuban reforms aimed at redistributing wealth were met by U.S. ultimatums to reverse those reforms. As we saw, that dialectical process, in which neither side would give in and the confrontation escalated, was what triggered vast new state expropriations of U.S. companies. This, in turn, opened the door to the further socialization of the economy and, together with U.S.-sponsored military threats, even to an intimate, strange new alliance between Cuba and the Soviet Union.

Despite Bundy's warnings against doing so, the Johnson administration persisted in its campaign of public deception and imperious maneuvering. It had such a sense of power that it sent former ambassador Martin to Puerto Rico to ask Bosch, as the former Dominican president later recalled, "to declare that the revolution had fallen into Communist hands, and therefore the landing of United States military forces was justified." "I told Martin that I could not issue the message he was asking for," Bosch later recalled. But this was not, the ambassador made clear, a request. "Martin answered that I *had* to make that declaration. My astonishment grew all the more. I said 'Pardon me, Mr. Ambassador, I am not an American functionary and Washington cannot dictate what I must do.'"[99]

After the invasion of the Dominican Republic, the U.S. press circulated stories of beheadings, church burning, and other horrors U.S. writers claimed had been perpetrated by Communist rebels. Martin mentioned these, too, when he met with Bosch, who recalled the ambassador saying "that heads had been cut off by the people" and "displayed." In a public speech in June, Johnson claimed the invasion had become necessary after "some fifteen hundred innocent people were murdered and shot, and their heads cut off." Afterward Johnson went so far as to ask the U.S. ambassador if he could find any headless cadavers as evidence. No decapitated bodies were ever discovered.[100]

One explanation offered by scholars for the invasion of the Dominican Republic in 1965 was that the Johnson administration mistakenly, but genuinely, believed that the Constitutionalist movement in some way or another entailed a Communist threat, and that this mistake was the product of intense paranoia shaped by the overall Cold War context and the recent Cuban Revolution. Reducing U.S. government action to Cold War paranoia, though, does not take into account the extent to which paranoia was mixed with pretense and convenient self-deception legitimating less noble motives. Furthermore, from a broader historical perspective, the 1965 U.S. invasion was of a piece with U.S. government policy going far back in time, all the way to 1898: the insistence on dutiful and effective allied leaders in the independent Caribbean and Central America. The particularities change over time. In this instance, U.S. officials and corporations rejected Bosch's 1963 presidency as contrary to U.S. interests, because he insisted on certain land reforms and he refused U.S. demands to repress the country's Communist parties, however minuscule, marginal, and lawful they were. Bosch's subsequent resurrection, with the strength of a powerful popular movement behind him, was more threatening to perceived U.S. interests. And the civil war endangered the cornerstone of the U.S. version of overseas empire—the powerful U.S.-friendly militaries created during early twentieth-century U.S. occupations. The alarm expressed by U.S. officials over Communism was the refraction of a logical, albeit imperialist, strategic concern about losing influence over whatever developed not only in the present moment but also in the future in the Dominican Republic and potentially in other parts of the Caribbean.[101]

With their troops now in control of the Dominican Republic, U.S. officials sought to select new leadership that would be more pliable and conservative than Bosch. Former U.S. ambassador Martin was brought in to manage the Dominican crisis after the invasion began. During the first week of May, he advised Johnson in blunt neocolonial fashion: "If we are going to stay in there, we're going to need some kind of puppet." For that role, the U.S. government chose General Antonio Imbert Barreras as head of the new "Government of National Reconstruction." In contrast to what had happened during the 1916 U.S. invasion of the country, the U.S. occupiers were able to find a cooperative figurehead. This gave U.S. leaders indirect control over the whole country, not just the capital where its troops disembarked.[102]

Much to Johnson's frustration, however, Bosch continued to resist U.S. dictates. When the U.S. president sent an envoy in mid-May to demand that Bosch give up the fight, Bosch refused. The U.S. official complained to Johnson: "This fellow Bosch is a complete Latin poet-hero type and he's completely devoted to this damn constitution." An enraged Johnson sent another official to deliver a personal message from him: "Tell that son of a bitch that unlike the young man who came before me"—that is, Kennedy—"I am not afraid to use what's on my hip"—that is, guns. But Bosch continued to ignore Washington's marching orders. And he and the rebels, U.S. observers conceded, were winning the battle for hearts and minds in the Dominican Republic.[103]

Even with popular support, however, the Constitutionalists could not win militarily. In the Santo Domingo neighborhoods where their troops prevailed, they were surrounded by U.S. soldiers, cordoned off, and then attacked by Dominican Loyalists working with U.S. military advisers. The working-class areas of the city that backed the Constitutionalists were devastated by these assaults. The Johnson administration claimed that it was a neutral party, but the reality of the situation was made vividly clear by one telling detail: the Dominican armed forces continuously played the U.S. national anthem, "The Star Spangled Banner," on their radio station. Decisive for the Loyalist victory, and in contrast to what happened during the first U.S. occupation earlier in the century, there was no rural rebellion against the U.S. invasion. Such an insurrection could potentially have created, as before, more sustained difficulties for the occupying U.S. forces, especially when combined, unlike then, with an armed urban resistance movement. This was, though, an altogether different time. For one, thanks to the first U.S. occupation—and the subsequent Trujillo dictatorship—the rural population was no longer well-armed, and its once deeply rooted anti-state forces had been vanquished.[104]

After four months of fighting and negotiation, an accord was hammered out and signed on August 31, 1965. The Constitutionalists were forced to back down from their demand for the return of Bosch. Instead, they agreed to a new provisional civil government presided over by Héctor García Godoy, a key ally of Balaguer who had been vice president of his Reformist Party. And they agreed to hold elections in the near future. From the point of view of U.S. leaders, their intervention had proceeded smoothly and effectively. The fifty-year-old U.S.-made Dominican army had been reconsolidated, and U.S.-trained officers and leaders were now essentially in control of the political situation. Only a relatively small number of U.S. soldiers had died—a reported forty-four (twenty-seven of whom perished in combat), along with 172 wounded. Not surprisingly, there was little criticism of the invasion by the U.S. public. The 1965 invasion of the Dominican Republic foregrounded the continuing power of U.S. empire, an innovative form of empire born out of the War of 1898 based on neither expansion nor colonialism but rather on interventions and occupations. The distinction between types of empire mattered little, though, from Bosch's perspective. U.S. intervention had ensured that the Dominican Republic remained, in his words, a "colonized territory."[105]

While perhaps more ideologically palatable for U.S. citizens than outright colonial rule, intervention was not necessarily any less bloody or imperial. In the war between the Constitutionalists and the U.S.-backed Loyalists in the streets of Santo Domingo, hundreds of Loyalists died in the fighting, while an estimated two thousand Constitutionalists and civilians perished and another three thousand were wounded. These deaths occurred not only in the summer of 1965, but also afterward. When Bosch, still holding out hope for a "revolutionary democracy," returned to Santo Domingo to run for president in the open elections of 1966, the Dominican military responded by murdering hundreds of Bosch supporters. Those slain included not only "political activists" but also members of the military who had previously sided with the Constitutionalist army. The Dominican armed forces perpetrated these acts of terror against Bosch's supporters with impunity during a continuing U.S. occupation. In fact, the Dominican military drew on the assistance of the CIA, the Federal Bureau of Investigation (FBI), and U.S. troops throughout the military's campaign of violence.[106]

Bosch feared that he himself was in danger of assassination, enough so that he never left his house to campaign. Instead, he broadcast speeches over the radio from his home. These did not have the same charismatic force that his speeches had in 1962, surely not only because of the venue—the impotence of internal exile—but also because there now seemed little hope for the democratic revolution he had earlier sought to lead. Many Dominicans suspected that Bosch's cause was hopeless, and, correctly, that supporting him could be fatal. The CIA had also concluded that the Dominican military would seize power before allowing Bosch to win. Should that happen, there might be a bloody repeat of 1965, one that a large part of the population surely was seeking to avoid. U.S. troops also spread the rumor of a cutoff of all U.S. aid if Bosch won the election. Through its intervention and ongoing interference in the election, the U.S. government, in effect, urged Dominicans to accept that the dream of carrying out popular socioeconomic reforms and of true national independence in a liberal democratic country remained an unrealizable fantasy in what U.S. leaders understood to be the U.S. "backyard."[107]

At the same time, Balaguer had some appeal as a candidate to many Dominicans despite his having been Trujillo's puppet president in the regime's final years. Balaguer had actually opposed the coup against Bosch in 1963 and the Triumvirate regime that followed it, and avoided taking a public position during the civil war. He seemed to promise a continuation of some of Trujillo's relatively popular economic public policies of agrarian reform and rural public works, but without the tyrant's terrible violence. Balaguer skillfully promised both "social reform" and something that Bosch could not: peace. He was, after all, Washington's candidate. The United States carried out covert operations in support of Balaguer throughout the campaign, including financial backing. Perhaps most importantly, the rural majority now threw its support behind Balaguer. With 70 percent of the population rural, one of the highest proportions in Latin America and the Caribbean at the time, a Balaguer win seemed possible, at least with U.S. help. U.S. covert operations included a major effort to bolster election turnout in rural areas.[108]

In the election on June 1, 1966, Balaguer won with 57 percent of the vote compared with Bosch's 39 percent. Bosch had prevailed in the capital. But in the countryside, where Bosch had lost much of the popular support he had in 1963, Balaguer won a substantial majority. Observers generally concluded that it had been a fair vote, but one that followed a farcically unfair and repressive campaign on behalf of Balaguer by the Dominican military with the help of U.S. covert assistance.[109]

With the U.S.-backed candidate successfully installed, U.S. troops withdrew from the Dominican Republic. Not only did U.S. interests have a seemingly dutiful representative as president of the Dominican Republic, but its government, as historian Frank Moya Pons recounts, was "dominated by some 400 U.S. officials and advisers who were working at every level of public administration; the military was practically run by a U.S. mission with 65 men." Another important new lever of control was a rise in U.S. economic assistance as well as a relatively high sugar quota at preferential prices in the U.S. market. There would be devastating economic costs as well as military and political threats if the Dominican government did not follow the U.S. line. Dominicans lived now with a sense of an "overwhelming U.S. presence" and a reality "very close to colonialism." Bosch himself understood his defeat as a story ultimately of empire: "The 1963 coup generated the 1965 uprising, and that uprising was the opportunity for the United States to take military, political, and economic control of this country," he later wrote, and for the Dominican Republic "to replace" Cuba's former role in the U.S. empire.[110]

U.S. as well as domestic investment now soared in the Dominican Republic, given the guarantee of pro-business policies. Foreign investment was particularly concentrated in mining, oil refinement, sugar, and manufacturing inside free-trade (tariff and tax-free) zones. The U.S. government, it could now be assumed, would make sure that nothing would be nationalized, as might have occurred under a Bosch government and had happened under Trujillo in the 1950s. Realizing that the path to large-scale U.S. investment was open to him, Balaguer provided incentives for a continued influx of capital.

From this position of strength, Balaguer carried out an enormously bloody suppression of leftist opposition. More than a thousand Constitutionalists, journalists, labor leaders, left-wing party members, and other opponents were murdered by his regime between 1966 and 1974. Balaguer, though, also secured a substantial measure of support and acquiescence in the 1970s among peasants, his erstwhile urban opponents, and business groups. He did so with the help, respectively, of some land distribution measures, co-option through state contracts and employment, and a period of economic growth between 1966 and 1978 that was among the highest in the world. That growth permitted expansion in both private and public sectors in ways that were politically useful. Engineers from opposition parties, for instance, were given public works contracts, and over a thousand professors and others gained employment at the Autonomous University of Santo

Domingo. Although Balaguer had campaigned and secured votes primarily in the countryside, he put money increasingly into the cities, especially into urban public works. This generated employment and showed development in the capital, building some support for Balaguer even among those who had fought against him fiercely and voted for Bosch. Members of the Dominican Communist party even participated in the regime, helping to implement certain agrarian reform measures, and Balaguer eventually fully legalized the party. This was, of course, another profound irony, given that Bosch's refusal to persecute members of Communist parties was one of the main rationales for U.S. opposition to his administration in 1963. The Balaguer state's anti-leftist violence, only moderate reforms, and pro-U.S. stance gave him more room to maneuver.[111]

Yet while Balaguer perpetuated Trujillo's rural populist discourse, he neglected rural roads, irrigation, and other needed infrastructure, imposed discriminatory pricing policies that hurt agriculturalists, and offered minimal credit for small farming. In that context, land distributed by the Balaguer regime to peasants was increasingly useless. A large portion of the areas given out fell idle, and more than a third of its beneficiaries were obliged to turn to wage labor for complementary income. As a result, by 1980 only 36 percent of occupied land was held by small and medium farmers compared with 70 percent in 1960 (even after the sugar expansion of the 1950s). A country that had been nearly self-sufficient in agriculture under Trujillo was moving in a different direction, importing an estimated one-fourth of its food by the early 1980s.[112]

Following years of state repression and co-option, the Dominican Revolutionary Party that Bosch had once led moved to a centrist rather than left-wing orientation. It renounced key goals, such as nationalization of the remaining large U.S. sugar company, the Central Romana, then owned by Gulf and Western. And it put forward a conservative candidate for the 1978 election, Antonio Guzmán, a prominent landowner with personal connections to both Dominican businessmen and U.S. foreign policy leaders. The party was now seeking political liberalization but neither socioeconomic reforms nor more independence from U.S. influence. As a result, it garnered support among those seeking democratization without threats to existing economic interests and aspirations.[113]

On election night in 1978, soldiers nonetheless stopped the vote counting when it looked like Balaguer was going to lose. The chief of police and the secretary of the armed forces supported a military coup. But numerous generals and political officials hesitated. Protesters poured into the streets.

And in this case, the U.S. government took a stand against a military coup to forestall Guzmán's democratic victory. At the U.S. State Department's request, the head of the U.S. Southern Command in Panama reportedly phoned the Dominican secretary of the armed forces to impress upon him the seriousness of U.S. opposition, indicating that it would not recognize a government brought to power by a coup to block Guzmán. In the face of U.S. as well as domestic pressure against a coup, the Dominican military gave in and let the election of Guzmán proceed—but not entirely. In return for accepting Guzmán's presidential victory, Balaguer insisted on an illegal reversal of the electoral outcome in four Senate races, so that his Reform Party could retain a majority in the Senate and its control over the appointment of judges.[114]

Why, in this case, did the United States intervene forcefully to support democracy, at least at the presidential level, when a military coup was threatened? Perhaps this reflected a more democratic impulse under the new U.S. president, Jimmy Carter. Also key, though, was that by 1978 the major left-wing Dominican organizations either had been decimated or were no longer advocating major economic reforms or nationalist positions. The Dominican Revolutionary Party was not the social democratic party it had once been. In this context, the U.S. government did not have to choose between support for democratic elections and opposition to a candidate who might win in a fair vote but was considered nonetheless unacceptable to Washington—too independent from the United States, as Bosch had been seen by U.S. leaders.

The political system in the Dominican Republic began a steady process toward liberal democracy after 1978, however imperfect it would long remain in terms of fully fair elections and civil rights. What was not achieved and had become harder to imagine were the substantive socioeconomic improvements that so many had long craved. The economy continued to move in the direction Balaguer had set: expanding foreign investment, tourism, free-trade zones, and remittances from Dominican emigrants. All this further weakened the state's concern with the peasantry and with agriculture in general. At the same time, rural Dominicans' growing contact with the city and international currents gave rise to new needs and desires for education and consumer goods, while schools and public services in the countryside suffered from state neglect. Large numbers migrated to the cities in search of new opportunities. In 1981, for the first time in Dominican history, the nation's population was primarily urban.[115]

But in urban as well as rural areas, Dominicans would face desperate conditions: dreadful health care, limited periods of electricity, increasing crime, and ubiquitous graft and corruption across the state. The lack of decent economic opportunities and conditions in the Dominican Republic pushed hundreds of thousands of Dominicans to migrate to the United States. In certain respects, conditions in the Dominican Republic in the 1980s represented the polar opposite of those in Cuba, where there were none of the desired political rights and civil liberties—the political freedoms people also craved—but welcome socioeconomic equality, well-being, and security that were remarkable for a lower-income nation.[116]

Life in 1980s Communist Cuba

By the 1980s, Cuba's Communist society had become relatively successful in socioeconomic terms. There was an impressive degree of guaranteed material well-being, a high level of equity, and extraordinary human capital that helped drive a solid economy overall. At the same time, no real external or internal political threats prevailed, and that corresponded, it seems, with a substantial decline in the number of political prisoners, even while tight repression continued.[117]

Cuba's relatively prosperous economy was highly dependent on Soviet trade and aid. By replacing the United States in 1961 as the guaranteed purchaser of Cuban sugar at preferential prices, the Soviet Union had insulated the Cuban economy from the devastating impact of the U.S. trade embargo. As importantly, perhaps, the U.S.S.R. protected Cuba from billions of dollars' worth of annual losses after the world market price of oil skyrocketed in 1973 by partially maintaining the preexisting terms of trade between the two economies. Despite an almost tenfold increase in oil prices between 1973 and 1982, and a concomitant decrease in world sugar prices, the purchasing power of Cuban sugar for Soviet oil was only halved. Cuban leaders used this support effectively. In the 1960s, Cuba's economy developed slowly, but in the 1970s and in the early 1980s, its growth rate was robust and appears to have outstripped that of Latin America overall.[118]

The clearest form of development in Cuban society between 1960 and 1990 is shown in quality-of-life indicators. Prior to the revolution, figures for health and education in Cuba were already high for Latin America and the Caribbean. Yet socialist Cuba was able to continue improving these levels, both in absolute terms and compared with other countries in the region, despite not expanding its relative per capita national income. High-quality health care and schooling became available to a far larger part of the population than ever before, including the remotest areas and formerly poorest neighborhoods. Cuba developed a world-class health care system and an abundance—surplus, even—of doctors. By the 1980s, Cuba had the highest life expectancy and the lowest level of infant mortality in Latin America, with both roughly the same as those in the United States. In 1980, life expectancy was seventy-three years in Cuba and seventy-four in the United States, in contrast, for instance, to sixty-one years and fifty-three years in the Dominican Republic and Haiti, respectively. Most dramatically, Cuba had evened out the once-stark inequities of medical care across class and the rural-urban divide.[119]

Similar investment in education almost eliminated illiteracy, dropping from a rate of 23 percent before the revolution to less than 8 percent of those ages fifteen and older by 1985. Only 4.5 percent of the labor force had a high school education in 1953 versus 38.7 in 1986. And university enrollment in 1983—roughly 200,000—was some ten times what it had been before the revolution.[120]

Although the statistics we have for income distribution are far from perfect, it is clear that Cuba went from being one of the most unequal nations in the Americas in the 1950s to being one of the most equal in the 1970s. Furthermore, by 1981 an extraordinary degree of socioeconomic parity across race had been achieved in key areas—health, education, and employment—a stark contrast from pre-1959 Cuba and other former slave societies, notably Brazil and the United States. Nonetheless, there remained significant failings in the Cuban government's legislation and discourses addressing racial inequality. Certain spaces of discrimination continued, as in the criminal justice system, where incarceration rates were grossly unequal. And prejudice was far from eliminated, however much it was silenced. Critiques of extant forms of racism—like critiques of the regime in general—were also silenced, making their defeat more difficult and improbable.[121]

The course of Cuban history, though, would change radically, once again, with the collapse of the U.S.S.R. in the early 1990s. When the old Soviet trade deals and aid were eliminated, the U.S. economic embargo began to have the intended devastating effect on the Cuban nation. Cuba faced an almost unimaginable blow at this time—the loss of three-fourths of its imports along with two-thirds of exports in just four years (1989–93). Because Cuba had never transcended the old plantation structure reliant on exporting essentially one crop to one key purchaser at preferential prices, its seemingly robust socialist economy remained nonetheless as dependent and vulnerable as the economy had been before the revolution.[122] The promise of simply changing one buyer for another, the Soviet Union for the United States, had been understandably seductive in that moment. But the Cuban Revolution's deal with the plantation devil worked only until it didn't. Cuba's economy all but died within a few years of the end of the Soviet trade and support, which the island had depended upon since the U.S. government prohibited Cuban sugar imports.

Facing economic collapse, the regime opened up forms of free enterprise and engaged in more state capitalist endeavors, such as tourism. And the government cut back on the socioeconomic benefits to which Cubans had grown accustomed. It would and could no longer ensure the same level of material well-being as in the past or the same degree of control over employment, wages, and promotions in the new hybrid economy. Novel structures of racial inequality also emerged. Because emigrants had been disproportionately white, lighter-skinned Cubans received more remittances from family members abroad. And white Cubans profited, too, from better housing stock in attractive neighborhoods, a legacy of prerevolutionary Cuba, in which to open restaurants in their homes.[123]

Cubans may yet gain the possibility of choosing public policies, freedoms, and political leaders desired by the majority of their population, rather than having them circumscribed by repressive Cuban and hostile U.S. governments. Still, old conflicts will remain on the island over national independence, how land should be used, and how to develop an economic model that fulfills popular aspirations for material well-being without sacrificing liberal freedoms that people also crave.

Cuba's seeming socioeconomic triumphs had been inspiring to many in the Caribbean in the 1960s and 1970s. These triumphs came, though, at the high price of never securing political freedom and of breaking relations with the superpower ninety miles away with which it shared deep economic and cultural ties. After the Cuban Revolution, many in the Caribbean, such as Juan Bosch, would seek to chart a different path and avoid those costs, which would also eventually include the near collapse of the Cuban economy.

The rupture between the United States and Cuba stemmed to a large degree from U.S. leaders' unwillingness to accept the Cuban government's egalitarian public policies, policies that hit U.S. interests hard. This left the Cuban government with little room to maneuver vis-à-vis popular demands for agrarian and other reforms and its own overall left-wing ideals. The history of U.S. intervention in the Dominican Republic, which prevented the restoration of a democratically elected reformist government, did not suggest much hope, either, for a different way of addressing the yearnings of people in the Caribbean for change. Yet the approach pursued during the Bosch era in the Dominican Republic, despite failure, was still for many the last best hope.

7 Transformation in Jamaica, Grenada, and Haiti

In the last decades of the twentieth century, the Caribbean saw multiple nations pursue dramatic efforts to transform state and society and to create new forms of equality. Left-wing leaders sought to carve out paths to equality that would provide an alternative to the Cuban model of a state socialist economy and close integration into the Communist world. In 1970s Jamaica, Prime Minister Michael Manley's government attempted to build a more socioeconomically equal society and to provide greater opportunities for the Jamaican majority while also sustaining liberal democracy and a capitalist economy. In these ways, his political philosophy would parallel that of Juan Bosch's short-lived democratic revolution in the Dominican Republic. The 1979 Grenada Revolution similarly focused on reforms benefiting the popular classes, but instead under leftist one-party rule. While that revolution was increasingly authoritarian and doctrinaire politically, it remained moderate and capitalist in economic terms. In 1990 Haiti, President Jean-Bertrand Aristide, a theologian-turned-politician, sought both to put an end to decades of state terror and to address the needs of the poor majority, as well as to affirm their dignity as equal members of the nation. Yet during his brief seven-month presidency, before he was overthrown by the army, Aristide never had great faith in being able to alter the old order in Haiti within a liberal democracy, however much support there was for doing so among the Haitian majority. In part as a result, he himself condoned popular political violence under certain circumstances, even while he was in office.

Manley, the Grenada Revolution, and Aristide all excited nearly unprecedented expectations of change in their nations and hope for a truly new day, much like the Cuban Revolution in this respect. They spearheaded popular projects for economic and social change, particularly for agrarian reform and improving public education and health care, and they embraced the popular classes as equal members of society as almost never before. The outcomes of reform efforts in Jamaica, Grenada, and Haiti varied from progress to tragedy, but none could fulfill the lofty political dreams they inspired. These powerful contradictions have given rise to contested memories of these transformational governments.

Jamaica, 1972–1980

Following independence from Britain in the 1960s and 1970s, much of the English-speaking Caribbean was brimming with expectations for deep changes in society. Many sought the type of egalitarian and nationalist reforms that had been envisioned and then quashed in the Dominican Republic under Juan Bosch in 1963. In Jamaica, the Caribbean's fourth-largest nation, many embraced Bosch's same dream of peaceful revolution and popular socioeconomic reform coupled with liberal democracy. Historian Thomas Holt draws a powerful analogy between this moment in Jamaican history after independence in 1962 and the period that followed the abolition of slavery in the 1830s. On the island, and in the Americas at large, both moments were critical ones during which "the meaning of freedom was in dispute." The question was: To what extent would and could freedom involve socioeconomic transformation? With independence, might real changes be possible that had been foreclosed before by colonial rule?[1]

In the newly independent Anglophone Caribbean, some in the better-off classes may have been content, and even sought, to limit the meaning of freedom to legal equality and self-rule. The majority of the population, however, also expected improved material conditions and greater equity in economic and social realms. This was what they had fought for since slavery's end. This had also been a driving force behind the movement for self-government, which had emerged in the context of escalating labor strikes and riots by the unemployed in the late 1930s. Many proponents of independence had "insisted that the transfer of political power was the first requisite to . . . social improvement for the masses." In the wake of independence, then, the "problem of freedom" was thus "both old *and* new," Holt notes. In his last public address in 1969, Norman Manley, the retiring leader of one of Jamaica's two main parties (the minority party in Parliament at the time) and the father of the soon-to-be prime minister, Michael Manley, framed freedom in this same way: "The mission of my generation was to win self-government for Jamaica, to win political power. . . . And what is the mission of this generation? . . . It is . . . reconstructing the social and economic society and life of Jamaica."[2]

That mission of reconstruction would be a challenge. Jamaica was now in a deepening and dependent relationship with the United States, rather than Britain, and home to a local conservative opposition. By freeing themselves from the trammels of British imperial rule, Anglophone Caribbean leaders had inevitably made their nations more vulnerable to U.S. empire.

U.S. leaders now saw the English-speaking Caribbean much more as part of the U.S. sphere of influence. To some extent, the experiences of the long-standing independent nations of the Caribbean—Haiti, the Dominican Republic, and Cuba—specifically, their subjection to U.S. control through economic and military means since 1898, would be echoed in the Anglophone Caribbean during the 1970s and 1980s. At the same time, though, the different histories of these new nations helped to constrain U.S. power, and their leaders more frequently affirmed their independence from U.S. dictates. Caribbean nations formerly colonized by Britain lacked large powerful militaries of any kind, let alone ones created by and still linked to the United States. It was those formidable U.S.-created militaries that had given rise to and protected dictatorships such as Trujillo's in the Dominican Republic and that continued to be a conduit for U.S. interests and influence. As a result, U.S.-supported coups, covert operations, and dictatorships were less likely in the independent English-speaking Caribbean. In fact, these lands would be blessed overall with stronger institutions of political democracy than existed in the islands that the United States had occupied.[3]

These contradictions produced complex political dynamics across the newly independent Caribbean. That complexity played out dramatically in Michael Manley's two terms as prime minister of Jamaica between 1972 and 1980. Manley, a former labor organizer and leader of the People's National Party that his father had founded, promised to advance socioeconomic equality and material well-being while maintaining liberal democratic government and a mostly private-sector economy. He would seek to do so through agrarian reform, expanding public education, and other legislative changes. These reforms, though, ran up against difficult constraints. Jamaica was a small, lower-income nation with only limited tax revenues available to pay for social programs. The Manley administration would have to contend, too, with the opposition of the U.S. government and eventually international financial institutions to its reform project. Furthermore, because Jamaica remained democratic with a mostly private-sector economy, entrepreneurs and merchants had powerful tools with which to oppose Manley's policies by disinvesting, slowing down commerce, and thereby undermining support for the government. These challenges ultimately helped lead to Manley's electoral defeat after eight years of governing. Still, these eight years were far from a tragic social democratic blip, as one might characterize Juan Bosch's government in the Dominican Republic. Manley remained in office for two full terms and spearheaded important economic and political-cultural transformations.

When Manley won in an electoral landslide in 1972 against a broadly unpopular incumbent, Hugh Shearer, conditions in Jamaica were difficult. Little had improved in the everyday lives of most Jamaicans since independence a decade before. Despite economic growth, the nation's severe income inequality had only increased, and unemployment was as high as 24 percent, roughly double what it had been at the time of independence. Average Jamaicans were not benefiting from the robust bauxite industry responsible for most of the country's exports. During the 1950s the industry took off, and Jamaica became the globe's biggest producer of this valuable ore, the mineral used for manufacturing aluminum. But the industry was owned entirely by U.S. and Canadian firms, which also controlled vast tracts of largely idle land around their mines. Meanwhile, small farmers, about 20 percent of Jamaica's population, were generally tilling parcels in the far and hilly reaches of the country, without needed infrastructure, irrigation, good local roads, or agricultural loans. These farmers, as well as many unemployed rural workers, were eager for new and better lands, whether those held by the mines, the sugar companies, or other large landowners.[4]

Independence had also failed in many people's minds to challenge the old order of things with regard to ideas of race and nation. Jamaicans increasingly sought to move past official constructs of the nation simply as a fusion of African, European, and Asian peoples—exemplified in the national motto "Out of Many, One People"—given that the country's population was overwhelmingly of African descent. After independence, many Jamaicans, more often and more visibly, embraced the notion of Jamaica as a black nation. This was not only a reflection of demographic realities. It was also an assertion of cultural pride following hundreds of years of white colonial domination and, for most of four centuries, enslavement of the nation's majority. The rejection of a "mixed" Jamaica corresponded, too, with contemporary conditions in which greater wealth, status, "beauty," and power continued to be correlated with relative lightness of skin color and other physical features associated with Europe, subjecting those of darker color to employment discrimination, among other forms of prejudice.[5]

The strengthening of black identity found expression in the country's expanding Rastafari movement, which had first developed in the 1930s, particularly among urban youth. Many of its adherents followed the doctrine that Africans were the Israelites described in the Old Testament and that Ethiopian emperor Haile Selassie was a living god. As the Rastafari movement grew in influence, F. S. J. Ledgister explains, its way of "challenging the white bias built into Jamaican society" spoke to growing numbers of

Jamaicans. New middle- and lower-class youth drawn to Rastafari, notes Rex Nettleford, began to "secularize the movement" by embracing its cultural more than religious dimensions. Still, when Selassie visited the island in 1966, he attracted great interest and enthusiasm. The soon-to-be reggae music superstars Bob Marley and the Wailers joined the Rastafari movement at this time, helping link them with another rising force of popular protest, reggae.[6]

Popular protest against antiblackness and economic deprivation also galvanized the Black Power movement in Jamaica, a movement then spreading widely across the United States and the Caribbean. The contours of "black power" demands varied from place to place, but at their core, they formed a searing critique of the interrelated structures of racism, imperialism, and class privilege. "Black power [in Jamaica] was often expressed in terms of nationalization of foreign property," writes Michael Kaufman. "The language of *Abeng*—the short-lived, but influential publication of the movement—focused on colour and imperialism." This was a movement demanding a decolonization that was truly transformative.[7]

In its critique of imperialism, Black Power in Jamaica dovetailed with the prominent ideas of the important Guyanese intellectual Walter Rodney on the whiteness of empire. It was not simply a coincidence, Rodney stressed, that "every country in the dominated colonial areas has an overwhelming majority of nonwhites, as in most of Asia, Africa and the West Indies." Even with independence and black political leadership, postcolonial structures sustained the status quo, he argued. "A black man ruling a dependent State within the imperialist system has no power." Rodney also criticized the relatively privileged brown, or mulatto, Caribbeans for supposedly selling out "to the bribes of white imperialism, often outdoing the whites in their hatred and oppression of blacks." Rodney placed Jamaicans of Asian descent in an analogous category to "blacks," arguing that as descendants of indentured workers, they shared similar histories of oppression with those whose forebears had been enslaved.[8]

In 1968, the History Department at the University of the West Indies in Jamaica hired Rodney to teach courses in African history, a subject that had not previously been part of the curriculum. Rodney also delivered public lectures in low-income urban neighborhoods and, less frequently, rural areas of the country. Offering new perspectives that moved beyond Eurocentric histories and opened up ideas about Black Power, Rodney quickly became a popular speaker. But a substantial number of Jamaicans continued to object to any racialized construction of the nation and brushed aside the relevance of Black Power ideas in a country and government composed predominantly of African-descended people, including the prime minister, Shearer. Political leaders began to fear the growing influence of this dramatic new transnational movement, and, at the end of 1968, the government declared Rodney persona non grata. When he attempted to return to Jamaica from a conference in Montreal, officials barred his reentry into the country.[9]

Student protests broke out at the University of the West Indies demanding that Rodney be permitted to return. These soon broadened into demonstrations among the urban poor. When police tried to stop the demonstrations, people rioted, attacking stores, cars, and government offices. Two people were killed. What may have appeared to some as a sudden explosion of popular violence in fact reflected the depth of long-term discontent in post-independence Jamaica.[10]

It was in this milieu of anger and frustration with the perceived failures of independence and with economic growth without growing equity that Manley forged his political career, beginning as a senator in 1962. When he ran for prime minister in 1972, he campaigned with the simple slogan "Better must come." The slogan was a savvy one, picked up from a recent reggae hit by Delroy Wilson: "I've been trying a long, long time. . . . Why they trying to keep me down. . . . Better must come one day." Independence should mean more than it had thus far, Manley would tell his audience. He promised to focus on "the sufferers" and to improve the lives of the Jamaican majority.[11]

Although Manley himself was a light-skinned person of African and European descent from the upper classes, his populist language and politics were shaped by Black Power as well as a long career as a labor leader. This led him to embrace black as well as other popular movements and to pay attention to their intersections. While prior government leaders had sought to repress the Rastas, he generally courted them. After taking office, he remarked that "Jamaica still has a grave psychological problem and that [is] it is not as yet fully at ease with itself in the question of race, particularly the question of blackness." He pushed for a growing emphasis on African history and culture in Jamaican schools. Manley later recalled: "Whereas our predecessors in office had banned much of the protest music of the ghetto, we opened the doors and, on the contrary, worked to assist in the promotion of the cultural energy of the ghetto as expressed in reggae music. Malcolm X was forbidden reading. We opened those doors too." As Stuart Hall frames it, the nation's black identity was "learned" in the

1970s. Manley helped consolidate this profound transformation in cultural politics.[12]

Manley's administration also brought concrete material change by enacting a sweeping legislative agenda. While in no sense radical or that far outside the mainstream even for the United States of the period, the Manley administration's policies benefited the popular classes at large. For instance, Manley galvanized thousands of Jamaicans to volunteer as literacy workers to address the needs of as many as 40 percent of the population who could not read or write. Volunteers taught some two hundred thousand people, roughly 10 percent of the population, new literacy skills. In a nation where only elementary school had been available to students without charge, Manley got through legislation making all education free, including universities. The government also improved health care. Infant deaths decreased from 3 percent to 1 percent annually between 1972 and 1979. Housing programs were also expanded. The government constructed tens of thousands of new homes distributed mostly by lottery to those in need.[13]

The Parliament passed important new labor laws as well, including the first across-the-board national minimum wage, an eight-hour workday, and a forty-hour work week. New legislation also strengthened the hand of unions. Under these new conditions, the income of wage laborers rose substantially between 1973 and 1976 while unemployment at least modestly declined. Overall, the popular sectors gained much in material terms during Manley's administration. But the gains of these new laws were also profound symbolically. Even those at the lowest rung of the labor market "were suddenly told that they had rights too," including those who labored within what Michael Manley identified as "that final citadel" of master-servant domination, the private homes of the wealthy. One of the leaders of Manley's party recalled: "People were saying . . . 'is black man time now.' For example, domestic servants, for the first time, felt entitled to walk through the front door."[14]

Some of Manley's policies focused on gender as well as class inequity. Manley condemned Jamaica's "systematic discrimination" and "deep-seated prejudices" against women as "an intolerable invasion of the principle of equality." He successfully pushed through an impressive maternity leave law, the foremost goal of the women's movement at the time, which was passed over the intense opposition of business interests. It guaranteed women's jobs after giving birth and granted at least eight weeks of leave with pay. The country's foremost newspaper, the *Daily Gleaner*, scoffed in sexist style that, as a result, "teachers would be spawning in the streets."

Manley's view was different: "At the very moment when . . . [a new mother's] financial needs were greatest . . . she faced the loss of everything," an unequal burden that fell on women. Manley also managed to pass the Status of Children Act, which eliminated legal distinctions between children born to parents who were legally married and those who were not. This made, he wrote, "the norm of . . . the great majority . . . the legal norm in society." Finally, the Equal Pay Act required that women and men be paid equally for the same work.[15]

Manley also initiated deep structural changes to the rural economy, ones that countered the island's plantation history. He both expanded the prospects for small farmers and experimented with innovative forms of workers' control and democracy. During Manley's two administrations, the government distributed some seventy-five thousand acres of both state and private lands to upwards of thirty-five thousand farmers, technically in the form of long-term leases. The initial leases were for five or ten years, but subsequent ones were for forty-nine years and conferred hereditary rights. In cases where the government could not renew a lease, farmers would be compensated for crops or other improvements left behind. Land reform benefited those with no land and others with small plots. By the end of Manley's second term, independent farmers working less than five acres possessed a third more land than they had previously. The reform also boosted the nation's food supply for the domestic market. Government agricultural loans were also made available to land recipients. Recognizing that state infrastructure was critical for successful small farming, the Manley administration formulated plans for new irrigation projects and roads to facilitate the transportation of crops to markets.[16]

Some of the distributed lands had already been owned by the state. But most were purchased from large foreign-owned sugar and bauxite corporations. Rarely did the government have to invoke forcible acquisition provisions of a new law requiring idle lands beyond one hundred acres be turned over to the state. Instead, the state generally offered reasonable sums to, and perhaps placed a measure of pressure on, landowners in order to acquire areas that were not indispensable to them. As a result, though, these were often not the country's best lands. Also, the government had only so much money available at any time to purchase or lease property, and this slowed down Manley's agrarian reform. Although much land had been distributed, it was still only a small portion of idle areas across the country. By revolutionary standards, agrarian reform proceeded at a snail's pace. By the standards of a low-income, liberal-democratic, capitalist country, however, things were moving along at a decent clip.[17]

For the land hungry, though, the agrarian reform was moving too slowly. Rather than wait for state largesse, many took matters into their own hands and "created a land reform from below." Thousands took over uncultivated lands for farming and building homes, bringing the country's total number of squatters to the tens of thousands. Police forces at times acted to stop the occupations. But squatters also often succeeded in gaining rights to the land, for their actions pressured the government—which was for the most part sympathetic—to purchase or at least lease the land for them from its owners.[18]

Rural workers also helped push the government into another type of agrarian reform under Manley. The year prior to his taking office, the government had purchased two of the country's large sugar companies. These companies were at the time losing money, so they were not reluctant to sell. Acquisitions continued under Manley. In retrospect, Manley was critical of his government's initial project vis-à-vis the sugar plantations. "When foreign properties were acquired," Manley recalled, "it was assumed that the lands would be divided up into reasonably big parcels to be owned and farmed by medium-sized cane farmers. For the sugar worker who had cut and watered the canes, who had ploughed, weeded and fertilized the land over the years, this would have meant exchanging the former employer whom he never saw for the kind he would see occasionally. Nothing else would change." But sugar workers organized and pushed the government in another direction, to "organize the workers themselves into co-operatives" and thus make "the worker . . . a full and equal partner." By the mid-1970s, one-third of Jamaica's second-largest export had been placed under the control of tens of thousands of workers. "It all belong to us now," a cane cutter rejoiced in 1976. And because "we share profit now," we "have better spirit" and "work harder."[19]

In their first few years, the cooperatives failed to make a profit. "The problems which had made the estates inefficient in the first place [when in foreign hands]: under-capitalization, over-staffing and cultivation of marginal lands, were never rectified," two scholars of Manley's policies, Evelyne Huber Stephens and John Stephens, recount. Also, "there was no education program to teach the workers about cooperatives." In 1979, a government committee recommended a series of changes to address the problems—for instance, developing a management education program and cutting the staff—that scholars argue would most likely have made the co-ops successful. In the end, though, there was not time to implement the changes, for Manley lost the 1980 election, and his successor ended the co-operatives.[20]

The biggest challenge in Jamaica to what Manley called the "democratic socialist" project was funding: to purchase land and provide infrastructure for farmers; to make the sugar co-ops thrive; and to pay for new public education, health care, and housing. Jamaica was a small, lower-income nation, and, to boot, Manley had the misfortune of becoming prime minister precisely at the time of one of the most seismic shocks in recent history to the world economy: the skyrocketing of global oil prices after 1973. The following year, Jamaica was hit hard with an oil bill ($178 million) that was nearly triple what it had been the year before, thus driving up prices and diminishing profits across much of the economy, depleting foreign exchange, and reducing government revenues. Manley's administration faced new fiscal headwinds just when the need for a major economic boost to pay for its new programs and investments became more pressing.[21]

To address these challenges, Manley opted to raise taxes on the mostly U.S.-owned bauxite and alumina industry. In 1974, the government imposed a major new levy on bauxite production that resulted in a sevenfold increase in revenues, bringing in almost $170 million that year and $210 million by 1980. Nor was the levy the only coup that Manley managed to pull off with the U.S. and Canadian bauxite firms. They agreed to sell the government majority ownership on favorable terms—at book value with low-interest loans. Under the agreements, the state would take over management of the corporations after a set period of time, usually seven years.[22]

The Manley administration's bauxite policies were a formidable achievement, enormously expanding the government's resources. They would come, though, at a high political cost: U.S. government opposition and restrictions on U.S. aid. Unlike most of the land purchases, the bauxite levy was imposed over the vehement protests of the bauxite companies. And the company executives made their displeasure clear to sympathetic U.S. government leaders.

When Manley first informed the aluminum corporations about his new tax plan, he quickly discovered, as he later recalled, that "they were clearly not prepared to deal with a small island that saw itself as clothed in the rights and dignity of sovereignty." Despite extended discussions, the corporate executives considered far too high the lowest levy to which Manley would agree. Manley surely hoped for compromise, especially given U.S.

Secretary of State Henry Kissinger's explicit warning of the "jeopardies of a unilaterally imposed solution." Unable to come to an agreement, the Jamaican Parliament approved the new levy anyway in May 1974. U.S. corporations had already invested $660 million in Jamaican mines. Half of all U.S. bauxite and alumina, an essential industrial material, came from Jamaica, and new sources for them would take years to develop. The corporations and the United States thus depended on Jamaica in this case as well as vice versa. This surely boosted the Manley administration's confidence in its ultimate negotiating power.[23]

U.S. State Department officials described the "unilateral" bauxite levy as a "radical action." In response, members of U.S. president Richard Nixon's administration considered retaliatory moves, beginning with a retrenchment in loans and assistance. Specifically, U.S. officials informed the Jamaican ambassador that a $9.1 million U.S. Agency for International Development (AID) loan to expand educational opportunities for the rural poor would not be executed until an agreement was reached with the U.S. bauxite corporations on the island. Furthermore, "meaningful dialogue" between U.S. leaders and the Jamaican government would be placed "largely in suspension 'pending substantial progress in the bauxite negotiations,'" a suspension that would continue under the Gerald Ford presidency after Richard Nixon resigned in August 1974.[24]

During Ford's brief term, a major additional problem developed in U.S.-Jamaican relations: Manley's growing independence and divergence from U.S. foreign policy dictates for the island. In April 1975, the U.S. ambassador expressed to Manley "serious concern that on matters that were not of great importance to the GOJ [Government of Jamaica] it had voted in UN forums against the U.S. position even after strong representation on our part." In response, one of Manley's advisers "interjected that the GOJ was not a party to steamroller tactics and bloc voting, to which the PM [prime minister] added that the GOJ's votes were determined by principle." The adviser also said, as the ambassador reported, "that it was important for Jamaica to preserve its credentials with its Third World allies if Jamaica was to retain their support on economic issues which Jamaica considered of great importance." Later that year, Manley traveled on an official visit to Cuba and, upon his return, lauded the social project and achievements of its revolution. It was not just the United States that objected to this, but many Jamaicans as well. Manley denounced these critics as individuals who sought to become millionaires and live in palaces. As the U.S. Embassy reported, he "invited them to note that there are daily flights to Miami where there is a different kind of society in which they might feel more comfortable."[25]

The Manley government's relations with Cuba and independence from U.S. foreign policy dictates were the product of rational economic forces as much as ideological or politically self-destructive proclivities. The U.S. government continued to hold up rather than expand aid while Jamaica faced an escalating fiscal crisis that threatened its social democratic project. In this context, it was logical that Manley would turn to other countries hoping for assistance, including Cuba as well as oil-rich Trinidad. The latter extended a $50 million loan to Jamaica in 1976. And while Cuba lacked financial wherewithal, it abounded in human capital that it was ready to share. In the years after Manley's visit, hundreds of Cubans came to assist Jamaicans in health care, fishing, aviculture, microdams, and affordable housing and school construction.[26]

At first, U.S. officials wisely perceived Manley's actions as part of an overall alignment with Third World nations more than the Communist bloc. "In a world outside his island," Manley "sees the growing solidarity among the less developed countries as providing a salubrious climate for independent behavior by a small nation," a CIA observer wrote. In this respect, "he is inspired by the example of new societies around the world, especially nearby Cuba." The U.S. ambassador to Jamaica described Manley as an aspiring "Third World prophet-philosopher-economist-reformer-teacher-leader," casting global politics as a struggle between high- and low-income countries and between the imperial and the (formerly) colonized nations.[27]

Most vexing to Washington, however, was Manley's eventual support for Cuba after Cuba dispatched armed forces to Angola in the fall of 1975. Regardless of Manley's motivations, this the State Department considered intolerable. The then infamous white-supremacist state in South Africa had invaded Angola to defeat the leading faction in that nation's civil war, one that was far more hostile to South Africa's apartheid rule than other factions. In response, roughly thirty-five thousand Cuban troops landed in Angola to oust the South African forces, ejecting them in expeditious fashion, for the time being at least. Piero Gleijeses argues that Cuba's motives for its overseas intervention were a mix of ideology—genuine opposition to racial injustice—and perceived long-standing needs for cultivating global allies in light of U.S. hostility against the island. In the eyes of Nelson Mandela, the leader of South Africa's struggle against its apartheid regime, Cuba's military intervention in Angola against South Africa represented a wonderful new day. "It was the first time that a country had come from another continent not to take something away," he wrote from his prison cell in South Africa, "but to help Africans to achieve their freedom." In Washington's eyes, though, this was an ominous new projection of Cuban might abroad. U.S. Secretary of State Kissinger demanded that Manley denounce or at the very least remain neutral about Cuba's intervention in Angola. But the Jamaican government nonetheless came out in support of it once Jamaica's leaders "were satisfied that they [the Cubans] were there because of the South African invasion."[28]

Manley had stood up to Kissinger and refused his imperious requests. The rift with the United States over Cuba, though, did not play well with some Jamaicans. Manley felt compelled to explain why "we [are] taking this risk to anger the United States of America." "We have that friendship with Cuba," Manley explained, "as part of a world alliance of Third World nations that are fighting for justice for poor people in the world." "As long as this party is in power," he declared with unflinching independence, "we intend to walk through the world on our feet and not on our knees."[29]

Yet the Jamaican economy was less robust than Manley's discourse. By 1976, the government appeared on the brink of financial collapse. Some U.S. officials suggested an economic carrot in this time of fiscal need to persuade Manley to pursue policies and international relations in line with U.S. wishes. "Significant economic assistance" could be "an inducement [for Manley] to stay out of the Socialist camp and keep his distance from Castro," some argued, specifically a $200 million loan Manley had been seeking from the United States. Other members of the Ford administration rejected the idea of using aid, doubtless in vain they argued, to "buy . . . good will" and supported instead covert action aimed at ousting the prime minister. Blocking nearly all aid to Jamaica remained U.S. policy, a stark contrast to the generous loans and assistance that would be extended to the island after Manley's time in office.[30]

The potential efficacy of any U.S. covert actions in Jamaica was also limited, though, a number of officials stressed. The U.S. government did not have the same tools and institutions in Jamaica to threaten a leader or condition elections that it had in the old independent Caribbean (excluding post-1959 Cuba). Jamaica had no powerful armed force organized by or responsive to U.S. demands, or for that matter domestic elite interests, but rather relatively weak security forces still tied to the United Kingdom, whose leaders maintained a proprietary stance toward its former Caribbean colonies. The U.S. government could pursue covert destabilization efforts to undermine support for Manley ahead of the upcoming elections—paying opposition leaders and groups, planting damaging stories in the press about Manley and conditions in Jamaica, or other similar activities. Such election interference, though, was unlikely to keep Manley out of office. In spite of the precarious economy, Manley's "charisma is untarnished and re-election . . . is a near certainty," a CIA analyst reported. And "as long as Manley moves within constitutional bounds, he has nothing to fear from the apolitical Jamaican Army."[31]

Better-off Jamaicans, among whom there was considerable opposition to Manley, had another potent weapon at their disposal. Although they could not defeat him at the polls, they could harm his government by voting with their feet and their capital. Thousands of entrepreneurs, professionals, and high-skilled workers took themselves and their money abroad amid the escalating economic crisis, political rift between the United States and Jamaica, and Jamaica's perceived anticapitalist direction, echoing the mass emigration from Cuba in the aftermath of the 1959 revolution. The exodus of people and capital was both an effect and a cause of a major economic crisis. The U.S. ambassador described conditions on the island: "There are serious threats of food shortages and there are persistent rumors of impending devaluation and drastic measures to reduce imports. There is a pervasive unease as demonstrated by [capital] flight and the length of visa lines." Foreign investment was at a "virtual standstill."[32]

Manley nonetheless won another landslide victory at the polls in 1976. What he had lost in support from better-off Jamaicans he had more than made up with votes from the popular classes and the poor. Jamaicans overall had seen improvements in their standard of living and life chances: greater access to land, increased wages, new labor rights, and expanded public education and health care. They had also participated in an ongoing transformation in prevailing ideas about race and nation that incorporated the Jamaican majority in powerful new ways.[33]

The 1976 reelection, though, would prove to be only a momentary victory. The worsening fiscal crisis soon forced Manley to reverse course, to pull back from his social democratic policies and the programs that had garnered him so much support. Arguably, what was an improbable dream of social democracy from the start in a country with limited revenues had become impossible due to hostile political forces. The new U.S. president Jimmy Carter had modestly increased aid to Jamaica to $32 million in 1977, hoping to improve relations and "indicate a new tolerance in U.S. foreign policy for ideological pluralism." This was not close, though, to the $200 million Jamaica had needed to meet its fiscal and foreign exchange obligations. And even that modest increase would soon be steadily reduced. U.S. leaders still objected to Jamaica's continuing close relations with Cuba and Manley's anti-imperialist rhetoric, including support for Puerto Rican independence. By late 1979, the Carter administration would again envisage covert operations against Manley, including damaging propaganda and funding for his opponents.[34]

Manley now felt compelled to turn to the International Monetary Fund (IMF). He considered this multilateral institution's loan terms an infringement on national sovereignty, for the IMF extended loans and offered its seal of approval for others to do the same only if a country adopted the IMF's particular economic model and set of policy prescriptions. Manley, though, clearly did not see another way to avoid a government collapse, because in 1977 he agreed to the IMF's terms. The agreement required Jamaica to make drastic changes in policy that led to a contraction in real wages by more than 25 percent within one year and a decline overall in the standard of living by roughly 50 percent in 1978 alone. The government devalued the currency, which dramatically raised the cost of imported goods. It ended subsidies and price controls for basic goods. And it imposed restrictions on wage growth that otherwise might have compensated for cost-of-living increases. The decline in people's purchasing power caused sales to drop, which in turn led to a series of layoffs and further decreased demand. And despite the IMF's supposed medicine for economic efficiency through free-market policies, the austerity and deregulation program did not pull Jamaica out of its economic tailspin. One part of the problem was the continuing unwillingness of businesses to invest in what they perceived to be an unstable political and economic environment.[35]

Manley was not reelected in 1980. The combination of economic stagnation with dramatic cuts to popular social programs pushed the electorate toward hopes that having a more pro-U.S., centrist prime minister, Edward Seaga, would facilitate economic improvement and foster stability. It is possible, too, that Carter's government interfered covertly in the Jamaican election and contributed to Manley's defeat, as Carter initially had proposed doing in 1979. Sensational claims of Cuban and Soviet agents in the Jamaican government made by the opposition party and mainstream conservative press may also have facilitated Seaga's victory. In sum, deeply intertwined domestic, U.S., and international financial interests that opposed Manley's economic and nationalist policies had aggravated the fiscal challenges inherent in a social democratic project in a low-income nation. Ultimately these challenges were too much for Jamaica, forcing policy reversals and causing a political crisis.[36]

Certainly Manley's final years in office were economically dismal. But Manley came closer than perhaps any other leader in a Caribbean or low-income nation anywhere to achieving what has been the preserve of wealthy nations: a genuine social democracy. For the first few years, the government fostered better material conditions for most Jamaicans and greater equity across society by raising taxes and reallocating state revenues. Thanks to Manley's successful negotiations with the large foreign bauxite and alumina industry, the government gained substantial new revenues that could be used to expand agrarian reform and public education, housing, and health care. The government also enhanced labor laws and rights, affording dignity to those at the lowest rung of the labor market. Overall, wages and the standard of living for the Jamaican majority went up dramatically during Manley's first term. The government also embraced a new collective black identity and pride in Jamaica's African roots. Manley achieved all this within a fully liberal-democratic system and without attacking the private sector. This history explains, Anthony Bogues writes, why "many Jamaicans remember him today in a favorable way. . . . While his efforts did not achieve their mark . . . they resonated with the ordinary Jamaican's deepest aspirations."[37]

Might Jamaica's social democratic system have thrived longer under different circumstances? What might have happened if there had been no economically devastating global oil crisis? What if the U.S. government had been supportive of rather than hostile to Manley's project of nationalist and egalitarian reforms? U.S. leaders might have seen aiding Manley as in their interests in the broader scheme of things, if his administration could make clear that substantial socioeconomic improvements in ordinary people's lives did not require recourse to socialism or communism, or acceptance of any type of dictatorship. When Manley met with Carter in 1977, Manley argued his case for U.S. aid, saying, "It is essential that Jamaica be helped to demonstrate that in a democracy, development and the raising of standards of living can occur; that democracies can satisfy both social and basic needs as well as maintain freedom." Instead, at the time, Manley's perceived failure doubtless discouraged supporters of change in the Caribbean and beyond from heading in the same direction.[38]

In 1979, the Anglophone Caribbean would see a rare exception to the overall liberal democratic trajectory the region followed after independence and witness its only revolution, that in Grenada. Its revolutionary leaders did not pursue Jamaica's social democratic model for change, but rather an authoritarian one, conceivably in part because Manley and his popular socioeconomic transformations were at the time failing while Communist Cuba's were thriving.

The Grenada Revolution, 1979–1983

In the late 1970s, the small Caribbean island of Grenada, with a population of roughly one hundred thousand, was the stage for a powerful revolutionary drama that captured global attention. The 1979 Grenada Revolution was the first successful armed uprising in the independent English-speaking Caribbean. It overthrew a nominally democratic but increasingly dictatorial and unpopular government and led to a left-wing, nondemocratic regime that enjoyed overwhelming popular support. Its new prime minister, Maurice Bishop, would be the sole head of state in the Anglophone Caribbean to be assassinated. And Grenada would become the only former British colony to be invaded by the United States. All these historical transformations, violent crosscurrents of change, reaction, and empire, occurred over four fast years.

The Grenada Revolution began in 1979 with a nearly bloodless civilian coup, when a group of young political leaders and activists forced then prime minister Eric Gairy out of office. Gairy had become a repressive as well as ineffective leader who terrorized his opponents and relied on voter fraud and intimidation to ensure his victory at the polls. Originally, Gairy had been a popular figure, beginning his career as a labor leader who organized cocoa workers in the island's first nationwide strike in 1951. He cast himself as a "black" leader from the rural majority, rather than the lighter-skinned Grenadian elite, and was the country's first prime minister after independence in 1974. Gairy also envisaged a major agrarian reform. The island had been starkly divided between large plantations and often extremely small farms. Independent farmers produced roughly half of the nation's three main exports—cocoa, bananas, and nutmeg (one-third of the world's supply)—but were constrained by the small size of their plots, a problem that agrarian reform could address. With the help of threats of state expropriation, Gairy's government managed to purchase some 40 percent of all properties over forty acres. An agrarian reform of this magnitude had the potential to transform the countryside.[39]

Yet decolonization under Gairy's government became a deeply frustrating and soon nightmarish, rather than euphoric, moment. First, the government never distributed or developed most of the newly obtained state lands, and the proportion of arable farmland under cultivation actually fell to just 55 percent. At the same time, unemployment skyrocketed. "It quickly became evident to a new generation of Grenadian poor," writes Brian Meeks, "that Gairyism held little benefit in it for them, [and] dissatisfaction began to grow in the lower classes, his traditional bedrock of support." Second, the government became increasingly repressive and corrupt. New legislation limited free speech. And Gairy organized a vicious paramilitary force, known as the Mongoose Gang, which worked with the army, then known as the Green Beast, to violently assault Gairy's critics. These included Black Power demonstrators, belying his claim to be a champion of black Grenadians. Rupert Bishop, the father of the future revolutionary leader, Maurice Bishop, was one of the people murdered by Gairy's men, gunned down when they attacked a peaceful rally against Gairy in 1974. People faced mortal danger if they offended the prime minister.[40]

It was during Gairy's rule, in the mid-1970s, that the New Jewel Movement (NJM) emerged, an outgrowth of the old JEWEL movement that had focused on the problems of land and agriculture in Grenada. ("JEWEL" was an acronym for Joint Endeavor for Welfare, Education and Liberation.) The NJM drew supporters from the island's black majority as well as the South Asian- and European-descended minorities. In 1976, the NJM sought change through the ballot box, and one of its leaders, the charismatic lawyer Maurice Bishop, won a seat in Parliament. Bishop was trained as a lawyer and had spent several years defending opponents of Gairy, Rastas, and others at odds with the status quo. He formed part of the democratic opposition in an election in which Gairy's party narrowly prevailed thanks to a measure of voter fraud. Parliament, though, was rarely in session, and when it did meet, it rubber stamped Gairy's bills and mocked his opponents. This experience only furthered Bishop's prior cynical views about Grenada's quasi-democratic system and pushed him, and the NJM, to the left. A more violent show of its farcical character came with rumors in March 1979 that Gairy had ordered the assassination of the NJM's leadership. At that point, NJM leaders decided that it was time to act against Gairy's dictatorial version of democracy. A group of some fifty NJM members attacked the main army barracks, eventually overpowering its troops, and captured the radio station. From there they called on the population to flood into the streets and demand the surrender of the police. Victory came swiftly.[41]

Despite Grenada's small size, its revolution inspired great hopes for a new day on the island and across the region—much like the Cuban Revolution had in 1959 and Aristide would in 1990 Haiti. Jamaican-born anthropologist David Scott recalls how "like many Caribbeans of my generation," he lived this moment as "a euphoric leap into the future . . . a revolutionary beginning." For Grenadians, the revolution promised "the possibility of breaking with the colonial and neocolonial Caribbean past, and of hope for egalitarian change and social and political justice."[42]

The new revolutionary government quickly focused the nation's attention on improving the lives of the Grenadian majority. It mobilized a massive literacy drive to help older Grenadians learn to read and write. It opened up new opportunities for people to acquire high school and university education. Overall expenditures on public education, health care, day care, and housing all skyrocketed, however modest still in absolute terms. The People's Revolutionary Government was wildly popular. The charismatic new prime minister Maurice Bishop would remain so in particular. One member of the NJM recalled how Bishop would "go into the shops in the villages and sit down with them and play cards and talk and laugh and at the same time give them . . . confidence that what we were trying to do in Grenada . . . could work, but it could only work with the people."[43]

As was the case with Fidel Castro after the Cuban Revolution, Bishop could easily have won in a fair vote and yet never held elections, and Castro was likely a model for him in this respect. Just two weeks after the NJM took over the government, Bishop told the U.S. ambassador that the revolution might not "continue with the current democratic model (which he termed 'farcical' and implanted by a foreign culture)," but rather "adopt a new system of 'peoples' assemblies.'" Soon afterward, the new regime dissolved Parliament and suspended the constitution indefinitely. The prime minister could now simply issue new laws—and, for that matter, arrest warrants—by fiat, following consultation with his cabinet. The government's problematic claim to popular representation would rest on its consulting and securing input from relevant organizations, such as trade unions, for major new legislation, rather than on elections, which the NJM dismissed as "five-second democracy."[44]

NJM authorities also brushed aside democratic principles when they shut down all media not controlled by the state. This was in part perhaps an effort to prevent manipulation of the press by opponents of "the Revo," as the revolution would popularly be called. The NJM leadership was aware of the ways the media had helped destabilize Jamaica under Manley, as well as Chile under Salvador Allende, whose democratic socialist government collapsed in a military coup in 1973 following years of U.S. actions against him.

In both cases, the press disseminated false and damaging information, sometimes with the aid of U.S. funding. "We think of the days when . . . [the U.S. government] landed Marines in somebody's country," Bishop proclaimed, "Arbenz in Guatemala in 1954, Dominican Republic in 1965 and dozens of other examples. . . . Destabilization is the name given to the most recently developed . . . method of controlling . . . a country through bullying, intimidation and violence." The government expressed concerns about U.S. intervention in popular culture as well, particularly oral poetry, which was performed in multiple venues. A young revolutionary and poet-turned-minister of culture and then of health, Chris "Kojo" DeRiggs, penned a poem titled "The Last Cowboy" (long before the U.S. invasion in 1983):

> Ronald Reagan, the ageing cowboy bandit man
> Cooked up a major bandit plan . . .
> Announced that he was riding down
> Through his backyard and islands in the sun
> To put more notches on his gun . . .
> For Ronald Reagan 'twas not strange
> To go gun-shooting on his range
> To shoot back all dese winds of change . . .
> No matter who protest, don't bother who gripe
> Dey all must bow down to de stars and stripes.[45]

The NJM leadership was right to be afraid of a U.S. intervention. Even under the liberal Carter administration in 1979, U.S. leaders immediately focused on Grenada, debating how to respond just two days after the NJM coup. Carter's National Security Affairs adviser hoped at that time that the "young (25–35), idealistic, and socialistically-inclined" new leadership "could be co-opted by the U.S." "But," he warned, "if we are not sensitive to their overtures, it is conceivable that they could turn to Cuba." As with Jamaica and Cuba, U.S. officials recognized that they had a choice: try to co-opt and alter the course of a left-wing government in the Caribbean with ample U.S. support or cut back aid and try to overturn the regime, potentially instead pushing it into Soviet—and in Jamaica's and Grenada's case, Cuban—arms. U.S. leaders consistently chose the latter approach.[46]

Less than a month after the revolution, the U.S. ambassador reported emphasizing to Bishop that although, in principle, the United States recognized that "Grenada was a fully independent country . . . he should have no doubts that developing close ties with Cuba would greatly complicate relations with friendly countries like the U.S." Shortly after, Bishop went on Grenadian radio to denounce such pressure: "No country has the right to tell us what to do or how to run our country, or who to be friendly with. We certainly would not attempt to tell any other country what to do. We are not in anybody's backyard, and we are definitely not for sale." The sentiments Bishop expressed, and even the precise words "we are not for sale," echoed earlier statements of Michael Manley. Both leaders gave voice to nationalist resentment of foreign interference in their countries. Their nations had moved in the blink of an eye from British rule to independence under the continual threat of U.S. intervention, becoming part of the long and perilous history of U.S. empire, covert operations, and occupations in the region. Although Jamaica and Grenada's left-wing political projects differed in fundamental ways, they shared this new reality.[47]

Around this same time, the U.S. government received reports that eight Cubans and some Cuban weaponry had arrived "covertly" on the island. Soon thereafter, Carter approved covert operations to "resist the Marxist totalitarian oriented government [in Grenada] and its . . . Cuban advisers" by funneling money to its opponents as well as "by disseminating non-attributable propaganda worldwide and in Grenada . . . in opposition to Cuban intervention." A few months later, Grenadian authorities arrested Winston Whyte, whom the CIA was then funding, in connection with a foiled coup attempt. Grenada's government protested to the U.S. State Department that "mercenaries, vessels, arms and money" had been provided for the coup "from sources in Miami," though U.S. officials denied any government involvement. In March 1980, U.S. leaders agreed that no financial assistance would be extended to Grenada and sought, with only modest success, to discourage aid to the island from U.S. allies. In 1981, the U.S. government took advantage of its 1898 annexation of the Puerto Rican island of Vieques to practice a mock military invasion off its coasts of "Amber and the Amberines," an imaginary nation whose name mirrored Grenada and the Grenadines. Grenada's leaders immediately protested and sought international support to express opposition to this threatening maneuver.[48]

The U.S. government's room for maneuver in Grenada was more limited than it had been in Haiti or the Dominican Republic. As in Jamaica, the U.S. government did not have a U.S.-built, allied, or dutiful military it could work through. And "in the first hours of the Revolution the Green Beast army of Gairy was completely disbanded," Bishop explained in an interview a couple of years later. "A new army came into being, an army of patriotic youth, young farmers and sections of the unemployed." "And that," he said optimistically, "proved to be a decisive factor" in the Revo's longevity, in spite of U.S. hostility.[49]

Unlike the United States, Cuba was a ready supporter of the new government. And Bishop turned increasingly to the Communist nation to help build the new Grenada, literally. Growing numbers of Cuban construction workers and engineers, nurses and doctors, and teachers—and eventually a few dozen military personnel—alighted on the small island to assist with government projects. Above all, they provided free labor and materials to assist with a major, potentially transformative, project for the island: the construction of a new large international airport to facilitate expansion of the tourist industry, a project that had been a major aspiration of Gairy's government as well. The existing airport's runway was too short for tourist jumbo jets, and it lacked lighting for night landings. As a result, many traveling to and from Grenada had to make stopovers, and commercial goods required trans-shipments, in other countries. During the decades prior to the revolution, the economy had been undergoing a slow transition, as planters shifted their capital from agriculture to tourism. For that reason, Grenada's leaders had long envisaged a new airport as key to the island's economic growth. In the 1970s, U.S. officials had indicated to Gairy that the U.S. government would help build one. But despite Gairy's lobbying hard for U.S. favor, reminding the U.S. secretary of state that "Grenada always voted with the United States in international fora . . . and that Grenada was the strongest in the Caribbean against Communism," U.S. aid for a new airport never materialized.[50]

After the 1979 revolution, Grenada was finally building the long-sought new airport, thanks in part to Cuban assistance. The excitement about the airport, and the Revo, was so great early on that many Grenadians volunteered to help build it. Large numbers of inspired Grenadians also assisted with other public works projects, from constructing prefabricated houses to repairing schools. Many, too, had faith at first that the rhetoric of "participatory" rather than parliamentary democracy meant something serious. They participated in numerous local meetings organized by the government to discuss local needs and public policy, such as budget allocations.[51]

Despite some of its radical allies and rhetoric, Grenada pursued largely free-market economic policies, reformist but not socialist, in stark contrast to Cuba. And thanks to the new airport and other construction efforts, together with aid from France, Canada, Venezuela, certain Arab states, and others—U.S. opposition notwithstanding—the economy looked robust. Yet

Bishop's emphasis on tourism as the engine of economic growth was an ironic choice given that much of the Caribbean left then was denouncing the industry as exploitative and analogous to old racist plantation and colonial structures. Furthermore, although the government continued Gairy's policies of purchasing or forcibly leasing the island's large estates, it still did little to restructure land tenure or to aid small farmers and the rural economy. Lands held by the state continued to languish. "Little was done for agriculture in an agricultural island," the Trinidadian writer V. S. Naipaul noted in an essay highly critical of Bishop's government. Its immediate priority, at least, was tourism, not helping farmers. (Perhaps Grenada's political leaders hoped that revenue from the former could contribute later to agricultural development.)[52]

The revolution's conventional economic program, which did little for most people in the countryside, was probably part of the reason for declining enthusiasm and growing opposition over time. The regime responded to these trends in repressive and counterproductive fashion. Scott describes how rising "internal dissent [was] met with draconian measures from the revolutionary state," which, in turn, produced more dissent. Soon the regime was holding hundreds of political prisoners. Not infrequently, those arrested and imprisoned were subjected to abuse and, in some cases, horrendous torture. This, again, surely generated only further opposition, particularly from friends and families of the victims. Police and others accused of and charged with such abuses were invariably found innocent following an investigation. Unsurprisingly, membership in the NJM declined over time. Perhaps surprisingly, though, this was not simply the consequence of waning support. Increasing numbers of people were unable to join because they did not meet new educational and ideological eligibility requirements. This growing "vanguardism" meant the end of even "participatory" democracy.[53]

Revolutionary support, pride, volunteerism, and inspiration were not extinguished. But they were certainly fading, even if Bishop remained popular nonetheless. And the regime's response was ultimately suicidal. In 1983, popular disillusionment with the revolution and sagging morale within the party provoked, or provided an excuse for, Deputy Prime Minister Bernard Coard and the party leadership to demand that Bishop now share power equally with Coard. The precise brew of political rivalry, personal ambition, and policy disagreements at work in this coup is not clear. What is obvious is that neither the people nor any institution other than the "vanguard" party had any role here in deciding on the country's leadership.

Moreover, this change was not what most Grenadians wanted. Although initially accepting the odd new power-sharing arrangement, Bishop quickly changed his mind and rejected this usurpation of his authority. In response, the party took severe action seemingly without hesitation. It ordered Bishop's arrest.[54]

A tragic cascading of events now followed in rapid succession. After soldiers placed Bishop under house arrest, mass protests sprung up demanding his restoration as prime minister. His supporters then forced their way past the soldiers guarding Bishop's residence, who chose not to shoot, and freed him. Bishop and the crowds proceeded to retake the country's military headquarters, Fort Rupert, renamed after Bishop's father. They would not hold the fort for long, though. Troops arrived from another base and, in the ensuing conflict, killed dozens of Bishop's civilian supporters. The soldiers then assassinated the prime minister and seven other national leaders, their bodies never to be found, identified, or honored. The divorce between the country's leadership and the people now felt complete to many Grenadians. "If they could kill the Prime Minister, imagine what they could do to us," one person who lived through these traumatic days later recounted.[55]

At will, the party leaders had deposed, arrested, and summarily executed the country's, and until very recently their party's, popular prime minister. The party was acting with seemingly absolute and terrifying discretion. There were no checks and balances or forms of accountability, as a well-functioning liberal democracy provides, to contain the power, desires, and decisions of individual leaders. The Grenada Revolution's chosen dictatorial mode of rule may have made it less vulnerable to the types of destabilization faced by Manley and other democratic governments attempting popular reforms, but it also had facilitated a bloody and horrifying internecine coup.

With a demoralized and horrified Grenadian population, the revolution was now politically vulnerable to intervention by the United States, whose leaders had long opposed it. U.S. leaders had sought the end of a regime in their perceived sphere of influence that sustained close relations with Cuba. As we have seen, this specific concern, though, formed part of a broader pattern of U.S. intervention in the independent Caribbean since 1898. U.S. intervention might ultimately be driven less by the specifics of a particular case (for instance, Cuban aid to Grenada) than by the U.S. government's demand for Caribbean leaders who could be trusted to act in accordance with U.S. strategic and economic interests in any contingency that might arise in the near or distant future. One U.S. official who worked in the Department of Defense in 1983 recalled: "Grenada was of potential military utility to the Soviet Union. . . . It was the potential . . . [its new] airport offered to the Soviets that worried American analysts."[56]

Some six thousand U.S. troops were dispatched to the tiny island of Grenada on a fleet led by the USS *Guam*—fittingly named after the small island colony in the Western Pacific that the United States seized from Spain in the War of 1898. The Grenadian armed forces were able to mobilize Cuban construction workers to fight alongside them to repel the invaders, but not its own disillusioned citizens. In light of the recent coup and the revolution killing its own beloved leader, there was, in fact, widespread support for the U.S. invasion. "Some Grenadians left their homes when they could to be on the streets showing visible, almost vengeful, support for the invasion. It was an almost gleeful betrayal of those whom they felt had betrayed them by their actions," writes the Grenadian poet Merle Collins. This presumably would not have been the case had the United States invaded the country just a few weeks back, when Bishop was still at the helm, even though from the U.S. point of view Bishop and Coard were one and the same enemy, the Grenada Revolution.[57]

Without popular support, the Grenadian military could not have defeated a covert operation like the Bay of Pigs, let alone a full-scale U.S. invasion. Despite the perhaps unprecedented mismatch between the two sides in this war, the U.S. military relied heavily on air power rather than troops on the ground. This inevitably made civilian deaths more likely. The most notorious incident in this case was "a direct hit on Grenada's mental hospital, killing more than a dozen patients. Several dozen others," Stephen Kinzer recounts, "stumbled away from the blazing ruins [and] . . . wandered the streets . . . as war swirled around them." A British artist, Sue Coe, made a nightmarish painting of this scene with the satirical title "US Military Successfully Bombs a Mental Hospital in Grenada." The work now hangs in New York's Metropolitan Museum of Art, simultaneously displaying the imposition of U.S. empire abroad and maintenance of freedom of speech at home.[58]

U.S. troops took the capital in about twenty-four hours, though fighting continued for a few more days, particularly in rural areas to where some Grenadian troops had retreated. Even though this was the battle of "the sledgehammer and the nutmeg," as one writer put it, Reagan would nonetheless boast, "Our days of weakness are over!" This was perhaps good politics after a string of U.S. "losses" and defeats over the last decade: not only a bombing of U.S. forces in Lebanon just days beforehand, killing over 220, but the Nicaraguan Revolution against the Somoza dictatorship, the Iranian

Revolution and hostage crisis, and the Vietnamese victory over the United States. This was, though, not how most of the world saw the U.S. invasion of Grenada. The United Nations voted 108 to 9 to condemn it.[59]

A year after the invasion, the U.S.-backed candidate for prime minister, Herbert Blaize, was democratically elected. Blaize's government ended the revolution's social welfare programs, repealed the agrarian reform legislation, and privatized state enterprises. Grenada also dutifully broke off diplomatic relations with Moscow. This conservative reaction was reminiscent of the victory of the U.S.-backed and pro-U.S. candidate Seaga over Manley in Jamaica in 1980 and the U.S.-backed Balaguer over Bosch in the Dominican Republic in 1966 following the U.S. occupation there. U.S. aid now flowed freely to Grenada, helping to put the finishing touches on the new international airport that Reagan had previously condemned as a "major military bastion to export terror and undermine democracy."[60]

Prime Minister Blaize commissioned a large stone memorial to be placed just outside the airport. The memorial contains a plaque honoring the U.S. soldiers killed in the invasion, whose "commitment and sacrifice returned freedom to Grenada." "With its scale and design, the monument announces US oversight of Grenadian space and postrevolutionary Grenadian acquiescence," writes cultural studies scholar Shalini Puri. In 2009, the airport was rechristened Maurice Bishop International Airport. Travelers to and from Grenada now confront the ironic joint commemoration of the Grenada Revolution and the U.S. empire of intervention that ended it.[61]

Haiti, 1986–1991

Probably at no time since the Haitian Revolution were hopes greater in Haiti for a new day than on February 7, 1991, when Jean-Bertrand Aristide was inaugurated as president. Popular enthusiasm for the charismatic leader mirrored that for Manley in 1972 Jamaica and for the Grenada Revolution seven years later. Aristide, a liberation theologian from a modest rural background, garnered two-thirds of the vote in the first truly free election in Haitian history, one in which more than 80 percent of eligible voters came to the polls. Only 14 percent voted for Marc Bazin, the U.S.-backed candidate and former finance minister from the Duvalier dictatorship, in spite of the fact that Bazin had received tens of millions of dollars from the U.S. government to help gain—or to buy—votes. In response to that aid, Aristide supporters chanted at his rallies during the campaign, "We're not here for the money, but our own free will."[62]

Democracy appeared to be taking root in the most infertile terrain. The 1990 election came after almost thirty-five years of brutal and bloody dictatorship. The dynasty of François and Jean-Claude Duvalier had prevailed from 1957 to 1986 with extremes of military repression and paramilitary terror beyond anything in the Haitian past since the days of slavery and colonial rule. And after their dynasty collapsed in 1986, tyranny continued in new form. Haiti was still ruled by an army that the United States had created during its 1915–1934 occupation of the country and by the militia and paramilitary forces, the Tonton Makouts, that François Duvalier had developed both to complement and to compete with the U.S.-made army. The post-Duvalier military governments gunned down political protesters and opponents. Hundreds were massacred, for instance, while protesting the seizure of their lands by powerful landowners. During the election held in 1987, the year after Duvalier fell, paramilitary forces opened fire, with the army's complicity, on those going to a polling site in Port-au-Prince, murdering seventeen. These forces also killed numerous others on the day of the vote in the capital and throughout the country. They acted to stop an election in which opponents of the military regime and of the Duvalierists were about to win.[63]

Ignoring the perils of doing so, Father Aristide had fearlessly spoken out against Duvalier in his regime's final years, and Aristide continued to condemn the terrors of military rule after Duvalier's fall. Aristide also condemned the extreme economic and social inequalities of Haitian society. The vast majority lived in areas without health care or the most basic public infrastructure, despite onerous taxes on them. And they farmed land that they could not legally call their own, even though land and property had been probably the deepest aspiration of generations of Haitians since the end of slavery during the Haitian Revolution. Haiti could also long boast of one of the Americas' most impressive and well-educated elites—one, though, that had never taken measures to address the material deprivation of its population at large. Aristide's championing of the Haitian majority and his capacity to inspire them was, arguably in and of itself, a threat to the old order. Aristide was not the only outspoken opponent at the time, but he seemed to connect uniquely with the Haitian people. The words in his sermons became famous across Port-au-Prince and beyond.[64]

Some of Aristide's sermons under Duvalier and the military dictatorship that followed prophesied and even embraced a popular revolution if Haitian leaders and the powers-that-be did not address the inequality and exclusion that oppressed the majority of the nation. In 1987, Aristide even preached to a packed congregation: "*Vive la guerre*! [Long live war!] So that we will all have bread. *Vive la guerre*! So that we will all have houses. *Vive la guerre*! So that we will all have land." No wonder he struck terror into the hearts of many, while swelling those of many more with hope and pride. After almost being assassinated by a man pretending to take communion from him, a would-be killer who was disarmed by Aristide's parishioners, Aristide fought back with a fiery sermon: "We are telling you today that we have anger in our veins, in our guts, but one day—we don't know when that day will arrive—one day we will put that anger into action. From one moment to the next, anything can happen, because when the winds of vicissitudes blow, when the winds of hunger blow, when the storm of injustice is raging, one fine day a people weighed down by all this human and inhuman suffering—this people will become a people marching toward justice." "One day the people," he later wrote, will "knock the table of privilege over, and take what rightfully belongs to them."[65]

Aristide's rousing, sometimes revolutionary sermons in a poor Port-au-Prince neighborhood, La Saline, made him a target of government assassins, who were responsible for several failed attempts on his life. The most notorious of these was an assault on him along with his entire congregation. In September 1988, a gang of two dozen men with automatic weapons and machetes charged into a church packed with around one thousand parishioners and went on a killing spree. The victims had come to hear Father Aristide preach, despite rumors that those who did would be attacked. At least thirteen were killed and over seventy people wounded, some of the dead still holding Bibles in their hands. Most managed to escape, though, including Aristide. The murderous band of paramilitaries torched the church and walked away, right past soldiers watching from a major army barracks next door. The following day, the attackers gave interviews on the radio and television, with even more surreal impunity, warning the population again: "What you saw yesterday was child's play. . . . Whatever parish lets Father Aristide lead a mass, there will be a pile of cadavers attending."[66]

Aristide continued, though, to condemn the dictatorship and existing order, which now included, from his perspective, the Catholic hierarchy and U.S. government. The Church and U.S. leaders had together turned against Duvalier in the mid-1980s and allied with the popular classes at the eleventh hour to force him out of office. That alliance, though, had broken down, and Aristide called out both for what he saw as a betrayal of the people. On the day of a general strike in November 1988, he took to the radio with revolutionary words:

Alone, we are weak.
Together, we are strong.
Together, we are the flood.
Let the flood descend, the flood of
Poor peasants and poor soldiers,
The flood of the poor jobless multitudes (and poor soldiers)

. . . To prevent the flood of the children of God from descending,
The imperialists in soutane [those within the Catholic Church] have
conspired with the imperialists of America.
This is why we Haitians must say to one another what Jesus declared
(Mark 2:11):
Arise! Go forth! Walk!

Aristide's labeling of some clerics as "imperialist" surely irritated Church authorities. But most Haitian bishops—appointed by Duvalier and ready to take the fight against Duvalierism only so far—were already opponents of Aristide. Many Church leaders also feared the community-based progressive Catholic movement in Haiti (born in the 1970s and known as the Little Church [*Ti Legliz*]) that Aristide helped build. Aristide received no support even from his superiors in his own order, the Salesians. To the contrary, they had almost blamed him for the slaughter at his church, he bitterly recalled, castigating him for getting "mixed up in politics" and demanding that he take up his work elsewhere, perhaps in Canada or Rome. When Aristide refused to leave Haiti and cease his searing critiques, he was expelled from the order in December 1988, with the Vatican's approval.[67]

Neither exclusion from the Church nor the regime's violence stopped the upsurge of support for Aristide. With each failed assassination effort, his following seemed to grow to new heights. People were transfixed by this small, frail man, who refused to be held back by fear and threats to his life and continued to denounce the dictatorship and injustice in captivating, often poetic, rhetoric. People called him "Titid," or "Little Tid [Aristide]," in Kreyòl. In general, the violence of the post-Duvalier regime increasingly backfired, especially following the church massacre. A broad spectrum of groups began pressuring the government to democratize, including the U.S. government. The Church, too, finally voiced criticism of the regime's human rights violations.[68]

In the face of overwhelming pressure, the government agreed to hold elections in 1990. Many Haitians were cynical about the prospects for a fair and peaceful vote following the 1987 massacre at the polls and a farcical election the next year. Aristide himself had never expressed optimism about a democratic path forward. He had warned before the 1987 vote that efforts at change through the ballot box would be met only with violence and bloodshed, with many dying in vain, as, in fact, occurred. And the people, he stated, sought not simply democracy but "a revolution that will change Haiti for once and for all." From where he stood, it was perhaps understandably hard to imagine that, even if there could be a fair election and popular reforms followed, the old military would not overthrow a democratic leader bringing about meaningful change.[69]

It was also hard to imagine that a military coup under those circumstances would not receive at least tacit U.S. support—thus making its occurrence more likely—given that the U.S. government had long supported the dynastic Duvalier dictatorship and maintained close relations with the army. Despite that regime's extraordinary state violence and terror, Jean-Claude Duvalier (François Duvalier's son) had been a close ally of the United States and recipient of bountiful U.S. and multilateral aid, because he was seen as boosting U.S. strategic and business interests. Only in the face of popular rebellion against Duvalier and fears that it would become a left-wing revolution if the dictator were not discharged did the U.S. government ultimately withdraw its support for Duvalier and pressure him to resign and head off into exile. To prevent "massive internal uprisings" and to "maintain the military as an institution, Duvalier had to be eased out," one U.S. military officer explained. The lesson Aristide may have learned was that change in Haiti could come about only through a powerful popular uprising.[70]

Unsurprisingly in this light, Aristide did not enter the presidential race at first in 1990. At the eleventh hour, though, two months before the election, his supporters and would-be allies persuaded him to do so. Aristide's change of heart was driven in part by new logistics. The United Nations and the Organization of American States had intervened and would now dispatch hundreds of election observers to ensure a fair vote and to prevent a repeat of the violence that took the lives of many voters in 1987.[71]

During Aristide's short campaign, he electrified crowds, traveling around the country in a borrowed car on a shoestring budget. "When you tell me that you are living in hunger, can you tell me that you are free?" Aristide asked. "No!," the crowds roared back. Optimism was in the air, as embodied in the electoral commission's new song. "We [the people] are the state . . . / the state is us." Perhaps the day was finally over when the state did not belong to the nation but only to a small elite of wealthy and powerful Haitians and the country's armed forces. Aristide named his party *Lavalas*, "the flood," a metaphor for the power of collective resistance that he had often used since the final Duvalier years.[72]

A free and fair election took place in November 1990, and Aristide triumphed, a now wildly popular and populist figure unlike any government leader Haiti had seen since the Haitian Revolution. There was an immediate but failed coup to prevent Aristide from coming to office, staged by the notoriously brutal ex-Duvalier minister of the interior, Roger Lafontant. Yet the popular forces fired by Aristide's election responded by attacking Lafontant's associates and businesses. It is important, too, that the U.S. ambassador made his opposition to the coup clear. At that point the military banded together to stop it. Once again, for Aristide the lesson learned may have been that any real change in Haiti required popular mobilization and possibly even violence.[73]

From the moment he took office, Aristide initiated a political-cultural revolution. People from the countryside, often called *moun andeyo* (literally "people from the outside"), were brought into the city, into public space, and integrated with *moun lavil* ("city people") in dramatic new fashion. It was a poor rural woman whom Aristide asked to place the presidential sash on him during the inauguration. Journalist Mark Danner recounted how Aristide "invited the poorest of the poor to come to the Palace" following the inauguration, "where on the vast green lawns he served them a copious meal of rice and beans. Or rather, he had his soldiers serve them—soldiers, serving the poor! It was unheard of in the history of the country." Aristide also signaled a new era by shuttering the infamous Fort Dimanche, where the army tortured and murdered prisoners in the past, and by turning it into a public memorial to its many victims. Suggesting perhaps the depths of contempt among the wealthy and powerful for the people at large, Haitians quickly embraced Aristide's simple new motto, "All people are people" and his modest promise to move people "from misery to poverty with dignity."[74]

During Aristide's inauguration, he called on six of the country's leading generals to retire. This indicated literally from day one that his administration would make it a high priority to reform the country's army—an important but obviously risky move. "A handful of soldiers were suspended from duty and even arrested following charges that they had killed or wounded civilians, denting the customary impunity enjoyed by the military," the non-governmental organization America's Watch reported. "Abusive commanders were transferred to obscure posts or dismissed." The new government also moved to crack down on violence and intimidation by members of the old secret police and mass militia, often both of which were referred to as Tonton Makouts or simply Makouts. Aristide's success in this regard would lead to the most obvious concrete improvement in people's lives after his inauguration. The nightly gunfire stopped, Haitians could walk freely, and the armed forces could no longer arrest and assault people with impunity. "Corpses would no longer be found on sidewalks at dawn," sociologist Alex Dupuy writes.[75]

The new government also quickly laid out public policy goals. Ten days after the inauguration, Prime Minister René Préval announced that extending public health care throughout the country, subsidizing and assisting small farmers, and developing infrastructure were the government's top priorities. These were the key concerns for Haitians as well, nearly three out of four of whom lived in rural areas and worked in agriculture as small farmers, tenants, or wage laborers. The rural population and economy had been severely neglected by most previous governments in Haitian history. And while the 1987 Haitian Constitution called for "an agrarian reform to benefit those who actually work the land," no legislation was passed toward this goal. Government budgets had also continued to allocate almost no resources for agricultural needs or public schools and health care for the rural majority.[76]

Implementing successful programs in health, education, and agrarian reform, though, was a tall order even if the political will was there. Haiti was a low-income nation with resources nothing close to Jamaica's under Manley or certainly Cuba's under Castro, let alone thriving European social democracies. The country had a small potential tax base. And even that was not realized because of tax evasion by the wealthy and a regressive tax structure that relied heavily on those with the least means, the peasantry (taxes on the coffee exports they produced, the food they sold in local markets, and necessities from abroad that they consumed). As a result, the state had almost no revenue with which to work.[77]

Undeterred by these overwhelming challenges, Aristide set out to raise revenues and reduce existing state expenditures in order to fund his administration's social project. The government targeted tax evasion, failure to pay back taxes, and loopholes and exemptions to increase internal revenues and customs receipts from levies on external trade. The government also went on a campaign against corrupt state officials who used their public position for personal gain. That included putting a stop to "zombie checks," government payments to deceased individuals that ended up in the hands of government officials and administrators or their fortunate associates. Aristide also laid off thousands of civil servants who either were not qualified or staffed bloated departments. The results were impressive. In just a few months, government expenditures were nearly halved, while revenues, which had been in decline for years, expanded.[78]

The Aristide administration sought to add to its increasing state revenues with external loans and aid. Given Aristide's sound fiscal policies and successful anticorruption measures, foreign governments (France and the United States), the World Bank, and the IMF promised loans and financial contributions totaling roughly $500 million. In an earlier incarnation, Aristide had scoffed at the IMF, dismissing it as, in fact, the International Misery Fund. But Haiti was a special case, for the IMF's austerity demands, which generally required eliminating social services and subsidies, did not affect most people as it did elsewhere. In Haiti, there were virtually no subsidies or social services to cut.[79]

Aristide also pushed a major minimum wage hike through Parliament. The government set ceilings on food prices, too, lowering the cost of living for most Haitians. These reforms, though, benefited mostly urban workers, while Haiti was still then a country predominantly of small farmers. Plots tended to be very small. Few people held title to the land they worked. And a good number had to engage in sharecropping. Although there were unproductive estates across the country, land scarcity was a product largely of an ever higher person-to-land ratio. There were a relatively small number of large landowners compared with the rest of Latin America and the Caribbean. The limited availability of vast rural estates and idle areas, the usual targets of agrarian reform, reduced the possibilities for land redistribution, as did the growing problem of deforestation and soil erosion. Haiti's high person-to-land ratio would surely require the development of avenues in addition to farming to provide a decent livelihood for everyone and to grow the country's overall wealth.[80]

Yet Aristide's administration nonetheless still saw agrarian reform as an essential avenue for social democratic change in a country as poor as Haiti. Certainly it would have made a world of difference to tenants and sharecroppers if they were made property owners instead. And if the state were able to distribute even small amounts of land to increase people's holdings, so recipients could cultivate two to three hectares instead of one, that also might have made a big difference. Even small plots would have been beneficial, too, given that people often combined agriculture and other work as, for instance, teachers or merchants. Land distribution promised beneficiaries greater economic autonomy and subsistence security. And if the state could provide agricultural and infrastructural support (irrigation, loans, reduced taxes, crop storage facilities, and new roads), small farming would have become more productive and profitable. Had international aid organizations been convinced to embrace this project, they could have helped finance such rural infrastructure.[81]

As an initial measure, Aristide pledged to help small farmers in a way that seemed within fiscal reach, by granting titles to those farming state lands as well as redistributing areas belonging to the state that had been enclosed by private landholders (well-off squatters, in other words). Aristide's administration also planned to draw on new revenue to provide subsidies for small farmers. Many, though, eager for land of their own, were not willing to wait for the government to act. Since the fall of Duvalier, some lands had been spontaneously taken over by poor farmers, resulting at times in violence. Aristide responded to one armed conflict by promising future land distribution and calling for peace and patience: "While we wait for the creation of the National Institute of Agrarian Reform and a solution . . . to these land problems, I ask each brother and each sister . . . to use their machetes to work the land and not to wound their fellow creatures."[82]

The patience Aristide asked for was not put to the test, nor was his vision for agrarian reform, at least not at this time. Instead, his government began to lose control and would soon fall to a military coup, just seven months after what for many had been a hopeful, even awe-inspiring, inauguration.[83] A large part of the better-off and the powerful and privileged in the military and paramilitary forces had not voted for Aristide in 1990, we can safely assume. Certainly as president, Aristide mobilized intense opposition among these groups. Dismissing military officers and arresting rank-and-file soldiers for human rights violations, firing thousands of civil servants and eliminating government graft, repressing the erstwhile supreme Makouts and attacking their lucrative drug and contraband industries, and making the wealthy pay taxes may have all been sound public policies. But they also galvanized virulent political opposition and resistance among powerful groups.[84]

Aristide's economic policy itself was far from radical. Still, the raise in the minimum wage was substantial, and it struck a blow against business classes. They surely sensed around them what they saw as ominous challenges to the old order. There was a "new confidence among the poor," one observer, David Nicholls, wrote, and growing popular mobilization. Under Aristide, "hardly a month went by without demonstrations or other actions—

sometimes violent—by one or another group or mass organization . . . [making] demands on the government: workers calling for higher wages, better working conditions . . . students for university reforms; peasants for land reform; consumers for lowering the high cost of living . . . citizens for more jobs, health care, education, and a literacy campaign; others for reversing deforestation and the degradation of the environment." "The bourgeoisie feared the empowerment of the social classes whose abject exploitation and suppression the dictatorships had guaranteed," writes Dupuy.[85]

Yet it was not only elite disdain for the Haitian majority and resistance to their growing demands and presence that fired anti-Aristide sentiments among the better-off classes. So, too, did several major acts or threats of popular political violence and, more ominously, Aristide's apparent unwillingness at times to denounce them. In one case, Roger Lafontant, the leader of the failed January coup to prevent Aristide from taking office, was on trial. Lafontant had been one of the most feared and loathed figures in Haiti, responsible for massacres under both the Duvalier dynasty and the post-Duvalier military regime. People surrounded the courthouse, with tires, matches, and gasoline in hand. These were the tools of what was known as *Pe Lebrun*: tires burned in protest and, in the worst instances, for "necklacing"—a type of lynching in which a burning tire is forced around a victim's neck. This form of popular "justice" started after Duvalier fled into exile. It was inflicted on military figures, Makouts, or simply common criminals believed to be guilty of horrendous crimes. Presumably swayed by the menacing crowds outside, the judge in the Lafontant case sentenced him to life imprisonment. Perhaps this was a fair punishment, but it was a stiffer one than that mandated by law. A few days after Lafontant's trial, at a student rally, Aristide lauded the protesters for ensuring that justice had been served. It's true that necklacing occurred no more frequently during Aristide's government than it had under the post-Duvalier military regime. Twenty-five would be lynched during Aristide's time in office in 1991. But what was different was that Aristide seemed to legitimate menacing popular protest and, in some instances, even violent actions against powerful opponents, at a time when he was the country's president, the person responsible for ensuring justice and order through the rule of law.[86]

The following month, protesters once again threatened violence in an effort to influence the state. When the National Assembly scheduled a no-confidence vote to unseat Prime Minister Préval, demonstrators enveloped the palace in an effort to forestall the vote. Some also vandalized the offices of Aristide opponents, and others beat up two deputies. The police acted to stop the rioters, and this time the Aristide administration condemned their actions. But the condemnation was scarcely convincing to Aristide's critics and of little significance at this point. The country was brimming with rumors of an imminent coup.[87]

In mid-September, soldiers attempted to seize Aristide after he returned from delivering a speech on democracy and equality at the United Nations in New York. The president discovered the plot in time and was able to escape. Soon everyone in Haiti knew of the failed military coup, and tens of thousands poured into the streets to demonstrate their support for Aristide. Desperate but defiant, Aristide spoke to enormous crowds that had gathered at the palace. His words were balanced on a razor's edge between calling and not quite calling for a revolution, as if he had given up on the existing political process as an avenue for change, as if he were instead living out his earlier prophesies that reform was not possible in Haiti through democracy, but rather only through a popular uprising against the powerful forces lined up against meaningful change. Those forces, Aristide suggested, had sought since he was inaugurated to strangle the economy and his administration through a type of business or capital strike, and now they were turning to military violence and dictatorship to rid themselves of his presidency. "Whenever you are hungry, turn your eyes in the direction of those people who aren't hungry. Whenever you are out of work, turn your eyes in the direction of those who can put people to work. . . . You who have money . . . you must invest your money . . . so that more people can find work, for . . . if you don't do it, I am sorry for you! It's not my fault, you understand. . . . That money in your possession, it is not really yours. You earned it in thievery . . . under an evil regime . . . and in all other unsavory ways. . . . If I speak to you in that way, it's because I've given you seven months to conform," that is, to play "according to the rules of the democratic game," yet to no avail. Finally, he threatened the Makouts, perhaps here referring to the old Duvalier repressive forces more broadly. If a Makout tried to gain political power, the people should not "hesitate to give him what he deserves," surely referring to *Pe Lebrun*. "What a beautiful tool! . . . It has a good smell [the burning tires], wherever you go you want to inhale it." He seemed to be reassuring the crowd that violence, even brutality, was a legitimate act in the service of popular justice.[88]

To some extent, Aristide's words were couched simply as a warning to the powerful that there would be a violent popular revolution if they did not accept peaceful democratic change. But Aristide also appeared to be calling on people to rise up in armed resistance if he were ousted by a coup.

He did not, though, take any steps to organize, arm, or provide direction to his supporters.

In any case, the armed forces and their civilian supporters were not deterred, but rather incited to violence by Aristide's menacing, amorphous threats. The military took almost immediate action after the speech, first shutting down the radio station to prevent Aristide from alerting people to the coup and calling on them to resist. Aristide was arrested, and following the mediation of the U.S. ambassador, the democratically elected president was whisked off to exile in Venezuela. The armed forces immediately commenced a preemptive slaughter, indiscriminately firing at people in areas seen as most likely to come out in support of Aristide. On the night of the coup, in Port-au-Prince's poor Cité Soleil neighborhood, 250 people were reportedly killed.[89]

Within a few days of the coup, the U.S. government made clear that while it favored a return to democracy, it did not necessarily wish to see Aristide president again, supposedly because of his recourse to "mob rule." U.S. newspapers backed up this portrait of Aristide. "The president is a hero to the desperate people who live in the slums of Port-au-Prince . . . [whom] he has organized . . . into an instrument of real terror," the *Washington Post* wrote in somewhat misleading fashion. It was doubtless easy for Haitians to see a State Department stance against Aristide as disingenuous—as, in fact, reflecting long-standing opposition to his policies and rhetoric—given that the U.S. government had for decades supported the Duvalier dictatorship despite its far greater state violence.[90]

In the years after the coup, large numbers of Aristide supporters, suspected ones, and others were killed by Haitian military and paramilitary forces. The number slain appears to have been in the thousands. Popular organizations were decimated, and residents of poor neighborhoods, including children, died in the attacks. Some of the killings were carried out by the Revolutionary Front for the Advancement and Progress of Haiti, or FRAPH, a paramilitary organization that received much of its weaponry in illegal shipments from Miami, Florida. The organization was run by the infamous Emmanuel Constant, then on the CIA payroll.[91]

For the near future, at least, the exhilarating dream of peaceful transformation that Aristide inspired would not be rekindled and realized in Haiti. That would be true even when a new U.S. administration, facing new political currents and opportunities, including a devastated Haitian left and a seemingly less formidable and charismatic Aristide, forcibly returned him to office in 1994 through a new U.S. military intervention. The obstacles to a successful social democratic project at that point were perhaps impossible to overcome, even more improbable than in 1990. This time, Aristide was not coming into office after years of inspiring David-over-Goliath triumphs and widespread hopes of a long-awaited new beginning. Instead, Aristide's government now depended on the very U.S. empire that he had condemned for its historic role in propping up Haitian dictators and relied on U.S. leaders who violently opposed his left-wing policies. At the same time, the economy was in shambles, and international financial institutions made it clear that loans would be made available only if Aristide followed a neoliberal economic program at odds with his social democratic agenda.[92]

· · · · · ·

In the second half of the twentieth century, a series of both peaceful and violent revolutions transformed the Caribbean, their supporters imagining profound popular change in diverse fashion and by diverse means. These began with the Cuban Revolution, whose triumph and impressive achievements inspired other national efforts at reform. At the same time, its failures and crises also provided a cautionary tale to many in the Caribbean and beyond for how revolutionary projects could lead down unwanted paths and how perhaps such paths might be avoided. The transformational Caribbean governments and their supporters that followed the Cuban Revolution—in particular, those led by Juan Bosch in the Dominican Republic (1963), Michael Manley in Jamaica (1972–80), Maurice Bishop in Grenada (1979–83), and Jean-Bertrand Aristide in Haiti (1991)—weighed this history as they experimented with different paths forward for reform. The paths chosen were diverse with regard to their democratic or authoritarian character, how much of the economy was taken over by the state, and how independent their foreign policies became from the U.S. government. Yet in terms of their social projects, these reformist governments shared a great deal with the Cuban Revolution and with each other. They all drew on powerful popular hopes and mobilization. And they all sought to improve the lives of everyday people and further socioeconomic equity by providing land and property to small farmers, by expanding public education and health care, and by promoting a new respect for all members of society. In retrospect, their achievements as well as their failures seem formidable. Certainly, these pasts reveal the powerful and particular ways Jamaicans, Grenadians, and Haitians—and Cubans and Dominicans—envisaged the contours of desirable change during the late twentieth century.

Epilogue

Caribbean Futures

· ·

Historical struggles over land and autonomy in the Caribbean have been about mapping the future. Agents of empire and too many national leaders in the region have, again and again, been capable of imagining only plantation futures. And yet multiple communities in the Caribbean have imagined other futures, too, rooted in their experiences and struggles within and against the colonial order. In the twenty-first century, with new economic, political, and environmental pressures reshaping the contours of possibility in the region, it is critical to imagine differently. We live in an era when alternatives to the existing order may be especially unclear, when what is has come to seem inevitable, perhaps inescapable. Yet once plantation slavery, too, seemed that way, and the enslaved in the Caribbean rewrote the possible. In the Caribbean, the broader global truth that the current order is environmentally unsustainable is particularly clear, with problems of flooding and deforestation wreaking havoc in many communities. An alternative path is vital and necessary. But how can it take root?

There has been, and continues to be, a persistent will to misunderstand, overlook, or silence these alternatives. Today, the dream of the plantation Caribbean is as strong as it ever was, with projects for industrial parks and tourist playgrounds sometimes taking the place of actual plantations, but largely with a similar structure of meaning and exploitation. In these projects, what the Caribbean is presumed to be able to offer is only its geography and a supply of cheap labor. That these are the solutions still being offered, after many centuries in which they have consistently led to marginalization and poverty, is a measure of a profoundly bankrupt imagination. Why has it been, and why does it remain, so difficult to instead create a vision for the future grounded in the experiences, practices, and hopes that have been created and sustained by Caribbean populations over centuries? The reasons are many. One reason is that the resources offered up by the history of the region are too often overlooked. Our hope is that this work, in a small way, can contribute to and help sustain the search for different futures.

The stories we have told in this book are meant both to account for the shape of things as they evolved and to emphasize that there have always been other possibilities. These possibilities have all too often been fore-closed, some crushed through brutal violence and others strangled through long-term structural forces and leadership decisions. Yet there is, always, a source for wonder in the history of the Caribbean. The process of navigating this reality in ways that keep opening up new possibilities has been one of remarkable invention. As the region's artists—writers, painters, and musicians—have always understood, history is a burden but not a trap, and stories are made to be rewritten.

Acknowledgments

This book would not have been possible without the support of our editor at the University of North Carolina Press, Elaine Maisner. We are grateful for her engagement with our ideas and her patience as we worked through how to tell histories from the Caribbean. The book has also benefited from the scholarly expertise and myriad insights offered by Hannah Rosen. Conversations with Katharine Dubois over many years shaped the approach and style of the work. Thanks go as well to Julie Skurski for key interventions, including help conceiving the book's title. We also appreciate Marlene Daut's thoughtful comments on several chapters. Yanique Hume provided helpful insight into the question of family land. Two readers for the University of North Carolina Press, Thomas Holt and Matthew Smith, made crucial contributions that helped us develop new frameworks and rethink the structure of the book, and we are deeply grateful. Matthew Smith's insights about Jamaican history were particularly helpful in chapter 7. Thank you also to Daniella Bassi for her expert editorial assistance.

We are grateful to William & Mary and to Duke University for generous support for subvention, editorial assistance, and research leave. Our students, too, shared perceptive comments on chapter drafts. Finally, we would like to thank the National Humanities Center for funding during the 2016–17 academic year. The Center's Delta, Delta, Delta Fellowship and William C. and Ida Friday Fellowship generously supported our final work on the book and provided a wonderful environment and community in which to write.

Notes

Introduction

1. B. W. Higman, *A Concise History of the Caribbean* (New York: Cambridge University Press, 2011), xi, 6–7. Higman's work is part of a broader tradition that has sought to provide a panoptic view of the region. This tradition includes classic works from the 1970s and 1980s: Eric Eustace Williams, *From Columbus to Castro: The History of the Caribbean, 1492–1969* (London: Deutsch, 1970); Franklin W. Knight, *The Caribbean, the Genesis of a Fragmented Nationalism* (New York: Oxford University Press, 1978); J. H. Parry, P. M. Sherlock, and A. P. Maingot, *A Short History of the West Indies* (New York: St. Martin's, 1987). More recent studies include Carrie Gibson, *Empire's Crossroads: A History of the Caribbean from Columbus to the Present Day* (New York: Atlantic Monthly, 2014); Gad J. Heuman, *The Caribbean: A Brief History*, 2nd ed. (London: Bloomsbury Academic, 2014); Joshua Jelly-Schapiro, *Island People: The Caribbean and the World* (New York: Alfred A. Knopf, 2016); Frank Moya Pons, *History of the Caribbean* (Princeton, N.J.: Markus Wiener, 2007); Mimi Sheller, *Consuming the Caribbean: From Arawaks to Zombies* (London: Routledge, 2003). Stephan Palmié and Francisco A. Scarano, in *The Caribbean: A History of the Region and Its Peoples* (Chicago: University of Chicago Press, 2011), offer a wide-ranging overview of the region's history through chapters written by specialists of different areas. The most detailed and complete history of the Caribbean produced over the course of two decades and involving a vibrant network of collaborators is the magisterial *General History of the Caribbean*, 6 vols. (Paris: UNESCO Publishing/Macmillan Education, 1997).

2. "If historians are to be anything other than representatives for the Colonial office and the planter class," Bolland notes, they must begin from an understanding of how land and autonomy have been conceptualized by the population at large. See O. Nigel Bolland, "Systems of Domination after Slavery: The Control of Land and Labor in the British West Indies after 1838," *Comparative Studies in Society and History* 23, no. 4 (October 1981): 614–15.

3. Jean Casimir, *La cultura oprimida* (Mexico City: Nueva Imagen, 1981); Yvonne Acosta and Jean Casimir, "Social Origins of the Counter-Plantation System in St. Lucia," in *Rural Development in the Caribbean*, ed. P. I. Gomes (New York: St. Martin's, 1985), 34–59; Ángel G. Quintero Rivera, *¡Salsa, sabor y control!: Sociología de la música "tropical"* (Mexico City: Siglo Veintiuno, 1998), 228–29.

Chapter One

1. Peter Hulme, *Colonial Encounters: Europe and the Native Caribbean, 1492–1797* (London: Methuen, 1986), 246; Peter Hulme, "Black, Yellow and White on St. Vincent: Moreau de Jonnès," in *The Global Eighteenth Century*, ed. Felicity Nussbaum (Baltimore: Johns Hopkins University Press, 2003), 191; Julie Chun Kim, "Natural Histories of Indigenous Resistance: Alexander Anderson and the Caribs of St. Vincent," *Eighteenth Century* 55, nos. 2–3 (Summer–Fall 2014): 226.

2. Tzvetan Todorov, *The Conquest of America: The Question of the Other* (New York: Harper and Row, 1984), 4.

3. Melanie J. Newton, "Returns to a Native Land: Indigeneity and Decolonization in the Anglophone Caribbean," *Small Axe* 17, no. 2 (July 2013): 108, 121; Melanie J. Newton, "'The Race Leapt at Sauteurs': Genocide, Narrative, and Indigenous Exile from the Caribbean Archipelago," *Caribbean Quarterly* 60, no. 2 (June 2014): 21.

4. Philip P. Boucher, *Cannibal Encounters: Europeans and Island Caribs, 1492–1763* (Baltimore: John Hopkins University Press, 1992); Richard White, *The Middle Ground: Indians, Empires, and Republics in the Great Lakes Region, 1650–1815* (Cambridge: Cambridge University Press, 1991); Francisco Scarano, *Puerto Rico: Cinco siglos de historia* (San Juan: McGraw-Hill, 1993), 179–81, 200; Carlos Esteban Deive, *La Española y la esclavitud del indio* (Santo Domingo: Fundación García Arévalo, 1995), 101.

5. Samuel M. Wilson, *Hispaniola: Caribbean Chiefdoms in the Age of Columbus* (Tuscaloosa: University of Alabama Press, 1990), 4.

6. See Louis Allaire, "Agricultural Societies in the Caribbean: The Lesser Antilles," in *Autochthonous Societies*, ed. Jalil Sued-Badillo, vol. 1 of *General History of the Caribbean* (Paris: UNESCO Publishing/Macmillan Education, 1997), 196–98, 204.

7. José M. Guarch-Delmonte and A. Gus Pantel, "The First Caribbean People," in *Autochthonous Societies*, ed. Jalil Sued-Badillo, vol. 1 of *General History of the Caribbean* (Paris: UNESCO Publishing/Macmillan Education, 1997), 93–137; Samuel Wilson, "Introduction to the Study of the Indigenous People of the Caribbean," in *Indigenous Peoples of the Caribbean*, ed. Samuel Wilson (Gainesville: University Press of Florida, 1997), 4–5; Jay B. Haviser, "Settlement Strategies in the Early Ceramic Age," in *Indigenous Peoples of the Caribbean*, ed. Samuel Wilson (Gainesville: University Press of Florida, 1997), 61–63.

8. Arie Boomert, "Agricultural Societies in the Continental Caribbean," in *Autochthonous Societies*, ed. Jued Sued-Badillo, vol. 1 of *General History of the Caribbean* (Paris: UNESCO Publishing/Macmillan Education, 1997), 135, 139, 189n18.

9. Hulme, *Colonial Encounters*, 60–61.

10. Boomert, "Agricultural Societies," 189n18; Hulme, *Colonial Encounters*, 60; Christopher Schmidt-Nowara, "Conquering Categories: The Problem of Prehistory in Nineteenth-Century Puerto Rico and Cuba," *CENTRO Journal* 13, no. 1 (Spring 2001): 8.

11. Allaire, "Agricultural Societies," 198, 202, 204; David Watters, "Maritime Trade in the Prehistoric Eastern Caribbean," in *Indigenous Peoples of the Caribbean*, ed. Samuel Wilson (Gainesville: University Press of Florida, 1997), 88.

12. Jalil Sued-Badillo, "The Indigenous Societies at the Time of Conquest," in *Autochthonous Societies*, ed. Jalil Sued-Badillo, vol. 1 of *General History of the Caribbean* (Paris: UNESCO Publishing/Macmillan Education, 1997), 260; David Noble Cook, "Disease and Depopulation of Hispaniola, 1492–1518," *Colonial Latin American Review* 2, no. 1–2 (1993): 213–46; Irving Rouse, *The Tainos: Rise and Decline of the People Who Greeted Columbus* (New Haven, Conn.: Yale University Press, 1992), 9; Emile Nau, *Histoire des caciques d'Haïti*, 2 vols. (Port-au-Prince: Editions Panorama, 1963), 2: 36, 157; David Noble Cook, *Born to Die: Disease and New World Conquest, 1492–1650* (Cambridge: Cambridge University Press, 1998), 23; Hugh Thomas, *Rivers of Gold: The Rise of the Spanish Empire* (London: Weidenfeld and Nicolson, 2003), 111.

13. Rouse, *Tainos*, 12–13; Ramón Pané, *An Account of the Antiquities of the Indians: Chronicles of the New World Encounter* (Durham, N.C.: Duke University Press, 1999), 18.

14. Rouse, *Tainos*, 13; Ricardo Alegría, "An Introduction to Taíno Culture and History," in *Taíno: Pre-Columbian Art and Culture from the Caribbean*, ed. Fatima Bercht (New York: Monacelli Press, 1997), 23; Pané, *Account*, 21; Jeffrey Walker, "Taíno Stone Collars, Elbow Stones, and Three-Pointers," in *Taíno: Pre-Columbian Art and Culture from the Caribbean*, ed. Fatima Bercht (New York: Monacelli, 1997), 80–105; Nau, *Histoire des caciques*, 1: 41–42.

15. Joanna M. Ostapkowicz, "To Be Seated with 'Great Courtesy and Veneration': Contextual Aspects of the Taíno Duho," in *Taíno: Pre-Columbian Art and Culture from the Caribbean*, ed. Fatima Bercht (New York: Monacelli Press, 1997), 63–67.

16. Pané, *Account*, 21, 28–29; Sued-Badillo, "Indigenous Societies," 273.

17. Edmundo O'Gorman, *The Invention of America: An Inquiry into the Historical Nature of the New World and the Meaning of Its History* (Bloomington: Indiana University Press, 1961); Kathleen A. Deagan and José María Cruxent, *Columbus's Outpost among the Taínos: Spain and America at La Isabela, 1493–1498* (New Haven, Conn.: Yale University Press, 2002), 9–13.

18. Christopher Columbus, *The Diario of Christopher Columbus's First Voyage to America, 1492–1493*, ed. O. C. Dunn and James E. Kelley (Norman: University of Oklahoma Press, 1989), 4–5; Hulme, *Colonial Encounters*, 17.

19. Michael Palencia-Roth, "Prisms of Consciousness: The 'New Worlds' of Columbus and García Márquez," in *Critical Perspectives on Gabriel García Márquez* (Lincoln, Neb.: Society of Spanish and Spanish-American Studies, 1986), 23.

20. Columbus, *Diario*, 57–61.

21. Columbus, 65.

22. Columbus, 67–69; William D. Phillips and Carla Rahn Phillips, *The Worlds of Christopher Columbus* (Cambridge: Cambridge University Press, 1992), 169–85.

23. Columbus, *Diario*, 67–69; Thomas, *Rivers of Gold*, 106–7; Anthony Pagden, *European Encounters with the New World: From Renaissance to Romanticism* (New Haven, Conn.: Yale University Press, 1993), 89–93.

24. Hulme, *Colonial Encounters*, 17; Wilson, *Hispaniola*, 56; Boucher, *Cannibal Encounters*, 15.

25. Columbus, *Diario*, 71.

26. Columbus, 75.

27. Deagan and Cruxent, *Outpost*, 14; William F. Keegan, *The People Who Discovered Columbus: The Prehistory of the Bahamas* (Gainesville: University Press of Florida, 1992), 225.

28. Columbus, *Diario*, 79; Hulme, *Colonial Encounters*, 40.

29. Columbus, *Diario*, 79.

30. Deagan and Cruxent, *Outpost*, 14–15.

31. See the introduction to Bartolome de las Casas, *An Account, Much Abbreviated, of the Destruction of the Indies*, ed. Franklin Knight (Indianapolis, Ind.: Hackette, 2003), xvii–xviii, xxii; Thomas, *Rivers of Gold*, 127.

32. Sued-Badillo, "Indigenous Societies," 276.

33. Lynne Guitar, "Cultural Genesis: Relationships among Indians, Africans and Spaniards in Rural Hispaniola, First Half of the Sixteenth Century" (Ph.D. diss., Vanderbilt University, 1998), 290–93; Stuart B. Schwartz, "Spaniards, *Pardos*, and the Missing Mestizos: Identities and Racial Categories in the Early Hispanic Caribbean," *New West Indian Guide* 71, nos. 1–2 (1997): 5–19; Thomas, *Rivers of Gold*, 197, 302–3; Jalil Sued-Badillo, "The Island Caribs: New Approaches to the Question of Ethnicity in the Early Colonial Caribbean," in *Wolves from the Sea: Readings in the Anthropology of the Native Caribbean*, ed. Neil L. Whitehead (Leiden: KITLV, 1995), 67; Moya Pons, *History*, 7–13; Scarano, *Puerto Rico*, 192–99.

34. Genaro Rodríguez Morel, *Orígenes de la economía de plantación de la Española* (Santo Domingo: Editora Nacional, 2012), 50; Pierre Chaunu, *Sevilla y América siglos XVI y XVII* (Seville: Secretariado de Publicaciones de la Universidad de Sevilla, 1983), 77.

35. Richard S. Dunn, *Sugar and Slaves: The Rise of the Planter Class in the English West Indies, 1624–1713* (Chapel Hill: University of North Carolina Press, 1972), 10–11.

36. Pierre Chaunu, *L'Amérique et les Amériques* (Paris: A. Colin, 1964), 113; Kris E. Lane, *Pillaging the Empire: Piracy in the Americas, 1500–1750* (Armonk, N.Y.: M. E. Sharpe, 1998).

37. Peter Hulme and Neil L. Whitehead, *Wild Majesty: Encounters with Caribs from Columbus to the Present Day: An Anthology* (Oxford: Clarendon, 1992), 10–11, 60; Dunn, *Sugar and Slaves*, 6.

38. Maurile de Saint Michel, *Voyage des îles camercanes en l'Amérique qui font partie des Indes occidentales* (Le Mans, France, 1652), 31–32.

39. Jean-Baptiste Du Tertre, *Histoire général des Antilles habitées par les françois*, 4 vols. (Paris: Thomas Jolly, 1667), esp. vol. 2; Edward Long, *The History of Jamaica, Or, General Survey of the Antient and Modern State of That Island with Reflections on Its Situation, Settlements, Inhabitants, Climate, Products, Commerce, Laws, and Government*, 3 vols. (London: Printed for T. Lowndes, 1774), 3: 792–94.

40. Long, *History of Jamaica*, 2: 42–43, 153–54; Michael Craton and James Walvin, *A Jamaican Plantation: The History of Worthy Park, 1670–1970* (Toronto: University of Toronto Press, 1970), 8.

41. M. L. E Moreau de Saint-Méry, *Description topographique, physique, civile, politique et historique de la partie française de l'isle Saint Domingue*, new ed., 3 vols. (Paris: Société de l'histoire des colonies françaises et Librairie Larose, 2004), 1: 244, 2: 1140–41.

42. David Brion Davis, *Inhuman Bondage: The Rise and Fall of Slavery in the New World* (Oxford: Oxford University Press, 2006), 99.

43. Arnold M. Highfield, "Some Observations on the Taíno Language," in *Indigenous Peoples of the Caribbean*, ed. Samuel Wilson (Gainesville: University Press of Florida, 1997), 157.

44. Samuel Wilson, "The Legacy of Indigenous People of the Caribbean," in *Indigenous Peoples of the Caribbean*, ed. Samuel Wilson (Gainesville: University Press of Florida, 1997), 206; Maya Deren, *Divine Horsemen: The Living Gods of Haiti* (New York: Documentext, 1959).

45. Nau, *Histoire des caciques*, 1: 12–13.

46. Jean Fouchard, *Langue et littérature des aborigènes d'Ayti* (Port-au-Prince: Henri Deschamps, 1988), 95–98.

47. Boucher, *Cannibal Encounters*, 15; Hulme, *Colonial Encounters*, 47; Newton, "Race Leapt," 8.

48. Hulme and Whitehead, *Wild Majesty*, 32; Hulme, *Colonial Encounters*, 19.

49. Neil Whitehead, "Carib Cannibalism: The Historical Evidence," *Journal de la Société des américanistes* 70 (1984): 70–72.

50. Whitehead, "Carib Cannibalism," 70–72; Richard Konetzke, *Colección de documentos para la historia de la formación social de Hispanoamérica, 1493–1810*, 5 vols. (Madrid: Consejo Superior de Investigaciones Científicas, 1953), 1: 14–16, 31–33, 36–38, 145–46; Juan de Castellanos, *Elegías de varones ilustres de Indias*, 2nd ed. (Madrid: M. Rivadeneyra, 1857), 279–80; Pascual de Andagoya, *Narrative of the Proceedings of Pedrarias Davila: In the Provinces of Tierra Firme, or Castilla del Oro and of the Discovery of the South Sea and the Coasts of Peru and Nicaragua* (London: Hakluyt Society, 1865), 3n2; Deive, *La Española*, 160, 176–81. On the concept of "slaving zones," see Jeff Fynn-Paul, "Introduction: Slaving Zones in Global History: The Evolution of a Concept," in Jeff Fynn-Paul and Damian Alan Pargas, eds., *Slaving Zones: Cultural Identities, Ideologies, and Institutions in the Evolution of Global Slavery* (Leiden: Brill, 2018), 1–19.

51. Whitehead, "Carib Cannibalism," 69; Hulme, *Colonial Encounters*, 246.

52. Laurence Verrand, *La vie quotidienne des Indiens caraïbes aux Petites Antilles (XVIIe siècle)* (Paris: Karthala, 2001), 13; Hulme and Whitehead, *Wild Majesty*, 3.

53. Christopher Taylor, *The Black Carib Wars: Freedom, Survival, and the Making of the Garifuna* (Jackson: University Press of Mississippi, 2012), 29–30.

54. Simone Dreyfuss, "Territoire et résidence chez les Caraïbes insulaires au XVIIème siècle," *Proceedings of the International Congress of Americanists* 42, no. 2 (1977): 37; Hulme and Whitehead, *Wild Majesty*, 51–52.

55. Hulme and Whitehead, *Wild Majesty*, 53–56.

56. Jean-Pierre Moreau, ed., *Un flibustier français dans la mer des Antilles, 1618–1620* (Paris: Seghers, 1990), 118–23.

57. Hulme and Whitehead, *Wild Majesty*, 68–69, 71–72; Dunn, *Sugar and Slaves*, 7.

58. Anne Pérotin-Dumon, "French, English and Dutch in the Lesser Antilles: From Privateering to Planting, c. 1550–c. 1650," in *New Societies: The Caribbean in the Long Sixteenth Century*, ed. German Carrera Damas and Pieter C. Emmer, vol. 2 of *General History of the Caribbean* (London: UNESCO Publishing/Macmillan Education, 1999), 123; Dunn, *Sugar and Slaves*, 17; Jerome S. Handler and Frederick W. Lange, *Plantation Slavery in Barbados: An Archaeological and Historical Investigation* (Cambridge, Mass.: Harvard University Press, 1978).

59. Dunn, *Sugar and Slaves*, 17; Gordon C. Merrell, *The Historical Geography of St. Kitts and Nevis, the West Indies* (Mexico City: Instituto Panamericano de Geografía e Historia, 1958), 15, 46; Hulme and Whitehead, *Wild Majesty*, 53.

60. Pérotin-Dumon, "French, English and Dutch," 123–24; Merrell, *Historical Geography*, 48–51.

61. Handler and Lange, *Plantation Slavery*, 15.

62. Boucher, *Cannibal Encounters*, 51, 67; Hulme and Whitehead, *Wild Majesty*, 89, 91–92.

63. Boucher, *Cannibal Encounters*, 79–80.

64. Boucher, 81; Hulme and Whitehead, *Wild Majesty*, 89, 102–3.

65. Jean-Baptiste Labat, *Voyage aux isles: Chronique aventureuse des Caraïbes: 1693–1705*, ed. Michel Le Bris (Paris: Phébus, 1993), 130–32; Taylor, *Black Carib Wars*, 38–39.

66. Hulme and Whitehead, *Wild Majesty*, 105–6.

67. Julie Chun Kim, "The Caribs of St. Vincent and Indigenous Resistance during the Age of Revolution," *Early American Studies* 11, no. 1 (Winter 2013): 123–24; Taylor, *Black Carib Wars*, 27.

68. Taylor, *Black Carib Wars*, 18–19, 23; Alexander Anderson, *Alexander Anderson's Geography and History of the West Indies* (London: Linnean Society of London, 1983), 5; Paul Christopher Johnson, *Diaspora Conversions: Black Carib Religion and the Recovery of Africa* (Berkeley: University of California Press, 2007), 65; Douglas MacRae Taylor, *The Black Carib of British Honduras* (New York: Wenner-Gren Foundation for Anthropological Research, 1951), 52; Douglas MacRae Taylor, "Loanwords in Central American Carib," *Word: Journal of the Linguistic Circle of New York* 4, no. 3 (1948): 187–95.

69. Taylor, *Black Carib Wars*, 15–16, 20.

70. Taylor, 105; Johnson, *Diaspora Conversions*, 64, 71; Virginia Kerns, *Women and the Ancestors: Black Carib Kinship and Ritual*, 2nd ed. (Urbana: University of Illinois Press, 1997), chaps. 9 and 10.

71. Richard H. Grove, *Green Imperialism: Colonial Expansion, Tropical Island Edens and the Origins of Environmentalism, 1600–1860* (Cambridge: Cambridge University Press, 1995), 65–70, 286–87, 290.

72. Grove, 266, 282, 286–87; Anderson, *Geography and History*, 6; Hulme and Whitehead, *Wild Majesty*, 244; Taylor, *Black Carib Wars*, 71, 103.

73. Grove, *Green Imperialism*, 266, 282, 286–87; Anderson, *Geography and History*, 6; Hulme and Whitehead, *Wild Majesty*, 244; Taylor, *Black Carib Wars*, 71, 103.

74. Grove, *Green Imperialism*, 284, 288–90.

75. Hulme, *Colonial Encounters*, 246; Hulme, "Black, Yellow and White," 191; Kim, "Natural Histories," 226.

76. Hulme, "Black, Yellow and White," 187, 193–94; Johnson, *Diaspora Conversions*, 70–71.

77. Hulme, *Colonial Encounters*, 242–45.

78. Hulme, "Black, Yellow and White," 184; Johnson, *Diaspora Conversions*, 77; Anderson, *Geography and History*, 11, 19; on the broader context surrounding the French alliance with the Caribs during this period, see Laurent Dubois, *A Colony of Citizens: Revolution and Slave Emancipation in the French Caribbean, 1787–1804* (Chapel Hill: University of North Carolina Press, 2004).

79. Nancie L. Solien González, *Sojourners of the Caribbean: Ethnogenesis and Ethnohistory of the Garifuna* (Urbana: University of Illinois Press, 1988), 52–57; Kerns, *Women and the Ancestors*, 32–33.

80. Johnson, *Diaspora Conversions*, 105–7, 112; Kerns, *Women and the Ancestors*, 150, 162; González, *Sojourners of the Caribbean*, 93.

81. Johnson, *Diaspora Conversions*, 153.

Chapter Two

1. Columbus renamed the island of Haiti or Quisqueya la Isla Española (the Spanish Island). The colony would begin to be called Santo Domingo as well in the sixteenth century, and this became more common over time. Later, the French colony on the western side of the island would be named "Saint Domingue." "Hispaniola" would eventually be the term used in English for the entire island, comprising both the Spanish and French colonies and subsequent nations of the Dominican Republic and Haiti.

2. Trevor G. Burnard and John D. Garrigus, *The Plantation Machine: Atlantic Capitalism in French Saint-Domingue and British Jamaica* (Philadelphia: University of Pennsylvania Press, 2016), 2.

3. Jennifer Morgan, *Laboring Women: Reproduction and Gender in New World Slavery* (Philadelphia: University of Pennsylvania Press, 2004), 3, 7, 12; Barbara Bush, *Slave Women in Caribbean Society, 1650–1838* (Kingston: Heinemann Caribbean, 1990); Marisa J. Fuentes, *Dispossessed Lives: Enslaved Women, Violence, and the Archive* (Philadelphia: University of Pennsylvania Press, 2016); David Eltis, *The Rise of African Slavery in the Americas* (Cambridge: Cambridge University Press, 2000), 100–105; Trevor Burnard, "Evaluating Gender in Early Jamaica, 1674–1784," *History of the Family* 12, no. 2 (2007): 81–91, esp. 87.

4. Russell R. Menard, *Sweet Negotiations: Sugar, Slavery, and Plantation Agriculture in Early Barbados* (Charlottesville: University of Virginia Press, 2006), 13; Antonio Benítez-Rojo, *The Repeating Island: The Caribbean and the Postmodern*

Perspective, 2nd ed. (Durham, N.C.: Duke University Press, 1996), 8; Burnard and Garrigus, *Plantation Machine*, 3, 41; Jean-Baptiste Labat, *Voyage aux isles: Chronique aventureuse des Caraïbes: 1693–1705*, ed. Michel Le Bris (Paris: Phébus, 1993), 38.

5. Benítez-Rojo, *Repeating Island*, 9, 39.

6. Benítez-Rojo, 9, 18; Herbert Klein, *The Atlantic Slave Trade*, 1st ed. (Cambridge: Cambridge University Press, 1999), 129–39.

7. Peter H. Wood, *Black Majority: Negroes in Colonial South Carolina from 1670 through the Stono Rebellion* (New York: Knopf, 1974); Andrew Jackson O'Shaughnessy, *An Empire Divided: The American Revolution and the British Caribbean*, Early American Studies (Philadelphia: University of Pennsylvania Press, 2000).

8. Michel-Rolph Trouillot, "Culture on the Edges: Creolization in the Plantation Context," *Plantation Society in the Americas* 5 (1988): 24, 28.

9. Roser Salicrú i Lluch, "Slaves in the Professional and Family Life of Craftsmen in the Late Middle Ages," in *La famiglia nell'economia europea, secc. XIII–XVIII: atti della "quarantesima Settimana di studi," 6–10 Aprile 2008 = The economic role of the family in the European economy from the 13th to the 18th centuries*, ed. Simonetta Cavaciocchi (Florence: Firenze University Press 2009), 325–26, 326n8; Sally McKee, "Domestic Slavery in Renaissance Italy," *Slavery and Abolition* 29, no. 3 (September 2008): 316; Charles Verlinden, "Les origines coloniales de la civilization atlantique," *Cahiers d'histoire mondiale* 1, no. 2 (1953): 385; Debra Blumenthal, *Enemies and Familiars: Slavery and Mastery in Fifteenth-Century Valencia* (Ithaca, N.Y.: Cornell University Press, 2009), 1, 9, 9n1, 10, 20; William D. Phillips Jr., *Slavery in Medieval and Early Modern Iberia* (Philadelphia: University of Pennsylvania Press, 2014), 24, 36–37, 61–62; Alfonso Franco Silva, *La esclavitud en Sevilla y su tierra a fines de la edad media* (Seville: Diputación Provincial de Sevilla, 1979), 47–51.

10. McKee, "Domestic Slavery," 308–11; Phillips, *Slavery*, 34, chap. 2; Blumenthal, *Enemies*, 1, 9–10; Steven A. Epstein, *Speaking of Slavery: Color, Ethnicity, and Human Bondage in Italy* (Ithaca, N.Y.: Cornell University Press, 2001); Bernard Lewis, *Race and Slavery in the Middle East: An Historical Enquiry* (New York: Oxford University Press, 1990), 11–15, 54–69; Iris Origo, "The Domestic Enemy: The Eastern Slaves in Tuscany in the Fourteenth and Fifteenth Centuries," *Speculum* 30, no. 3 (July 1955): 321–66; Alan W. Fisher, "Muscovy and the Black Sea Trade," *Canadian-American Slavic Studies* 6, no. 4 (Winter 1972): 576–78; David Brion Davis, *Challenging the Boundaries of Slavery* (Cambridge, Mass.: Harvard University Press, 2003), 17–21; Charles Verlinden, *The Beginnings of Modern Colonization* (Ithaca, N.Y.: Cornell University Press, 1970), 28–29; David Brion Davis, *Inhuman Bondage: The Rise and Fall of Slavery in the New World* (Oxford: Oxford University Press, 2006), 82; Verlinden, "Origines," 385; Jacques Heers, *Esclaves et domestiques au moyen-age dans le monde méditerranéen* (Paris: Fayard, 1981), 69–70; Alice Rio, *Slavery after Rome, 500–1100* (Oxford: Oxford University Press, 2017), 24–40, 165–67.

11. J. H. Galloway, "The Mediterranean Sugar Industry," *Geographical Review* 67, no. 2 (April 1977): 177–94; Sidney W. Mintz, *Sweetness and Power: The Place of Sugar in Modern History* (New York: Penguin Books, 1986), 23.

12. Galloway, "Mediterranean Sugar Industry," 190; Mintz, *Sweetness and Power*, 23.

13. Galloway, "Mediterranean Sugar Industry," 177, 194; Mintz, *Sweetness and Power*, 23.

14. Phillips, *Slavery*, 22; A. J. R. Russell-Wood, "Before Columbus: Portugal's African Prelude to the Middle Passage and Contribution to Discourse on Race and Slavery," in *Race, Discourse and the Origin of the Americas: A New World View*, ed. Vera Lawrence Hyatt and Rex Nettleford (Washington, D.C.: Smithsonian Institution Press, 1995), 148–49; Verlinden, "Origines," 385; Galloway, "Mediterranean Sugar Industry"; Mintz, *Sweetness and Power*, 23; Halil Inalcik, *An Economic and Social History of the Ottoman Empire*, vol. 1, *1300–1600* (Cambridge: Cambridge University Press, 1994), 274–85; Alan W. Fisher, "Chattel Slavery in the Ottoman Empire," *Slavery and Abolition* 1, no. 1 (May 1980): 34–35.

15. Davis, *Inhuman Bondage*, 82–84; Verlinden, "Origines," 385; Alejandro de la Fuente, *Havana and the Atlantic in the Sixteenth Century* (Chapel Hill: University of North Carolina Press, 2008), 35; Rodríguez Morel, *Orígenes de la economía de plantación de la Española* (Santo Domingo: Editora Nacional, 2012), 43, 54.

16. Anthony M. Stevens-Arroyo, "The Inter-Atlantic Paradigm: The Failure of Spanish Medieval Colonization of the Canary and Caribbean Islands," *Comparative Studies in Society and History* 35, no. 3 (July 1993): 515–43; Felipe Fernández-Armesto, *The Canary Islands after the Conquest: The Making of a Colonial Society in the Early Sixteenth Century* (Oxford: Clarendon, 1982), 10, 36, 201–6; Kathleen A. Deagan and José María Cruxent, *Columbus's Outpost among the Taínos: Spain and America at La Isabela, 1493–1498* (New Haven, Conn.: Yale University Press, 2002), 8–9; Willian D. Phillips and Carla Rahn Phillips, *The Worlds of Christopher Columbus* (Cambridge: Cambridge University Press, 1992), 224; Hugh Thomas, *Rivers of Gold: The Rise of the Spanish Empire* (London: Weidenfeld and Nicolson, 2003), 58–59, 383; Hugh Thomas, *The Slave Trade: The Story of the Atlantic Slave Trade, 1440–1870* (New York: Simon and Schuster, 1997), 84; Vicenta Cortés Alonso, *Los cautivos canarios* (San Cristóbal de La Laguna, Spain: Universidad de La Laguna, 1970), 6–8; Blumenthal, *Enemies*.

17. Thomas, *Rivers of Gold*, 58–59, 383; Thomas, *Slave Trade*, 84; Cortés Alonso, *Los cautivos canarios*, 6–8; Stevens-Arroyo, "Inter-Atlantic Paradigm"; Fernández-Armesto, *Canary Islands*.

18. Sidney M. Greenfield, "Madeira and the Beginnings of New World Sugar Cane Cultivation and Plantation Slavery: A Study in Institution Building," in *Comparative Perspectives on Slavery in New World Plantation Societies*, ed. Vera Rubin and Arthur Tuden (New York: New York Academy of Sciences, 1977), 537; Frank Moya Pons, *History of the Caribbean* (Princeton, N.J.: Markus Wiener, 2007), 23, 313n4; Thomas, *Rivers of Gold*, 52.

19. Davis, *Inhuman Bondage*, 84–86.

20. Sidney M. Greenfield, "Plantations, Sugar Cane and Slavery," in *Roots and Branches: Current Directions in Slave Studies*, ed. Michael Craton (Toronto: Pergamon, 1979), 85–119.

21. Blumenthal, *Enemies*, 19–20; Phillips, *Slavery*, 23–27; Sally McKee, "The Familiarity of Slaves in Medieval and Early Modern Households," in *Mediterranean Slavery Revisited (500–1800)—Neue Perspektiven Auf Mediterrane Sklaverei (500–1800)*, ed. Stefan Hanß and Juliane Schiel (Zurich: Chronos Verlag, 2014), 501–14; Carlos Esteban Deive, *La Española y la esclavitud del indio* (Santo Domingo: Fundación García Arévalo, 1995).

22. Thomas, *Rivers of Gold*, 179; Deive, *La Española*, 58, 63; Rodríguez Morel, *Orígenes*, 95, 97–99, 111–17; de la Fuente, *Havana*, 35–37; Moya Pons, *History*, 12, 18.

23. Rodríguez Morel, *Orígenes*, 129; Moya Pons, *History*, 8; Deive, *La Española*; Genaro Rodríguez Morel, "The Sugar Economy of Española in the Sixteenth Century," in *Tropical Babylons: Sugar and the Making of the Atlantic World*, ed. Stuart B. Schwartz (Chapel Hill: University of North Carolina Press, 2004), 103–4, 107, 113; Jalil Sued-Badillo, "The Island Caribs: New Approaches to the Question of Ethnicity in the Early Colonial Caribbean," in *Wolves from the Sea: Readings in the Anthropology of the Native Caribbean*, ed. Neil L. Whitehead (Leiden: KITLV Press, 1995), 67; O. Nigel Bolland, "Colonization and Slavery in Central America," *Slavery and Abolition* 15, no. 2 (1994): 11–25, 13–15; Thomas, *Rivers of Gold*, 303–4; Deagan and Cruxent, *Columbus's Outpost*, 216–22; Richard Konetzke, *Colección de documentos para la historia de la formación social de Hispanoamérica, 1493–1810*, 5 vols. (Madrid: Consejo Superior de Investigaciones Científicas, 1953), 1: 14–15.

24. Konetzke, *Colección*, 1: 134–46, 215–18, 247–48, 291–92, 459–60, 531–32, 592–93, 626–28; Tatiana Seijas, *Asian Slaves in Colonial Mexico: From Chinos to Indians* (New York: Cambridge University Press, 2014), 63, chap. 7; Nancy E. van Deusen, "Indios on the Move in the Sixteenth-Century Iberian World," *Journal of Global History* 10, no. 3 (November 2015): 387–409, 388; Deive, *La Española*, 359–67; Andrés Reséndez, *The Other Slavery: The Uncovered Story of Indian Enslavement in America* (Boston: Houghton Mifflin Harcourt, 2016), 91, 122, 132–48.

25. The estimated enslaved population ranged in this period between fifteen and twenty-five thousand. Al Emperador, Melchor de Castro, escribano de minas, Santo Domingo, July 25, 1543, Biblioteca Nacional José Martí de Cuba (BNJM), Manuscritos, Colección Morales, tomo (T.) 81; Rodríguez Morel, *Orígenes*, 129–30, 209; Genaro Rodríguez Morel, "Esclavitud y vida rural en las plantaciones azucareras de Santo Domingo: Siglo XVI," *Anuario de Estudios Americanos* 49 (1992): 94, 99–100; Rodríguez Morel, "Sugar Economy," 103–4; Juan de Echagoian, "Relación de la isla Española enviada al Rey D. Felipe II por el Lic. Echagoian," *Boletín del Archivo General de la Nación* 4, no. 19 (1941): 446; Pierre Chaunu, *Sevilla y América siglos XVI y XVII* (Seville: Secretariado de Publicaciones de la Universidad de Sevilla, 1983), 77; Esteban Mira Caballos, "Otros sectores productivos y económicos," in *Historia general del pueblo dominicano*, vol. 1, ed. Genaro Rodríguez Morel (Santo Domingo: Academia Dominicana de la Historia, 2013), 426–27; Frank

Moya Pons, *El oro en la historia dominicana* (Santo Domingo: Academia Dominicana de la Historia, 2016).

26. Javier Malagón Barceló, *Código Negro Carolino (1784)* (Santo Domingo: Taller, 1974), 143; Carlos Esteban Deive, *Los guerrilleros negros: Esclavos fugitivos y cimarrones en Santo Domingo* (Santo Domingo: Fundación Cultural Dominicana, 1989), 43; Deive, *La Española*, 359; Rodríguez Morel, *Orígenes*, 118–31; Moya Pons, *History*, 18–20; Lynne Guitar, "Cultural Genesis: Relationships among Indians, Africans and Spaniards in Rural Hispaniola, First Half of the Sixteenth Century" (Ph.D. diss., Vanderbilt University, 1998), 290–93; Stuart B. Schwartz, "Spaniards, *Pardos*, and the Missing Mestizos: Identities and Racial Categories in the Early Hispanic Caribbean," *New West Indian Guide* 71, no. 1–2 (1997): 5–19.

27. Frank Moya Pons, *The Dominican Republic: A National History*, 3rd ed. (Princeton, N.J.: Markus Wiener, 2010), 18–21, 39–40; Pierre-François-Xavier de Charlevoix, *Histoire de l'isle Espagnole ou de S. Domingue. Ecrite particulierement sur des memoires manuscrits du P. Jean-Baptiste Le Pers, Jesuite, missionnaire a Saint Domingue, et sur les pieces originales, qui se conservent au Dépôt de la Marine* (Amsterdam: L'Honoré, 1733), 253; Rodríguez Morel, *Orígenes*, 114–57; Justicia y Regimiento de Santo Domingo (the *Cabildo* or City Council) to the Emperor, February 10, 1545, BNJM, Manuscritos, Colección Morales, T. 81.

28. Rodríguez Morel, *Orígenes*, 177; Rodríguez Morel, "Sugar Economy," 107; Stephan Palmié, "Toward Sugar and Slavery," in *The Caribbean: A History of the Region and Its People*, ed. Stephan Palmié and Francisco Scarano (Chicago: University of Chicago Press, 2011), 137.

29. Moya Pons, *History*, 21–25, 77–82; Moya Pons, *Dominican Republic*, 50; Chaunu, *Sevilla*, 68–80; Mira Caballos, "Otros sectores," 444–46; Bethany Aram, "Carribbean Ginger and Atlantic Trade, 1570–1648," *Journal of Global History* 10, no. 3 (2015); Carlos Larrazábal Blanco, *Los negros y la esclavitud en Santo Domingo* (Santo Domingo: Julio D. Postigo e hijos, 1975), 184. For another portrait of the postplantation period, see David Wheat, *Atlantic Africa and the Spanish Caribbean, 1570–1640* (Chapel Hill: University of North Carolina Press, 2016).

30. de la Fuente, *Havana*, 72–73; Ada Ferrer, Freedom's Mirror (New York: Cambridge University Press, 2014), 10, 25.

31. de la Fuente, 73–77.

32. de la Fuente, 52, 127–34.

33. de la Fuente, 99, 116, 180.

34. de la Fuente, 86–88, 101, 103, 105, 106–7; Seijas, *Asian Slaves*, esp. 14, 50–54, 251.

35. Maurile de Saint Michel, *Voyage des îles camercanes en l'Amérique qui font partie des Indies Occidentales* (Le Mans, France, 1652), 38–39, 45, 64–65, 75.

36. Laurence Verrand, "Fortifications militaires de Martinique, 1635–1845," *Journal of Caribbean Archaeology*, Special Publication no. 1, "Historical Archaeology in the French Caribbean" (2004): 16.

37. Richard S. Dunn, *Sugar and Slaves: The Rise of the Planter Class in the English West Indies, 1624–1713* (Chapel Hill: Published for the Institute of Early American

History and Culture at Williamsburg, Va., by the University of North Carolina Press, 1972), 18, 26.

38. Dunn, 5–6, 19.

39. Dunn, 53–55, 59, 77, 89; Menard, *Sweet Negotiations*, 12; Jerome S. Handler and Frederick W. Lange, *Plantation Slavery in Barbados: An Archaeological and Historical Investigation* (Cambridge, Mass.: Harvard University Press, 1978), 13, 15.

40. Dunn, *Sugar and Slaves*, 53–55, 59, 77, 89; Menard, *Sweet Negotiations*, 12; Handler and Lange, *Plantation Slavery*, 13, 15.

41. Dunn, *Sugar and Slaves*, 62; Sidney W. Mintz, *Sweetness and Power: The Place of Sugar in Modern History* (New York: Penguin Books, 1986).

42. Dunn, *Sugar and Slaves*, 59, 66–67, 83; Handler and Lange, *Plantation Slavery*, 8, 17.

43. Colin Palmer, "Slave Trade, African Slavers and Demographers to 1750," in *The Slave Societies of the Caribbean*, ed. Franklin W. Knight, vol. 3 of *General History of the Caribbean* (London: UNESCO Publishing/Macmillan Education, 1997), 37; Dunn, *Sugar and Slaves*, 46–48, 85.

44. Burnard and Garrigus, *Plantation Machine*, chap. 4, esp. 88–89.

45. Dunn, *Sugar and Slaves*, 151–52; Michael Craton and James Walvin, *A Jamaican Plantation: The History of Worthy Park, 1670–1970* (Toronto: University of Toronto Press, 1970), 9, 12–14; Edward Long, *The History of Jamaica, Or, General Survey of the Antient and Modern State of That Island with Reflections on Its Situation, Settlements, Inhabitants, Climate, Products, Commerce, Laws, and Government*, 3 vols. (London: Printed for T. Lowndes, 1774), 1: 221–34.

46. Michael Craton, *Testing the Chains: Resistance to Slavery in the British West Indies* (Ithaca, N.Y.: Cornell University Press, 1982), 69–70; Kenneth M. Bilby, *True-Born Maroons* (Gainesville: University Press of Florida, 2005), 87, 101.

47. "Proclamation of Oliver Cromwell Relative to Jamaica, 1655" and "Extract from Cromwell's Instructions to the Commissioners, 1656," in Edward Long, *The History of Jamaica, Or, General Survey of the Antient and Modern State of That Island with Reflections on Its Situation, Settlements, Inhabitants, Climate, Products, Commerce, Laws, and Government*, 3 vols. (London: Printed for T. Lowndes, 1774), 1: 213–15.

48. Ned Ward, "A Trip to Jamaica: With a True Character of the People and the Island (1700)," in *Five Travel Scripts, Commonly Attributed to Edward Ward; Reproduced from the Earliest Editions Extant*, ed. Howard W. Troyer (New York: Facsimile Text Society by Columbia University Press, 1933), 4, 8–9, 11–13, 16.

49. Long, *History of Jamaica*, 1: 139–43; Kris E. Lane, *Blood and Silver: A History of Piracy in the Caribbean and Central America* (Oxford: Signal, 1999), 106, 172–73.

50. Long, *History of Jamaica*, 1: 139–43; Lane, *Blood and Silver*, 106, 172–73.

51. Long, *History of Jamaica*, 1: 143–46; Jean Besson, *Martha Brae's Two Histories: European Expansion and Caribbean Culture-Building in Jamaica* (Chapel Hill: University of North Carolina Press, 2002), 58–59.

52. Besson, *Martha Brae's Two Histories*, 59–61; Douglas V. Armstrong, *The Old Village and the Great House: An Archaeological and Historical Examination of Drax*

Hall Plantation, St. Ann's Bay, Jamaica (Urbana: University of Illinois Press, 1990), 26–27, 207.

53. Craton and Walvin, *Jamaican Plantation*, 82, 93n45; John Rashford, "The Search for Africa's Baobab Tree in Jamaica," *Jamaica Journal* 20, no. 2 (July 1987): 3–7.

54. The unpublished poems are cited in Jean Fouchard, *Plaisirs de Saint-Domingue* (Port-au-Prince: Impr. de l'État, 1955), 87.

55. Trevor G. Burnard, *Mastery, Tyranny, and Desire: Thomas Thistlewood and His Slaves in the Anglo-Jamaican World* (Chapel Hill: University of North Carolina Press, 2004), 104, 106, 111.

56. Jack P. Greene, "Liberty, Slavery, and the Transformation of British Identity in the Eighteenth-Century West Indies," *Slavery and Abolition* 21, no. 1 (2000): 11.

57. Long, *History of Jamaica*, 2: 254.

58. Heather V. Vermeulen, "Thomas Thistlewood's Libidinal Linnean Project: Slavery, Ecology, and Knowledge Production," *Small Axe* 22, no. 1 (March 2018): 18, 23, 29.

59. Burnard and Garrigus, *Plantation Machine*, 58; Dominique Rogers and Stewart King, "Housekeepers, Merchants, Rentières: Free Women of Color in the Port Cities of Colonial Saint-Domingue, 1750–1790," in *Women in Port: Gendering Communities, Economies, and Social Networks in Atlantic Port Cities, 1500–1800*, ed. Douglas Catterall and Jodi Campbell (Leiden: Brill, 2012), 357–97.

60. Fuentes, *Dispossessed Lives*, 21, 27, 38–39, 101–2, 117, 119.

61. Elsa V. Goveia, *The West Indian Slave Laws of the 18th Century* (Kingston: Caribbean Universities Press, 1970), 20, 35, 58, 60; Fuentes, *Dispossessed Lives*, 107–9.

62. Palmer, "Slave Trade," 33; Vincent Brown, *The Reaper's Garden: Death and Power in the World of Atlantic Slavery* (Cambridge, Mass.: Harvard University Press, 2008); Burnard and Garrigus, *Plantation Machine*, 235.

63. Bilby, *True-Born Maroons*, 71–72.

64. Max G. Beauvoir, *Le Grand Recueil sacré, ou répertoire des chansons du vodou haïtien* (Port-au-Prince: Edisyon Près Nasyonal d'Ayiti, 2008), 94; Burnard and Garrigus, *Plantation Machine*, 60.

65. Long, *History of Jamaica*, 3: 137; Jerome S. Handler, "Slave Medicine and Obeah in Barbados, Circa 1650 to 1834," *New West Indian Guide* 74, no. 1–2 (2000): 62.

66. Handler, "Slave Medicine," 58, 61, 83–84.

67. Handler, 58, 61, 83–84.

68. Kenneth J. Kinkor, "Flibustiers Noirs," in *L'Aventure de la flibuste*, ed. Michel Le Bris (Paris: Hoëbeke, 2002), 97–118, quote on 108; Peter Linebaugh and Marcus Rediker, *The Many-Headed Hydra: Sailors, Slaves, Commoners, and the Hidden History of the Revolutionary Atlantic* (Boston: Beacon, 2000); Kris E. Lane, *Pillaging the Empire: Piracy in the Americas, 1500–1750* (Armonk, N.Y.: M. E. Sharpe, 1998); W. Jeffrey Bolster, *Black Jacks: African American Seamen in the Age of Sail* (Cambridge, Mass.: Harvard University Press, 1997).

69. Armstrong, *Old Village*, 21.

70. B. W. Higman, *Montpelier, Jamaica: A Plantation Community in Slavery and Freedom, 1739–1912* (Kingston: University Press of the West Indies, 1998), 79, 298–99.

71. Higman, *Montpelier*, 132–36.

72. Sidney W. Mintz, "The Origins of the Jamaican Market System," in *Caribbean Transformations* (New York: Columbia University Press, 1989), 180–215; Woodville Marshall, "Provision Ground and Plantation Labour in Four Windward Islands: Competition for Resources during Slavery," in *The Slaves' Economy: Independent Production by Slaves in the Americas*, ed. Ira Berlin and Philip D. Morgan (London: Frank Cass, 1991), 48–67.

73. Higman, *Montpelier*, 196–97.

74. John S. Brierley, "Kitchen Gardens in the Caribbean, Past and Present: Their Role in Small-Farm Development," *Caribbean Geography* 3, no. 1 (March 1991): 17; Riva Berleant-Schiller and Lydia M. Pulsipher, "Subsistence Cultivation in the Caribbean," *New West Indian Guide* 60, no. 1–2 (1986): 20.

75. Marshall, "Provision Ground," 55; Brierley, "Kitchen Gardens," 17; Theo Hills, "The Caribbean Peasant Food Forest, Ecological Artistry or Random Chaos," in *Small Farming and Peasant Resources in the Caribbean*, ed. John S. Brierley and Hymie Rubenstein, Manitoba Geographical Studies, vol. 10 (Winnipeg: Department of Geography, University of Manitoba, 1988), 4, 9, 13.

76. Long, *History of Jamaica*, 3: 787, 740, 782. John Luffman, *A Brief Account of the Island of Antigua* (London: T. Cadell, 1789), quoted in Roger D. Abrahams and John F. Szwed, eds., *After Africa: Extracts from British Travel Accounts and Journals of the Seventeenth, Eighteenth, and Nineteenth Centuries Concerning the Slaves, Their Manners, and Customs in the British West Indies* (New Haven, Conn.: Yale University Press, 1983), 23–24.

77. Sidney Wilfred Mintz, "Small Farming and Peasant Resources in the Caribbean," in *Roots and Branches: Current Directions in Slave Studies*, ed. Michael Craton (Toronto: Pergamon, 1979), 219.

78. Marshall, "Provision Ground," 56–60.

79. Marshall, 60.

80. Laurent Dubois, *A Colony of Citizens: Revolution and Slave Emancipation in the French Caribbean, 1787–1804* (Chapel Hill: University of North Carolina Press, 2004), 30–31, 44; Dale Tomich, "Une Petite Guinée: Provision Ground and Plantation in Martinique, 1830–1848," *Slavery and Abolition* 12, no. 1 (1991): 77; Dale W. Tomich, *Slavery in the Circuit of Sugar: Martinique and the World Economy, 1830–1848* (Baltimore: Johns Hopkins University Press, 1990), 274 and chap. 8 generally.

81. Jean Besson, "Free Villagers, Rastafarians and Modern Maroons," in *Born Out of Resistance: On Caribbean Cultural Creativity*, ed. Wim Hoogbergen (Utrecht: ISOR-Publications, 1995), 303; Jean Besson, "Land, Kinship and Community in the Post-Emancipation Caribbean: A Regional View of the Leewards," in *Small Islands, Large Questions: Society, Culture and Resistance in the Post-Emancipation Caribbean*, ed. Karen Fog Olwig (London: Frank Cass, 1995), 73–99, 84; Tomich, "Une Petite Guinée," 69, 80; Edouard Glissant, *Caribbean Discourse: Selected Essays* (Charlottesville: University of Virginia Press, 1989).

82. Trouillot, "Culture on the Edges," 25–26.

83. Morgan, *Laboring Women,* 62; Natasha Lightfoot, *Troubling Freedom: Antigua and the Aftermath of British Emancipation* (Durham, N.C.: Duke University Press, 2015), 58, 80.

84. Lightfoot, *Troubling Freedom,* 58, 65–68.

85. Jean Casimir, *La Culture opprimée* (Delmas, Haïti: Impr. Lakay, 2001); Yvonne Acosta and Jean Casimir, "Social Origins of the Counter-Plantation System in St. Lucia," in *Rural Development in the Caribbean,* ed. P. I. Gomes (New York: St. Martin's, 1985), 34–59.

Chapter Three

1. Kenneth M. Bilby, *True-Born Maroons* (Gainesville: University Press of Florida, 2005), 106.

2. Richard Price, ed., *Maroon Societies: Rebel Slave Communities in the Americas,* 3rd ed. (Baltimore: Johns Hopkins University Press, 1996), 1–3.

3. Bilby, *True-Born Maroons,* 87, 101.

4. Barbara Klamon Kopytoff, "The Early Political Development of Jamaican Maroon Societies," *William and Mary Quarterly,* 3rd ser., 35, no. 2 (April 1978): 287–307; Barbara Klamon Kopytoff, "Colonial Treaty as Sacred Charter of the Jamaican Maroons," *Ethnohistory* 26, no. 1 (Winter 1979): 45–64.

5. Bilby, *True-Born Maroons,* 130, 136; Price, *Maroon Societies,* 10.

6. Bilby, *True-Born Maroons,* 258.

7. Michael Craton, *Testing the Chains: Resistance to Slavery in the British West Indies* (Ithaca, N.Y.: Cornell University Press, 1982), 64; Bilby, *True-Born Maroons,* 416.

8. Eric Williams, *Capitalism and Slavery* (Chapel Hill: University of North Carolina Press, 1994).

9. The foundational critique of Williams is Seymour Drescher, *Econocide: British Slavery in the Era of Abolition* (Chapel Hill: University of North Carolina Press, 2010), originally published in 1977. Barbara L. Solow and Stanley L. Engerman, eds., in *British Capitalism and Caribbean Slavery: The Legacy of Eric Williams* (Cambridge: Cambridge University Press, 1987), offer a range of evaluations of the Williams thesis. Selwyn Carrington, *The Sugar Industry and the Abolition of the Slave Trade, 1775–1810* (Gainesville: University Press of Florida, 2002), builds on and defends the Williams thesis about the decline of slavery's profitability.

10. C. L. R. James, *The Black Jacobins: Toussaint L'Ouverture and the San Domingo Revolution* (New York: Vintage, 1963); Robin Blackburn, *The Overthrow of Colonial Slavery, 1776–1848* (London: Verso, 1988); David Brion Davis, *Inhuman Bondage: The Rise and Fall of Slavery in the New World* (Oxford: Oxford University Press, 2006), chap. 11.

11. Antonio Benítez-Rojo, *The Repeating Island: The Caribbean and the Postmodern Perspective,* 2nd ed. (Durham, N.C.: Duke University Press, 1996), chap. 2; Richard Gray, "The Papacy and the Atlantic Slave Trade: Lourenço Da Silva, The Capuchins, and the Decisions of the Holy Office," *Past and Present* 115 (May 1987): 52.

12. Thomas C. Holt, *The Problem of Freedom: Race, Labor, and Politics in Jamaica and Britain, 1832–1938* (Baltimore: Johns Hopkins University Press, 1992), 20–21; Rebecca Scott, *Slave Emancipation in Cuba: The Transition to Free Labor, 1860–1899* (Princeton, N.J.: Princeton University Press, 1985).

13. David Patrick Geggus, "The Slaves and Free Coloreds of Martinique during the Age of the French and Haitian Revolutions: Three Moments of Resistance," in *The Lesser Antilles in the Age of European Expansion*, ed. Robert Paquette and Stanley Engerman (Gainesville: University Press of Florida, 1996), 280–83; Sue Peabody, "'A Dangerous Zeal': Catholic Missions to Slaves in the French Antilles, 1635–1800," *French Historical Studies* 25, no. 1 (Winter 2002): 89.

14. Laurent Dubois and John D. Garrigus, *Slave Revolution in the Caribbean, 1789–1804: A Brief History with Documents*, 2nd ed. (New York: Bedford/St. Martin's, 2017), 51–55.

15. Geggus, "Slaves and Free Coloreds," 284–85; Dubois and Garrigus, *Slave Revolution*, 51–53.

16. Laurent Dubois, "An Enslaved Enlightenment: Re-Thinking the Intellectual History of the French Enlightenment," *Social History* 31, no. 1 (February 2006): 1–14.

17. David Barry Gaspar, *Bondsmen and Rebels: A Study of Master-Slave Relations in Antigua, with Implications for Colonial British America* (Baltimore: Johns Hopkins University Press, 1985); João José Reis, *Slave Rebellion in Brazil: The Muslim Uprising of 1835 in Bahia* (Baltimore: Johns Hopkins University Press, 1995); Emilia Viotti da Costa, *Crowns of Glory, Tears of Blood: The Demerara Slave Rebellion of 1823* (New York: Oxford University Press, 1994); John K. Thornton, "I Am the Subject of the King of Congo: African Political Ideology and the Haitian Revolution," *Journal of World History* 4 (Fall 1993): 181–214. For an account of the end of slavery that places slave insurrections, particularly those that were part of the Haitian Revolution, at the center of the story, see Robin Blackburn, *The Overthrow of Colonial Slavery, 1776–1848* (London: Verso, 1988).

18. See, for instance, Michael P. Johnson, "Denmark Vesey and His Co-Conspirators," *William and Mary Quarterly*, 3rd ser., 58, no. 4 (October 2001): 915–76; and John K. Thornton, "War, the State, and Religious Norms in Coromantee Thought," in *Possible Pasts: Becoming Colonial in America*, ed. Robert Blair St. George (Ithaca, N.Y.: Cornell University Press, 2000), 181–200. For a discussion of the issues surrounding archival and historiographical silences in the Haitian Revolution, see Michel-Rolph Trouillot, *Silencing the Past: Power and the Production of History* (Boston: Beacon, 1995).

19. Julius S. Scott, "The Common Wind: Currents of Afro-American Communication in the Era of the Haitian Revolution" (Ph.D. diss., Duke University, 1986).

20. Scott, "Common Wind."

21. Ranajit Guha, *Elementary Aspects of Peasant Insurgency in Colonial India* (Durham, N.C.: Duke University Press, 1999), 227, 257–61, 264; Steven Hahn, "'Extravagant Expectations' of Freedom: Rumour, Political Struggle, and the Christmas Insurrection Scare of 1865 in the American South," *Past and Present* 157 (November 1997): 124 and 134.

22. Gaspar, *Bondsmen and Rebels*, 245, 249–54; on revolts during the 1730s, see also David Barry Gaspar, "A Dangerous Spirit of Liberty: Slave Rebellion in the West Indies in the 1730s," in *Origins of the Black Atlantic*, ed. Laurent Dubois and Julius S. Scott (New York: Routledge, 2010), 11–25; Richard Price, *First-Time: The Historical Vision of an Afro-American People* (Baltimore: Johns Hopkins University Press, 1983); Peter Linebaugh and Marcus Rediker, *The Many-Headed Hydra: Sailors, Slaves, Commoners, and the Hidden History of the Revolutionary Atlantic* (Boston: Beacon, 2000).

23. Linebaugh and Rediker, *Many-Headed Hydra*, 193; Scott, "Common Wind," 117; Gabriel Debien, *Les Esclaves aux Antilles françaises, XVIIe–XVIIIe siècles* (Basse-Terre: Société d'histoire de la Guadeloupe, 1974), 387; Lucien Peytraud, *L'Esclavage aux Antilles françaises avant 1789* (Paris: Librarie Hachette, 1897), 372.

24. Scott, "Common Wind," 153–55, 21–23, 133–34.

25. Carolyn E. Fick, *The Making of Haiti: The Saint Domingue Revolution from Below*, 1st ed. (Knoxville: University of Tennessee Press, 1990), 83; Yves Benot, "La chaîne des insurrections d'esclaves dans les Caraïbes de 1789 à 1791," in *Les abolitions de l'esclavage de L. F. Sonthonax à V. Schoelcher, 1793, 1794, 1848*, ed. Marcel Dorigny (Paris: Presses universitaires de Vincennes, 1995), 182–83; Catin Dubois, "Certificat relatif au décret des gens de couleur, déposé entre les mains d'un députeé de l'Assemblée nationale," *Le Patriote français* 773 (September 22, 1791): 355–56; Jean Baptiste Lamarque to M. Lambert, January 3, 1791, Lamarque Papers, box 1, folder 1, Phillips Library, Peabody Essex Museum.

26. Frédéric Régent, *Esclavage, métissage, liberté: La Révolution française en Guadeloupe, 1789–1802* (Paris: Grasset, 2004), 219–21.

27. Fick, *Making of Haiti*, 91–92, 127–28; Thornton, "Subject of the King of Congo," 183.

28. See the letter of Hayo Baucage in "Lettres écrites à M. De Viomenil . . . au sujet de la révolte des nègres, 11–19 November 1789," in Marie-Hélène Leotin, ed., *La Martinique au temps de la Révolution française, 1789–1794* (Fort-de-France: Archives départementales, 1989), 35–39.

29. "St. Domingo Disturbances," *Philadelphia General Advertiser*, October 10, 1791, and October 11, 1791; "Le début de la révolte de Saint Domingue dans la Plaine du Cap, vécu par Louis de Calbiac," *Généalogie et histoire de la Caraïbe* 48 (April 1993): 776.

30. Governor Clugny to the Minister, 21 May 1791, Archives Nationales Section Outre Mer (ANSOM), C^{7A} 45, 5.

31. Victor Collot, "Insurrection de St. Anne," in *Précis d'événements qui se sont passés à la Guadeloupe pendant l'administration de Georges Henri Victor Collot*, ANSOM C^{7A} 46, 15–40; "Procès-verbal dressé par la municipalité de Sainte-Anne du soulèvement d'esclaves, survenu sur son territoire le 26 Août 1793," Archives nationales (AN) D^{XXV} 121, dossier 959, repr. in Anne Pérotin-Dumon, *Etre patriote sous les tropiques: La Guadeloupe sous la Révolution française* (Basse-Terre: Société d'histoire de la Guadeloupe, 1986), 278–82. "Etat des esclaves jugés et exécutés depuis le 31 Août 1792 au 12 Septembre courant," AN D^{XXV} 121, dossier 958.

32. Yves Benot, *La Révolution et la fin des colonies* (Paris: La Découverte, 1989); Laurence Boudouard and Florence Bellivier, "Des droits pour les bâtards, l'enfant naturel dans les débats révolutionnaires," in *La Famille, la loi, l'etat de la Révolution au Code civil*, ed. Irène Théry and Christian Biet (Paris: Imprimerie nationale, 1989), 122–44.

33. Laurent Dubois, *A Colony of Citizens: Revolution and Slave Emancipation in the French Caribbean, 1787–1804* (Chapel Hill: University of North Carolina Press, 2004), pt. 1.

34. The most detailed account of this is Jeremy D. Popkin, *You Are All Free: The Haitian Revolution and the Abolition of Slavery* (New York: Cambridge University Press, 2010); see also Fick, *Making of Haiti*, chap. 7; Laurent Dubois, *Avengers of the New World: The Story of the Haitian Revolution* (Cambridge, Mass.: Belknap Press of Harvard University Press, 2004), chaps. 4 and 5. For Sonthonax's statement, see "Sonthonax, ci-devant Commissaire Civil, Délegué de St. Domingue, à la Convention Nationale," 2 Fructidor an II, AN, AD^{VII}, 20A.

35. Laurent Dubois, "'The Price of Liberty': Victor Hugues and the Administration of Freedom in Guadeloupe," *William and Mary Quarterly*, 3rd ser., 56, no. 2 (April 1999): 363–92; Laurent Dubois, "Citizen-Soldiers: Emancipation and Military Service in the Revolutionary French Caribbean," in *The Arming of Slaves: From Classical Times to the Modern Age*, ed. Christopher Brown and Philip Morgan (New Haven, Conn.: Yale University Press, 2006), 233–54; Pedro M. Arcaya, *Insurrección de los negros en la Serranía de Coro* (Caracas: Instituto Panamericano de Geografía e Historia, 1949).

36. Blackburn, *Overthrow of Colonial Slavery, 1776–1848*; David P. Geggus, ed., *The Impact of the Haitian Revolution in the Atlantic World* (Columbia: University of South Carolina Press, 2001).

37. Williams, *Capitalism and Slavery*, 203.

38. Michael Craton, "Proto-Peasant Revolts? The Late Slave Rebellions in the British West Indies, 1816–1832," *Past and Present* 85 (November 1979): 101, 104, 107, 119; Hillary Beckles, "Emancipation by Law or War: Wilberforce and the 1816 Barbados Rebellion," in *Abolition and Its Aftermath: The Historical Context*, ed. David Richardson (London: Frank Cass, 1985), 92–94; *Brief Remarks on the Slave Registry Bill; and upon a Special Report of the African Institution, Recommending That Measure* (London, 1816), 574; for a comparison of slave revolts in the United States and the British Caribbean, see Davis, *Inhuman Bondage*, chap. 11.

39. Williams, *Capitalism and Slavery*, 203; Craton, "Proto-Peasant Revolts?," 119; Mary Turner, *Slaves and Missionaries: The Disintegration of Jamaican Slave Society, 1787–1834* (Urbana: University of Illinois Press, 1982).

40. Viotti da Costa, *Crowns of Glory, Tears of Blood*, 169, 177–79, 196.

41. Viotti da Costa, 179, 182–83, 187.

42. Viotti da Costa, 197, and generally chaps. 6 and 7.

43. Mary Turner, "The Jamaica Slave Rebellion of 1831," *Past and Present* 40 (July 1968): 110–11, 113–16, 125; Turner, *Slaves and Missionaries*, 160, and generally chap. 6; Holt, *Problem of Freedom*, 14–16.

44. Mary Turner, "The Baptist War and Abolition," *Jamaican Historical Review* 13 (1982): 31–41, 34; Turner, *Slaves and Missionaries*, 172–73.

45. Williams, *Capitalism and Slavery*, 206.

46. Holt, *Problem of Freedom*, 17.

47. Jean Besson, *Martha Brae's Two Histories: European Expansion and Caribbean Culture-Building in Jamaica* (Chapel Hill: University of North Carolina Press, 2002), 122.

48. Besson, *Martha Brae's Two Histories*, 113–14.

49. Sidney Mintz, "Historical Sociology of the Jamaican Church-Founded Free Village System," *De West-Indische Gids* 38, no. 1/2 (September 1958): 47–48; Yvonne Acosta and Jean Casimir, "Social Origins of the Counter-Plantation System in St. Lucia," in *Rural Development in the Caribbean*, ed. P. I. Gomes (New York: St. Martin's, 1985), 40–41.

50. O. Nigel Bolland, "The Politics of Freedom in the British Caribbean," in *The Meaning of Freedom: Economics, Politics and Culture after Slavery*, ed. Seymour Drescher and Frank McGlynn (Pittsburgh: University of Pittsburgh Press, 1992), 113; David Lowenthal, "Caribbean Views of Caribbean Land," *Canadian Geographer* 5, no. 2 (Summer 1961): 4; Jean Besson, "Land, Kinship and Community in the Post-Emancipation Caribbean: A Regional View of the Leewards," in *Small Islands, Large Questions: Society, Culture and Resistance in the Post-Emancipation Caribbean*, ed. Karen Fog Olwig (London: Frank Cass, 1995), 75, 78; Jean Besson, "Free Villagers, Rastafarians and Modern Maroons," in *Born Out of Resistance: On Caribbean Cultural Creativity*, ed. Wim Hoogbergen (Utrecht: ISOR-Publications, 1995), 301–14.

51. Douglas Hall, *Free Jamaica, 1838–1865: An Economic History* (New Haven, Conn.: Yale University Press, 1959), 62, 171, 188; O. Nigel Bolland, "Systems of Domination after Slavery: The Control of Land and Labor in the British West Indies after 1838," *Comparative Studies in Society and History* 23, no. 4 (October 1981): 599.

52. Besson, "Land, Kinship and Community," 85–86; Acosta and Casimir, "Social Origins," 36; Patrick Chamoiseau, *Texaco* (New York: Vintage, 1992); Bolland, "Politics of Freedom," 139.

53. Bolland, "Politics of Freedom," 121, 123, 126; Mintz, "Historical Sociology," 49–50, 53, 55.

54. Swithin Wilmot, "The Road to Morant Bay: Politics in Free Jamaica, 1838–1845," *Journal of Caribbean History* 50, no. 1 (2016): 3–6; Holt, *Problem of Freedom*.

55. Edith Clarke, *My Mother Who Fathered Me: A Study of the Families in Three Selected Communities of Jamaica* (Kingston: The Press of the University of the West Indies, 1999), 23–24; Besson, "Free Villagers," 310; Erna Brodber, *The Second Generation of Freemen in Jamaica, 1907–1944* (Gainesville: University Press of Florida, 2004), 110.

56. Jean Besson, "Agrarian Relations and Perceptions of Land in a Jamaican Peasant Village," in *Small Farming and Peasant Resources in the Caribbean*, ed. John S. Brierley and Hymie Rubenstein, Manitoba Geographical Studies, vol. 10 (Winnipeg:

Department of Geography, University of Manitoba, 1988), 43–45; Besson, "Land, Kinship and Community," 79; Clarke, *My Mother Who Fathered Me*, 22.

57. Besson, "Agrarian Relations," 44–45, 48; Jean Besson, "A Paradox in Caribbean Attitudes to Land," in *Land and Development in the Caribbean*, ed. Jean Besson and Janet Momsen (London: Macmillan, 1997), 14–15, 18.

58. Karen Fog Olwig, "Caribbean Family Land: A Modern Commons," *Plantation Society in the Americas* 4, nos. 2–3 (Fall 1997): 142–46; Karen Fog Olwig, *Cultural Adaptation and Resistance on St. John: Three Centuries of Afro-Caribbean Life* (Gainesville: University of Florida Press, 1985).

59. Olwig, "Caribbean Family Land," 151; Lowenthal, "Caribbean Views," 4.

60. Lowenthal, "Caribbean Views," 5; Bolland, "Politics of Freedom," 142.

61. Besson, "Land, Kinship and Community," 79, 93.

62. Holt, *Problem of Freedom*, 351.

63. Holt, 348–49.

64. Holt, 348.

65. Holt, 350–53.

66. Frank Taylor, *To Hell with Paradise: A History of the Jamaican Tourist Industry* (Pittsburgh: University of Pittsburgh Press, 1993), 87; Polly Pattullo, *Last Resorts: The Cost of Tourism in the Caribbean* (New York: Monthly Review Press, 2005), 20.

67. W. J. Hanna, "Tourist Travel to Jamaica in the 1890s," *Jamaica Journal* 22, no. 3 (October 1989): 19; Krista A. Thompson, *An Eye for the Tropics: Tourism, Photography, and Framing the Caribbean Picturesque* (Durham, N.C.: Duke University Press, 2006), 4–5, 8.

68. Thompson, *Eye for the Tropics*, 10, 13.

69. Harry Hamilton Johnston, *Photos and Phantasms: Harry Johnston's Photographs of the Caribbean* (London: British Council, 1998), 44, 55; Thompson, *Eye for the Tropics*, 309n15.

70. Thompson, *Eye for the Tropics*, 1, 12.

71. Laurent Dubois, *Haiti: The Aftershocks of History* (New York: Metropolitan Books, 2012), 112–18; Georges Anglade, *Atlas critique d'Haïti* (Montréal, Québec: Groupe d'études et de recherches critiques d'espace, UQAM, 1982); Gusti-Klara Gaillard, *L'expérience haïtienne de la dette extérieure, ou, une production caféière pillée: 1875–1915* (Port-au-Prince: Impr. H. Deschamps, 1990); Michel-Rolph Trouillot, *Haiti, State against Nation: The Origins and Legacy of Duvalierism* (New York: Monthly Review Press, 1990).

72. Serge Larose, "The Haitian Lakou: Land, Family and Ritual," in *Family and Kinship in Middle America and the Caribbean: Proceedings of the 14th Seminar of the Committee on Family Research of the International Sociological Association, Curaçao, September 1975*, ed. Arnaud F. Marks and Rene A. Romer (Willemstad: Institute of Higher Studies in Curaçao, 1975), 482, 486, 494, 506; Dubois, *Haiti*, chap. 1. The most detailed study of land tenure in Haiti over the long term is Drexel G. Woodson, "Tout Mounn Se Mounn, Men Tout Mounn Pa Menm: Microlevel Sociocultural Aspects of Land Tenure in a Northern Haitian Locality" (Ph.D. diss., Johns Hopkins University, 1990).

73. Larose, "Haitian Lakou," 489–91, 511.

74. Larose, 491–92; Karen McCarthy Brown, *Mama Lola: A Vodou Priestess in Brooklyn* (Berkeley: University of California Press, 1991).

75. Larose, "Haitian Lakou," 498–99; for detailed studies of Haitian market women's economic and social roles, see Sidney W. Mintz, "The Employment of Capital by Haitian Market Women," in *Capital, Savings and Credit in Peasant Societies*, ed. Raymond Firth and Basil Yamey (Chicago: Aldine, 1964), 256–86; Sidney Mintz, "Les Rôles économiques et la tradition culturelle," in *La Femme de couleur en Amérique latine*, ed. Roger Bastide (Paris: Éditions Anthropos, 1974), 115–48.

76. Larose, "Haitian Lakou," 508.

Chapter Four

1. Samuel Hazard, *Santo Domingo, Past and Present: With a Glance at Hayti* (New York: Harper and Bros., 1873), 419.

2. Juan Bosch, *The Social Composition of the Dominican Republic* (New York: Routledge, 2016), 225; Frank Moya Pons, *Manual de historia dominicana* (Santo Domingo: Caribbean Publishers, 1995), 468–89.

3. Richard Lee Turits, *Foundations of Despotism: Peasants, the Trujillo Regime, and Modernity in Dominican History* (Stanford, Calif.: Stanford University Press, 2003).

4. Purchased in 1867 from Russia, the giant Alaskan territory was perhaps the first U.S. territory not envisaged as a future state in the union. Its people were deemed "uncivilized native tribes," who would be subject to the will of the federal government and not offered "the rights, advantages, and immunities of citizens of the United States." Stuart Banner, *Possessing the Pacific: Land, Settlers, and Indigenous People from Australia to Alaska* (Cambridge, Mass.: Harvard University Press, 2007), 293. For an interesting discussion of the territory clause in a very different context, see Don E. Fehrenbacher, *The Dred Scott Case: Its Significance in American Law and Practice* (Oxford: Oxford University Press, 1978), 373–84; U.S. Const. art. IV, § 3, cl. 2; Stephen Kinzer, *Overthrow: America's Century of Regime Change from Hawaii to Iraq*, 1st ed. (New York: Times Books, 2006), 15, 22; Ralph S. Kuykendall and A. Grove Day, *Hawaii: A History from Polynesian Kingdom to American Statehood* (Englewood Cliffs, N.J.: Prentice Hall, 1976), 195; Christina Duffy Burnett, "United States: American Expansion and Territorial Deannexation," *University of Chicago Law Review* 72, no. 3 (Summer 2005): 797–897; Christina Duffy Burnett and Burke Marshall, "Between the Foreign and the Domestic: The Doctrine of Territorial Incorporation, Invented and Reinvented," in *Foreign in a Domestic Sense: Puerto Rico, American Expansion, and the Constitution*, ed. Christina Duffy Burnett and Burke Marshall (Durham, N.C.: Duke University Press, 2001), 1–36.

5. Burnett and Marshall, "Between Foreign and Domestic," 12, 33n52.

6. During the first two decades of the twentieth century, a number of prominent U.S. leaders and officials, though, referred to the new territories as "colonies." Daniel Immerwahr, *How to Hide an Empire: A History of the Greater United States*

(New York: Farrar, Straus and Giroux, 2019), 7; Downes v. Bidwell, 182 U.S. 244 (May 27, 1901); see the judgment of Justice Edward Douglass White; Francisco Scarano, *Puerto Rico: Cinco siglos de historia* (San Juan: McGraw-Hill, 1993), 552–57, 574–76; Fernando Picó, *History of Puerto Rico: A Panorama of Its People* (Princeton, N.J.: Markus Wiener Publishers, 2006), 234–41; Luis Muñoz Rivera, "Al pueblo de Puerto Rico (Manifiesto del Partido Federal), 5 Oct. 1899," in *Campañas políticas*, ed. Luis Muñoz Marín (Madrid: Editorial Puerto Rico, 1925), 241–48; Luis Martínez-Fernández, "Puerto Rico in the Whirlwind of 1898: Conflict, Continuity, and Change," *OAH Magazine of History* 26 (Spring 1998): 24–29; Francisco Scarano, "Intervention or Possession?: Puerto Rico, the War of 1898, and the American Colonial Periphery," in *Whose America?: The War of 1898 and the Battles to Define the Nation*, ed. Virginia Marie Bouvier (Westport, Conn.: Praeger, 2001), 161–70; Sarah H. Cleveland, "Powers Inherent in Sovereignty: Indians, Aliens, Territories, and the Nineteenth Century Origins of Plenary Power over Foreign Affairs," *Texas Law Review* 81, no. 1 (November 2002): 229.

7. Although Congress' declaration in 1917 that Puerto Ricans would now be considered citizens might appear transformative, without statehood its significance was essentially symbolic. The law did not enfranchise Puerto Ricans, and the Supreme Court had already affirmed their right, as residents of a U.S. territory, to unrestricted travel to the mainland. Sam Erman, *Almost Citizens: Puerto Rico, the U.S. Constitution, and Empire* (Cambridge: Cambridge University Press, 2019), 6, 141–45; César J. Ayala and Rafael Bernabe, *Puerto Rico in the American Century: A History since 1898* (Chapel Hill: University of North Carolina Press, 2007); Burnett, "Untied States"; Victor Bulmer-Thomas, *Empire in Retreat: The Past, Present, and Future of the United States* (New Haven, Conn.: Yale University Press, 2018), 123.

8. Mark Twain, "To the Person Sitting in Darkness," *North American Review* 172, no. 531 (February 1901): 170; Paul A. Kramer, *The Blood of Government: Race, Empire, the United States, and the Philippines* (Chapel Hill: University of North Carolina Press, 2006), 93–97; Nick Cullather, "The American Century in the Philippines," *CultureFront* (Spring 1998): 16.

9. Kramer, *Blood of Government*, 93, 138–45, 157, 456; Brian McAllister Linn, "Taking up 'The White Man's Burden': U.S. Troop Conduct in the Philippine War, 1899–1902," in *1898: Enfoques y perspectivas*, ed. Luis E. González Vales (San Juan: Academia Puertorriqueña de la Historia, 1997), 111–42; Eric Tyrone Lowery Love, *Race over Empire: Racism and U.S. Imperialism, 1865–1900* (Chapel Hill: University of North Carolina Press, 2004), 198; Cullather, "American Century"; Stuart Creighton Miller, *"Benevolent Assimilation": The American Conquest of the Philippines, 1899–1903* (New Haven, Conn.: Yale University Press, 1982), 9, 182–92; Richard Welch Jr., "American Atrocities in the Philippines: The Indictment and the Response," *Pacific Historical Review* 43, no. 2 (May 1974): 245; "Testimony of Grover Flint," April 29, 1902, in U.S. Congress Senate Committee on the Philippines, *Affairs in the Philippine Islands*," 57th U.S. Congress, 1st sess., 1902, S. Doc. 331, vol. 3, 1765–84; Immerwahr, *How to Hide an Empire*, 227–41.

10. Twain, "To the Person Sitting in Darkness," 169.

11. Already by 1870, Spain had declared a "free womb law," the Moret Law, which aimed to end slavery not by emancipation but by freeing all those born since 1868, effective upon their twenty-second birthday. Ultimately, Spain was compelled by 1880 to free those who were enslaved and declare universal freedom, though there was supposed to be a period of "wardship," of semifreedom, between 1880 and 1886. Ada Ferrer, *Insurgent Cuba: Race, Nation, and Revolution* (Chapel Hill: University of North Carolina Press, 1999), esp. 44–68, 143–44; Rebecca Scott, *Slave Emancipation in Cuba: The Transition to Free Labor, 1860–1899* (Princeton, N.J.: Princeton University Press, 1985), 63–83, 123–24, pt. 3. For the Moret Law, see http://college .cengage.com/history/world/keen/latin_america/8e/assets/students/sources/pdfs /44moret_law.pdf.

12. Louis A. Pérez, *The War of 1898: The United States and Cuba in History and Historiography* (Chapel Hill: University of North Carolina Press, 1998), esp. 10–18; Louis A. Pérez, *Cuba between Empires, 1878–1902* (Pittsburgh: University of Pittsburgh Press, 1982), 167–69; John Lawrence Tone, *War and Genocide in Cuba, 1895–1898* (Chapel Hill: University of North Carolina Press, 2006), 9, 97, 267–71.

13. Verena Martínez-Alier, *Marriage, Class and Colour in Nineteenth-Century Cuba: A Study of Racial Attitudes and Sexual Values in a Slave Society* (Ann Arbor: University of Michigan Press, 1989), 58.

14. Pérez, *War of 1898*, 5; Lars Schoultz, *That Infernal Little Cuban Republic: The United States and the Cuban Revolution* (Chapel Hill: University of North Carolina Press, 2009), 18–19; Henry Cabot Lodge, "Our Duty to Cuba," *Forum* (May 1896): 278–80; Richard H. Immerman, *Empire for Liberty: A History of American Imperialism from Benjamin Franklin to Paul Wolfowitz* (Princeton, N.J.: Princeton University Press, 2010), 5; Louis A. Pérez, *Cuba in the American Imagination: Metaphor and the Imperial Ethos* (Chapel Hill: University of North Carolina Press, 2008).

15. A similar fate befell Grant's effort to annex the Danish Virgin Islands with the promise of the "liberties and rights of American citizens" and a "path to statehood." Love, *Race over Empire*, 53–54, 59, 62–63, 67; Lars Schoultz, *Beneath the United States: A History of U.S. Policy toward Latin America* (Cambridge, Mass.: Harvard University Press, 1998), 82–83; Erman, *Almost Citizens*, 12.

16. José Martí, "Cuba and the United States," in José Martí, *Our America: Writings on Latin America and the Struggle for Cuban Independence*, ed. Philip Sheldon Foner and trans. Elinor Randall (New York: Monthly Review Press, 1977), 226–34; Schoultz, *Beneath the United States*, 78–90.

17. Ferrer, *Insurgent Cuba*, 3; Pérez, *Cuba between Empires*, 16–17, 107, 135–37, 385; Arcadio Díaz Quiñones, "1898," *Hispanic American Historical Review* 78, no. 4 (November 1998): 577–81; Tone, *War and Genocide*, 36; Joanna Swanger, "Lands of Rebellion: Oriente and Escambray Encountering Cuban State Formation, 1934–1974" (Ph.D. diss., University of Texas at Austin, 1999), 149–223; Rebecca Scott, "Reclaiming Gregoria's Mule: The Meanings of Freedom in the Arimao and Caunao Valleys, Cienfuegos, Cuba, 1880–1899," *Past and Present* 170 (February 2001): 183.

18. Scott, "Gregoria's Mule," 183; Aline Helg, *Our Rightful Share: The Afro-Cuban Struggle for Equality, 1886–1912* (Chapel Hill: University of North Carolina Press,

1995), 80. For use of the phrase "another Haiti or Santo Domingo" also during the Ten Years' War, see Ferrer, *Insurgent Cuba*, 48, 59.

19. Pérez, *War of 1898*, chap. 2.

20. Pérez, *Cuba between Empires*, 311–12, 325; Pérez, *War of 1898*, chap. 2, esp. 34; Louis A. Pérez, *Army Politics in Cuba, 1898–1958* (Pittsburgh: University of Pittsburgh Press, 1976), 77–85, 92; Matthew Casey and Alejandro de la Fuente, "Race and the Suffrage Controversy in Cuba, 1898–1901," in *Colonial Crucible: Empire and the Making of the Modern American State*, ed. Alfred W. McCoy and Francisco Scarano (Madison: University of Wisconsin Press, 2009), 228–29; Alejandro de la Fuente, *A Nation for All: Race, Inequality, and Politics in Twentieth-Century Cuba* (Chapel Hill: University of North Carolina Press, 2001), 54; Ferrer, *Insurgent Cuba*.

21. Leopoldo Cancio, Rafael Cruz Pérez, and Octavio Giberga, "No. 62," *Gaceta de la Habana*, March 5, 1902; Louis A. Pérez, *Lords of the Mountain: Social Banditry and Peasant Protest in Cuba, 1878–1918* (Pittsburgh: University of Pittsburgh Press, 1989), 96–104; Antero Regalado, *Las luchas campesinas en Cuba* (Havana: Departamento de Orientación Revolucionario del Comité Central del Partido Comunista de Cuba, 1974), 44–58; Duvon Corbitt, "Mercedes and Realengos: A Survey of the Public Land System in Cuba," *Hispanic American Historical Review* 19, no. 3 (August 1939): 262–85; Pérez, *War of 1898*, 19–21, 25.

22. Cancio, Pérez, and Giberga, "No. 62"; Francisco Scarano, "Liberal Pacts and Hierarchies of Rule: Approaching the Imperial Transition in Cuba and Puerto Rico," *Hispanic American Historical Review* 78, no. 4 (November 1998): 601; Pérez, *Lords of the Mountain*, esp. 69–73, 103–4; Swanger, "Lands of Rebellion," 149–223; Corbitt, "Mercedes and Realengos."

23. Robert P. Porter, "United States and Cuba," *New York Times*, February 11, 1901, 6; César J. Ayala, *American Sugar Kingdom: The Plantation Economy of the Spanish Caribbean, 1898–1934* (Chapel Hill: University of North Carolina Press, 1999), 70; Gillian McGillivray, *Blazing Cane: Sugar Communities, Class, and State Formation in Cuba, 1868–1959* (Durham, N.C.: Duke University Press, 2009), 30, 79, 87; Pérez, *Cuba between Empires*, 357–60; Joshua Nadel, "Processing Modernity: Social and Cultural Adaptation in Eastern Cuba, 1902–1933" (Ph.D. diss., University of North Carolina at Chapel Hill, 2007), chap. 1, esp. 53; Pérez, *Lords of the Mountain*, 96–111; Carmen Diana Deere, "Here Come the Yankees! The Rise and Decline of United States Colonies in Cuba, 1898–1930," *Hispanic American Historical Review* 78, no. 4 (November 1998): 735–38.

24. Robert H. Holden and Eric Zolov, *Latin America and the United States: A Documentary History* (New York: Oxford University Press, 2000), 81–82; Jana Lipman, *Guantánamo: A Working-Class History between Empire and Revolution* (Berkeley: University of California Press, 2008).

25. Pérez, *Cuba between Empires*, 324–27; Louis A. Pérez Jr., *Cuba: Between Reform and Revolution*, 1st ed. (New York: Oxford University Press, 1988), 265–70.

26. J. Fred Rippy, "The Initiation of the Customs Receivership in the Dominican Republic," *Hispanic American Historical Review* 17, no. 4 (November 1937): 420–23. See also Noel Maurer, *The Empire Trap: The Rise and Fall of U.S. Intervention to*

Protect American Property Overseas, 1893–2013 (Princeton, N.J.: Princeton University Press, 2013), 64–65.

27. Rippy, "The Initiation," 420–22.

28. Turits, *Foundations*, chap. 2; Pedro Mir, *Cuando amaban las tierras comuneras* (Santo Domingo: Siglo Veintiuno, 1978), 183–84.

29. Mats Lundahl, *The Haitian Economy: Man, Land and Markets* (London: Croom Helm, 1983), 70–97; Mats Lundahl, *The Political Economy of Disaster: Destitution, Plunder and Earthquake in Haiti* (New York: Routledge, 2013), 19–29; Laurent Dubois, *Haiti: The Aftershocks of History* (New York: Metropolitan Books, 2012), chap. 3, esp. 107; for a detailed study of the postindependence economy in Haiti, see Johnhenry Gonzalez, *Maroon Nation: A History of Revolutionary Haiti* (New Haven, Conn.: Yale University Press, 2019).

30. W. E. B. Du Bois, *The Negro* (1915; New York: Cosimo Classics, 2007), 106; David Levering Lewis, *W. E. B. Du Bois: The Fight for Equality and the American Century, 1919–1963* (New York: Henry Holt, 2009), 18.

31. Turits, *Foundations*, chap. 2. *Gavillero* translates as "gang," but *caco* has no general meaning in Kreyòl. Some hypothesize that it is derived from the Kreyòl word *taco*, a species of bird that is seen as particularly fierce. Dubois, *Haiti*, 222; Brenda Gayle Plummer, *Haiti and the United States: The Psychological Moment* (Athens: University of Georgia Press, 1992), 90. Others state that it is derived from the Spanish word *caco*, meaning "thief," and that it was used in colonial Santo Domingo to describe putative bandits among those escaping from enslavement in Saint-Domingue. Roger Gaillard, *Le Cacoïsme bourgeois contre Salnave (1867–1870): Inclus le récit commenté de Ducis Viard: La dernière étape* (Port-au-Prince: Fondation Roger Gaillard, 2003), 43–44.

32. Bosch, *Social Composition*, 225; Moya Pons, *Manual*, 468–69; Ellen D. Tillman, *Dollar Diplomacy by Force: Nation-Building and Resistance in the Dominican Republic* (Chapel Hill: University of North Carolina Press, 2016), 17–18, 36–55.

33. Turits, *Foundations*, chap. 2, esp. 61–62.

34. Turits, chaps. 2 and 4, esp. 71, 208–9; María Filomena González Canalda, "Gavilleros, 1904–1924," *Ecos* 4, no. 5 (1996): 129–40; Julie Franks, "The Gavilleros of the East: Social Banditry as Political Practice in the Dominican Sugar Region, 1900–1924," *Journal of Historical Sociology* 8, no. 2 (1995): 158–81; Humberto García-Muñiz, "The South Porto Rico Sugar Company: The History of a United States Multinational Corporation in Puerto Rico and the Dominican Republic, 1900–1921" (Ph.D. diss., Columbia University, 1997), 414–28.

35. Lundahl, *Haitian Economy*, 70–97; Lundahl, *Political Economy of Disaster*, 19–29, 49–50, 277.

36. Roger Gaillard, *Premier écrasement du cacoïsme* (Port-au-Prince: R. Gaillard, 1981), 12, quoted in Dubois, *Haiti*, 208–11.

37. Franks, "Gavilleros," 161; Turits, *Foundations*, 209; Marvin Chochotte, "The Twilight of Popular Revolutions: The Suppression of Peasant Armed Struggles and Freedom in Rural Haiti during the US Occupation, 1915–1934," *Journal of African American History* 103, no. 3 (Summer 2018): 285–87.

38. Tillman, *Dollar Diplomacy*, chap. 3; Roger Gaillard, *Charlemagne Péralte le caco* (Port-au-Prince: R. Gaillard, 1982), 122; Marvin Chochotte, "The History of Peasants, *Tonton Makouts*, and the Rise and Fall of the Duvalier Dictatorship in Haiti" (Ph.D. diss., University of Michigan, 2017), chap. 1; Maurer, *Empire Trap*, 95; Turits, *Foundations*, 71, 208–10, 292n89, 332n8; Bruce J. Calder, *The Impact of Intervention: The Dominican Republic during the U.S. Occupation of 1916–1924*, 1st ed. (Austin: University of Texas Press, 1984), 118.

39. Rippy, "Customs Receivership," 420–22; *New York Times*, February 20, 1893, 6, quoted in Cyrus Veeser, *A World Safe for Capitalism: Dollar Diplomacy and America's Rise to Global Power* (New York: Columbia University Press, 2002), 3.

40. Calder, *Impact*, xxi; Maurer, *Empire Trap*, 91; Hans Schmidt, *The United States Occupation of Haiti, 1915–1934* (New Brunswick, N.J.: Rutgers University Press, 1995), 41.

41. Maurer, *Empire Trap*, 3–4, 91; Eric Williams, *From Columbus to Castro: The History of the Caribbean* (New York: Vintage, 1984), 428–42, quoted in Ayala, *American Sugar Kingdom*, 6, 70; Kuykendall and Day, *Hawaii*, 189–90; Scarano, *Puerto Rico*, 614–15; Kramer, *Blood of Government*, 392–95.

42. Schmidt, *Occupation*, 36–60; Dubois, *Haiti*, 173–74, 200–201; Nancy Mitchell, *The Danger of Dreams: German and American Imperialism in Latin America* (Chapel Hill: University of North Carolina Press, 1999); Mary A. Renda, *Taking Haiti: Military Occupation and the Culture of U.S. Imperialism, 1915–1940* (Chapel Hill: University of North Carolina Press, 2001), 96.

43. Mitchell, *Danger of Dreams*, 1; Schmidt, *Occupation*, 56.

44. J. Adam Tooze, *The Deluge: The Great War and the Remaking of Global Order, 1916–1931* (London: Allen Lane, 2014); Calder, *Impact*, 7; Tillman, *Dollar Diplomacy*, chap. 3, esp. 74–75; Renda, *Taking Haiti*, 11; Chantalle F. Verna, *Haiti and the Uses of America: Post-U.S. Occupation Promises* (New Brunswick, N.J.: Rutgers University Press, 2017), chap. 2.

45. Calder, *Impact*, 6–7; Moya Pons, *Manual*, 467.

46. Bosch, *Social Composition*, 225–31; Moya Pons, *Manual*, 468–69; Juan A. Senior and Antonio Hoepelman, *Documentos históricos que se refieren a la intervención armada de los Estados Unidos de Norte-América y la implantación de un gobierno militar americano en la República Dominicana* (Santo Domingo: Imprenta de J.R. Vda. García, 1922), 5, 290; Dubois, *Haiti*, 214–15.

47. Senior and Hoepelman, *Documentos históricos*, 283–84, 291–94; Unión Nacional Dominicana, December 24, 1920, quoted in Lauren Hutchinson Derby, *The Dictator's Seduction: Politics and the Popular Imagination in the Era of Trujillo* (Durham, N.C.: Duke University Press, 2009), 28.

48. David Nicholls, *From Dessalines to Duvalier: Race, Colour and National Independence in Haiti* (New Brunswick, N.J.: Rutgers University Press, 1996), 145–47; Dubois, *Haiti*, 204–27, 243–48; Schmidt, *Occupation*, 71–74; Veeser, *World*, chaps. 8 and 9; Eric Roorda, *The Dictator Next Door: The Good Neighbor Policy and the Trujillo Regime in the Dominican Republic, 1930–1945* (Durham, N.C.: Duke University Press, 1998), 13–15.

49. Calder, *Impact*, 16–19, 24–25.

50. Roorda, *Dictator Next Door*, 16–17; Maurer, *Empire Trap*, 102; Calder, *Impact*, 21, 24; Tillman, *Dollar Diplomacy*, 131.

51. Tillman, *Dollar Diplomacy*, 127–29; Calder, *Impact*, 25; Alan L. McPherson, *The Invaded: How Latin Americans and their Allies Fought and Ended U.S. Occupations* (New York: Oxford University Press, 2014), 43; Roorda, *Dictator Next Door*, 16–17.

52. Calder, *Impact*, 12–16, 28–29, 183–98; Tillman, *Dollar Diplomacy*, 72, 122, 149–51; McPherson, *Invaded*, 38.

53. Tillman, *Dollar Diplomacy*, 122; Moya Pons, *Manual*, 484; Sumner Welles, *Naboth's Vineyard: The Dominican Republic, 1844–1924*, 2 vols. (New York: Payson and Clarke, Ltd., 1928), 2, 823, quoted in Calder, *Impact*, 183–89; Dubois, *Haiti*, chap. 6, esp. 275–77; Millery Polyné, *From Douglass to Duvalier: U.S. African Americans, Haiti and Pan Americanism, 1870–1964* (Gainesville: University Press of Florida, 2010); Trygve Throntveit, *Power without Victory: Woodrow Wilson and the American Internationalist Experiment* (Chicago: University of Chicago Press, 2017), 249.

54. Chochotte, "Twilight," 301; Benoît Rameau, in Gaillard, *Premier écrasement*, 105, 109, quoted in Dubois, *Haiti*, 223–31.

55. Renda, *Taking Haiti*, 32–33, 141–51; Schmidt, *Occupation*, 100–106; Dubois, *Haiti*, esp. 238–43, 249; Chochotte, "Twilight," 299.

56. Matthew Casey, *Empire's Guestworkers: Haitian Migrants in Cuba during the Age of US Occupation* (Cambridge: Cambridge University Press, 2017), 82–84; Landon Yarrington, "The Paved and the Unpaved: Toward a Political Economy of Infrastructure, Mobility, and Urbanization in Haiti," *Economic Anthropology* 2, no. 1 (January 2015): 185–204; Charlemagne Péralte, reprinted in *Conjonction*, no. 115 (1971): 102, quoted in Nicholls, *From Dessalines to Duvalier*, 149; Dubois, *Haiti*, 243, 249, 254.

57. Calder, *Impact*, chaps. 5–7, esp. 115, 145, 171; Chochotte, "Twilight," 302; Tillman, *Dollar Diplomacy*, 92, 165.

58. Lundahl, *Haitian Economy*, 99, 54; Casey, *Empire's Guestworkers*, 73; Dubois, *Haiti*, 244–47, 267–71, 298; Frank Moya Pons, *History of the Caribbean* (Princeton, N.J.: Markus Wiener, 2007), 294–98; Plummer, *Haiti*, 110–14; Guy Pierre, "La industria azucarera de Haití entre 1915–1918 y 1938–1939," *Boletín del Archivo General de la Nación* 41, no. 144 (January–April 2016): 109–61.

59. According to Plummer, Washington eventually favored awarding property titles on the basis of "prescription" ("squatters") rights. But unlike in the Dominican Republic (see below), few if any steps appear to have been taken in this direction. Plummer, *Haiti*, 112–13; Schmidt, *Occupation*, 179; Lundahl, *Haitian Economy*, 99.

60. Plummer, *Haiti*, 112–13; Casey, *Empire's Guestworkers*, 67.

61. Plummer, *Haiti*, 111–12; Casey, *Empire's Guestworkers*, 139; Lundahl, *Haitian Economy*, 100–103; Matthew Casey, "Haitians, Labor and Leisure on Cuban Sugar Plantations: The Limits of Company Control," *New West Indian Guide* 85, no. 1–2 (2011): 6; Franklin Knight, "Jamaican Migrants and the Cuban Sugar Industry, 1930–1934," in Manuel Moreno Fraginals, Frank Moya Pons, and Stanley Engerman, eds., *Between Slavery and Free Labor: The Spanish-Speaking Caribbean in the Nineteenth Century* (Baltimore: Johns Hopkins University Press, 1985), 94–114;

Marc McLeod, "Undesirable Aliens: Race, Ethnicity, and Nationalism in the Comparison of Haitian and British West Indian Immigrant Workers in Cuba, 1912–1939," *Journal of Social History* 31, no. 3 (1998): 599–623; Samuel Martínez, "From Hidden Hand to Heavy Hand: Sugar, the State, and Migrant Labor in Haiti and the Dominican Republic," *Latin American Research Review* 34, no. 1 (1999): 57–84, 61–68. For a close treatment of the vast British Caribbean diaspora across Cuba, Panama, the United States, Venezuela, and elsewhere, see Lara Putnam, *Radical Moves: Caribbean Migrants and the Politics of Race in the Jazz Age* (Chapel Hill: University of North Carolina Press, 2013).

62. The Cuban government deported some forty thousand Haitian immigrants between 1928 and 1940, often without letting them take their money or belongings with them. Casey, *Empire's Guestworkers*, 75–76, 87, 235–36; Lundahl, *Haitian Economy*, 103–6.

63. Casey, *Empire's Guestworkers*, esp. 63–67, 75; Michel-Rolph Trouillot, *Haiti, State against Nation: The Origins and Legacy of Duvalierism* (New York: Monthly Review Press, 1990), 61; Lundahl, *Political Economy of Disaster*, 49; Lundahl, *Haitian Economy*, 98–99.

64. Lundahl, *Haitian Economy*, 98; Trouillot, *Haiti*, 61.

65. Jesse Hoffnung-Garskof, *A Tale of Two Cities: Santo Domingo and New York after 1950* (Princeton, N.J.: Princeton University Press, 2008), 31–33, 69. In the 1960s, 70 percent of the population still lived in the countryside, not far, comparatively speaking, from the 83 percent in 1935. Turits, *Foundations*, 265n3. María Filomena González Canalda, "Desiderio Arias y el caudillismo," *Estudios Sociales* 18, no. 61 (September 1985): 29–50; Canalda, "Gavilleros"; McPherson, *Invaded*, 70–71; Roorda, *Dictator Next Door*, 17, 247n24.

66. Turits, *Foundations*, chap. 2; Calder, *Impact*, 120–21, 171–72, 175.

67. Turits, *Foundations*, 71–79.

68. Thomas Snowden, "Proclama," March 30, 1920, *Gaceta Oficial*, April 7, 1920; Calder, Impact, 99.

69. Snowden, "Proclama"; Turits, *Foundations*, chap. 2.

70. "Agriculture Director's Report," Archivo General de la Nación (AGN), Santo Domingo, Gobierno Militar, Correspondencia, 1917–1924, leg. 49; Evan Young to Sec. of State, May 31, 1929, National Archives and Records Administration (NARA), College Park, Md., Record Group (RG) 59, 839.52.

71. Turits, *Foundations*, 77.

72. Calder, *Impact*, 121, 136; Turits, *Foundations*, 208–9.

73. Calder, *Impact*, 125–26, 148–50, 154; McPherson, *Invaded*, 93.

74. Tillman, *Dollar Diplomacy*, 100–101; McPherson, *Invaded*, 91–110; Calder, *Impact*, 123–47; "The 'Water Torture' and Other Abuses: US Senate, Hearings before a Select Committee on Haiti and Santo Domingo," in Eric Paul Roorda, Lauren H. Derby, and Raymundo González, eds., *The Dominican Republic Reader: History, Culture, Politics* (Durham, N.C.: Duke University Press, 2014), 252–59; Select Committee on Haiti and Santo Domingo Congress, *Inquiry into Occupation and Administration of Haiti and Santo Domingo* (Washington, D.C.: United States Congress, 1921).

75. Renda, *Taking Haiti*, 32–33, 141–51, 158, 160–62; Schmidt, *Occupation*, 100–106; Dubois, *Haiti*, 235–36, 250–54, 259; Chochotte, "Twilight," 298.

76. John Houston Craige, *Cannibal Cousins* (New York: Minton, Balch, 1934), 124, quoted in Renda, *Taking Haiti*, 154, 163; Erica Caple James, *Democratic Insecurities: Violence, Trauma, and Intervention in Haiti* (Los Angeles: University of California Press, 2010), 54; Dubois, *Haiti*, 237; Calder, *Impact*, 124, 132; McPherson, *Invaded*, 186. The comments from the 1990s were expressed in oral histories collected by Richard Turits in 1992. A 1935 census of the Dominican Republic recorded 13 percent of the population as "white," 19 percent "black," and 68 percent "*mestizo*" (meaning mulatto here). Jean Price-Mars, *La República de Haití y la República Dominicana: Diversos aspectos de un problema histórico, geográfico y etnológico* (Madrid: Industrias Gráficas España, 1958), 181.

77. Tillman, *Dollar Diplomacy*, 162–64; Calder, *Impact*, 123–27, 135–36, 150–51, 166, 169, 284n46; Dubois, *Haiti*, chap. 6.

78. Calder, *Impact*, 175–76, 173, 246, 250; Tillman, *Dollar Diplomacy*, 151, 162–64.

79. Stephen Fuller and Graham Cosmas, *Marines in the Dominican Republic, 1916–1924* (Washington, D.C.: Marine Corps, 1974), 38–43; Calder, *Impact*, 51, 136, 140, 148, 150, 159–69, 171–81, 295n88; McPherson, *Invaded*, 48–49.

80. "Convention between the United States and the Dominican Republic to Replace the Convention of February 8, 1907, between the Two Governments Providing for the Assistance of the United States in the Collection and Application of the Customs Revenues of the Dominican Republic," *American Journal of International Law* 20, no. 1 (January 1926): 1–4; Calder, *Impact*, 63, 79–80, 115, 174–81, 204–50; Moya Pons, *Manual*, 444–45, 478, 520–21; Fuller and Cosmas, *Marines*, 40–45; Roorda, *Dictator Next Door*, 13–19; Frank Moya Pons, *The Dominican Republic: A National History*, 3rd ed. (Princeton, N.J.: Markus Wiener, 2010), 333.

81. Moya Pons, *Dominican Republic*, 335; Roorda, *Dictator Next Door*, 20.

82. Casey, *Empire's Guestworkers*, 89; Schmidt, *Occupation*, 86–87; Dubois, *Haiti*, 256–62, 269.

83. Plummer, *Haiti*, 118; Matthew J. Smith, *Red and Black in Haiti: Radicalism, Conflict, and Political Change, 1934–1957* (Chapel Hill: University of North Carolina Press, 2009), 9; Verna, *Haiti*, 60–62; Schmidt, *Occupation*, 87; Dubois, *Haiti*, 260–67.

84. Dubois, *Haiti*, 238, 265–67.

85. Calder, *Impact*, 55, 59, 63, 79–80; Roorda, *Dictator Next Door*, 18–19; Valentina Peguero, "Trujillo and the Military: Organization, Modernization and Control of the Dominican Armed Forces, 1916–1961" (Ph.D. diss., Columbia University, 1993), esp. 71, 122.

86. Tillman, *Dollar Diplomacy*, 96–98, 103, 158, 166; Valentina Peguero, *The Militarization of Culture in the Dominican Republic, from the Captains General to General Trujillo* (Lincoln: University of Nebraska Press, 2004), 36; Calder, *Impact*, 58; Robert Crassweller, *Trujillo: The Life and Times of a Caribbean Dictator* (New York: Macmillan, 1966), 42–44.

87. Unsigned letter to Major General John A. Lejeune, Commandant, U.S. Marine Corps, October 25, 1921, quoted in April Mayes, *The Mulatto Republic: Class, Race,*

and Dominican National Identity (Gainesville: University Press of Florida, 2014), 107–8; Mil. Gov. Samuel Robison to Lejeune, October 25, 1921, quoted in Calder, *Impact*, 55–59; Tillman, *Dollar Diplomacy*, 97–103.

88. Turits, *Foundations*, chap. 1; Tillman, *Dollar Diplomacy*, 2, 188–90, 205; Calder, *Impact*, 55–56.

89. Peguero, *Militarization of Culture*, 41; Michel Gobat, *Confronting the American Dream: Nicaragua under U.S. Imperial Rule* (Durham, N.C.: Duke University Press, 2005).

90. Calder, *Impact*, 49–53, 61–63, 79–80; McPherson, *Invaded*, 155, 188; Tillman, *Dollar Diplomacy*, esp. 93; Moya Pons, *Manual*, 480–81.

91. "El catastro nacional y un nuevo impuesto," *La Opinión*, January 29, 1929; *Censo agro-pecuario, 1940: Resumen nacional* (Ciudad Trujillo: Dirección General de Estadística Nacional, 1940), 4–5; Ayala, *American Sugar Kingdom*, 70.

92. Roorda, *Dictator Next Door*, 43, 45, 50.

93. Roorda, 51–57, 165–67.

94. Roorda, 58–59.

95. See, for instance, Joseph Cotton, Dept. of State, to Curtis, U.S. Legation, March 19, 1930, NARA, RG 59, 389.00/3355.

96. Pérez, *Cuba: Between*, 268–70.

97. Pérez, 266–75.

98. Frank Argote-Freyre, *Fulgencia Batista: From Revolutionary to Strongman* (New Brunswick, N.J.: Rutgers University Press, 2006), esp. 230–74.

99. "La alarmante amenaza de las factorías azucareras: La República Dominicana y Haití, antes dos estados soberanos, conviértense en dos colonias yankis," *La Información*, July 6, 1927; Rafael Vidal, "Las hipérboles de 'Patria,'" *Listín Diario*, September 2 and 3, 1926; Turits, *Foundations*, 77–89.

100. Franklin Frost to Sec. of State, no. 566, August 6, 1927, NARA, RG 59, 839.52; Turits, *Foundations*, chap. 3, esp. 88.

101. Turits, *Foundations*, chaps. 2–4, esp. 106–7, 215–16.

102. Turits, 232–36; Pedro San Miguel, *Los campesinos del Cibao: Economía de mercado y transformación agraria en la República Dominicana, 1880–1960* (San Juan: Editorial de la Universidad de Puerto Rico, 1997), 305–41; Walter Cordero, *Tendencias de la economía cafetalera dominicana, 1955–1972* (Santo Domingo: Editora de la Universidad Autónoma de Santo Domingo, 1975), 19, 73–109; Orlando Inoa, *Estado y campesinos al inicio de la Era de Trujillo* (Santo Domingo: Librería La Trinitaria, 1994), 204.

103. Turits, *Foundations*, esp. 5–7; Richard Lee Turits, "A World Destroyed, a Nation Imposed: The 1937 Haitian Massacre in the Dominican Republic," *Hispanic American Historical Review* 82, no. 3 (August 2002): 589–635.

104. Smith, *Red and Black*; Dubois, *Haiti*, 311–24, 324–49.

105. Marvin Chochotte, "Making Peasants Chèf: The *Tonton Makout* Militia and the Moral Politics of Terror in the Haitian Countryside during the Dictatorship of François Duvalier, 1957–1971," *Comparative Studies in Society and History* (forthcoming); Chochotte, "The History of Peasants"; Dubois, *Haiti*, 347.

106. James, *Democratic Insecurities*, 57–65; Michel-Rolph Trouillot, *Haiti, State against Nation: The Origins and Legacy of Duvalierism* (New York: Monthly Review Press, 1990), 166–69.

107. Chochotte, "Making Peasants Chèf"; Chochotte, "The History of Peasants"; Trouillot, *Haiti*, 189–91; Dubois, *Haiti*, 335–36.

108. Chochotte, "Making Peasants Chèf"; Chochotte, "The History of Peasants"; Trouillot, *Haiti*, 189–91.

109. Chochotte, "Making Peasants Chèf"; Chochotte, "The History of Peasants," 85–105; Greg Chamberlain, "Up by the Roots," *NACLA Report on the Americas* 21, no. 3 (1987): 16, quoted in Trouillot, *Haiti*, 189–91.

110. Turits, *Foundations*, chap. 8; Moya Pons, *Dominican Republic*, 373.

111. Bernardo Vega, "La Era de Trujillo, 1930–1961," in *Historia de la República Dominicana*, ed. Frank Moya Pons (Santo Domingo: Academia Dominicana de la Historia, 2010), 503; Moya Pons, *Dominican Republic*, 381–83.

112. Dubois, *Haiti*, 334–39.

Chapter Five

1. Nancy Stout, *One Day in December: Celia Sánchez and the Cuban Revolution* (New York: Monthly Review Press, 2013), 108, 157–58.

2. Lillian Guerra, *Heroes, Martyrs, and Political Messiahs in Revolutionary Cuba, 1946–1958* (New Haven, Conn.: Yale University Press, 2018), 123, 127; Hugh Thomas, *Cuba, or, The Pursuit of Freedom*, updated ed. (New York: Da Capo Press, 1998), 824–28, 835, 838, 1560–61; Louis A. Pérez Jr., *Cuba: Between Reform and Revolution*, 4th ed. (New York: Oxford University Press, 2011), 221; Carlos Franqui, ed., *Diary of the Cuban Revolution*, trans. Georgette Felix, Elaine Kerrigan, Phyliss Freeman, Hardie St. Martin (New York: Viking, 1980), 85; Tad Szulc, *Fidel: A Critical Portrait* (New York: Avon Books, 1986), 257, 262–81; Fidel Castro, *History Will Absolve Me* (Secaucus, N.J.: Citadel Press, 1984), 77; Dirk Kruijt, *Cuba and Revolutionary Latin America: An Oral History* (London: Zed Books, 2017), 49.

3. Lorraine Bayard de Volo, *Women and the Cuban Insurrection: How Gender Shaped Castro's Victory* (Cambridge: Cambridge University Press, 2018), 50.

4. Fidel Castro, "This Is Democracy," May 1, 1960, in Fidel Castro, *Our Power Is That of the Working People: Building Socialism in Cuba* (New York: Pathfinder, 1983), 30–33. See also chapter 6.

5. Szulc, *Fidel*, 96–104; Luis Martínez-Fernández, *Revolutionary Cuba: A History* (Gainesville: University Press of Florida, 2015), 22; Thomas, *Cuba*, 803–10.

6. Szulc, *Fidel*, 155–57; Robert D. Crassweller, *Trujillo: The Life and Times of a Caribbean Dictator* (New York: Macmillan, 1966), 214–16, 236–39; Thomas, *Cuba*, 803–10. See also Guerra, *Heroes*, 46–49.

7. Marifeli Pérez-Stable, *The Cuban Revolution: Origins, Course and Legacy*, 3rd ed. (New York: Oxford University Press, 2012), 50–52; Guerra, *Heroes*, 27, 42–44, 63–73, 74, 140–41; Thomas, *Cuba*, 741–43; Memorandum of a Conference, Dept. of State, December 31, 1958, U.S. Department of State, *Foreign Relations*

of the United States (FRUS), 1958–1960, vol. 6, *Cuba*, ed. John P. Glennon (Washington, D.C.: U.S. Government Printing Office, 1991), doc. no. 201; Domínguez, *Cuba*, 113.

8. Communism was no longer "the immediate historical task of our party," stressed one Cuban Communist leader in 1944, but rather "economic progress" and "social security." Fitting this reformist orientation, the Communist party had been rechristened the Popular Socialist Party. The party had formerly been named the Communist Revolutionary Union and, prior to that, the Cuban Communist Party. Thomas, *Cuba*, 733; Guerra, *Heroes*, 50–55, 76; Szulc, *Fidel*, 147–51; Frank Argote-Freyre, *Fulgencio Batista: From Revolutionary to Strongman* (New Brunswick, N.J.: Rutgers University Press, 2006), 230–74; Mervyn J. Bain, *From Lenin to Castro, 1917–1959* (New York: Lexington Books, 2013), 8–9, 52–53; Steve Cushion, *A Hidden History of the Cuban Revolution: How the Working Class Shaped the Guerrillas' Victory* (New York: Monthly Review Press, 2016), 21; Jorge I. Domínguez, *Cuba: Order and Revolution* (Cambridge, Mass.: Harvard University Press, 1978), 113.

9. Guerra, *Heroes*, 74–121; "Cuba: 'Dictator with the People,'" *Time*, April 21, 1952, 38–42; Thomas, *Cuba*, 785–802; Franqui, *Diary*, 44; Pérez, *Cuba*, 221; Michelle Chase, *Revolution within the Revolution: Women and Gender Politics in Cuba, 1952–1962* (Chapel Hill: University of North Carolina Press, 2015), 21; Stout, *One Day*, 32–33.

10. Guerra, *Heroes*, 92, 124, 134–35, 140–41; Aviva Chomsky, *A History of the Cuban Revolution*, 2nd ed. (Hoboken, N.J.: John Wiley and Sons, 2015), 37; Pérez-Stable, *Cuban Revolution*, 47–49; Julia Sweig, *Inside the Cuban Revolution: Fidel Castro and the Urban Underground* (Cambridge, Mass.: Harvard University Press, 2002), 124; Thomas, *Cuba*, 838–42; Pérez, *Cuba*, 221, 236–59; Szulc, *Fidel*, 274.

11. Fidel Castro, *La historia me absolverá: Autodefensa de Fidel Castro ante el Tribunal de Urgencia de Santiago de Cuba el 16 de Octubre de 1953* (Havana: Imprenta Nacional de Cuba, 1961), 50–68, 121–26; Castro, *History Will Absolve Me*, 7–13; Thomas, *Cuba*, 830, 847–48; Guerra, *Heroes*, 136–37, 160–61.

12. Castro, *La historia me absolverá*, 50, 56; Thomas, *Cuba*, 831.

13. Thomas, *Cuba*, 831; Pérez, *Cuba*, 245; Franqui, *Diary*, 78, 80, 85; Castro, *La historia me absolverá*, 50–59.

14. Castro, *La historia me absolverá*, 55–56.

15. Castro, *La historia me absolverá*, 55–56, 59–60.

16. Miguel Centeno, lecture, Princeton University, February 27, 2003; Castro, *La historia me absolverá*, 129.

17. Franqui, *Diary*, 65–90, esp. 67 and 76; Castro, *La historia me absolverá*, 49–50; José Martí, *Versos sencillos. Estudio de Gabriela Mistral* (Havana: Secretaría de Educación, 1939), 45.

18. Richard Turits, "Trade, Debt, and the Cuban Economy," *World Development* 15, no. 1 (January 1987): 163–80; Pérez, *Cuba*, 224–30; Lars Schoultz, *That Infernal Little Cuban Republic: The United States and the Cuban Revolution* (Chapel Hill: University of North Carolina Press, 2009), 52–54; Jorge G. Castañeda, *Compañero: The Life and Death of Che Guevara* (New York: Knopf, 1997), 79–80; Carmelo Mesa-Lago, *Market, Socialist, and Mixed Economies: Comparative Policy and Performance,*

Chile, Cuba, and Costa Rica (Baltimore: Johns Hopkins University Press, 2000), 172, 193, 385.

19. Joanna Swanger, "Lands of Rebellion: Oriente and Escambray Encountering Cuban State Formation, 1934–1974" (Ph.D. diss., University of Texas at Austin, 1999), 149–223; Thomas, *Cuba*, 905–8; Bert Useem, "Peasant Involvement in the Cuban Revolution," *Journal of Peasant Studies* 5, no. 1 (October 1977): 99–111.

20. Louis A. Pérez, *On Becoming Cuban: Identity, Nationality, and Culture* (Chapel Hill: University of North Carolina Press, 1999), 166–69, esp. 167.

21. Dennis Merrill, *Negotiating Paradise: U.S. Tourism and Empire in Twentieth-Century Latin America* (Chapel Hill: University of North Carolina Press, 2009), 103–38; Christine Skwiot, *The Purposes of Paradise: U.S. Tourism and Empire in Cuba and Hawai'i* (Philadelphia: University of Pennsylvania Press, 2010), 146–47, 155; Peter Moruzzi, *Havana before Castro: When Cuba Was a Tropical Playground* (Salt Lake City: Gibbs Smith, 2008), 113, 124, 170–81; Rosalie Schwartz, *Pleasure Island: Tourism and Temptation in Cuba* (Lincoln: University of Nebraska Press, 1997), 125; Jon Lee Anderson, *Che Guevara: A Revolutionary Life* (New York: Grove, 1997), 377; Graham Greene, *Ways of Escape* (New York: Simon and Schuster, 1980), 206–7; Denis Smyth, "*Our Man in Havana*, Their Man in Madrid: Literary Invention in Espionage Fact and Fiction," *Intelligence and National Security* 5, no. 4 (1990): 118.

22. Richard Turits and Laura Gotkowitz, "Socialist Morality: Sexual Preference, Family, and State Intervention in Cuba," *Socialism and Democracy* 6 (1988): 7–29; Lourdes Arguelles and Ruby Rich, "Homosexuality, Homophobia, and Revolution: Notes toward an Understanding of the Cuban Lesbian and Gay Male Experience, Part I," *Signs* 9, no. 4 (Summer 1984): 686–87; Merrill, *Negotiating Paradise*, 128–38; Tomás Fernández Robaina, *Recuerdos secretos de dos mujeres públicas* (Havana: Editorial Letras Cubanas, 1983); Oscar Lewis, Ruth M. Lewis, and Susan M. Rigdon, *Four Women* (Urbana: University of Illinois Press, 1977); Moruzzi, *Havana before Castro*, esp. 124–37; Joseph L. Scarpaci, Mario Coyula, and Roberto Segre, *Havana: Two Faces of the Antillean Metropolis* (Chapel Hill: University of North Carolina Press, 2002), 114; Pérez, *Becoming Cuban*, 468–69, 472–73, 566n51, and 566n52; Thomas, *Cuba*, 972.

23. Interview with Retamar in the film *Cuba: In the Shadow of Doubt* (Jim Burroughs, 1986), transcription provided by Dan Weltsch of Alexander Street Press/Filmakers Library and Professor Peter Winn, one of the two writers of the film's narration; Thomas, *Cuba*, 954; Sweig, *Inside*, 146.

24. Thomas, *Cuba*, 852–62, 874; Schoultz, *Infernal*, 61; Pérez, *Cuba*, 221–22.

25. Thomas, *Cuba*, 863–69, 868n19, 913; Anderson, *Che*, 169; Jules Dubois, *Fidel Castro: Rebel—Liberator or Dictator?* (Indianapolis: Bobbs-Merrill, 1959), 172; Bayard de Volo, *Women*, 7–9, 38–39; Stout, *One Day*, 52; Guerra, *Heroes*, 182–84.

26. Thomas, *Cuba*, 876; Anderson, *Che*, 129.

27. Anderson, *Che*, 3–20, 49–52, 128–74; Thomas, *Cuba*, 878–79; Castañeda, *Compañero*, chap. 3; Paul Jaime Dosal, *Comandante Che: Guerrilla Soldier, Commander, and Strategist, 1956–1967* (University Park: Pennsylvania State University Press, 2003), chap. 2.

28. Thomas, *Cuba*, 879; Dosal, *Comandante Che*, 36, 39; Piero Gleijeses, *Shattered Hope: The Guatemalan Revolution and the United States, 1944–1954* (Princeton, N.J.: Princeton University Press, 1991), 150–64; Castañeda, *Compañero*, 63–64, 71–73; Anderson, *Che*, 126; Stephen C. Schlesinger and Stephen Kinzer, *Bitter Fruit: The Story of the American Coup in Guatemala* (Cambridge, Mass.: Harvard University Press, 1999).

29. Gleijeses, *Shattered Hope*, 306–39, 372, 391n12; Stephen Kinzer, *Overthrow: America's Century of Regime Change from Hawaii to Iraq*, 1st ed. (New York: Times Books, 2006), 141–42; Castañeda, *Compañero*, 71–73; Anderson, *Che*, 165–166.

30. Gleijeses, *Shattered Hope*, 306–8, 320–21, 326–28, 338–39, 372, 391n12.

31. Dosal, *Comandante Che*, 42; Gleijeses, *Shattered Hope*, 391n12; Castañeda, *Compañero*, 70.

32. Anderson, *Che*, 162–75; Castañeda, *Compañero*, 84–85; Franqui, *Diary*, 269; Dosal, *Comandante Che*, 64.

33. John J. Dwyer, *The Agrarian Dispute: The Expropriation of American-Owned Rural Land in Postrevolutionary Mexico* (Durham, N.C.: Duke University Press, 2008), 164–66, 182–88. For comparative purposes, see Kevin Young, *Blood of the Earth: Resource Nationalism, Revolution, and Empire in Bolivia* (Austin: University of Texas Press, 2017).

34. Szulc, *Fidel*, 330–32, 360–63.

35. Franqui expressed concerns in 1957 about Castro's potential revolutionary authoritarianism. Franqui, *Diary*, 96, 98, 136, 200–201.

36. Thomas, *Cuba*, 876; Dosal, *Comandante Che*, 8, 49.

37. Thomas, *Cuba*, 876; Dosal, *Comandante Che*, 8, 49; Szulc, *Fidel*, 325–26.

38. Szulc, *Fidel*, 325–27; Dosal, *Comandante Che*, 49–57.

39. Thomas, *Cuba*, 894; Anderson, *Che*, 204, 220; Castañeda, *Compañero*, 98–99; Dosal, *Comandante Che*, 73.

40. Stout, *One Day*, 40–45, 54–63, 97–101; Bayard de Volo, *Women*, 100, 111n89.

41. Franqui, *Diary*, 127–29; Szulc, *Fidel*, 379, 383, 386, 389, 416; Thomas, *Cuba*, 897, 900–903, 908; Bayard de Volo, *Women*, 80; Stout, *One Day*, 57–59, 64–67.

42. Dosal, *Comandante Che*, 6–10; Anderson, *Che*, 212–13, 216; Castañeda, *Compañero*, 99.

43. Stout, *One Day*, 117–25; Franqui, *Diary*, 127–29.

44. Domínguez, *Cuba*, 423–32, 435–36; Swanger, "Lands of Rebellion," 149–223; Useem, "Peasant Involvement," 105–6; Szulc, *Fidel*, 379, 383, 386, 389, 416; Thomas, *Cuba*, 897, 900–908; Ramón Leocadio Bonachea Hernández and Marta San Martín, *The Cuban Insurrection, 1952–1959* (New Brunswick, N.J.: Transaction Books, 1974), 89.

45. Domínguez, *Cuba*, 423–36; Swanger, "Lands of Rebellion," 149–223; Useem, "Peasant Involvement," 105–6.

46. Swanger, "Lands of Rebellion," chaps. 3 and 5; Domínguez, *Cuba*, 424–31, 437; Useem, "Peasant Involvement"; Thomas, *Cuba*, 905–8, 920, 1122.

47. Szulc, *Fidel*, 380–90, 393, 404; Thomas, *Cuba*, 906, 914–15, 924, 936–37; Dosal, *Comandante Che*, 103–4; Domínguez, *Cuba*, 437–38.

48. Szulc, *Fidel*, 394–95; Dosal, *Comandante Che*, 74–78; Thomas, *Cuba*, 913–14.

49. Herbert L. Matthews, "Cuban Rebel Is Visited in Hideout: Castro Is Still Alive and Still Fighting in Mountains," *New York Times*, February 24, 1951, 1; Stout, *One Day*, 148–49; Thomas, *Cuba*, 911–22.

50. Matthews, "Cuban Rebel," 1, 34; Thomas, *Cuba*, 911–22. See also Hart Philips, "Cubans Debating Rebel Interview: Public Tends to Accept Story While Regime Continues to Discount It," *New York Times*, March 1, 1957, 8.

51. "Rebel Urges U.S. Stop Arming Cuba," *New York Times*, May 20, 1957, 8; Thomas, *Cuba*, 920, 924, 938; Szulc, *Fidel*, 421; Kruijt, *Cuba*, 48–51.

52. Stout, *One Day*, 32, 182–83; Thomas, *Cuba*, 936; Szulc, *Fidel*, 419–20; Kruijt, *Cuba*, 220n2; Bayard de Volo, *Women*, 24–29; "Rebel Urges U.S. Stop Arming Cuba," *New York Times*, May 20, 1957, 8.

53. Herbert L. Matthews, "Castro Rebels Gain in Face of Offensive by the Cuban Army," *New York Times*, June 9, 1957, 1, 13; Dosal, *Comandante Che*, 93; Thomas, *Cuba*, 938–40.

54. Matthews, "Castro Rebels Gain," 1, 13; Thomas, *Cuba*, 923–24, 935–36; Dosal, *Comandante Che*, 78–93; Pérez, *Cuba*, 222–23; Domínguez, *Cuba*, 437.

55. Dubois, *Fidel Castro*, 163; Jorge Domínguez, "The Batista Regime in Cuba," in *Sultanistic Regimes*, ed. H. E. Chehabi and Juan J. Linz (Baltimore: Johns Hopkins University Press, 1998), 127–28; Chase, *Revolution within the Revolution*, 20, 81–82; Bayard de Volo, *Women*, 149–50.

56. Bayard de Volo, *Women*, 34, 114–34, 139n87, 152–56; Franqui, *Diary*, 443–44.

57. Thomas, *Cuba*, 909–12, 917–18, 925.

58. Echeverría mistakenly announced Batista's execution on the radio and was subsequently shot by police. Bonachea Hernández and San Martín, *Cuban Insurrection*, 51–52; Thomas, *Cuba*, 925–33; Dubois, *Fidel Castro*, 162; Sweig, *Inside*, 19, 79, 97; Guerra, *Heroes*, 168, 172, 180, 186, 221–22.

59. Thomas, *Cuba*, 926, 932–33, 942–46, 956–60; Lillian Guerra, *Visions of Power in Cuba: Revolution, Redemption, and Resistance, 1959–1971* (Chapel Hill: University of North Carolina Press, 2012), 53; Sweig, *Inside*, 26; Dubois, *Fidel Castro*, 184–87; *La solución que conviene a Cuba* (Havana: Partido Social Popular, 1958), quoted in Samuel Farber, *The Origins of the Cuban Revolution Reconsidered* (Chapel Hill: University of North Carolina Press, 2006), 155–57; Guerra, *Heroes*, 234; Bain, *From Lenin to Castro*, 61.

60. Herbert L. Matthews, "Situation in Cuba Found Worsening; Batista Foes Gain," *New York Times*, June 16, 1957; Thomas, *Cuba*, 942–43, 946, 961–65, 1149.

61. Leland L. Johnson, "U.S. Business Interests in Cuba and the Rise of Castro," *World Politics* 17, no. 3 (April 1965): 442–43, 453; Schoultz, *Infernal*, 86; John Foran, "Theorizing the Cuban Revolution," *Latin American Perspectives* 36, no. 2 (March 2009): 16–30, 18.

62. Sweig, *Inside*, 78; Ernesto Guevara to René Ramos Latour, December 14, 1957, in Franqui, *Diary*, 268–70.

63. Dubois, *Fidel Castro*, 170; Thomas, *Cuba*, 954.

64. Guevara to Ramos Latour, December 14, 1957, in Franqui, *Diary*, 268–70.

65. Sweig, *Inside*, 46.

66. Thomas, *Cuba*, 969, 972, 975, 1044, 1044n21; Dosal, *Comandante Che*, 98; Sweig, *Inside*, 78, 100; Guerra, *Visions*, 43.

67. Thomas, *Cuba*, 951, 965, 973–74, 994; Sweig, *Inside*, 78; Neill Macaulay, "The Cuban Rebel Army: A Numerical Survey," *Hispanic American Historical Review* 58, no. 2 (May 1978): 289; Dosal, *Comandante Che*, 91, 104–13, 131; Franqui, *Diary*, 284–85; Bayard de Volo, *Women*, 8; Kruijt, *Cuba*, 51.

68. Thomas, *Cuba*, 951, 973–74; Szulc, *Fidel*, 433–35; Bayard de Volo, *Women*, 165–76; Stout, *One Day*, 60–61; Mary-Alice Waters, ed., *Marianas in Combat: Teté Puebla, the Mariana Grajales Women's Platoon in Cuba's Revolutionary War, 1956–1958* (New York: Pathfinder, 2003), 30; Franqui, *Diary*, 232–33; Guerra, *Heroes*, 253–59.

69. Yale University's Manuscripts and Archives collection contains a somber photograph of a small-town pharmacist, Olga Suárez, prior to her execution taken by a U.S. journalist living with the rebels. Franqui, *Diary*, 233–35; Guerra, *Heroes*, 245, 253–59.

70. Thomas, *Cuba*, 951, 973–74; Szulc, *Fidel*, 433–35; Franqui, *Diary*, 232–33.

71. Bayard de Volo, *Women*, 102, 189, 202–4, 210–28; Guerra, *Heroes*, 255.

72. Carlos Franqui, ed., *Diario de la revolución cubana* (Paris: Ruedo Ibérico, 1976), 389, 719–20; Thomas, *Cuba*, 992–95; Bonachea Hernández and San Martín, *Cuban Insurrection*, 190, 267, 271–73, 276; Szulc, *Fidel*, 434; Sweig, *Inside*, 105; Domínguez, *Cuba*, 437; Macaulay, "The Cuban Rebel Army," 289.

73. Guerra, *Heroes*, 225–26, 235; Sweig, *Inside*, 104–8, 112; Szulc, *Fidel*, 439; Thomas, *Cuba*, 978, 983.

74. Thomas, *Cuba*, 980–81; Sweig, *Inside*, 111–12; Guerra, *Heroes*, 280.

75. Herbert L. Matthews, "Castro Rebels Gain in Face of Offensive by the Cuban Army," *New York Times*, June 9, 1957, 1, 13; Szulc, *Fidel*, 429, 438–39, 446–49; Thomas G. Paterson, *Contesting Castro: The United States and the Triumph of the Cuban Revolution* (New York: Oxford University Press, 1994), 145; Thomas, *Cuba*, 939–47, 957–60, 967, 986, 990–91, 995, 1009; Schoultz, *Infernal*, 66–67, 75, 85; Sweig, *Inside*, 42, 47; Earl Smith, *The Fourth Floor: An Account of the Castro Communist Revolution* (New York: Random House, 1962), 100–101; Dosal, *Comandante Che*, 112; Domínguez, "Batista Regime," 129–30.

76. Sweig, *Inside*, 108, 131–53, 176; Dosal, *Comandante Che*, 117–18; Thomas, *Cuba*, 988–91; Domínguez, *Cuba*, 121–22; Fidel Castro to Celia Sánchez, April 16, 1958, in Franqui, *Diary*, 300–302.

77. Dosal, *Comandante Che*, 131–32; Szulc, *Fidel*, 445–46; Thomas, *Cuba*, 997; Macaulay, "Cuban Rebel Army," 285.

78. Franqui, *Diario*, 720; Eulogio A. Cantillo, "Plan de operaciones," July 26, 1958, in Ernesto Guevara, *Che* (Havana: Instituto del Libro, Editorial de Ciencias Sociales, 1969), 254–57, 255; Dosal, *Comandante Che*, 134; Macaulay, "Cuban Rebel Army," 286–89; Thomas, *Cuba*, 992–97; Szulc, *Fidel*, 445, 448.

79. Dosal, *Comandante Che*, 139–42; Thomas, *Cuba*, 997–1000; Szulc, *Fidel*, 447–48; Domínguez, "Batista Regime," 130; Louis A. Pérez Jr., *Army Politics in Cuba, 1898–1958* (Pittsburgh: University of Pittsburgh Press, 1976), 154–56.

80. Eulogio A. Cantillo, "Plan de operaciones," July 26, 1958, in *Che*, 255; Thomas, *Cuba*, 998-1000; Pérez, *Army Politics*, 156; Domínguez, *Cuba*, 126; Dosal, *Comandante Che*, 140-45; Szulc, *Fidel*, 447-48; Domínguez, "Batista Regime," 130; Lowry Nelson, *Rural Cuba* (New York: Octagon Books, 1970), 56.

81. Interview with Mariano Lesme in *Cuba: In the Shadow of Doubt*; Szulc, *Fidel*, 448; Sweig, *Inside*, 164, 173; Thomas, *Cuba*, 998; Bonachea Hernández and San Martín, *Cuban Insurrection*, 251-62, 272-73; Che Guevara, "Interview in the Escambray Mountains," in Ernesto Guevara, *Che: Selected Works of Ernesto Guevara*, ed. Rolando B. Bonachea and Nelson Valdés (Cambridge: MIT Press, 1969), 366-67; Domínguez, "Batista Regime," 130.

82. Bonachea Hernández and San Martín, *Cuban Insurrection*, 272-73; Sweig, *Inside*, 172-74, 177.

83. Thomas, *Cuba*, 842, 922-23, 1002-13; Chomsky, *History*, 37, 41; Sweig, *Inside*, 124-25; Anderson, *Che*, 296-98; Bonachea Hernández and San Martín, *Cuban Insurrection*, 264-65; Pérez-Stable, *Cuban Revolution*, 40; Franqui, *Diario*, 728.

84. Szulc, *Fidel*, 455-56; Thomas, *Cuba*, 978-80, 1005, 1013; Bonachea Hernández and San Martín, *Cuban Insurrection*, 174-87, 266-90, 383; Dosal, *Comandante Che*, 147; John Dorschner and Roberto Fabricio, *The Winds of December* (New York: Coward, McCann and Geoghegan, 1980), 177; Sweig, *Inside*, 106, 130; Macaulay, "Cuban Rebel Army," 291. On Camilo Cienfuegos, the child of early twentieth-century Spanish immigrants, see Carlos Franqui, *Camilo Cienfuegos* (Barcelona: Seix Barral, 2001), esp. 60-61, 75-76.

85. Dosal, *Comandante Che*, 146-52; Bonachea Hernández and San Martín, *Cuban Insurrection*, 266, 268-77; Thomas, *Cuba*, 1008-9, 1021; Castañeda, *Compañero*, 119.

86. Castañeda, *Compañero*, 123-24; Thomas, *Cuba*, 1010-11, 1013.

87. Ernesto Guevara, "Interview in the Escambray Mountains," in Guevara, *Che*, 367.

88. Bonachea Hernández and San Martín, *Cuban Insurrection*, 277-78; Thomas, *Cuba*, 868, 1012.

89. Memorandum of a Conference, Dept. of State, December 31, 1958, *FRUS, 1958-1960*, doc. no. 201; Pérez, *Cuba*, 235; Bonachea Hernández and San Martín, *Cuban Insurrection*, 288-89; Paterson, *Contesting Castro*, chaps. 18 and 19, esp. 171, 195-99, 213, 221; Thomas, *Cuba*, 1014-17, 1019-21; Jules R. Benjamin, *The United States and the Origins of the Cuban Revolution: An Empire of Liberty in an Age of National Liberation* (Princeton, N.J.: Princeton University Press, 1990), 155-66.

90. "We regard Cuba as an issue of domestic politics," Arthur Schlesinger, who was President John Kennedy's adviser during the early 1960s, put it starkly even in 1996. James G. Blight and Peter Kornbluh, *Politics of Illusion: The Bay of Pigs Invasion Reexamined* (Boulder, Colo.: Lynne Rienner, 1998), 22, 55, 72, 118; Schoultz, *Infernal*, 18, 86, 122; Louis A. Pérez, *The War of 1898: The United States and Cuba in History and Historiography* (Chapel Hill: University of North Carolina Press, 1998), 5; Susan Eckstein, "The Cuban Revolution in Comparative Perspective," in *Constructing Culture and Power in Latin America*, ed. Daniel H. Levine (Ann Arbor: University of Michigan Press, 1993), 433.

91. Quoted in Samuel Farber, "The Cuban Communists in the Early Stages of the Cuban Revolution: Revolutionaries or Reformists?" *Latin American Research Review* 18, no. 1 (1983): 59–83, 61.

92. Blight and Kornbluh, *Politics of Illusion*, 42.

93. Hugh Thomas, "Cuba: The United States and Batista, 1952–58," *World Affairs* 149, no. 4 (Spring 1987): 169–75, 171, 173; Sweig, *Inside*, 178–79; Thomas, *Cuba*, 995; Paterson, *Contesting Castro*, chaps. 18 and 19.

94. S. Everett Gleason, Memorandum of Discussion at the 392nd Meeting of the National Security Council, December 23, 1958, U.S. Department of State, *FRUS, 1958–1960*, doc. no. 188; Benjamin, *Origins*, 164–65.

95. Franqui, *Diary*, 469–71; Pérez, *Army Politics*, 172; Paterson, *Contesting Castro*, 216–19; Thomas, *Cuba*, 1021–23. On the 1933 popular uprising and joint civil-military coup, see chapter 4.

96. Dosal, *Comandante Che*, 159–60; Bonachea Hernández and San Martín, *Cuban Insurrection*, 296–301; Thomas, *Cuba*, 1021–23; Crassweller, *Trujillo*, 344–48; Martínez-Fernández, *Revolutionary Cuba*, 41–42.

97. Crassweller, *Trujillo*, 344–48; Richard Lee Turits, *Foundations of Despotism: Peasants, the Trujillo Regime, and Modernity in Dominican History* (Stanford, Calif.: Stanford University Press, 2003), 251–52, 260; Martínez-Fernández, *Revolutionary Cuba*, 42.

98. Thomas, *Cuba*, 1028; Bonachea Hernández and San Martín, *Cuban Insurrection*, 319–20; Schoultz, *Infernal*, 82.

99. Thomas, *Cuba*, 1028–30, 1099; Franqui, *Diary*, 504; Bonachea Hernández and San Martín, *Cuban Insurrection*, 322–25; Paterson, *Contesting Castro*, 230; Dosal, *Comandante Che*, 162.

100. Dosal, *Comandante Che*, 162.

Chapter Six

1. Castro, quoted in Carlos Franqui, ed., *Diario de la revolución cubana* (Paris: Ruedo Ibérico, 1976), 695; Carlos Franqui, ed., *Diary of the Cuban Revolution*, trans. Georgette Felix, Elaine Kerrigan, Phyliss Freeman, Hardie St. Martin (New York: Viking, 1980), 489; Herbert L. Matthews, "Castro Aims Reflect Character of Cubans. He Is a Creature of His Country and He Is Followed as a Hero," *New York Times*, January 18, 1959.

2. Franqui, *Diario*, 695.

3. Louis A. Pérez, *Cuba: Between Reform and Revolution*, 4th ed. (New York: Oxford University Press, 2006), 241.

4. Pérez, *Cuba*, 238, 241; Hugh Thomas, *Cuba, or, The Pursuit of Freedom*, updated ed. (New York: Da Capo Press, 1998), 1193, 1353.

5. Pérez, *Cuba*, 241; Thomas, *Cuba*, 849–50, 1196.

6. Pérez, *Cuba*, 241; Thomas, *Cuba*, 1108–9; Jorge I. Domínguez, *Cuba: Order and Revolution* (Cambridge, Mass.: Harvard University Press, 1978), 440–41.

7. Devyn Spence Benson, "Cuba Calls: African American Tourism, Race, and the Cuban Revolution, 1959–61," *Hispanic American Historical Review* 93, no. 2 (May 2013):

239–71, 239, 244–45, 245n17; Alejandro de la Fuente, *A Nation for All: Race, Inequality, and Politics in Twentieth-Century Cuba* (Chapel Hill: University of North Carolina Press, 2001), 260–76, 307–8; on demands for racial equality during the Cuban War of Independence, see Ada Ferrer, *Insurgent Cuba: Race, Nation and Revolution* (Chapel Hill: University of North Carolina Press, 1999).

8. Pérez, *Cuba*, 241–42.

9. Thomas, *Cuba*, 1030, 1065–69, 1075; Julia Sweig, *Inside the Cuban Revolution: Fidel Castro and the Urban Underground* (Cambridge, Mass.: Harvard University Press, 2002), 180–82; Franqui, *Diary*, 503; Jules R. Benjamin, *The United States and the Origins of the Cuban Revolution: An Empire of Liberty in an Age of National Liberation* (Princeton, N.J.: Princeton University Press, 1990), 165–66; Pérez, *Cuba*, 237; Thomas G. Paterson, *Contesting Castro: The United States and the Triumph of the Cuban Revolution* (New York: Oxford University Press, 1994), 232–33; Jon Lee Anderson, *Che Guevara: A Revolutionary Life* (New York: Grove Press, 1997), 383.

10. Matthews, "Castro Aims"; comments by Prof. Alfred Stephan and Dr. Wayne Smith and scenes reproduced in *Cuba: In the Shadow of Doubt* (Jim Burroughs, 1986); Thomas, *Cuba*, 1030–34, 1065, 1087, 1193, 1195; Pérez, *Cuba*, 238–42; Sweig, *Inside*, 179–81; Ramón Leocadio Bonachea Hernández and Marta San Martín, *The Cuban Insurrection, 1952–1959* (New Brunswick, N.J.: Transaction Books, 1974), *Cuban Insurrection*, 328–30; Paterson, *Contesting Castro*, 233; Benjamin, *Origins*, 165–66; Anderson, *Che*, 383.

11. Luis Martínez-Fernández, *Revolutionary Cuba: A History* (Gainesville: University Press of Florida, 2015), 52; Thomas, *Cuba*, 1030, 1065–69, 1075, 1214.

12. Thomas, *Cuba*, 785–800, 1197; Domínguez, *Cuba*, 110–13; Pérez, *Cuba*, 244; Lars Schoultz, *That Infernal Little Cuban Republic: The United States and the Cuban Revolution* (Chapel Hill: University of North Carolina Press, 2009), 88; Lillian Guerra, *Heroes, Martyrs, and Political Messiahs in Revolutionary Cuba, 1946–1958* (New Haven, Conn.: Yale University Press, 2018), 27, 42–44, 63–73, 74, 140–41.

13. Louis A. Pérez, *Army Politics in Cuba, 1898–1958* (Pittsburgh: University of Pittsburgh Press, 1976), 165; Thomas, *Cuba*, 1071–73.

14. Anderson, *Che*, 384–89, 392; Thomas, *Cuba*, 1044, 1072–75, 1202–03; Michelle Chase, "The Trials: Violence and Justice in the Aftermath of the Cuban Revolution," in *A Century of Revolution: Insurgent and Counterinsurgent Violence during Latin America's Long Cold War*, ed. Greg Grandin and Gilbert M. Joseph (Durham, N.C.: Duke University Press, 2010), 163–98; Schoultz, *Infernal*, 87, 594n18; William M. LeoGrande and Peter Kornbluh, *Back Channel: The Hidden History of Negotiations between Washington and Havana* (Chapel Hill: University of North Carolina Press, 2016), 12; Martínez-Fernández, *Revolutionary Cuba*, 50, 61.

15. R. Hart Phillips, "Reds' Alleged Role in Castro's Regime Alarming Havana," *New York Times*, April 22, 1959, 1, 4; Pérez, *Cuba*, 242–44; Thomas, *Cuba*, 1200–1201, 1206, 1228; Martínez-Fernández, *Revolutionary Cuba*, 52, 62–64; Noel Maurer, *The Empire Trap: The Rise and Fall of U.S. Intervention to Protect American Property Overseas, 1893–2013* (Princeton, N.J.: Princeton University Press, 2013), 320; Lillian Guerra, *Heroes*, 285.

16. De la Fuente, *Nation for All*, 260–79; Lillian Guerra, *Visions of Power in Cuba: Revolution, Redemption, and Resistance, 1959–1971* (Chapel Hill: University of North Carolina Press, 2012), 49–54; *Constitución de la República de Cuba* (Havana: Compañía Editora de Libros y Folletos O'Reilly, 1940), 5; Pérez, *Cuba*, 243; Oscar Lewis, Ruth M. Lewis, and Susan M. Rigdon, *Four Women* (Urbana: University of Illinois Press, 1977), 254.

17. De la Fuente, *Nation for All*, 268–69, 279, 300–308; Devyn Spence Benson, *Antiracism in Cuba: The Unfinished Revolution* (Chapel Hill: University of North Carolina Press, 2016), 94, 126; Pérez, *Cuba*, 243; Guerra, *Visions*, 54–56; Guerra, *Hereos*, 241.

18. De la Fuente, *Nation for All*, 264–78; Benson, *Antiracism in Cuba*, 125–31; Guerra, *Visions*, 54–56; Pedro Pérez Sarduy and Jean Stubbs, *AfroCuba: An Anthology of Cuban Writings on Race, Politics and Culture* (Melbourne: Ocean Press, 1993), 9.

19. De la Fuente, *Nation for All*, 279–96, 307–16, 322–29; Benson, "Cuba Calls," 249; Benson, *Antiracism in Cuba*, 23, 92–101, 133–34.

20. E. W. Kenworthy, "U.S. Warns Cuba on Land Reform," *New York Times*, June 11, 1959; "Primera Ley de Reforma Agraria," *Calibán: Revista cubana de pensamiento e historia*, June 2009, 142–61; Pérez, *Cuba*, 245; Thomas, *Cuba*, 1215–17, 1216, 1221, 1223, 1229; Schoultz, *Infernal*, 95, 597n59; Martínez-Fernández, *Revolutionary Cuba*, 53. On Puerto Rico, see Fernando Picó, *History of Puerto Rico: A Panorama of Its People* (Princeton, N.J.: Markus Wiener, 2006), 242, 253–55; Francisco Scarano, *Puerto Rico: Cinco siglos de historia* (San Juan: McGraw-Hill, 1993), 584–93, 670–83, 716–19; Ismael García Colón, *Land Reform in Puerto Rico: Modernizing the Colonial State, 1941–1969* (Gainesville: University Press of Florida, 2009), 50.

21. Articles 17–18, 22, "Primera Ley de Reforma Agraria."

22. "Primera Ley de Reforma Agraria," 142–61; Thomas, *Cuba*, 1216; Domínguez, *Cuba*, 423–24, 432, 438; Rebecca Scott, *Slave Emancipation in Cuba: The Transition to Free Labor, 1860–1899* (Princeton, N.J.: Princeton University Press, 1985), 208–12; Fe Iglesias, *Del ingenio al central* (Havana: Editorial de Ciencias Sociales, 1999), 99.

23. Thomas, *Cuba*, 1218, 1324–26, 1425.

24. Telegram from the Embassy in Cuba to the Department of State, June 12, 1959, and Editorial Note, *Foreign Relations of the United States (FRUS), 1958–1960*, vol. 6, *Cuba*, ed. John P. Glennon (Washington, D.C.: United States Government Printing Office, 1991), doc. nos. 320 and 318; Thomas, *Cuba*, 1216–18, 1222, 1228; Carlos Franqui, *Family Portrait with Fidel: A Memoir* (New York: Random House, 1984), 78; Martínez-Fernández, *Revolutionary Cuba*, 53, 90.

25. Joanna Swanger, "Lands of Rebellion: Oriente and Escambray Encountering Cuban State Formation, 1934–1974" (Ph.D. diss., University of Texas at Austin, 1999), 391n34; Domínguez, *Cuba*, 440.

26. Philip Bonsal, "Airgram from the Embassy in Cuba to the Department of State," August 2, 1959, *FRUS, 1958–1960*, doc. no. 349; Thomas, *Cuba*, 1242, 1242n21.

27. Thomas, *Cuba*, 1206–7, 1219–22; Schoultz, *Infernal*, 91–92; LeoGrande and Kornbluh, *Back Channel*, 13–21.

28. According to the Cuban government's calculations based on the 1946 National Agricultural Census, 1.5 percent of owners held 46 percent of landed property. "Primera Ley de Reforma Agraria," 142–43; Schoultz, *Infernal*, 98; Leland L. Johnson, "U.S. Business Interests in Cuba and the Rise of Castro," *World Politics* 17, no. 3 (April 1965): 451–52; LeoGrande and Kornbluh, *Back Channel*, 38.

29. Editorial Note, *FRUS, 1958–1960*, doc. no. 318; Articles 29, 31, "Primera Ley de Reforma Agraria," 151–52; Maurer, *Empire Trap*, 317. In Japan after World War II, the U.S. government provided compensation in the form of twenty-five-year bonds yielding an annual 3.5 percent, as Cuban officials pointed out to the U.S. ambassador. Note from Minister of State Roa to the Ambassador in Cuba (Bonsal), June 15, 1959, *FRUS, 1958–1960*, doc. no. 321.

30. Telegram from the Department of State to the Embassy in Cuba, June 1, 1959, and Telegram from the Embassy in Cuba to the Department of State, June 12, 1959, *FRUS, 1958–1960*, doc. nos. 311 and 320; Kenworthy, "U.S. Warns Cuba"; "Text of the U.S. Statement on Cuba," *New York Times*, June 11, 1959; LeoGrande and Kornbluh, *Back Channel*, 22, 24; Schoultz, *Infernal*, 99.

31. LeoGrande and Kornbluh, *Back Channel*, 24, 41.

32. Memorandum of a Conversation, Department of State, September 24, 1959, and Memorandum from Richard G. Cushing of the Office of the Public Affairs Adviser, Bureau of Inter-American Affairs, to the Deputy Director of the United States Information Agency (Washburn), April 5, 1960, *FRUS, 1958–1960*, doc. nos. 363 and 497; Maurer, *Empire Trap*, 318; Schoultz, *Infernal*, 95–100, 121–22, 428–29; Stephen G. Rabe, *The Killing Zone: The United States Wages Cold War in Latin America* (Oxford: Oxford University Press, 2012), 63; Thomas, *Cuba*, 1219–23, 1229; Richard Turits, "Trade, Debt, and the Cuban Economy," *World Development* 15, no. 1 (January 1987): 169; Susan Eckstein, "The Cuban Revolution in Comparative Perspective," in *Constructing Culture and Power in Latin America*, ed. Daniel H. Levine (Ann Arbor: University of Michigan Press, 1993), 433; Pérez, *Cuba*, 227.

33. Schoultz, *Infernal*, 106; Aleksandr Vasil'evich Fursenko and Timothy J. Naftali, *"One Hell of a Gamble": Khrushchev, Castro, and Kennedy, 1958–1964* (New York: W. W. Norton, 1997), 18; Thomas, *Cuba*, 1221–22; Piero Gleijeses, *Shattered Hope: The Guatemalan Revolution and the United States, 1944–1954* (Princeton, N.J.: Princeton University Press, 1991).

34. James G. Blight and Peter Kornbluh, *Politics of Illusion: The Bay of Pigs Invasion Reexamined* (Boulder, Colo.: Lynne Rienner, 1998), 55, 60–64, 77; Samuel Farber, *The Origins of the Cuban Revolution Reconsidered* (Chapel Hill: University of North Carolina Press, 2006), 38, 150, 155; Guerra, *Heroes*, 22, 201–2; Schoultz, *Infernal*, 106–7.

35. Enrique Krauze, "Cuba: The New Opening," *New York Review of Books*, April 2, 2015; Tom Gjelten, *Bacardi and the Long Fight for Cuba: The Biography of a Cause* (New York: Viking, 2008), 161, 219, 231–32.

36. Memorandum from the Assistant Secretary of State for Inter-American Affairs (Rubottom) to the Under Secretary of State for Political Affairs (Murphy), October 23, 1959, and attached Current Basic United States Policy towards Cuba

(October 1959), *FRUS, 1958–1960*, doc. no. 376; LeoGrande and Kornbluh, *Back Channel*, 24, 28.

37. Blight and Kornbluh, *Politics of Illusion*, 24–25; Alejandro Portes and Alex Stepick, *City on the Edge: The Transformation of Miami* (Berkeley: University of California Press, 1993), 100–103; Pérez, *Cuba*, 255–56, 261–62; Martínez-Fernández, *Revolutionary Cuba*, 72–73; Gjelten, *Bacardi*, 230.

38. Memorandum from Richard G. Cushing of the Office of the Public Affairs Adviser, Bureau of Inter-American Affairs, to the Deputy Director of the United States Information Agency (Washburn), April 5, 1960, *FRUS, 1958–1960*, doc. no. 497; Pérez, *Cuba*, 251; Thomas, *Cuba*, 1348–49, 1351, 1353; Peter Kornbluh, *Bay of Pigs Declassified: The Secret CIA Report on the Invasion of Cuba* (New York: New Press, 1998), 120.

39. Memorandum of Discussion of the 464th Meeting of the National Security Council, Washington, D.C., October 20, 1960, *FRUS, 1958–1960*, doc. no. 596; Kornbluh, *Bay of Pigs*, 110, 117, 120, 151–52; Swanger, "Lands of Rebellion," 384–402; Domínguez, *Cuba*, 441–45; Guerra, *Visions*, 182–88.

40. Kornbluh, *Bay of Pigs*, 7; Pérez, *Cuba*, 241, 253–54; Thomas, *Cuba*, 1108–9, 1336, 1333; Martínez-Fernández, *Revolutionary Cuba*, 53.

41. Guerra, *Visions*, 158–68; Pérez, *Cuba*, 273; Thomas, *Cuba*, 1339–41, 1344; Michelle Chase, *Revolution within the Revolution: Women and Gender Politics in Cuba, 1952–1962* (Chapel Hill: University of North Carolina Press, 2015), chap. 6.

42. Guerra, *Visions*, 158, 164; Lorraine Bayard de Volo, *Women and the Cuban Insurrection: How Gender Shaped Castro's Victory* (Cambridge: Cambridge University Press, 2018), 240.

43. Fidel Castro, "This Is Democracy," May 1, 1960, in Fidel Castro, *Our Power Is That of the Working People: Building Socialism in Cuba* (New York: Pathfinder, 1983), 25–37.

44. Castro, "This Is Democracy," 30.

45. On the other hand, trade and relations with the Soviet Union did not require or signify an entering of the Soviet political orbit. Argentina and Brazil would be important trading partners of the Soviet Union in the Americas even when they were ruled by right-wing dictatorships in the 1970s. Raúl Castro reportedly took steps toward initiating relations with the Soviet Union as early as April 1959, before Cuba's split with the United States was known. Fursenko and Naftali, *"One Hell of a Gamble,"* 11–13. Evelyne Huber Stephens and John D. Stephens, *Democratic Socialism in Jamaica: The Political Movement and Social Transformation in Dependent Capitalism* (Princeton, N.J.: Princeton University Press, 1986), 315–16.

46. Farber, *Origins*, 143–54; Fursenko and Naftali, *"One Hell of a Gamble,"* 22–29, 40.

47. Memorandum of Discussion at the 435th Meeting at the National Security Council, February 18, 1960, *FRUS, 1958–1960*, doc. no. 456; Thomas, *Cuba*, 1252, 1252n53, 1258–59, 1262, 1267, 1316; Schoultz, *Infernal*, 110, 114; LeoGrande and Kornbluh, *Back Channel*, 29; Maurer, *Empire Trap*, 320; Blight and Kornbluh, *Politics of Illusion*, 36–37; Fursenko and Naftali, *"One Hell of a Gamble,"* 38, 42, 45.

48. Memorandum of Discussion at the 432d Meeting of the National Security Council, January 14, 1960, *FRUS, 1958–1960*, doc. no. 423; Thomas, *Cuba*, 1269; Martínez-Fernández, *Revolutionary Cuba*, 69; LeoGrande and Kornbluh, *Back Channel*, 32–33.

49. Kornbluh, *Bay of Pigs*, 2, 24–26, 97; Schoultz, *Infernal*, 115–17; Thomas, *Cuba*, 1276–77, 1279; Piero Gleijeses, "Cuba and the Cold War, 1959–1980," in *The Cambridge History of the Cold War*, vol. 2, ed. Melvyn P. Leffler and Odd Arne Westad (Cambridge: Cambridge University Press, 2010), 329.

50. Schoultz, *Infernal*, 119–21; Thomas, *Cuba*, 1279–80; Maurer, *Empire Trap*, 323; Johnson, "Business Interests," 458; LeoGrande and Kornbluh, *Back Channel*, 36; Fursenko and Naftali, *"One Hell of a Gamble,"* 47–48.

51. Pérez, *Cuba*, 247–48; Schoultz, *Infernal*, 120–21, 125, 139–41, 144; Maurer, *Empire Trap*, 322–26; LeoGrande and Kornbluh, *Back Channel*, 36–37.

52. Memorandum from the Attorney General (Kennedy) to President Kennedy, April 19, 1961, *Foreign Relations of the United States (FRUS), 1961–1963*, vol. 10, *Cuba, January 1961–September 1962*, ed. Louis J. Smith (Washington, D.C.: United States Government Printing Office, 1997), doc. no. 157; Blight and Kornbluh, *Politics of Illusion*, 18; Schoultz, *Infernal*, 126–27; Thomas, *Cuba*, 1312–22, 1336, 1384; LeoGrande and Kornbluh, *Back Channel*, 37; Robert S. Walters, "Soviet Economic Aid to Cuba, 1959–1964," *International Affairs (Royal Institute of International Affairs)* 42, no. 1 (January 1966): 74, 76–78, 82; Pérez, *Cuba*, 248.

53. Schoultz, *Infernal*, 126.

54. Schoultz, 120–21, 125, 139–41; Maurer, *Empire Trap*, 320, 322–26; Johnson, "Business Interests," 442, 446, 453; Pérez, *Cuba*, 247–48, 250; Martínez-Fernández, *Revolutionary Cuba*, 70; Walters, "Economic Aid," 74, 76–78, 82; Thomas, *Cuba*, 1315–16, 1336, 1376; Rabe, *The Killing Zone*, 63.

55. Pérez, *Cuba*, 261–65; Thomas, "Cuba," 1382; Franqui, *Family Portrait*, 71.

56. Pérez, *Cuba*, 247–48; Thomas, *Cuba*, 1333; Lewis, Lewis, and Rigdon, *Four Women*, 285.

57. Thomas, *Cuba*, 1317; Kornbluh, *Bay of Pigs*, esp. 24–25; Memorandum of Discussion at the 432d Meeting of the National Security Council, January 14, 1960, *FRUS, 1958–1960*, doc. no. 423.

58. Memorandum from the Chairman of the Board of National Estimates (Kent) to Director of Central Intelligence Dulles, November 3, 1961, *FRUS, 1961–1963*, doc. no. 271; Schoultz, *Infernal*, 143–44, 148–51; Kornbluh, *Bay of Pigs*, 52, 55; Pérez, *Cuba*, 251; Thomas, *Cuba*, 1321. In March 1960, the CIA estimated two-thirds of Cubans supported Castro. Kornbluh, *Bay of Pigs*, 7.

59. Memorandum from the Assistant Secretary of State for Inter-American Affairs (Mann) to Secretary of State Rusk, February 15, 1961, and Memorandum from the President's Special Assistant (Schlesinger) to President Kennedy, April 14, 1961, *FRUS, 1961–1963*, doc. nos. 45 and 101; Schoultz, *Infernal*, 162–63, 616n63; Fursenko and Naftali, *"One Hell of a Gamble,"* 91. See also Kornbluh, *Bay of Pigs*, 30, 35, 48–55, 117, 120, 131, 151–52; Schoultz, *Infernal*, 148–51.

60. Memorandum from the Deputy Director of the C.I.A. (Cabell) to General Maxwell D. Taylor, May 9, 1961, *FRUS, 1961–1963*, doc. no. 108; Thomas, *Cuba*,

1355–71; Schoultz, *Infernal*, 166–67; Kornbluh, *Bay of Pigs*, 1, 37–41; Blight and Kornbluh, *Politics of Illusion*, 70, 72–73, 236; Frederick Kempe, *Berlin 1961: Kennedy, Khrushchev, and the Most Dangerous Place on Earth* (New York: G. P. Putnam's Sons, 2011), 171.

61. Memorandum for the Records, April 25, 1961, *FRUS, 1961–1963*, doc. no. 175; Kornbluh, *Bay of Pigs*, 2, 37–41; Martínez-Fernández, *Revolutionary Cuba*, 79.

62. Telegram from the Embassy in the Soviet Union to the Department of State, April 18, 1961, Memorandum from the President's Special Assistant for National Security Affairs (Bundy) to President Kennedy, April 18, 1961, Letter from President Kennedy to Chairman Khrushchev, April 18, 1961, and Editorial Note, *FRUS, 1961– 1963*, doc. nos. 117, 119, 130, and 170; Schoultz, *Infernal*, 152–53, 83; Kempe, *Berlin 1961*, 139–53, 174; "Presidente Kennedy Respalda Invasión (AP)," *El Caribe* (Santo Domingo), April 19, 1961.

63. Memorandum from the President's Assistant Special Counsel (Goodwin) to President Kennedy, August 22, 1961, *FRUS, 1961–1963*, doc. no. 257; LeoGrande and Kornbluh, *Back Channel*, 43–47.

64. Pérez, *Cuba*, 252, 262, 278; Franqui, *Family Portrait*, 78, 121; Thomas, *Cuba*, 1373, 1383–87; Domínguez, *Cuba*, 202, 445; Robert S. McNamara, "Foreword" in Laurence Chang and Peter Kornbluh, *The Cuban Missile Crisis, 1962* (New York: New Press, 1992), xi–xiii; Schoultz, *Infernal*, 186–87; Ernest R. May and Philip Zelikow, *The Kennedy Tapes: Inside the White House during the Cuban Missile Crisis*, concise ed. (New York: Norton, 2002), 421; Blight and Kornbluh, *Politics of Illusion*, 65–66; José Álvarez, "Transformations in Cuban Agriculture after 1959," Electronic Data Information Source, FE481, Department of Food and Resource Economics, University of Florida, 2004, http://edis.ifas.ufl.edu/fe481; Carmelo Mesa-Lago, *Market, Socialist, and Mixed Economies: Comparative Policy and Performance, Chile, Cuba, and Costa Rica* (Baltimore: Johns Hopkins University Press, 2000), 342, 347.

65. Martínez-Fernández, *Revolutionary Cuba*, esp. 10–11; Domínguez, *Cuba*, 438.

66. Turits, "Trade," 168; Mesa-Lago, *Economies*, 193, 385; Brian H. Pollitt, "The Rise and Fall of the Cuban Sugar Economy," *Journal of Latin American Studies* 36, pt. 2 (May 2004): 323, 327.

67. Volker Skierka, *Fidel Castro: A Biography* (Malden, Mass.: Polity Press, 2004), 219; Carrie Hamilton, *Sexual Revolutions in Cuba: Passion, Politics, and Memory* (Chapel Hill: University of North Carolina Press, 2012), 38–44; José Yglesias, "The Case of Heberto Padilla," *New York Review of Books*, June 3, 1971; Guerra, *Visions*, 353–56; Aviva Chomsky, *A History of the Cuban Revolution*, 2nd ed. (Hoboken, N.J.: John Wiley and Sons, 2015), 113, 146–47; Nicola Miller, "The Intellectual in the Cuban Revolution," in *Intellectuals in the Twentieth-Century Caribbean*, ed. Alistair Hennessey (London: Macmillan, 1992), 89–93; Thomas, *Cuba*, 1463; Mayra Gómez, *Human Rights in Cuba, El Salvador, and Nicaragua: A Sociological Perspective on Human Rights Abuse* (New York: Routledge, 2003), 99–122.

68. Jonathan Hartlyn, *The Struggle for Democratic Politics in the Dominican Republic* (Chapel Hill: University of North Carolina Press, 1998), 68, 73, 76, 78; Piero

Gleijeses, *The Dominican Crisis: The 1965 Constitutionalist Revolt and American Intervention* (Baltimore: Johns Hopkins University Press, 1978), 86; Matías Bosch Carcuro, *Juan Bosch: El golpe de estado; Antología* (Santo Domingo: Fundación Juan Bosch, 2018), 151; Tad Szulc, "After Trujillo, a Reformer with a Mission," *New York Times*, September 8, 1963, 114.

69. Bernardo Vega, *Kennedy y Bosch: Aporte al estudio de las relaciones internacionales del gobierno constitucional de 1963* (Santo Domingo: Fundación Cultural Dominicana, 1993), 21, 54.

70. Much to the church's chagrin, the constitution also legalized informal unions, facilitated divorce, affirmed the equality of women and men, and eliminated privileges that the church had enjoyed in the past, such as benefits for Catholic schools. Memorandum of a Conversation, January 10, 1963, *FRUS, 1961–1963*, doc. no. 353; Hartlyn, *Struggle*, 81–82; Gleijeses, *Dominican Crisis*, 88, 91; Vega, *Kennedy y Bosch*, 33, 69, 71, 73, 86, 91, 175–79, 191, 208, 218, 362; John Bartlow Martin, *Overtaken by Events: The Dominican Crisis from the Fall of Trujillo to the Civil War* (New York: Doubleday, 1966), 316–17, 501.

71. John F. Kennedy, "Address on the First Anniversary of the Alliance for Progress," March 13, 1962, http://www.presidency.ucsb.edu/ws/?pid=9100.

72. Vega, *Kennedy y Bosch*, 21–29; John H. Coatsworth, *Central America and the United States: The Clients and the Colossus* (New York: Twayne, 1994), 90; Martin, *Overtaken*, 563–64; Szulc, "After Trujillo," 30.

73. Vega, *Kennedy y Bosch*, 69, 86, 91, 160, 175–79, 185, 206, 218; Martin, *Overtaken*, 459, 465, 501; Turits, *Foundations*, chap. 8.

74. Martin, *Overtaken*, 309, 353, 355–56, 459, 464, 471–73, 477; Gleijeses, *Dominican Crisis*, 96.

75. Vega, *Kennedy y Bosch*, 191, 208; Martin, *Overtaken*, 355–56, 459; Marlin D. Clausner, *Rural Santo Domingo: Settled, Unsettled, and Resettled* (Philadelphia: Temple University Press, 1973), 232–37, 251; Luis Gómez, *Relaciones de producción dominantes en la sociedad dominicana, 1875/1975* (Santo Domingo: Alfa y Omega, 1984), 102–5.

76. Vega, *Kennedy y Bosch*, 191, 208, 237–39, 245, 284–85, 363; Martin, *Overtaken*, 355–56, 459, 464, 471–73, 489, 495; Clausner, *Rural Santo Domingo*, 232–37, 251; Gleijeses, *Dominican Crisis*, 90–91; Gómez, *Relaciones*, 102–5.

77. Martin, *Overtaken*, 389; Gleijeses, *Dominican Crisis*, 96–97.

78. Gleijeses, *Dominican Crisis*, 88–89, 95–103, 108–14, 365n204; Vega, *Kennedy y Bosch*, 83, 91, 151, 197, 200, 205–11; Martin, *Overtaken*, 415, 419, cf. 454, 470, 477–78, 562–65, 570; "Crecimiento de la población dominicana desde 1844 a 1980," in Frank Moya Pons, *Manual de historia dominicana* (Santiago, Dominican Republic: Universidad Católica Madre y Maestra, 1984); José Antonio Moreno, *Barrios in Arms: Revolution in Santo Domingo* (Pittsburgh: University of Pittsburgh Press, 1970), 118–20.

79. Martin, *Overtaken*, 562–67, 570–74.

80. Vega, *Kennedy y Bosch*, 357–58, 402; Gleijeses, *Dominican Crisis*, 107, 115, 370n49; Frank Moya Pons, *The Dominican Republic: A National History*, 3rd ed. (Princeton, N.J.: Markus Wiener, 2010), 385–86; Martin, *Overtaken*, 11; Bernardo

Vega, *Addendum: El gobierno de Kennedy y el de Bosch, un análisis más profundo* (Santo Domingo: Fundación Cultural Dominicana, 2017), 19–20.

81. Piero Gleijeses, "Hope Denied: The US Defeat of the 1965 Revolt in the Dominican Republic," The Cold War International History Project Working Paper Series, Woodrow Wilson International Center for Scholars, no. 72 (November 2014): 8; Vega, *Kennedy y Bosch*, 370–71, 377, 392, 406; Gleijeses, *Dominican Crisis*, 108, 114, 96–97, 369–70n49; Hartlyn, *Struggle*, 85; "Military Seizes Dominican Rule," 3.

82. Vega, *Kennedy y Bosch*, 403, 418; Gleijeses, *Dominican Crisis*, 108, 367.

83. Hartlyn, *Struggle*, 88–89, 309; Moya Pons, *Dominican Republic*, 386–87; Eric Thomas Chester, *Rag-Tags, Scum, Riff-Raff, and Commies: The U.S. Intervention in the Dominican Republic, 1965–1966* (New York: Monthly Review Press, 2001), 42; Moreno, *Barrios in Arms*, 24–28; Alex Von Tunzelmann, *Red Heat: Conspiracy, Murder, and the Cold War in the Caribbean* (New York: Henry Holt, 2011), 339.

84. Chester, *Rag-Tags*, 43; Bernardo Vega, *Negociaciones políticas durante la intervención militar de 1965* (Santo Domingo: Fundación Cultural Dominicana, 1993), 487; Tunzelmann, *Red Heat*, 339; Hartlyn, *Struggle*, 88–89; Moya Pons, *Dominican Republic*, 386–87.

85. Gleijeses, *Dominican Crisis*, 189, 212–13, 288; Moreno, *Barrios in Arms*, 24–28; Howard Wiarda, "The United States and the Dominican Republic: Intervention, Dependency, and Tyrannicide," *Journal of Interamerican Studies and World Affairs* 22, no. 2 (May 1980): 254–56; Gleijeses, "Hope Denied," 14.

86. Some U.S. observers at the time described this as a rebellion of junior officers against an old military guard viewed as corrupt Trujillistas monopolizing military benefits and privileges. But while motives were surely multiple and varied, there was ample Constitutionalist sentiment among the rebel soldiers. One of the leaders of the countercoup, Lt. Col. Rafael Fernández Domínguez, had been plotting to return Bosch to the presidency since the day he was overthrown. Wiarda, "United States and the Dominican Republic," 251, 254–56; Abraham F. Lowenthal, "The Political Role of the Dominican Armed Forces: A Note on the 1963 Overthrow of Juan Bosch and on the 1965 'Revolution,'" *Journal of Interamerican Studies and World Affairs* 15, no. 3 (August 1973): 355–67; Gleijeses, *Dominican Crisis*, 180–81, 246, 289; Gleijeses, "Hope Denied," 9, 11, 14.

87. Telegram from the White House Situation Room to President Johnson at Camp David, April 25, 1965, *Foreign Relations of the United States (FRUS), 1964–1968*, vol. 32, *Dominican Republic, Cuba, Haiti, Guyana*, ed. Daniel Lawler and Carolyn Lee (Washington, D.C.: United States Government Printing Office, 2005), doc. no. 21; Telephone Conversation between the Under Secretary of State for Economic Affairs (Mann) and President Johnson, April 26, 1965, *FRUS, 1964–1968*, doc. no. 22; Moreno, *Barrios in Arms*, 25–27, 32–33.

88. Telephone Conversation between the Under Secretary of State for Economic Affairs (Mann) and President Johnson, April 27, 1965, *FRUS, 1964–1968*, doc. no. 23; Moreno, *Barrios in Arms*, 28–29; G. Pope Atkins and Larman C. Wilson, *The Dominican Republic and the United States: From Imperialism to Transnationalism*

(Athens: University of Georgia Press, 1998), 146; Gleijeses, *Dominican Crisis*, 218, 253; Moya Pons, *Dominican Republic*, 388; Theodore Draper, "The Dominican Intervention Reconsidered," *Political Science Quarterly* 86, no. 1 (March 1971): 6–7; Chester, *Rag-Tags*, 53; Alan L. McPherson, "Misled by Himself: What the Johnson Tapes Reveal about the Dominican Intervention of 1965," *Latin American Research Review* 38, no. 2 (2003): 133, 136; Wiarda, "United States and the Dominican Republic," 251–52.

89. Telephone Conversation between the Under Secretary of State for Economic Affairs (Mann) and President Johnson, April 26, 1965, *FRUS, 1964–1968*, doc. no. 22; McPherson, "Misled," 133, 136; "The President of the United States Chooses the Next President of the Dominican Republic: Lyndon Johnson," in Eric Paul Roorda, Lauren H. Derby, and Raymundo González, eds., *The Dominican Republic Reader: History, Culture, Politics* (Durham, N.C.: Duke University Press, 2014), 352–54.

90. Juan Bosch, "A Tale of Two Nations," *New Leader* 48, no. 13 (June 21, 1965): 4; Gleijeses, *Dominican Crisis*, 289; Draper, "Intervention Reconsidered"; Moreno, *Barrios in Arms*, 30–31, 33; Gleijeses, "Hope Denied," 44.

91. The Communist Role in the Dominican Republic, May 7, 1965, *FRUS, 1964–1968*, doc. no. 60; Moreno, *Barrios in Arms*, 28, 30–31, 94–95; Jesse Hoffnung-Garskof, *A Tale of Two Cities: Santo Domingo and New York after 1950* (Princeton, N.J.: Princeton University Press, 2008), 35.

92. William Bennett, Telegram from the Embassy in the Dominican Republic to the Department of State, April 28, 1965; William Bennett, Telegram from the Embassy in the Dominican Republic to the Director of the National Security Agency (Carter), April 28, 1965; and William Bennett, Telegram from the Embassy in the Dominican Republic to the Director of the National Security Agency (Carter), April 28, 1965, *FRUS, 1964–1968*, doc. nos. 27, 32, and 36; Chester, *Rag-Tags*, 77–78; Gleijeses, *Dominican Crisis*, 289; Vega, *Negociaciones*, 499–500, 504.

93. The 14th of June Movement would garner only 4,427 votes in an election in 1966. Moreno, *Barrios in Arms*, 114–23; Chester, *Rag-Tags*, 341–43; Vega, *Kennedy y Bosch*, 210–11; Gleijeses, "Hope Denied," 16, 25.

94. Editorial Note, *FRUS, 1964–1968*, doc. no. 30; Wiarda, "United States and the Dominican Republic," 253; Michael Grow, *U.S. Presidents and Latin American Interventions: Pursuing Regime Change in the Cold War* (Lawrence: University Press of Kansas, 2008), 75–79, 85, 88–89, 216, 220n51.

95. Wiarda, "United States and the Dominican Republic," 251; Jerome Slater, *Intervention and Negotiation: The United States and the Dominican Revolution* (New York: Harper and Row, 1970), 54–55; McPherson, "Misled," 128; "Crecimiento de la población dominicana desde 1844 a 1980," in Moya Pons, *Manual*.

96. McPherson, "Misled," esp. 139–41.

97. Minutes of Meeting with Congressional Leadership on Dominican Republic, April 28, 1965; Telephone Conversation between Director of Central Intelligence Raborn and President Johnson, April 29, 1965; and Editorial Note, *FRUS, 1964–1968*, doc. nos. 35, 39, and 48; McPherson, "Misled," 137–44.

98. Bosch, "Tale of Two Nations," 4–5.

99. Bosch, 7.

100. Bosch, 5–6; Peter G. Felten, "The Path to Dissent: Johnson, Fulbright, and the 1965 Intervention in the Dominican Republic," *Presidential Studies Quarterly* 26, no. 4 (Fall 1996): 1012; Tunzelmann, *Red Heat*, 351, 419n60.

101. Gaddis Smith, *The Last Years of the Monroe Doctrine, 1945–1993* (New York: Hill and Wang, 1994), 126–28; Alan L. McPherson, *Yankee No!: Anti-Americanism in U.S.-Latin American Relations* (Cambridge, Mass.: Harvard University Press, 2003), 151; Slater, *Intervention*, 57–58. For a compelling alternative perspective on the causal efficacy of U.S. leaders' Cold War paranoia, see Gleijeses, "Hope Denied."

102. McPherson, *Yankee No!*, 151–52; Slater, *Intervention*, 57–58; Moya Pons, *Dominican Republic*, 387–90; Hartlyn, *Struggle*, 89–91.

103. Telegram From the Embassy in the Dominican Republic to the Department of State, May 10, 1965, *FRUS, 1964–1968*, doc. no. 62; Tunzelmann, *Red Heat*, 352–53; Moya Pons, *Dominican Republic*, 387–90; Hartlyn, *Struggle*, 89–91; Atkins and Wilson, *Dominican Republic and the United States*, 146.

104. Slater, *Intervention*, 53–55, 57; Moya Pons, *Dominican Republic*, 387–90; Hartlyn, *Struggle*, 89–91; Hoffnung-Garskof, *Tale of Two Cities*, 35; Atkins and Wilson, *Dominican Republic and the United States*, 146.

105. Moya Pons, *Dominican Republic*, 387–90; Hartlyn, *Struggle*, 89–91; McPherson, *Yankee No!*, 151–52, 161–62; Tunzelmann, *Red Heat*, 354; Vega, *Negociaciones*, 505; Atkins and Wilson, *Dominican Republic and the United States*, 146; Bosch, *Juan Bosch*, 120. On the 1898 intervention, see chapter 4.

106. Moya Pons, *Dominican Republic*, 387–90; Hartlyn, *Struggle*, 89–91; Slater, *Intervention*, 53–55, 57; Hoffnung-Garskof, *Tale of Two Cities*, 35; Atkins and Wilson, *Dominican Republic and the United States*, 146.

107. Memorandum Prepared for the 303 Committee, December 30, 1965, and Memorandum from the Representative to the Organization of American States (Bunker) to President Johnson, March 9, 1966, *FRUS, 1964–1968*, doc. nos. 152 and 162; Bernardo Vega, "Las campañas sucias," *Hoy*, February 29, 2012; Hartlyn, *Struggle*, 90–91, 94, 281; Gleijeses, *Dominican Crisis*, 280, 299; Moya Pons, *Dominican Republic*, 390.

108. "The odds . . . were formidably stacked against Bosch," writes Piero Gleijeses, "but for the United States this was not certainty enough. 'The President [Johnson] wants to win the elections, and he expects the Agency [the CIA] to arrange for this to happen,' the Acting CIA director, Richard Helms, reminded the Deputy Director for Plans." Later Helms reported that "every effort" was "being made to see" that it did. Gleijeses, "Hope Denied," 45; Memorandum from William G. Bowdler of the National Security Council Staff to President Johnson, March 25, 1966, *FRUS, 1964–1968*, doc. no. 165; Hartlyn, *Struggle*, 90–91; Gleijeses, *Dominican Crisis*, 280–81; Turits, *Foundations*, 265n3.

109. Editorial Note, *FRUS, 1964–1968*, doc. no. 178; Hartlyn, *Struggle*, 90–91, 281; Atkins and Wilson, *Dominican Republic and the United States*, 143.

110. Frank Moya Pons, "Las relaciones económicas domínico-americanas," in *El pasado dominicano* (Santo Domingo: Editora Fundación Corripio, 1986), 336–38; Moya Pons, *Dominican Republic*, 397–99; Bosch Carcuro, *Juan Bosch*, 19.

111. Moya Pons, "Relaciones económicas," 344–45, 340–41; Atkins and Wilson, *Dominican Republic and the United States*, 152–53; Moya Pons, *Dominican Republic*, 391–92, 394–96, 399–400; Hartlyn, *Struggle*, 90, 104, 109–13; Turits, *Foundations*, 261–63, passim.

112. Turits, *Foundations*, 262–63.

113. Hartlyn, *Struggle*, 118–20.

114. Hartlyn, 120–23; Moya Pons, *Dominican Republic*, 402–3.

115. Rafael Francisco de Moya Pons, "Industrial Incentives in the Dominican Republic, 1880–1983" (Ph.D. diss., Columbia University, 1987), 571–72; Rosario Espinal and Jonathan Hartlyn, "The Dominican Republic: The Long and Difficult Struggle for Democracy," in *Democracy in Developing Countries*, ed. Larry Diamond et al. (Boulder, Colo.: Lynne Rienner, 1999), 469–517; Pedro San Miguel, *El pasado relegado: Estudios sobre la historia agraria dominicana* (Santo Domingo: Librería La Trinidad, 1999), 152–57; Peggy Levitt, *The Transnational Villagers* (Berkeley: University of California Press, 2001), 45–46; Moya Pons, "Relaciones económicas," 34–41; Vargas-Lundius, *Peasants in Distress*, 317–27.

116. The U.S. Immigration and Naturalization Service counted nearly six hundred thousand Dominicans immigrants to the United States between 1980 and 2000. Jorge Duany, *Blurred Borders: Transnational Migration Between the Hispanic Caribbean and the United States* (Chapel Hill: University of North Carolina Press, 2011), 173–74.

117. The number of political prisoners dropped from probably well over twenty thousand in the 1960s to several thousand in the 1970s to several hundred known prisoners in the 1980s. Gómez, *Human Rights*, 99–122; Thomas, *Cuba*, 1356–65; Franqui, *Family Portrait*, 127–28; Claes Brundenius, "The Role of Capital Goods Production in the Economic Development of Cuba," *Political Power and Social Theory* 6 (1987): 67–85.

118. Turits, "Trade," 163–65, 175; Claes Brundenius, *Revolutionary Cuba: The Challenge of Economic Growth with Equity* (Boulder, Colo.: Westview, 1984), 121; Claes Brundenius, "Revolutionary Cuba at 50: Growth with Equity Revisited," *Latin American Perspectives* 36, no. 2 (March 2009): 32, 42–43; Susan Eckstein, "The Cuban Revolution in Comparative Perspective," in *Constructing Culture and Power in Latin America*, ed. Daniel H. Levine (Ann Arbor: University of Michigan Press, 1993), esp. 431.

119. World Bank, *World Development Report 1982* (New York: Oxford University Press, 1982), 150–51; Julie M. Feinsilver, "Cuba as a 'World Medical Power': The Politics of Symbolism," *Latin American Research Review* 24, no. 2 (1989): esp. 5–16, 24–25; Brundenius, *Revolutionary Cuba*, 121; Brundenius, "Revolutionary Cuba at 50," 35–39; Eckstein, "Comparative Perspective," 448–51, 456; Pérez, *Cuba*, 274–78; Sean Brotherton, *Revolutionary Medicine: Health and the Body in Post-Soviet Cuba* (Durham, N.C.: Duke University Press, 2012), 61–72, 176–80; Mirien Uirarte, *Cuba, Social Policy at the Crossroads: Maintaining Priorities, Transforming Practice* (Boston: Oxfam, 2002), 9.

120. World Bank, "School enrollment, secondary (% gross)" and "School enrollment, tertiary (% gross)," https://data.worldbank.org/indicator/SE.SEC.NENR ?view=chart; Mesa-Lago, *Economies*, 225, 287, 336–37; Brundenius, "Revolutionary

Cuba at 50," 35–37; Pérez, *Cuba*, 273–74; Brundenius, "The Role of Capital Goods," 69, 84.

121. Mesa-Lago, *Economies*, 193, 385; de la Fuente, *Nation for All*, 279, 307–16, 322–29.

122. Jorge Domínguez, "Your Friend, Fidel: A Letter from Cuba," *Harvard Magazine*, August 2000, 35; Pérez, *Cuba*, 291–99, 313–16, 319–20; Brundenius, "Revolutionary Cuba at 50," 42; Turits, "Trade."

123. Pérez, *Cuba*, 305–12, 320–22, 332; Chomsky, *History*, 154–68; Brotherton, *Revolutionary Medicine*, 157–68; Schoultz, *Infernal*, 462–63; Brundenius, "Revolutionary Cuba at 50," 35–41; de la Fuente, *Nation for All*, 318–22.

Chapter Seven

1. Thomas Holt, *The Problem of Freedom: Race, Labor, and Politics in Jamaica and Britain, 1832–1938* (Baltimore: Johns Hopkins University Press, 1992), 399.

2. Holt, *Problem of Freedom*, 396, 399, 401; for Manley's quote, see "Norman Washington Manley," Jamaica Information Service, n.d., http://jis.gov.jm/information/heroes/norman-washington-manley/.

3. Evelyne Huber Stephens and John D. Stephens, *Democratic Socialism in Jamaica: The Political Movement and Social Transformation in Dependent Capitalism* (Princeton, N.J.: Princeton University Press, 1986), 231, 241, 338.

4. Stephens and Stephens, *Democratic Socialism in Jamaica*, 64–65; Norman Girvan, Richard Bernal, and Wesley Hughes, "The IMF and the Third World: The Case of Jamaica," *Development Dialogue* 2 (1980): 115; Kate Quinn, "Black Power in Caribbean Context," *Black Power in the Caribbean*, ed. Kate Quinn (Gainesville: University Press of Florida, 2014), 34; Michael Kaufman, *Jamaica under Manley* (Westport, Conn.: Lawrence Hill, 1985), 11–12, 65n4; Stephens and Stephens, *Democratic Socialism in Jamaica*, 26–27, 28–29, 36; Anthony Payne, "Jamaica: The 'Democratic Socialist' Experiment of Michael Manley," in Anthony Payne and Paul Sutton, eds., *Dependency under Challenge: The Political Economy of the Caribbean* (Manchester: Manchester University Press, 1983), 19–20; Kaufman, *Jamaica under Manley*, 11–12; Holt, *Problem of Freedom*, chaps. 4 and 5.

5. F. S. J. Ledgister, *Michael Manley and Jamaican Democracy, 1972–1980: The Word Is Love* (Lanham, Md.: Lexington Books, 2014), 4–10, 22; Colin A. Palmer, "Identity, Race, and Black Power in Independent Jamaica," in *The Modern Caribbean*, ed. Franklin W. Knight and Colin A. Palmer (Chapel Hill: University of North Carolina Press, 1989), 111–14, 124–26; Stephens and Stephens, *Democratic Socialism in Jamaica*, 35–38; Kaufman, *Jamaica under Manley*, 44; Jack Alexander, "The Culture of Race in Middle-Class Kingston, Jamaica," *American Ethnologist* 4, no. 3 (August 1977): 413–35.

6. Palmer, "Identity," 114; Stephens and Stephens, *Democratic Socialism in Jamaica*, 55–56; Ledgister, *Michael Manley and Jamaican Democracy*, 5; Barry Chevannes, *Rastafari: Roots and Ideology* (Syracuse, N.Y.: Syracuse University Press, 1994), 263; Joshua Jelly-Schapiro, *Island People: The Caribbean and the World* (New

York: Alfred A. Knopf, 2016), 52; Girvan, Bernal, and Hughes, "IMF and the Third World," 115.

7. Kaufman, *Jamaica under Manley*, 62.

8. Palmer, "Identity," 117–18; Quinn, "Black Power," 29, 35, 46, 47n35.

9. Palmer, "Identity," 117–25; Ledgister, *Michael Manley and Jamaican Democracy*, 6–7, 22; Kaufman, *Jamaica under Manley*, 62–63; Quinn, "Black Power," 38; Matthew Smith, personal communication, April 14, 2019.

10. Palmer, "Identity," 117–19; Ledgister, *Michael Manley and Jamaican Democracy*, 6–7, 22; Kaufman, *Jamaica under Manley*, 62–63. These events paralleled disturbances two years later led by Black Power activists in Trinidad and Tobago, where postcolonial grievances gave rise to a massive two-month-long demonstration that shut the country down. Those events came to be known as the "Black Power Revolt." Herman Bennett, "The Challenge to the Post-Colonial State: A Case Study of the February Revolution in Trinidad," in *The Modern Caribbean*, ed. Franklin W. Knight and Colin A. Palmer (Chapel Hill: University of North Carolina Press, 1989), 129, 134; Anthony Maingot, "Independence and Its Aftermath: Suriname, Trinidad, and Jamaica," in *The Caribbean: A History of the Region and Its People*, ed. Stephan Palmié and Francisco A. Scarano (Chicago: University of Chicago Press, 2011), 529.

11. Kaufman, *Jamaica under Manley*, 205, 221; Michael Manley, *Jamaica: Struggle in the Periphery* (London: Third World Media, 1982), 75; Holt, *Problem of Freedom*, 401. For a recent political biography of Manley, see Godfrey Smith, *Michael Manley: The Biography* (Kingston: Ian Randle, 2016). For lyrics to "Better Must Come," listen at https://www.youtube.com/watch?v=rKtcRFWjup4, accessed April 29, 2019.

12. Jelly-Schapiro, *Island People*, 52–53, 74; Kaufman, *Jamaica under Manley*, 63; Ledgister, *Michael Manley and Jamaican Democracy*, 8–11, 26; Manley, *Jamaica*, 80; Stuart Hall, "Minimal Selves," in *Black British Cultural Studies: A Reader*, ed. Houston A. Baker Jr., Manthia Diawara, and Ruth H. Lindeborg (Chicago: University of Chicago Press, 1996), 116; Anthony Bogues, "Michael Manley, Equality, and the Jamaican Labour Movement," *Caribbean Quarterly* 48, no. 1 (March 2002): 78, 91. Even under Manley some reggae songs were banned (several of which are by Bob Marley). Matthew Smith, personal communication, April 14, 2019.

13. Stephens and Stephens, *Democratic Socialism*, 74, 292, 293; Manley, *Jamaica*, 77; David Panton, *Jamaica's Michael Manley: The Great Transformation (1972–1992)* (Kingston: LMH, 1993), 45.

14. Stephens and Stephens, *Democratic Socialism*, 70–71, 286, 292, 293; Manley, *Jamaica*, 40–41, 91, 92; Richard L. Bernal, "The IMF and Class Struggle in Jamaica, 1977–1980," *Latin American Perspectives* 11, no. 3 (Summer 1984): 63; Ana Kasafi Perkins, *Justice as Equality: Michael Manley's Caribbean Vision of Justice* (New York: Peter Lang, 2010), 33.

15. A. Lynn Bolles, "Michael Manley in the Vanguard towards Gender Equality," *Caribbean Quarterly* 48, no. 1 (March 2002), 45–56; Kaufman, *Jamaica under Manley*,

175; Manley, *Jamaica*, 174; Stephens and Stephens, *Democratic Socialism*, 292–93; Perkins, *Justice as Equality*, 29.

16. Stephens and Stephens, *Democratic Socialism*, 74, 110, 164, 274–77; Kaufman, *Jamaica under Manley*, 98–99; Evelyne Huber Stephens and John D. Stephens, "Democratic Socialism in Dependent Capitalism: An Analysis of the Manley Government in Jamaica," *Politics and Society* 12, no. 3 (1983): 389–90; Manley, *Jamaica*, 94.

17. Stephens and Stephens, *Democratic Socialism*, 74, 164, 274–77; Kaufman, *Jamaica under Manley*, 98–99; Stephens and Stephens, "Democratic Socialism," 389–90; Manley, *Jamaica*, 94.

18. Kaufman, *Jamaica under Manley*, 99–100.

19. Soon private corporations would be responsible for only one-fourth of the country's sugar output. Kaufman, *Jamaica under Manley*, 100–104, 180; Stephens and Stephens, *Democratic Socialism*, 391; Stephens and Stephens, "Democratic Socialism," 283–84; Manley, *Jamaica*, 44, 85, 95; Bernal, "IMF and Class Struggle," 62; Bogues, "Michael Manley," 89.

20. Stephens and Stephens, "Democratic Socialism," 391–92; Stephens and Stephens, *Democratic Socialism*, 284; Kaufman, *Jamaica under Manley*, 167–73.

21. Payne, "Jamaica," 27; Panton, *Jamaica's Michael Manley*, 57.

22. To put the revenue generated by the bauxite levy in perspective, income taxes provided $166 million (150 million Jamaican dollars) in 1973. Bernal, "IMF and Class Struggle," 57; Manley, *Jamaica*, 45, 89–90, 98, 101, 103; Stephens and Stephens, *Democratic Socialism*, 79; Kaufman, *Jamaica under Manley*, 83; Stephens and Stephens, "Democratic Socialism," 386, 388.

23. Manley, *Jamaica*, 101, 102; State Dept. to Sec. of State Henry Kissinger, May 1, 1974; State Dept. to Embassy in Jamaica, May 26, 1974; Interagency Intelligence Memo., July 19, 1976; and Asst. Sec. of State for Inter-American Affairs to Sec. of State Kissinger, November 8, 1976, *Foreign Relations of the United States (FRUS), 1969–1976*, vol. E-11, part 1, *Documents on Mexico, Central America, and the Caribbean, 1973–1976*, ed. Halbert Jones (Washington, D.C.: United States Government Printing Office, 2015), doc. nos. 444, 445, 465, and 471; Stephens and Stephens, *Democratic Socialism*, 79.

24. Director of the Office of Caribbean Affairs to Asst. Sec. of State for Inter-American Affairs, June 7, 1974; Asst. Sec. of State for Inter-American Affairs and Asst. Sec. of State for Economic and Business Affairs to Sec. of State Kissinger, June 24, 1974; and Embassy in Jamaica to State Dept., April 11, 1975, *FRUS, Mexico, Central America, and the Caribbean, 1973–1976*, doc. nos. 446, 448, and 451.

25. Embassy in Jamaica to State Dept., April 11, 1975, and Embassy in Jamaica to State Dept., July 17, 1975, *FRUS, Mexico, Central America, and the Caribbean, 1973–1976*, doc. nos. 451 and 453.

26. Asst. Sec. of State for Inter-American Affairs to Sec. of State Kissinger, November 8, 1976, *FRUS, Mexico, Central America, and the Caribbean, 1973–1976*, doc. no. 471; Manley, *Jamaica*, 157–58; Dirk Kruijt, *Cuba and Revolutionary Latin America: An Oral History* (London: Zed Books, 2017), 153; Memo., March 3, 1977, *Foreign Relations of the United States (FRUS), 1977–1980*, vol. 23, *Mexico, Cuba, and the*

Caribbean, ed. Alexander O. Poster (Washington, D.C.: United States Government Publishing Office, 2016), doc. no. 175.

27. CIA Memorandum, March 5, 1976, and Embassy in Jamaica to State Dept., December 24, 1975, *FRUS, Mexico, Central America, and the Caribbean, 1973–1976,* doc. nos. 461 and 458.

28. Max Bearak, "Fidel Castro, African Hero," *Washington Post,* November 28, 2016; Piero Gleijeses, "The View from Havana: Lesson from Cuba's African Journey, 1959–1976," in *In from the Cold: Latin America's New Encounters with the Cold War,* ed. Gilbert Joseph and Daniela Spenser (Durham, N.C.: Duke University Press, 2008), 112–33; Piero Gleijeses, *The Cuban Drumbeat* (London: Seagull Books, 2009). For a comprehensive treatment of smaller-scale training of and assistance to guerrillas by Cubans in many areas of Latin America during the 1960s, see Jonathan C. Brown, *Cuba's Revolutionary World* (Cambridge, Mass.: Harvard University Press, 2017); Manley, *Jamaica,* 116–17; Embassy in Jamaica to State Dept., November 21, 1977, *FRUS, 1977–1980,* doc. no. 181.

29. Speeches shown in the BBC film *Blood and Fire* (Robert Beckford, 2002).

30. Embassy in Jamaica to State Dept., September 17, 1975; Memorandum, March 23, 1976; National Security Council to the Deputy Asst. for National Security Affairs, August 17, 1976; and Asst. Sec. of State for Inter-American Affairs to Under Sec. of State for Political Affairs, September 20, 1976, *FRUS, Mexico, Central America, and the Caribbean, 1973–1976,* doc. nos. 454, 462, 466, and 468. The year prior to Manley's first election, 1971, it had been at $23 million. (These figures, though, do not take inflation into account.) Stephens and Stephens, *Democratic Socialism,* 397.

31. National Security Council to the Deputy Asst. for National Security Affairs, August 17, 1976; Asst. Sec. of State for Inter-American Affairs to Under Sec. of State for Political Affairs, September 20, 1976; CIA Memorandum, March 5, 1976; and Memo., June 9, 1976, *FRUS, Mexico, Central America, and the Caribbean, 1973–1976,* doc. nos. 466, 468, 461, and 464. Stephens and Stephens, *Democratic Socialism,* 231, 241, 338; Stephen Kinzer, *Overthrow: America's Century of Regime Change from Hawaii to Iraq,* 1st ed. (New York: Times Books, 2006), 233. The U.S. government had intervened in the English-speaking Caribbean before, but it had been exceptional, limited, and with Britain's blessing. During World War II, the United States established a military based in Trinidad to forestall German actions in the region, a base that some Trinidadians called an "occupation," but that was nonetheless accepted and supported by most. See Harvey R. Neptune, *Caliban and the Yankees: Trinidad and the United States Occupation* (Chapel Hill: University of North Carolina Press, 2007). And in 1964, the U.S. government covertly helped foment instability in British Guiana to prevent the reelection of Prime Minister Cheddi Jagan, a left-wing leader who was unique in Latin America and the Caribbean at the time for his outspoken support of the Cuban Revolution. Here they acted, though, in concert with the British, who were actually the main force behind the destabilization campaign. Gordon Lewis, *Grenada: The Jewel Despoiled* (Baltimore: Johns Hopkins University Press, 1987), 92; Kruijt, *Cuba,* 152.

32. "By 1977, it was conservatively estimated that some $300 million had left the country illegally." Manley, *Jamaica,* 151. See also Panton, *Jamaica's Michael Manley,*

61. Embassy of Jamaica to State Dept., September 28, 1976, and Embassy in Jamaica to State Dept., December 24, 1975, *FRUS, Mexico, Central America, and the Caribbean, 1973–1976,* doc. nos. 470 and 458.

33. Kaufman, *Jamaica under Manley,* 125–27; Bernal, "IMF and Class Struggle," 63; Stephens and Stephens, *Democratic Socialism,* 292–93; Perkins, *Justice as Equality,* 33; Manley, *Jamaica,* 92.

34. Memo., National Security Council Staff, February 11, 1977, *FRUS, 1977–1980,* doc. no. 174; Stephens and Stephens, *Democratic Socialism,* 397; *FRUS, 1977–1980,* doc. nos. 192–214.

35. Sec. of the Treasury to President Carter, June 16, 1977, *FRUS, 1977–1980,* doc. no. 179; Stephens and Stephens, "Democratic Socialism," 380–83; Bernal, "IMF and Class Struggle," 64–71.

36. In September 1979, Carter issued instructions to the State Department to take action against Manley: "We should rap him in a way to strengthen his opposition." But the following month, he lamented and conceivably reversed his call, in his words, to "knock the hell out of Manley and support a moderate group," for he feared that "we may be on the verge of driving Manley and Jamaica irrevocably to Cuba." Asst. for National Security Affairs to Secretary of State, September 24, 1979, and Editorial Note, *FRUS, 1977–1980,* doc. nos. 195, 199. For more on this history, see *FRUS, 1977–1980,* doc. nos. 192–214. Stephens and Stephens, "Democratic Socialism," 380–83; Bernal, "IMF and Class Struggle," 64–71.

37. Payne, "Jamaica," 37–38; Michael Kaufman, "Democracy and Social Transformation in Jamaica," *Social and Economic Studies* 37, no. 3 (September 1988): 45–73; Bogues, "Michael Manley," 90.

38. Memo. of Conversation, December 16, 1977, *FRUS, 1977–1980,* doc. no. 184.

39. Brian Meeks, *Caribbean Revolutions and Revolutionary Theory: An Assessment of Cuba, Nicaragua, and Grenada* (Kingston: University of West Indies Press, 1993), 136–40, 164; Fitzroy Ambursley, "Grenada: The New Jewel Revolution," in *Crisis in the Caribbean,* ed. Fitzroy Ambursley and Robin Cohen (New York: Monthly Review Press, 1983), 195–97; Lewis, *Grenada,* 11–15; Kinzer, *Overthrow,* 223; Shalini Puri, *The Grenada Revolution in the Caribbean Present: Operation Urgent Memory* (New York: Palgrave Macmillan, 2014), 31.

40. Meeks, *Caribbean Revolutions,* 140, 141; Lewis, *Grenada,* 13–14, 17; Puri, *Grenada Revolution,* 31, 31–35.

41. Puri, *Grenada Revolution,* 33–34; Meeks, *Caribbean Revolutions,* 145–57; Lewis, *Grenada,* 13–14; Kinzer, *Overthrow,* 224–25.

42. David Scott, *Omens of Adversity: Tragedy, Time, Memory, Justice* (Durham, N.C.: Duke University Press, 2014), 4, 16.

43. Lewis, *Grenada,* 33, 70; Merle Collins, "What Happened? Grenada: A Retrospective Journey," *Social and Economic Studies* 62, nos. 3–4 (2013): 15–44, 28; Chris Searle, *Grenada: The Struggle against Destabilization* (New York: W. W. Norton, 1983), 93, 97–98, 122; Meeks, *Caribbean Revolutions,* 130, 164.

44. Robert Pastor of the National Security Staff to the President's Asst. for National Security Affairs (NSA) and the President's Dep. Asst. for NSA, March 27, 1979, *FRUS, 1977–1980,* doc. no. 314; Ambursley, "Grenada," 201–3, 208–13; Richard

Hart, *The Grenada Revolution: Setting the Record Straight* (London: Caribbean Labor Solidarity and Socialist History Society, 2005), 23–24, 31–32; Kinzer, *Overthrow*, 227; Puri, *Grenada Revolution*, 79; Quinn, "Black Power," 33.

45. Ambursley, "Grenada," 212; Kinzer, *Overthrow*, 226; Searle, *Grenada*, 93, 97–98.

46. President's Assistant for National Security Affairs (NSA) to President Carter, March 15, 1979, *FRUS, 1977–1980*, doc. no. 313.

47. Embassy in Barbados to the Dept. of State, April 11, 1979, *FRUS, 1977–1980*, doc. no. 317; Scott, *Omens*, 16, 182n47; Michael Witter, "Lessons from the IMF experiences," *The Gleaner* (Kingston, Jamaica), July 8, 2012.

48. Robert Pastor of the National Security Staff to the President's Asst. for NSA and the President's Dep. Asst. for NSA, April 14, 1979; Jimmy Carter, Presidential Finding, July 3, 1979; Conclusions of a Special Coordination Committee, June 26, 1979; Director of Central Intelligence to the President's Dep. Asst. for NSA et al., October 9, 1979; Grenadian Embassy to Dept. of State, November 9, 1979; Memorandum from the Dep. Director of Central Intelligence to the President's Deputy Asst. for NSA et al., November 23, 1979; and State Dept. to Embassy in Barbados, March 18, 1980, *FRUS, 1977–1980*, doc. nos. 318, 325, 324, 328, 330, 331, and 332; Meeks, *Caribbean Revolutions*, 165; Kruijt, *Cuba*, 155; Ambursley, "Grenada," 214, 218; and Scott, *Omens*, 182n48, 132.

49. Searle, *Grenada*, 128.

50. Meeks, *Caribbean Revolutions*, 165; Kruijt, *Cuba*, 155; Lewis, *Grenada*, 101; Ambursley, "Grenada," 204–5; and Memo. of a Conversation, June 14, 1977, *FRUS, 1977–1980*, doc. no. 301.

51. Puri, *Grenada Revolution*, 43–49.

52. Ambursley, "Grenada," 218, 197, 205–7; Meeks, *Caribbean Revolutions*, 160–67, esp. 164; Lewis, *Grenada*, 29; V. S. Naipaul, "An Island Betrayed," *Harper's*, March 1, 1984, 70.

53. Scott, *Omens*, 16; Puri, *Grenada Revolution*, 79–84; Meeks, *Caribbean Revolutions*, 129–79, esp. 130; Collins, "What Happened?," 29–30, 34–35; Lewis, *Grenada*, 34; Hart, *Grenada Revolution*, 23–24, 31–32.

54. Puri, *Grenada Revolution*, 39–50, 82–87; Scott, *Omens*, 40–43; Meeks, *Caribbean Revolutions*, esp. 130; Lewis, *Grenada*, 35, 193.

55. After the collapse of the Grenada Revolution, Fort Rupert was named once again "Fort George." Scott, *Omens*, 16–17, 39–45, 51–65; Meeks, *Caribbean Revolutions*, 165–79; Lewis, *Grenada*, chap. 10; Kinzer, *Overthrow*, 228–30; Puri, *Grenada Revolution*, 19, 100, 140; Audre Lord, "Grenada Revisited: An Interim Report," *Black Scholar* 15, no. 1 (January–February, 1984): 27.

56. Meeks, *Caribbean Revolutions*, 130; Lewis, *Grenada*, 106.

57. Kinzer, *Overthrow*, 231–32, 237; Lewis, *Grenada*, 100–102, esp. 101; Collins, "What Happened?," 33, 35; Puri, *Grenada Revolution*, 99–100.

58. Lewis, *Grenada*, 101; Kinzer, *Overthrow*, 236; Puri, *Grenada Revolution*, 118–19.

59. Kinzer, *Overthrow*, 238; Lewis, *Grenada*, 101, 106. A documentary film treating this tragic denouement and the Grenada Revolution overall is *Forward Ever: The*

Killing of a Revolution (New York: Third World Newsreel, 2013), directed by the Trinidadian filmmaker Bruce Paddington.

60. On the other hand, that aid was modest, and Grenada no longer profited from growing Soviet purchases of nutmeg as it had when Bishop was prime minister. Lewis, *Grenada*, 106, 183–84; Kinzer, *Overthrow*, 227, 303–5; Ambursley, "Grenada," 215; Alan McPherson, *A Short History of U.S. Interventions in Latin America and the Caribbean* (Oxford: Wiley Blackwell, 2016), 166; Seth Mydans, "Nutmeg Diplomacy in Grenada: The Aftermath of Invasion," *New York Times*, January 22, 1984.

61. Puri, *Grenada Revolution*, 128–32, 141–42.

62. David Nicholls, *From Dessalines to Duvalier: Race, Colour and National Independence in Haiti* (New Brunswick, N.J.: Rutgers University Press, 1996), xxix; Peter Hallward, *Damming the Flood: Haiti and the Politics of Containment* (London: Verso, 2007), 32; Kim Ives, "The Unmaking of a President," *NACLA Report on the Americas* 27, no. 4 (January 1994): 16–29, 19; Brenda Gayle Plummer, *Haiti and the United States: The Psychological Moment* (Athens: University of Georgia Press, 1992), 196.

63. Erica Caple James, *Democratic Insecurities: Violence, Trauma, and Intervention in Haiti* (Los Angeles: University of California Press, 2010), chap. 1; Mark Danner, "The Prophet," *New York Review of Books*, November 18, 1993, secs. 5 and 6; Robert Fatton, *Haiti's Predatory Republic: The Unending Transition to Democracy* (Boulder, Colo.: Lynn Rienner, 2002), 66; Hallward, *Damming the Flood*, 16, 27–29; Marvin Chochotte, "The History of Peasants, *Tonton Makouts*, and the Rise and Fall of the Duvalier Dictatorship in Haiti" (Ph.D. diss., University of Michigan, 2017).

64. Hallward, *Damming the Flood*, 23–24, 133; Laurent Dubois, *Haiti: The Aftershocks of History* (New York: Metropolitan Books, 2012); Amy Wilentz, "Foreword," in Jean-Bertrand Aristide, *In the Parish of the Poor: Writings from Haiti* (New York: Orbis Books, 1994), ix–xxiv; *The Agronomist* (New York: ThinkFilm, 2003), directed by Jonathan Demme.

65. Mark Danner, "Haiti on the Verge," *New York Review of Books*, November 4, 1993, pt. 2; Mark Danner, *Stripping Bare the Body: Politics, Violence, War* (New York: Nation Books, 2009), 8–9; Mark Danner, "The Struggle for a Democratic Haiti," *New York Times*, June 21, 1987; Fatton, *Haiti's Predatory Republic*, 68–69; Danner, "Prophet," sec. 7; Hallward, *Damming the Flood*, 24.

66. Danner, *Stripping Bare*, 109–11; Danner, "Prophet," sec. 7.

67. Elsewhere, Aristide criticized the United States for having "set up the Haitian Army" during the U.S. Occupation (1915–34) and "trained it to work against the people." Aristide, *In the Parish*, 59, 101–5; Wilentz, "Foreword," ix–xvii; Mark Danner, "The Fall of the Prophet," *New York Review of Books*, December 2, 1993; Danner, "Prophet," sec. 5; Alex Dupuy, *The Prophet and Power: Jean-Bertrand Aristide, the International Community, and Haiti* (Lanham, Md.: Rowman and Littlefield, 2007), 75; Nicholls, *From Dessalines to Duvalier*, xxx; Wilentz, "Foreword," x–xvii.

68. Dubois, *Aftershocks*, 356, 362; Dupuy, *Prophet and Power*, 67–73; Fatton, *Haiti's Predatory Republic*, 68, 69.

69. Fatton, *Haiti's Predatory Republic*, 66; Hallward, *Damming the Flood*, 27–29; Danner, "Fall of the Prophet."

70. Dubois, *Aftershocks*, 351–58; Hallward, *Damming the Flood*, 15–16; Fatton, *Haiti's Predatory Republic*, 59, 62–63.

71. Fatton, *Haiti's Predatory Republic*, 67; Hallward, *Damming the Flood*, 31–32; Danner, "Fall of the Prophet."

72. Jean-Bertrand Aristide, speech of December 5, 1990, in the film *Haiti: Killing the Dream*, directed by Ossie Davis, Babeth Mondini-VanLoo, Katharine Kean, Hath Perry, and Rudi Stern (New York: Crowing Rooster Productions, 1992); Dubois, *Aftershocks*, 362. We are drawing here from the title of Michel-Rolph Trouillot's book, *Haiti, State against Nation: The Origins and Legacy of Duvalierism* (New York: Monthly Review Press, 1990).

73. Dupuy, *Prophet and Power*, 72, 104; Fatton, *Haiti's Predatory Republic*, 84, 100n35.

74. Americas Watch Committee, National Coalition for Haitian Refugees and Caribbean Rights, *Haiti, the Aristide Government's Human Rights Record* (New York: Americas Watch, 1991), 4; Danner, "Fall of the Prophet"; Dupuy, *Prophet and Power*, 110; Jean-Bertrand Aristide and Christophe Wargny, *Tout moun sé moun/ Tout homme est un homme* (Paris: Éditions du Seuil, 1992); Fatton, *Haiti's Predatory Republic*, 84, 86.

75. Danner, "Fall of the Prophet," pt. 7. After the coup against Aristide in September of 1991, one colonel referred back to the generals' retirement as Aristide's "first mistake." It made clear that "we were going to have trouble with this guy." Ossie Davis, Babeth Mondini-VanLoo, Katharine Kean, Hath Perry, and Rudi Stern, dirs., *Haiti: Killing the Dream* (New York: Crowing Rooster Productions, 1992). America's Watch, "The Aristide Government's Human Rights Record," 4; Dupuy, *Prophet and Power*, 114–16, esp. 116; Mats Lundahl, *The Political Economy of Disaster: Destitution, Plunder and Earthquake in Haiti* (New York: Routledge, 2013), 55; Trouillot, *Haiti*, 189–91; Danner, "Fall of the Prophet," pt. 8.

76. Dupuy, *Prophet and Power*, 108; Haitian Const. of 1987, art. CCXLVIII (superseded 2012), http://pdba.georgetown.edu/Constitutions/Haiti/haiti1987.html; Fatton, *Haiti's Predatory Republic*, 69, 70, 77, 120.

77. Lundahl, *Political Economy of Disaster*, 33, 49–50, 69, 78.

78. Dupuy, *Prophet and Power*, 113–20; Nicholls, *From Dessalines to Duvalier*, xxxii; Danner, "Fall of the Prophet," pt. 8.

79. Dupuy, *Prophet and Power*, 119–20; Fatton, *Haiti's Predatory Republic*, 79–80; Danner, "Fall of the Prophet," pt. 8.

80. Dupuy, *Prophet and Power*, 118–21; Lundahl, *Political Economy of Disaster*, 26, 87–89, 176, 277–78; Mats Lundahl, *The Haitian Economy: Man, Land and Markets* (London: Croom Helm, 1983), 67–93; Robert Fatton, *Haiti: Trapped in the Outer Periphery* (Boulder, Colo.: Lynne Rienner Publishers, 2014), 171.

81. Lundahl, *Political Economy of Disaster*, 89, 278–79; Timothy T. Schwartz, *Travesty in Haiti: A True Account of Christian Missions, Orphanages, Fraud, Food Aid and Drug Trafficking* (Charleston, S.C.: BookSurge Publishing, 2010), 99; Fatton,

Haiti, 101–5, 171–72. On successful small farming in the Dominican Republic in the mid-twentieth century, see Richard Lee Turits, *Foundations of Despotism: Peasants, the Trujillo Regime, and Modernity in Dominican History* (Stanford, Calif.: Stanford University Press, 2003), 234–35, passim.

82. Dupuy, *Prophet and Power*, 113, 122, 108, 113; Fatton, *Haiti's Predatory Republic*, 86; Americas Watch, "Aristide Government's Human Rights Record," 33.

83. Dupuy, *Prophet and Power*, 117.

84. Dupuy, 117.

85. Danner, "Fall of the Prophet," pt. 8; Nicholls, *From Dessalines to Duvalier*, xxx–xxxii; Dupuy, *Prophet and Power*, 117.

86. Dupuy, *Prophet and Power*, 122–25; Danner, "Fall of the Prophet," pt. 8; Americas Watch, "Aristide Government's Human Rights Record," 5–6, 17, 20–26.

87. Americas Watch, "Aristide Government's Human Rights Record," 18–19; Dupuy, *Prophet and Power*, 126–27; Danner, "Fall of the Prophet," pt. 8.

88. Danner, "Fall of the Prophet," pt. 8; Jean-Bertrand Aristide, September 27, 1991, speech, trans. *Haiti Observateur*, http://faculty.webster.edu/corbetre/haiti/history/recent/lebrun.htm.

89. Danner, "Fall of the Prophet," pt. 8; Hallward, *Damming the Flood*, 40.

90. Ives, "Unmaking of a President," 16.

91. Plummer, *Haiti*, 234; Allan Nairn, "The Eagle Is Landing," *The Nation*, October 3, 1994; Allan Nairn, "Behind Haiti's Paramilitaries," *The Nation*, October 24, 1994; Allan Nairn, "He's Our S.O.B.," *The Nation*, October 31, 1994; and David Corn, "Loose Spooks," *The Nation*, October 31, 1994; Allan Nairn, "Haiti under the Gun," *The Nation*, January 8, 1996; Larry Rohter, "Cables Show US Deception on Violence in Haiti," *New York Times*, February 6, 1996; Hallward, *Damming the Flood*, 40.

92. Fatton, *Haiti's Predatory Republic*, 88–96, 107–9; Dubois, *Aftershocks*, 363; Aristide, *In the Parish*, 59, 101–5.

Index

Abeng, 285

abolition of slavery, 4, 79, 90, 92, 94–97, 146–47; and the Baptist church, 118–19, 123–24; in the British Caribbean, 114–21; causes of, 97–101, 114; in Cuba, 57, 145–46, 345n11; explanation of, in *Capitalism and Slavery* (Williams), 114; in the French Empire, 50, 120; in Guadeloupe, 50; rumors of, 101–14; in Saint-Domingue, 57, 97, 105, 136; in the Spanish Empire, 345n11; in the United States, 57, 147. *See also* antislavery thought

Account, Much Abbreviated, of the Destruction of the Indies, An (Las Casas), 25

African-Atlantic slave trade, 3, 20, 53–54, 56–60, 62–64, 66–69, 73

Agency for International Development (AID), 261, 291

agrarian reform, 5, 187, 193–94, 200–201, 213, 221–22, 281; in Cuba during 1933 revolution, 181; of Cuban rebels during Cuban War of Independence (1895–98), 148–51, 204–5; in the Dominican Republic under Joaquín Balaguer, 273–75; in the Dominican Republic under Juan Bosch, 258, 260; in the Dominican Republic under Trujillo, 142, 182–84, 206; in Grenada, 297–98, 303; in Jamaica, 281, 288–89, 294, 297; in Haiti, 184, 281, 307, 312–14; in post-1959 Cuba, 189, 234–41, 243, 254–55; of rural guerrillas in 1950s Cuban insurrection, 212–13, 214, 221, 226, 229

Agüero, Luis Conte, 198

Agwe, 82–83

Akan, 108

All Slave-Keepers That Keep the Innocent in Bondage, Apostates (Lay), 100

Allaire, Louis, 16

Alekseev, Aleksandr, 246–48

Allende, Salvador, 299

Alliance for Progress, 258

alumina. *See* bauxite.

"American Sugar Kingdom," 158, 167

Anacoana, 17

Andalusia (Spain), 68

Anderson, Alexander, 9, 44, 48, 50

Angola: and the slave trade, 62, 67–69; and the Cuban Revolutionary Government, 292–93

Antigua, 14, 36, 41, 47, 88, 108; abolition of slavery in, 92, 123

antislavery thought, 79, 96–101

Arawak, 15, 49

Arada (or Arara), 68

Árbenz, Jacobo, 200–202, 223, 240, 299, 300

areitos, 19

Argentina, 364n45

Arias, Desiderio, 160

Aristide, Jean-Bertrand, 281, 299, 308; coup against, 316–17, 375n75; 1994 return to office of, 317; political ideas and speeches of, 306–18. *See also* Haiti

Aruba, 29

Asian-descended Caribbeans, 3, 298; contract laborers, 285; enslaved people, 68

avocado, 85–86

Cuba (to 1959) (cont.)
149–50, 181, 229, 233; racial and class
demographics in, 146–48, 229, 234,
243, 269; renamed Fernandina, 29;
renamed Juana, 29; repression in,
191, 231, 242; revolution of 1933 in,
181; sex workers in, 197–98, 210;
slavery in, 56–57, 63, 66–68, 74, 114;
small farming in, 149, 229, 243;
squatters in, 150, 197, 204–6, 209,
229; structure of land tenure in, 148,
150–51, 197, 205–6, 208–9, 243, 269;
sugar workers in, 148, 196, 229, 243;
Ten Years' War (independence war)
in, 101, 145–46, 346n18; tourism in,
197–99, 226; U.S. annexation
aspirations for, 147–48; U.S. invasion
and occupation of (1898–1902),
149–51, 283; U.S. sugar companies in,
148, 151, 197, 239; universal male
suffrage in, 149–50; War of Independence (1895–98) in, 101, 146, 148–50,
206, 208, 227, 229; women in, 181;
women's suffrage in, 181
Cuba (since 1959), 5, 227–56, 277–81,
312, 318; agrarian reform in, 189,
234–36, 242, 249–50, 254–55; and
the Dominican Republic, 256–62,
265, 267–69; economy of, 233,
235–36, 238, 241, 243, 249–50,
254–55, 277, 279; education in, 233,
244, 277–78; emigration to the
United States from, 242, 254, 279,
294; and Grenada, 298, 302, 304;
health care in, 233, 255, 277–78; and
U.S. business interests, 237–41,
247–50, 269; intervention in Angola
of, 292–93; and Jamaica, 292–93;
plantation agriculture in, 236–37,
254–55; political violence and
repression in, 242–43, 246, 255–56,
371n117; post-1990 economic and
socialist collapse of, 278–79; race
and racism in, 233–34, 244, 278–79;
and the Soviet Union, 246–50, 254,
269, 277–79, 364n45; and the United
States, 211, 237–42, 247–51, 253–54,
269, 279–80; small farmers in,
235–37; sugar workers in, 233,
236–37, 255; tourism in, 279; U.S.
economic embargo on, 247–50, 277;
urban reform in, 232–33, 243, 250
Cuban Communist party (Popular
Socialist Party), 181, 192, 220, 240,
269, 354n8
Cuban Missile Crisis, 254
Cuban Revolution (1950s insurrection),
5, 186, 189–226, 228–29; and the
Communist party (Popular Socialist
Party), 220, 222, 354n8; and Cuban
military, 208–9, 214, 218–19, 221,
224, 232; harm to business interests
of, 235–39, 269; race and racism in,
202, 233–34; professional classes in,
211–13, 242; rebel government of,
214–15, 217–18, 221; rebel government's agrarian reform, 214, 221;
Revolutionary Student Directorate,
210–11, 212–13, 221; rural guerrillas
in, 188, 204–9, 211, 213–16, 218,
220–21, 226, 229–30, 235; sex
workers in, 210; small farmers in,
208, 215, 221, 229, 234; squatters in,
205, 209, 212, 222, 229, 234; upper
classes in, 210–12, 226, 230, 242–43;
urban guerrillas in, 199, 209–11,
216–17, 222–23; wage laborers in,
222, 225, 229, 243; women and
gender in, 202, 203–5, 208–10,
214–15
Cuervo, Pelayo, 211
Curtis, Charles, 179–80
Cyprus, 59
Czechoslovakia, 247–48

Danish Virgin Islands, 108, 127, 140,
144, 159, 345n15
Davis, David Brion, 29, 58, 60, 99
Declaration of the Rights of Man and
Citizen, 111

and speeches of, 221; military and political strategies of, 224–25, 246, 253–54

Guha, Ranajit, 107

Guiana (British and French), 15, 38–39, 109, 375n31. *See also* Guyana.

Guinea (also Guinée), 83, 89

Guyana, 122

Guzmán, Antonio, 175–76

haciendas comuneras (jointly owned estates), 150–51, 155, 169–70;

Hahn, Steven, 119

Haiti (island): indigenous name of, 30; indigenous populations of, 16–18; See also la Española; la Isla Española; Hispaniola; Quisqueya

Haiti: demographics of, 153, 165, 312–13; Aristide regime in, 228, 281, 306–18, 375n75; *cacos* in, 154, 156–57, 159, 161, 164, 175–76; coffee production in, 153, 184; deforestation in, 313; Duvalier regime in, 152, 281, 307–10; emigration from, to Cuba, 167, 350n62; emigration from, to the Dominican Republic, 155, 167; foreign aid to, 313, 318; Germans in, 133–34, 159; indigenous peoples in, 14, 17–18, 30–31; *lakou* system in, 133–36; as metaphor, 125, 149, 346n18; naming of, after revolution; 1980s conditions in, 312; plantation agriculture in, 28, 55–56, 66, 153, 166; race and racism in, 153; repression in, 307–9, 314–17; sisal plantation in, 166; small farming in, 133–36, 153–54, 156, 165–68, 176, 184, 312; structure of land tenure in, 153, 156, 165–66, 307, 312–13, 349n59; sugar plantations in, 153; sugar production in, 166; and the United States, 306, 310, 316–18, 349n59; U.S.-created military of, 175–76, 178, 184–85, 283, 307, 310–12, 316–17, 375n75; U.S. invasion of (1994); U.S. occupation of (1915–1934), 139–42,

149–87, 265; U.S. sugar companies and business interests in, 139, 141, 155, 158, 165, 167–68; women and gender in, 136. *See also* Haitian Revolution

Haitian American Sugar Company (HASCO), 166, 176

Haitian Revolution, 31, 56, 66, 97, 101, 105–6, 114, 120, 125, 187; and abolitionism, 97, 102–5; and *lakou* system, 134, 136; negative perceptions of, 149–50; role of rumor in, 105–6

Hall, Douglas, 122–23

Hall, Stuart, 286–87

hammocks, 38, 42–43, 52

Harlan, John Marshall, 144.

Havana: and Cuban Revolution, 190–92, 196–98, 207, 209–11, 220–21, 224–25, 230–31, 238, 244, 246–48; emergence of, 66–68, 72

Hawai'i, 140, 143, 158

Hazard, Samuel, 139

Higman, B. W., 1, 85, 99

Hispaniola, 15, 19, 24–25, 78, 158, 329n1; small farming in, 153–54. *See also* la Isla Española; Haiti; Santo Domingo

"History Will Absolve Me" speech (Castro), 193–95, 212, 230–32, 244

Holt, Thomas, 119–20, 129, 142, 282

Honduras, 45, 50–51

Hoover, Herbert, 180

Hulme, Peter, 15, 20, 24, 35, 41, 49

hurricanes, 29, 45, 76, 132

Iberian slave trade, 58, 60

indentured servitude, 54, 70–71, 285

indigenous Americans: enslavement of, 9, 11, 26–27, 33–35, 40, 42, 48, 62–64; native Caribbeans, 9–52

indigo, 53, 69

Inhuman Bondage (Davis), 58, 99

Insular Cases in U.S. Supreme Court. *See* Downes v. Bidwell

International Monetary Fund (IMF), 263, 295, 313; and Cuba, 213; and the Dominican Republic, 263; and Haiti, 313; and Jamaica, 295

Iran: coup in, 223; revolution of, 305–6.

irrigation, 17, 156, 167, 182, 184, 260, 275, 284, 288, 314

Isidro Jimenes, Juan, 160

la Isla Española, naming of, 17, 24, 329n1. *See also* la Española; Hispaniola; Dominican Republic; Santo Domingo; Quisqueya, Haiti (island)

Jagan, Cheddi, 375n31

Jamaica, abolition of slavery in, 101, 104, 114–20; bauxite and alumina industry in, 284, 288, 290–91, 296, 374n22; colonization of, 40–41, 54–56; and Cuba, 228, 292–93; decolonization of, 282–85; economy of, 283–84, 287–90, 293–96, 375n30; emigration to the United States from, 294; and foreign aid, 292–96; and Grenada, 299; Manley government of (1972–80), 281–96, 318, 330; maroons in, 93–96, 108; nationalism and anti-imperialism in, 284–85, 296; 1960s conditions in, 284, 287; People's National Party, 283; plantation agriculture in, 28, 55–56, 73–88, 134, 289–90; postemancipation society of, 121–34, 139; race and racism in, 284–87, 296; Rastafari movement in, 284–87; reggae in, 285; slavery in, 54–56, 63, 73–88; small farming in, 74, 80, 85–88, 87, 121–32, 134, 284, 288; structure of land tenure in, 284; trade with the United States, 130; and Trinidad, 292; and the United States, 282–83, 291–95, 376n36; U.S. corporations in, 288–91

James, C. L. R., 99

Jefferson, Thomas, 147

JEWEL (Joint Endeavor for Welfare, Education and Liberation) movement (Grenada), 298

Johnson, James Weldon, 163

Johnson, Lyndon Baines, 239, 263–71

Johnson, Paul, 44, 45–46, 49, 52

Johnston, Harry, 133

Jonnès, Alexandre Moreau de, 49

Kalinago, 9, 35, 51. See *Garifuna*

Kaufman, Michael, 285

Kelly, Hugh, 152, 157–58

Kennedy, John F.: and Cuba, 251–254; and the Dominican Republic, 258–63, 271

Kerns, Virginia, 51

Khrushchev, Nikita, 246, 253

Kim, Julie Chun, 43–44

Kingston (Jamaica), 76, 80, 119

Kissinger, Henry, 291, 293

Kleberg, Robert, 239

Labat, Jean-Baptiste, 13, 42–44, 55

Lafontant, Roger, 311, 315

lakou (family land) 133–136

la Rivière, Romaine, 110–11

Larose, Serge, 136–38

Las Casas, Bartolomé de, 13, 20–21, 25, 34, 99

Las Casas, Pedro de, 25

Lay, Benjamin, 100

Lebanon, 305

Ledgister, F. S. J., 284

Lee, Harry, 176

liberation theology, 306

Lightfoot, Natasha, 91

Lisbon (Portugal), 25, 99

literacy rates: in Cuba, 244, 278; in Jamaica, 287

literacy campaigns: in Cuba, 244; in Grenada, 299; in Haiti, 315; in Jamaica, 287

Little Church movement (Haiti). See *Ti Legliz* movement

Lobo, Julio, 211–12

London (England), 41–42, 76–78, 104, 116, 120

Long, Edward, 28, 55, 76, 79, 83

53, 56, 63, 66; territorial status of, 143–44

Puri, Shalini, 306

Quakers, 100
Quevedo, José, 218
Quintero Rivera, Ángel, 2
Quisqueya, 17–18. *See also* Haiti; Hispaniola; la Isla Espanola, Santo Domingo

Raborn, William, 268
race and racism, 9, 26, 28, 49, 78, 84; color and colorism, 22, 37, 153, 177, 284; in the Dominican Republic, 153; and free people of color, 67–68; in Grenada, 297–98, 303; in Haiti, 153, 161; in Jamaica, 284–87, 296; and pirates, 84; and slavery, 53, 54, 58, 60, 62–63, 68; during U.S. occupation in Cuba (1898–1902), 149–50, 229; during U.S. occupation in the Dominican Republic (1916–24), 173, 177; during U.S. occupation in Haiti (1915–34), 173
Rameau, Benoît, 164
Rastafari, 284–85
Reagan, Ronald, 300, 305–6
Rebel Radio, 221, 225
Reformist Party (Dominican Republic), 266, 272
Refuge (Haiti), 121
reggae, 285–86
Reid Cabral, Donald, 262–65
Revolutionary Front for the Advancement and Progress of Haiti (FRAPH) (Haiti), 317
Revolutionary Student Directorate (Cuba), 210–12, 221
Rochefort, César de, 33
Rodney, Walter, 285–86
Rodríguez, Carlos Rafael, 220
Roosevelt, Franklin D., 181, 196, 241
Roosevelt, Theodore, 152
Rowe, Mann, 95

rumors, and emancipation, 99, 101–20; and Aristide government, 308, 316; in Cuba, 199, 294; in Grenada, 298; in Haiti, 105–6; in Martinique, 101–4, 111–12; and Michael Manley government, 294
Rusk, Dean, 260
Russian Revolution, 241

Saint-Domingue. *See* Haiti
Saint-Michel, Maurile de, 27, 69
Samoa, 140
Sánchez, Celia, 188–89, 192, 199, 204–5, 207–8, 215
Sans-Souci Palace, 30, 140
Santa María, 24–25
Santamaría, Haydée, 199
Santiago de Cuba, 188–89, 199, 204, 208–9, 217, 220–21, 225, 228, 231
Santo Domingo (city), 162, 170, 172, 177, 179–80, 191, 257, 262, 264, 266–67, 271–72
Santo Domingo (colony): multiple names for, 329n1; open-range economy in, 65–66; post-plantation peasantry of, 66; sixteenth-century demographics of, 64, 332n25; sixteenth-century slave plantation economy in, 3, 33, 53, 56, 60, 62–66, 332n25. *See also* Dominican Republic; la Española; la Isla Española; Quisqueya; Haiti (island)
São Tomé, 62
Schmidt, Hans, 159
Schoelcher, Victor, 90, 120
Schlesinger, Arthur, Jr., 252
Schurz, Carl, 147
Scott, David, 299, 303
Scott, Julius, 106, 121
Scott, Rebecca, 149
Seaga, Edward, 295, 306
Selassie, Haile, 284–85
Seville (Spain), 25, 60, 64, 68
sexual violence and rape: by the Batista regime, 215; by *cacos*, 156; by the Duvalier regime, 185; against

enslaved women, 79–80; by *gavilleros*, 156; by the Trujillo regime, 183; by U.S. forces in the Dominican Republic, 172; by U.S. forces in Haiti, 173

sex work, 197–98, 210

Sierra Maestra (Cuba), geography of, 188, 204, 208–9, 214–16, 218–19, 221

Sierra Manifesto, 213

sisal, 156

slavery, 53–58; 81–82; and the American Revolution, 57; in Antigua, 47, 91–92; in Barbados, 44, 71–72, 80–81; in Brazil, 58; in Canary Islands, 60–61; in Cuba, 56–57, 63, 66–68, 74, 114; in Cyprus, 59; demographics of, 54; escape from, 2–4, 31, 41, 44–45, 66, 69, 74, 80, 82, 84–85, 93–96, 133, 146, 156; in French Caribbean, 54, 70, 104, 112–13, 120; in Guadeloupe, 73; of Guanches (native Canary Islanders), 60–61; of indigenous Americans, 9, 11, 26–27, 33–35, 40, 42, 48, 62–64; in Italy, 58–59; in Jamaica, 28, 54–56, 63, 73–88; in late medieval and early modern Southern Europe and the Atlantic islands, 3, 54, 58; in Madeira, 61–63; in Mallorca, 58; in Martinique, 70, 73; in the Middle East; in Morocco, 59; of Muslim Spaniards and North Africans, 58–60; of Orthodox Christians (Eastern Europeans, Eurasians, and Greeks), 58, 60; of people of African descent, 26, 28–31, 40, 44–46, 53–136; of people of Asian descent, 68; and punishment and torture, 55, 78–81, 105; and race and racism, 53, 54, 58, 60, 62–63, 68; rebellions against, 101–20; in Portugal, 58, 60; in Puerto Rico, 53, 56, 63, 66; in Santo Domingo (colony and city), 3, 33, 53, 56, 60, 62–66; in St. Christopher, 69; in St. Vincent, 45; in São Tomé, 62; and sexual assault, 79–80; and "slaving zones," 33, 34, 69; in Spain, 58, 60;

and women, 54–55, 79–80, 91–92. *See also* abolition of slavery; African-Atlantic slave trade; Black Sea slave trade; trans-Saharan slave trade

small farming: in Cuba, 149, 229, 235–37, 243; in the Dominican Republic, 153, 169–70, 182–83, 269, 275; in Grenada, 297–98; in Haiti, 133–36, 153–54, 156, 165–68, 176, 184, 312; in Jamaica, 74, 80, 85–88, 87, 134; and provision grounds, 42, 47, 80, 85–92, 96, 121, 124; in Santo Domingo, 65–66. *See also* counter-plantation system; open–range lands; *lakou*; family land; open-range economy

Smith, Earl, 217

Société des Amis des Noirs, 102

Soler, William, 209

Somoza dynasty, 252, 305

South Porto Rico Sugar Company, 171

Sonthonax, Léger Félicité, 113

South Africa, 292–93

Soviet Union, 191, 201, 230, 240–41, 246, 248–50, 253–54, 269, 277, 279, 305, 378n60

Spain, 20, 22, 24, 32, 58–69, 100–101, 108, 144–46, 149, 163, 190, 203, 305, 345n11

Spanish-American War, 143–46

St. Anne, 110–12

St. Christopher, 39–40, 69

St. John, 108, 127

St. Lucia, 38–39, 109, 114, 123

St. Pierre, 101

St. Vincent, 9–11, 32, 35, 41–52, 114

Stephens, Evelyne Huber, 289

Stephens, John, 289

Stout, Nancy, 204

Sudre Dartiguenave, Philippe, 161–62

sugar production, 28–29, 40, 56, 58, 91, 97–98, 133; in Antigua; in Barbados, 40, 70–72; in Brazil, 53, 65, 71–72; in the British Caribbean, 97; in Canary Islands, 59, 61, 63; in Cuba, 56, 66,

ers and merchants in Haiti, 136; as members of Tonton Makouts, 185–86; as owners of family land in Jamaica, 126–27; as pirates, 84; in post-1959 Cuba, 244, 367n70; reforms under Michael Manley in Jamaica relating to, 287–88; sexual assaults on, by the Batista regime, 215; sexual assaults on, by the Duvalier regime, 185; sexual assaults on enslaved women, 79–80; sexual assaults on, by *gavilleros* and *cacos*, 156; sexual assaults on, by the Trujillo regime, 183; sexual assaults on, by U.S. forces in Cuba and the Dominican Republic, 172; sexual assaults on, by U.S. forces in Haiti, 173; and slavery, 54–55, 79–80

World Bank: and Haiti, 313; and Cuba, 197, 277–78

yellow fever, 132
Young, William, 45

zemis, 18–19, 28, 30
Zumba, Marie Jeanne, 136

Printed in the USA
CPSIA information can be obtained
at www.ICGtesting.com
CBHW030904290624
10807CB00003B/77

9 781469 672557